# Classic Reviews in Tourism

# ASPECTS OF TOURISM

**Series Editors:** Professor Chris Cooper, *University of Queensland, Australia,*
Dr Michael Hall, *University of Otago, Dunedin, New Zealand*
and Dr Dallen Timothy, *Arizona State University, Tempe, USA*

**Aspects of Tourism** is an innovative, multifaceted series which will comprise
authoritative reference handbooks on global tourism regions, research volumes, texts
and monographs. It is designed to provide readers with the latest thinking on tourism
world-wide and in so doing will push back the frontiers of tourism knowledge. The
series will also introduce a new generation of international tourism authors, writing
on leading edge topics. The volumes will be readable and user-friendly, providing
accessible sources for further research. The list will be underpinned by an annual
authoritative tourism research volume. Books in the series will be commissioned that
probe the relationship between tourism and cognate subject areas such as strategy,
development, retailing, sport and environmental studies. The publisher and series
editors welcome proposals from writers with projects on these topics.

**Other Books in the Series**
Dynamic Tourism: Journeying with Change
    *Priscilla Boniface*
Journeys into Otherness: The Representation of Differences and Identity in Tourism
    *Keith Hollinshead and Chuck Burlo (eds)*
Marine Ecotourism: Issues and Experiences
    *Brian Garrod and Julie C. Wilson (eds)*
Natural Area Tourism: Ecology, Impacts and Management
    *D. Newsome, S.A. Moore and R. Dowling*
Progressing Tourism Research
    *Bill Faulkner, edited by Liz Fredline, Leo Jago and Chris Cooper*
Tourism Collaboration and Partnerships
    *Bill Bramwell and Bernard Lane (eds)*
Tourism and Development: Concepts and Issues
    *Richard Sharpley and David Telfer (eds)*
Tourism Employment: Analysis and Planning
    *Michael Riley, Adele Ladkin, and Edith Szivas*
Tourism in Peripheral Areas: Case Studies
    *Frances Brown and Derek Hall (eds)*

**Other Books of Interest**
Global Ecotoursim Policies and Case Studies
    *Michael Lück and Torsten Kirstges (eds)*

**Please contact us for the latest book information:**
**Channel View Publications, Frankfurt Lodge, Clevedon Hall,**
**Victoria Road, Clevedon, BS21 7HH, England**
**http://www.channelviewpublications.com**

**ASPECTS OF TOURISM 8**
*Series Editors*: Chris Cooper (*University of Queensland, Australia*),
Michael Hall (*University of Otago, New Zealand*)
and Dallen Timothy (*Arizona State University, USA*)

# Classic Reviews in Tourism

Edited by
Chris Cooper

**CHANNEL VIEW PUBLICATIONS**
Clevedon • Buffalo • Toronto • Sydney

b 2264596
o 1240997
70108503

**Library of Congress Cataloging in Publication Data**
A catalog record for this book is available from the Library of Congress.

**British Library Cataloguing in Publication Data**
A catalogue entry for this book is available from the British Library.

ISBN 1-853150-45-8 (hbk)
ISBN 1-853150-44-X (pbk)

**Channel View Publications**
An imprint of Multilingual Matters Ltd

*UK*: Frankfurt Lodge, Clevedon Hall, Victoria Road, Clevedon BS21 7SJ.
*USA*: 2250 Military Road, Tonawanda, NY 14150, USA.
*Canada*: 5201 Dufferin Street, North York, Ontario, Canada M3H 5T8.
*Australia*: Footprint Books, PO Box 418, Church Point, NSW 2103, Australia.

Typeset by Archetype-IT Ltd (http://www.archetype-it.com).
Printed and bound in Great Britain by the Cromwell Press.

# Contents

Contributors . . . . . . . . . . . . . . . . . . . . . . . . . . . . vii

1 Progress in Tourism Research
  *Chris Cooper* . . . . . . . . . . . . . . . . . . . . . . . . . . 1
2 The Sociology of Tourism
  *John Urry* . . . . . . . . . . . . . . . . . . . . . . . . . . . 9
3 The Economics of Tourism
  *M. Thea Sinclair, Adam Blake and Guntur Sugiyarto* . . . . . . . . . . 22
4 The Statistical Measurement of Tourism
  *John Latham and Chris Edwards* . . . . . . . . . . . . . . . . . 55
5 Perspectives on Temporal Change and the History of
  Tourism and Recreation
  *Geoff Wall* . . . . . . . . . . . . . . . . . . . . . . . . . . 77
6 Marketing of the Service Process: State of the Art in the
  Tourism, Recreation and Hospitality Industries
  *Frank Go and Michael Haywood* . . . . . . . . . . . . . . . . . 87
7 Comprehensive Human Resource Planning: An Essential
  Key to Sustainable Tourism in Small Island Settings
  *Michael V. Conlin and Tom Baum* . . . . . . . . . . . . . . . . 115
8 Competitive Strategies for a 'New Tourism'
  *Auliana Poon* . . . . . . . . . . . . . . . . . . . . . . . . . 130
9 Urban Tourism: Still an Imbalance in Attention?
  *Gregory Ashworth* . . . . . . . . . . . . . . . . . . . . . . . 143
10 Revisiting 'Heritage: A Key Sector of the (then) "New"
  Tourism' – Out With the 'New' and Out With 'Heritage'?
  *Richard Prentice* . . . . . . . . . . . . . . . . . . . . . . . 164
11 Environmental Auditing: A Means to Improving Tourism's
  Environmental Performance
  *Brian Goodall* . . . . . . . . . . . . . . . . . . . . . . . . . 192

12  Alternative Tourism – A Deceptive Ploy
    *Brian Wheeller* . . . . . . . . . . . . . . . . . . . . . . . . . . . . 227
13  Gender and Tourism
    *Geoff Wall and Joanne Norris*. . . . . . . . . . . . . . . . . . . . . 235

# Contributors

**Gregory Ashworth** is Professor of Heritage Management and Tourism at the University of Groningen, Netherlands. His research interests focus on the themes of urban tourism, heritage management, and city centre planning and management.

**Tom Baum** is Professor and Head in the Scottish Hotel School, University of Strathclyde, Glasgow, UK. His research interests are in the twin areas of human resource management planning and tourism in peripheral areas.

**Adam Blake** is Research Fellow at the Christel DeHaan Tourism and Travel Research Institute, University of Nottingham, UK. He has a PhD from the School of Economics, University of Nottingham and his research interests are in the evaluation of the economic impact of tourism and the effects of tourism taxation.

**Michael V Conlin** is the Chief Executive and Dean of the Australian International Hotel Management School, Canberra, Australia. He has organised a number of international forums dealing with Island Tourism and is co-author of *Island Tourism: Management Principles and Practice* (with Tom Baum).

**Chris Cooper** is Foundation Professor of Tourism Management and Head of the School of Tourism and Leisure Management in the University of Queensland, Brisbane, Australia. His research interests lie in the areas of resort development, tourism education and training, and the knowledge management of tourism research.

**Chris Edwards** is a Senior Lecturer in Southampton Business School at Southampton Institute, UK. His research interests are in assessing marketing effectiveness and customer satisfaction in the tourism context.

**Frank Go** is the Bewetour Chair Professor in Tourism Management at the Rotterdam School of Management, Erasmus University, Netherlands. His current research interests include interfacing and organisational flexibility in travel and hospitality networks and the construction of organisational and community identity.

**Brian Goodall** is Professor of Geography and Dean of Urban and Regional Studies and Director of the Tourism Research and Policy Unit at the University of Reading, UK. His research interests focus on environmental performance in tourism, holiday choice and behaviour and the creation of inclusive tourism environments, particularly in response to disability discrimination legislation.

**Michael Haywood** is a Professor in the School of Hotel and Food Administration, University of Guelph, Canada. His research interests lie in the area of tourism development and the strategic management of tourist enterprises.

**John Latham** is Professor of Business Analysis and Dean of Southampton Business School, Southampton, UK. His research interests lie in the statistical measurement of tourism, the monitoring and interpretation of demand for the tourism product, market analysis, and methodology associated with market research.

**Joanne Norris** is Director of Social Returns at Social Capital Partners, a venture philanthropy organization based in Toronto Canada. She is an expert on enterprise development projects and has published on issues in tourism, community economic development and gender issues.

**Auliana Poon** heads Tourism Intelligence International, the research and consulting arm of Caribbean Futures Ltd. She is the author of *Tourism Technology and Competitive Strategies*.

**Richard Prentice** is Professor of Heritage Interpretation and Cultural Tourism in the University of Sunderland, UK. His research interests are in the areas of heritage and cultural tourism, especially in response to marketing and consumer development.

**M. Thea Sinclair** is Professor of Economics and Director of Research at the Christel DeHaan Tourism and Travel Research Institute, University of Nottingham, UK. She has undertaken considerable research on the economics of tourism, including research for the United Nations and the World Bank. Her research interests are currently in tourism demand modelling, tourism impact modelling, tourism taxation policy, economic development and sustainability.

**Gunter Sugiyarto** is a Researcher at the Christel DeHaan Tourism and Travel Research Institute, University of Nottingham, UK. He has a PhD from the School of Economics, University of Nottingham and his research interests are in the modelling of the economic impact of tourism and the distributional implications of tourism in conjunction with issues such as globalisation, trade liberalisation and taxation.

**John Urry** is Professor of Sociology at the University of Lancaster, UK. He is the author of *The Tourist Gaze*; *Consuming Places*; *Touring Cultures* (edited with C. Rojek); Contested Natures (co-authored with P. Macnaghten); *Sociology Beyond Societies*; and *Bodies of Nature* (co-edited with P. Macnaghten).

**Geoff Wall** is Professor of Geography and Associate Dean for Graduate Studies and Research at the University of Waterloo, Ontario, Canada. His research interests are in coastal zone management, eco-planning and environmental management.

**Brian Wheeller** is Senior Lecturer in Tourism at the Centre for Urban and Regional Studies, University of Birmingham, UK. His research interests include international planning and development issues, eco/sustainable tourism, popular culture and tourism and the relationship between fish, fishing and travel and tourism.

## Chapter 1

# Progress in Tourism Research

CHRIS COOPER

*Progress in Tourism, Recreation and Hospitality Management* was launched in 1989 and ran to six volumes before reinventing itself as a quarterly refereed journal *Progress in Tourism and Hospitality Research*, now the *International Journal of Tourism Research*. In a sense the history of the publication reflects the development of the subject areas, partly as it was responsive to the needs of the research community, but also in an attempt to provide leadership and direction.

In the first editorial preface, I was critical of existing research in the field. Back in the late 1980s it was possible to identify a range of issues that are still familiar today:

- The field of tourism research remains bedevilled by conceptual weakness and fuzziness (Cooper, 1989; Cohen, 1974; Britton, 1979; Dann, Nash and Pearce, 1988). For example, there remains confusion and no real agreement over terminology, and this has led to a deep-rooted lack of rigour.
- Lack of focus remains an issue (Pearce, 1993). Research interests and foci sprawl across both the sectors of tourism and academic subject area, reinforcing the need for a disciplined approach and a more tightly focused research agenda.
- Tourism is still a relative newcomer to the academic world. Much of the research remains descriptive, often based upon one-off case studies, specific destinations or problems, still concerned with measurement but only exceptionally making links and identifying relationships (Sheldon *et al.*, 1987; Pearce, 1999). Attempts to build a core of theory or to make generalisations are rare, accentuating the fragmentation and lack of an organising framework that has characterised tourism research in the late twentieth and early twenty-first century.

- As if these issues were not enough, tourism research remains handi-
  capped by problems with data sources, although the work of the
  World Tourism Organization has done much to improve matters
  since the first volume of *Progress* was published. Nonetheless, the
  quality and compatibility of much tourism data remain problematic
  and hold back the field from serious research and statistical manipulation.

It can be argued that these characteristics of tourism research condemn it
to the 'pre-science' or 'pre-paradigmatic' stage of the development of a
subject area (Echtner & Jamal, 1997; Pearce, 1993). Taking Kuhn's (1970)
notion of paradigms, the current stage of the development of tourism
research clearly does not fit the concept of a fully fledged paradigm. Kuhn's
approach would therefore suggest that the danger for tourism research is
that if it remains fragmented amongst myriad disciplines and subjects, who
often do not speak the same academic language, then it will remain a
shallow and loosely articulated body of knowledge. It will thus lack the
defining characteristics of a paradigm; namely a 'shared constellation of
beliefs, values, techniques . . . models and examples' (Kuhn, 1970: 175).

However, the current direction of tourism research refutes these fears,
and indeed, there is much room for optimism to brighten the gloom that
may accompany Kuhn's analysis. There are two main reasons for this
optimism:

(1) A newly emergent wave of tourism research, drawn from varied disci-
    plinary backgrounds, is extending the boundaries of tourism research
    through their *disciplinary insights*.
(2) The traditional schism between academic and industry-based research
    is closing as research *commercialisation agendas* are articulated and
    developed.

## Disciplinary Insights

It has to be recognised that Kuhn was developing his ideas at a time
when there was greater rigidity and structure in academic subject areas
(Ryan, 1997). In the early years of the twenty-first century – with the unlim-
ited bibliographic and information access facilitated by technology – fields,
subjects and disciplines are more free flowing with blurring boundaries
and greater borrowing of ideas, theories and literature. Pearce (1993)
argues that this is a strength for tourism and that we should not be concerned that tourism does not fit the Kuhn model. If this is the case then
'tourism should have a greater tolerance for eclectic and diverse approaches to investigation' (Echtner & Jamal, 1997: 869).

The debate is taken further by Echtner and Jamal (1997: 877) suggesting that the key issue for tourism studies is to diversify away from previously inappropriate approaches:

> ... the evolution of tourism studies might be seen to be plagued by the same phobia that dominates all of the social sciences, namely the need to become more 'scientific' and the resulting attachment to more traditional positivist methods.

There is resonance here across the writing of a number of researchers. For example, Ryan (1997: 3) wonders 'if we were not entrenched in a positivist tradition that was blinding us, as a group of scholars, to developments in the other social sciences'. In these other social sciences there are refreshing examples of the development of tourism research that rejects the positivist approach. For example, in tourism, Rojek and Urry's (1997) book *Touring Cultures* is overtly written from the standpoint of rejecting positivism and economic abstraction, whilst in leisure, Rojek's (1995) book *Decentring Leisure* is equally robust in challenging traditional approaches.

Franklin and Crang (2001) are more outspoken in their criticism of earlier tourism research, characterising it as stale and unexciting. They identify three reasons for this:

- The rapid growth of tourism has led researchers to simply record and document tourism in a series of case studies, examples and industry-sponsored projects, undertaken by a group of researchers 'whose work has become petrified in standardized explanations, accepted analyses and foundational ideas [with] . . . a tendency for studies to follow a template . . . ' (p. 6).
- The understanding of tourism has been reduced to a set of economic activities.
- Tourism is framed for study as a series of discrete local events where destinations are viewed as the passive recipient of tourism activity.

Tourism researchers must therefore *break the meniscus* of the poverty of tourism studies by taking the many conceptual and theoretical approaches to tourism that have yet to be tested. By freeing tourism research from the straitjacket of positivism, and opening up the subject to other approaches we can build upon the strengths of the contributory disciplines to analyse and understand the nature of tourism and the tourist (Hall, 1998). Two examples illustrate the potential richness of this approach:

(1) Crouch (1999: 12) takes contemporary geographical concepts and applies them to tourism. He argues that current concepts of tourism are too narrow and should be broadened to a concept of 'leisure / tourism'

given the overlap and hybrid nature of the two fields. Central to his approach is tourism as an 'encounter':

> Enlarging the qualitative and ethnographic investigation of what people do, and make sense of, in leisure practices will improve the critical texture of understanding. There is a much needed extension of practices, spaces and knowledge towards a greater understanding of their social distinctiveness and relativity.

(2) Franklin and Crang's (2001) review of the sociological literature suggests that a new research agenda is urgently needed, an agenda which recognises that tourism studies is about mobilities, the hybrid nature of both the activity and the academic approach and above all, should reflect the activity of tourism itself and be 'enjoyable'. In pursuing this agenda we should not

> . . . be in the business of importing wholesale theories from some other topics in some fit of 'theory envy' . . . tourist studies should be fertile ground for testing and developing social theory (Franklin & Crang, 2001: 18).

## Commercialisation Agendas

The tension between academic and industry-based research in tourism is a constant. As an applied field of study, it is inevitable that academics are involved in supplying research to the tourism sector, both industry and government. However, the tension between the two types of research is rooted in the different aims and objectives of the groups involved (Cobanoglu & Moreo, 2001). Jenkins (1999) provides an insightful articulation of the debate between academic and practitioner research in tourism. Academics he suggests, are employed as technicians and specialists to support practitioners. But it is the practitioners who formulate and implement policy and decisions. As such, the academic literature has little impact upon the tourism practitioner (see Table 1.1).

Much of the tension is caused by poor communication between academics and industry. As tourism matures as an industry it is vital that it adopts a 'knowledge-based' platform upon which to make its commercial and policy decisions (Jafari, 1990, 2000; Smith, 1995). Ritchie (2000) provides a useful framework here, categorising the different types of research and their appropriate use by the industry. In part what is needed in tourism is the true development of learning organisations (Flood, 1999) allowing tourism organisations to be ready for the unpredictable and to harness intellectual property in order to be more competitive, profitable and

**Table 1.1** The differing approaches of academic and practitioner tourism Researchers

| *Academics* | *Practitioners* |
|---|---|
| Advance knowledge and understanding of the subject | Work in a contractual, project specific and profit driven environment |
| Disseminate information through teaching, publications and conferences | Disseminate information through project specific reports, plans and studies that are commissioned and have a limited circulation |
| Educate and influence students, academics and the industry | Aim to develop their expertise and reputation to secure further work |

*Source*: Jenkins (1999)

responsive to events such as the 11th September terrorist attacks on the USA.

The work of Tribe (1997) is helpful here. He reworks traditional models of the discipline/subject debate in tourism. He proposes that tourism can be conceptualised as two fields – 'the business of tourism' and 'the non-business of tourism' – each of which are approached by four main methods of enquiry (Figure 1.1). In Figure 1.1 the outer band is formed of the key contributory disciplines to tourism; the middle band represents the two tourism fields of business and non-business of tourism; and between the two is band k where tourism theories and concepts are distilled. For the centre of the diagram Tribe draws upon the work of Gibbons *et al.* (1994). They view the production of knowledge as:

- 'mode 1' which is primarily generated in the disciplinary areas; or
- 'mode 2', which is developed from the application of research to specific problems outside of the disciplinary framework. In tourism this would be industry-generated research completed by governments, consultants, industry and professional bodies.

In tourism research the tension between academics and practitioners is effectively that between these two modes of knowledge production. This approach neatly encapsulates the two key issues identified in this chapter: (i) the expansion of the research agenda to take account of developments across other disciplines by a new wave of research in the outer bands of Figure 1.1; and (ii) the tension between a business management, industry-focused approach and other approaches in tourism research.

The way forward to resolve this tension is clear: where appropriate, the academic tourism research community needs to embrace concepts of

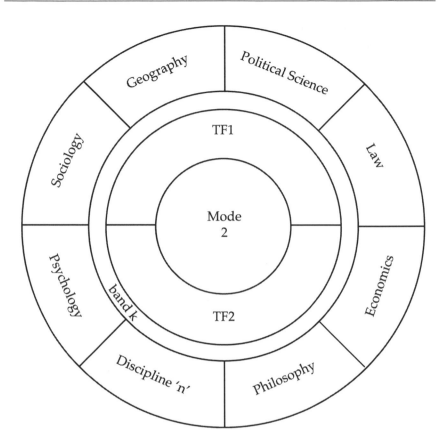

**Figure 1.1** The creation of tourist knowledge. Outer circle = Disciplines and subdisciplines; Middle circle = Fields of tourism; Inner circle = World of tourism; TFI = Business interdisciplinarity; TF2 = Non-business related tourism

*Source*: Tribe (1997)

research commercialisation and diffusion of their intellectual property (IP) to the tourism sector. Here, the Cooperative Research Centre for Sustainable Tourism in Australia has taken a lead in this approach, working out detailed commercialisation and diffusion strategies for tourism research projects and IP undertaken by academics (Cooper *et al.*, 2002; Scott, 1999). By adopting a commercialisation process, tourism research developed in the outer bands of Figure 1.1 can be developed for, and utilised by, the tourism business and government community, thus closing the traditional gap between tourism academics and the tourism industry.

## Progress in Tourism Research

This chapter is optimistic for the future of tourism research. Given the interdisciplinary nature of tourism studies and the new approaches and material now being published, there is a need to constantly synthesise and draw material together for researchers, teachers and students. This was the original concept of the *Progress* book series and the tradition is updated and continued in this volume of 'classic reviews'. *Progress* aimed to provide 'state of the art' reviews of research in the subject area. If anything, this need is even greater in the early years of the twenty-first century as new researchers enter the field, journals proliferate and tourism is taken seriously by a range of disciplines and subject areas.

This book revisits the leading authors and reviews from the first six volumes of *Progress* and provides updated 'state of the art' reviews. There is no doubt that many of the papers in the original *Progress* book series have stood the test of time and become oft-cited classics. The earliest of the updated reviews first appeared 15 years ago and the books are now out of print; I therefore felt that there was real value in identifying these influential papers and asking the authors to revisit them. Each author has interpreted this challenge in a different way, some staying very close to the original review, others radically changing their stance. The 'classic reviews' range from updated extensive subject area literature reviews – economics, sociology, statistics, history, human resources and marketing – to classic essays on gender, alternative tourism, urban tourism, heritage tourism, environmental auditing and Auliana Poon's 'new tourism'.

### References

Britton, R. (1979) Some notes on the geography of tourism. *Canadian Geographer* 33 (3), 276–82.

Cobanoglu, C. and Moreo, P.J. (2001) Hospitality research: Educators' perceptions. *Journal of Hospitality and Tourism Education* 13 (5), 9–20.

Cohen, E. (1974) Who is tourist? A conceptual classification. *Sociological Review* 22 (4), 527–55.

Cooper, C. (1989) Editorial Preface. In C. Cooper (ed.) *Progress in Tourism, Recreation and Hospitality Management 1* (pp. 1–3). London: Belhaven.

Cooper, C., Prideaux, B. and Ruhanen, L. (2002) *Destination Management Framework: Final Report*. Brisbane: Cooperative Research Centre for Sustainable Tourism.

Crouch, D. (1999) Introduction: Encounters in leisure/tourism. In D. Crouch (ed.) *Leisure/Tourism Geographies* (pp. 1–16). London: Routledge.

Dann, G.M.S., Nash, D. and Pearce, P.L. (1988) Methodology in tourism research. *Annals of Tourism Research* 15 (1), 1–28.

Echtner, C.M. and Jamal, T.B. (1997) The disciplinary dilemma of tourism studies. *Annals of Tourism Research* 21 (4), 868–83.

Flood, R.L. (1999) *Rethinking the Fifth Discipline. Learning Within the Unknowable*. London: Routledge.

Franklin, A, and Crang, M. (2001) The trouble with tourism and travel theory? *Tourist Studies* 1 (1), 5–22.

Gibbons, M., Limoges, C., Nowotny, H., Schwartzman, S., Scott, P. and Trow, M. (1994) *The Production of New Knowledge*. London: Sage.

Hall, C.M. (1998) Editor's Introduction. *Current Issues in Tourism* 1 (1), 1.

Jafari, J. (1990) Research and scholarship: The basis of tourism education. *Journal of Tourism Studies* 1 (1), 33–41.

Jafari, J. (2000) Introduction. In J. Jafari (ed.) *Encyclopedia of Tourism* (pp. xvii–xxiii). London: Routledge.

Jenkins, C. (1999) Tourism academics and tourism practitioners. Bridging the great divide. In D.G. Pearce, and R.W. Butler (eds) *Contemporary Issues in Tourism Development* (pp. 52–63). London: Routledge.

Kuhn, T. (1970) *The Structure of Scientific Revolutions* (2nd edn). Chicago: University of Chicago Press.

Pearce, D.G. (1999) Introduction. Issues and approaches. In D.G. Pearce and R.W. Butler (eds) *Contemporary Issues in Tourism Development* (pp. 1–12). London: Routledge.

Pearce, P. (1993) Defining tourism study as a specialism: A justification and implications. *TEORUS International* 1 (1), 25–32.

Ritchie, J.R.B. (2000) Research and the tourism industry: Building bridges of understanding and insight. *Tourism Recreation Research* 25 (1) 1–8.

Rojek, C (1995) *Decentring Leisure. Rethinking Leisure Theory*. London: Sage.

Rojek, C. and Urry, J. (1997) Transformations of travel and theory. In C. Rojek and J. Urry (eds) *Touring Cultures: Transformations of Travel and Theory* (pp. 1–19). London: Routledge.

Ryan, C. (1997) Tourism – A mature discipline? *Pacific Tourism Review* 1 (1), 3–5.

Scott, N. (1999) *Tourism Research in Australia*. Brisbane: Cooperative Research Centre for Sustainable Tourism Work in Progress, Report Series 11.

Sheldon, P.J., Juanita, C.L. and Gee, C.Y. (1987) The status of research in the lodging industry. *International Journal of Hospitality Management* 6 (2), 89–96.

Smith, S.L.J.(1995) *Tourism Analysis: A Handbook* (2nd edn). Harlow: Longman.

Tribe, J. (1997) The indiscipline of tourism. *Annals of Tourism Research* 24 (3), 638–57.

Chapter 2

# The Sociology of Tourism

JOHN URRY

## Introduction

The sociology of tourism has been a rapidly developing specialism over the past decade or so. This development has stemmed from:

- the growing interest in services as they become of overwhelming employment significance in Western economies;
- the belated recognition of the complex nature of tourist-related services;
- the increased attention being paid to the 'culture' of societies and hence to the variety of possible images and meanings conveyed by different tourist sites; and
- the rapid changes in the tourist industry, such as the growth of industrial, green, city centre and 'dark' tourisms which have induced interest in the sociological causes and consequences of such unexpected and often somewhat bizarre developments (see Lennon & Foley, 2000, on the 'dark tourism' of Auschwitz, assassination and murder sites, prisoner-of-war camps and so on).

The discipline is, however, characterised by intellectual underdevelopment. Still the best book is MacCannell's *The Tourist* (1989; and see 1992). Empirical studies abound, but until recently, few of them contributed to a sophisticated corpus of research findings (the best are in the *Annals of Tourism Research*). In the last few years, however, the sociology of tourism has been strengthened by an increasing input from other sociological sub-disciplines, from cultural and leisure studies, industrial sociology, urban and regional sociology, museum studies and the sociology / anthropology of culture. Overall, the sociology of tourism is gradually adapting to the dramatic transformations occurring within those social practices we conventionally classify as 'tourism'; but this is being achieved through drawing on, and in part incorporating, a variety of literatures and debates taking place in social science generally and within other branches of sociology in particular. This will be shown through elaborating some key areas of sociological debate within tourism and travel.

## Authenticity

The predominant issue has been that of authenticity, beginning with Boorstin's (1964) analysis of the pseudo-event. Isolated from the host environment and local people, the mass tourist travels in guided groups, cocooned within an environmental bubble. The tourist is said to find pleasure in inauthentic, contrived attractions, gullibly enjoying pseudo-events and disregarding the 'real' world. Over time the images generated within tourism come to constitute a self-perpetuating system of illusions, which may appear as quaint to the local inhabitants as they do to the tourists themselves (Duncan, 1978: 277). Turner and Ash (1975) elaborate on the manufacturing of this highly circumscribed world of the tourist. Surrogate parents, travel agents, tour operators and hoteliers, relieve the tourists of responsibility for their actions. Eco (1986) has famously examined the 'hyper-real', those simulated designed places that have the appearance of being more 'real' than the original. With hyper-reality the sense of vision is reduced to a limited array of features, is then exaggerated and comes to dominate the other senses. Hyper-real places are characterised by surface appearances that do not respond to or welcome the viewer. The sense of sight is reduced to the most immediate and visible aspects of the scene, such as the seductive if wholly inauthentic façades of Main Street in Disneyland (Bryman, 1995; Fjellman, 1992).

Cohen (1972; 1979; 1988) has challenged such a dystopic view, by maintaining that there are in fact a wide variety of types of tourist experience. He develops a typology based on parallels drawn from the sociology of religion, noting that 'experiential', 'experimental' and 'existential' tourists depend neither upon environmental bubbles nor wish to avoid entirely the 'strangeness' of people and places being visited.

MacCannell (1989) also criticises Boorstin and others on the grounds that this viewpoint reflects an upper-class view that other people are 'tourists' while oneself is a 'traveller' (see Buzard, 1993, more generally on the power of this distinction). MacCannell maintains that people do not seek inauthentic pseudo-events. Rather, tourists embody a quest for authenticity; they are a kind of contemporary pilgrim, especially to view the 'real lives' of others. Such lives, however, are only found backstage and are not immediately obvious to visitors. Large numbers of gazing tourists would in fact be far too intrusive and so over time the people being observed and local tourist entrepreneurs come to construct backstages, tourist spaces, that are contrived and artificial. MacCannell (1973) terms this production, 'staged authenticity'. Such a staging results from the social relations of tourism and not from an individualistic search for the inauthentic. Pearce and Moscardo (1986) have argued in criticism that it is necessary to distinguish between the authenticity of the setting from the authenticity of the persons that are observed, and between different elements of the experience relevant to each tourist (see also Pearce, 1982, and critique in Turner & Manning, 1988).

Based on research at New Salem where Abraham Lincoln spent some years in the 1830s, Bruner (1994) has distinguished further between various conflicting senses of the authentic:

- First, there is the authentic in the sense of a small town that 'looks' like it has appropriately aged over the previous 170 years, whether the buildings are actually that old or not.
- Second, there is the town that appears as it would have looked in the 1830s, that is, mostly comprised of 'new' buildings.
- Third, there are the buildings and artefacts that literally 'date' from the 1830s and have been there since then.
- Fourth, there are those buildings and artefacts that have been authorised as 'authentic' by the Trust that oversees 'heritage' within that town.

Holderness (1988) has similarly described the processes in Stratford-upon-Avon by which the Shakespeare Birthplace Trust has come to exert a hegemonic role in the town, determining which buildings, places and artefacts are authentically part of 'Shakespeare's heritage' and those which are not so 'authenticated' (see Lash & Urry, 1994: 264–6). Bruner also notes that New Salem now is wholly different from the 1830s since in the previous period there would not have been camera-waving tourists wandering about in large numbers excitedly staring at actors dressed up as though they were residents of a previous long since disappeared epoch.

The implication then is that the 'search for authenticity' is too simple a foundation for explaining contemporary tourism. There are multiple discourses and processes of the 'authentic'. Feifer (1985) also talks of the development of 'post-tourists', people who almost delight in the inauthenticity of the normal tourist experience. The post-tourist finds pleasure in the multitude of tourist games that can be played, in the knowledge that there is no real, authentic experience, and in their awareness that any apparent authenticity has been elaborately staged.

Crick (1988) also argues that in a sense all cultures are 'staged' or inauthentic. They are continually being remade, reinvented and their elements reorganised, whether or not they are viewed or may be viewed by tourists (see various examples in Rojek & Urry, 1997). For example, since the mid-nineteenth century, travel to see the key sites, texts, exhibitions, buildings, landscapes and achievements of a society has been part of the development of a national culture (McCrone, 1998: 53–5). Almost all cultures have invented (and re-invented) an 'authentic' culture, with the founding of national museums, the development of national artists, architects, musicians, playwrights, novelists, historians and archaeologists and the location of the nation's achievements within various world exhibitions. This last feature began with the Great Exhibition in London in 1851, and has then been followed by many other events where the invented national culture is on display, as with the so-called 'mega-events' such as the Sydney Olympics analysed by Roche (2000).

## Pilgrimage

Such visits have often taken something of the form of a pilgrimage to see the nation's sacred sties. Thus a further line of research has been concerned with the specific nature of the tourist experience as pilgrimage; this also drawing on literature from the sociology of religion. Turner (1973, 1974) analysed pilgrimages in terms of the *rites de passage* involved in movement from one stage to another. First, there is social and spatial separation from the normal place of residence and conventional social ties. Second, there is the liminal zone where the individual finds him/herself in an 'anti-structure', out of time and space, which provides an intensive social bonding or 'communitas', as well as the direct experience of the sacred. And third, there is reintegration as the individual re-enters the previous social group, usually with a higher social status. Various parallels have been drawn between pilgrimages and tourism (Cohen, 1988; Eade and Sallnow, 1991). The tourist moves from a familiar place to a far place and then returns to the familiar place. At the far place there is the worshipping at sacred shrines and the tourist is supposedly uplifted through intensive social bonding in which everyday obligations are suspended or inverted. In the liminal zone there is a licence for permissive or playful behaviour. And then there is return with enhanced social status.

Shields (1991) uses this notion of pilgrimage in his analysis of tourism within what he calls 'places on the margin'. At Niagara Falls, for example, honeymooners found themselves in an ideal liminal zone characterised by the relaxation of strict bourgeois social conventions, by relative anonymity and freedom from collective scrutiny, and by the awesome sublime experience of the Falls themselves. A similar analysis is provided of Brighton beach. In the middle of the nineteenth century it changed from a health resort to a pleasure beach, providing a built-in escape from the patterns and rhythms of everyday urban life. The beach had a further characteristic as a site for carnival, becoming noisy and crowded, full of unpredictable social mixing, involving the inversion of social hierarchies and moral codes, particularly with regard to extravagant bodily display.

Some writers have adopted the view that such 'ludic' behaviour is restitutive or compensatory, revitalising the tourists for their return to the familiar places of home and work (Lett, 1983). Other writers, though, maintain that notions of liminality and inversion have to be given a more specific content. It is necessary to consider exactly the social and cultural patterns in the tourist's day-to-day existence that has had to be inverted. And Edensor (1998) has elaborated the wide variety of different kinds of spatial practices that various kinds of tourists demonstrate at a single tourist site, in his case the Taj Mahal in India. His account undermines any single 'theory' of tourist practice.

## Visuality

*The Tourist Gaze* nevertheless argues for the fundamentally visual nature of tourism experiences (Urry, 2002; and see 1995). Gazes organise the encounters of visitors with the 'other', providing some sense of competence, pleasure and structure to those experiences. The gaze demarcates an array of pleasurable qualities to be generated within particular times and spaces. It is the gaze that orders and regulates the relationships between the various sensuous experiences while away, identifying what is visually out-of-ordinary, which establish 'difference' and what is 'other'. There are various contrasts: the seeing of a unique object, like the Eiffel Tower, which is famous for being famous; the seeing of particular signs, such as the typical German beer garden; the seeing of unfamiliar aspects of what had been thought familiar, such as museums of rural life; the seeing of ordinary aspects of social life undertaken by people in unusual contexts; the carrying out of familiar activities within an unfamiliar environment; and the seeing of particular signs which make it clear who for example lived in a specific house or painted a particular painting.

However, various writers have criticised this argument. Some have argued that the notion of the gaze is insufficiently developed in relationship to its Foucauldian legacy and especially to the related notion of the medical gaze (Hollingshead, 2000; but see Urry, 1992). Many holiday experiences are said to be physical or corporeal and are not merely visual (Veijola & Jokinnen, 1994). Relatedly, it is argued that the notion of the gaze is too static and passive and ignores performance and adventure (Perkins & Thorns, 1998). And finally, the gaze does not capture the moving, mobile, fleeting character of seeing or 'glancing' the other – it focuses upon the tourist while at 'rest' rather than gazing or glancing while walking, or looking out from a train or looking through a car windscreen (Larsen, 2001; Urry, 2002: Postscript).

Recently, the connections between the tourist gaze and photography have been further elaborated by especially Taylor (1994) and Osborne (2000). Photography has been shown to be crucial in the development of tourism. They are not separate processes but each derives from and enhances the other, an 'ensemble' according to Osborne (2000). If photography had not been 'invented', then contemporary tourism based upon the gaze would have been wholly different (see Crawshaw & Urry (1997), on the 'romantics' desire to fix fleeting images). Indeed there would not be anything like the contemporary global tourism industry at all. Osborne (2000: 70) describes: 'the ultimate inseparability of the medium [of photography] from tourism's general culture and economy and from the varieties of modern culture of which they are constitutive'.

Photography has been enormously significant in democratising various kinds of mobilities, making notable whatever gets photographed (Barthes, 1981: 34). Photography also gives shape to travel so that journeys consist of one 'good view' to capture on film, to a series of others. The objects and technologies of cameras and films have constituted the very nature of travel, as sites turn into sights, and have constructed what is worth going to 'sightsee' and what images and memories should be brought back (see Taylor, 1994, for many examples). The camera turns nature and society into a set of graspable objects: 'the snapshot transforms the resistant aspect of nature into something familiar and intimate, something we can hold in our hands and memories. In this way, the camera allows us some control over the visual environments of our culture' (Wilson, 1992: 122). Nature, other environments and humans are transformed into objects that are passed from person to person. They are put on walls to decorate a house, they structure reminiscences and they create images of place (Taylor, 1994).

An example of how photography and tourism are intricately connected can be seen in late nineteenth-century Egypt. Gregory (1999) has described the processes of 'kodakisation', as Egypt became scripted as a place of constructed visibility, with multiple, enframed theatrical scenes set up for the edification, entertainment and visual consumption of 'European' visitors. Cairo became 'no more than a Winter Suburb of London' (Löfgren 2000: 162). Studies have shown how this produced a 'new Egypt' available for visually consuming visitors. Such an Egypt consisted of the Suez Canal, of 'Paris-on-the-Nile', of Thomas Cook and Sons, of a cleaned-up 'ancient Egypt', of the exotic oriental 'other' and of convenient vantage-points and viewing platforms for the gaze (see Brendon, 1991, on the iconic role of Thomas Cook).

## Heritage

Particularly significant in the British sociology of tourism has been a concern with heritage and the establishment of links with museum studies. It has been noted how contemporary museums have been transformed. These used to be based on the aura of the authentic historical artefact. Home (1984) describes tourists as having been modern 'pilgrims' who carried guide books as devotional texts. In museums there was a ceremonial agenda, in which it was specified what objects should be seen, the order in which such viewing should occur and sense of awe to be displayed.

There are three main ways in which the auratic museum has been undermined. First, there has been a marked broadening of the objects deemed worthy of preservation as alternative or vernacular histories have proliferated. Visitors are increasingly attracted by representations of the 'ordinary' or the 'popular' as museums have shifted from aura to nostalgia (see Lumley, 1988). Samuel (1994) has documented in Britain the new democratic, familial, workerist, femininist, consumerist and domestic heritages that various social organisations have saved and laid out for display (see Macdonald, 1997, on the Aros Gaelic heritage centre on the Isle of Skye).

Second, museums themselves have changed. Visitors are no longer expected to stand in awe of the exhibits. Participation is encouraged as museums are now found out-of-doors, sometimes even with sounds and smells. Many glass cases have disappeared and visitors are expected not just to see, but on occasions to touch, hear and remember. In come cases actors play historical roles and interact with visitors in simple historical sketches (see Hewison, 1987, for an excoriating critique of such vulgar 'heritage').

Third, the relationship between museums and other social institutions is being transformed. Institutions such as shops, restaurants and pubs/bars increasingly look like museums. And in turn museums seem to look more and more like commercial institutions, with cafes, shops, and displays designed to entertain rather than to celebrate an unchanging national heritage (Vergo, 1989). Post-modern museums are said increasingly to provide 'edutainment', a mixture of popular education and commercial entertainment (see Judd & Fainstein's, 1999 account of *The Tourist City* which examines the production of many such 'places to play').

The development of such 'experience' sites of vernacular heritage has been analysed in the case of Welsh coal mining communities. Dicks (2000) notes how the only remaining colliery building in the Rhondda valley, a valley iconic of Welshness where there were once 66 deep mines, is now the Rhondda Heritage Park. This is based in the previous Lewis Merthyr mine. The heritage park resulted from extensive local campaigning through the discourse of what she calls 'memorialism' and it provides the only significant public memorial in the Rhondda to the once totally dominant mining industry (Dicks, 2000: chapters 6 and 7). However, the development of the Heritage Park involved huge disagreements over the scale and form of the memorial and the degree to which it should be turned from a memorial into a much broader tourism/heritage project which, it is said, only weakly captures the voices of the local community.

## Consumption

This last point in turn relates to the burgeoning interest in the changing nature of consumption. Campbell (1987) for example, in his examination of the importance of consumerism for the growth of capitalism, argues that individuals acquire satisfaction, not from their actual selection, purchase and use of objects, but from anticipation and daydreaming, from imaginative pleasure-seeking. People thus seek to experience 'in reality' the pleasurable dramas that have already emerged in their daydreams, but 're-ality' always turns out to be deeply disappointing and so consumers are continually turning to ever-new products or new places to visit.

One problem in Campbell's analysis is that he treats modern consumerism as relatively unchanging. However, various commentators have argued that there is a sea-change taking place in the organisation of contemporary Western societies, involving the shift from 'Fordism' to 'Post-Fordism' (Harvey, 1989; Urry, 2002). Part of this involves the change in typical modes of consumption, from mass consumption to more individual patterns, with greater differentiation and volatility of consumer preferences and a heightened need for producers to be consumer-driven and to segment markets more systematically. One example of this has been the change in the name of British holiday camps – once the paradigm case of Fordist tourism – which have now been renamed as centres or holiday-worlds in which freedom for different segments of the market is highlighted (Ward & Hardy, 1986). Poon (1993; and see Chapter 8 this volume) describes these changes in terms of a shift from *old tourism*, which involved packaging, regimentation and standardisation, to *new tourism*, which is segmented, flexible and customised.

One difficulty faced by the providers of various tourist services is that holiday-makers are only partly interested in consuming these services. They are often incidental to the particular experience that the tourist is seeking, such as the view of a magnificent Alpine mountain or of the strip on Las Vegas or of Niagara Falls. The consumption is at least partly visual and there is a rather unclear relationship between that gaze and the wide range of services which tourists happen to purchase around that unique and special experience (see Urry, 2002).

## Services

Indeed with manufactured commodities it is normally clear what the product is. By contrast, it is often difficult to specify the boundary and content of many services (Mars & Nicod, 1984). This is because the expenditure of labour is central to services and this involves some intentional social process in which interaction occurs between one or more producers and one or more consumers. The quality of this social interaction is itself part of the service. To buy the service is to buy a particular social or sociological experience. Many tourist-related services are especially high-contact systems and hence are difficult to rationalise (see Pine, 1987). Part of what is purchased is a particular social composition of those serving in the front line, and hence the service is infused with particular social characteristics of gender, class, race, generation, education, and so on (see Hochschild, 1983; Wouters, 1989, on changes in the case of flight attendants). Moreover, what is generally bought in a tourist-related service is a particular social composition of the other consumers. This is because the consumption of the service normally takes time, it occurs in close proximity to others, and its social meaning is unclear except via the markers provided by the social characteristics of fellow consumers (see Urry, 2002, chapter 4).

Such services also require 'emotional labour', the need to smile in a pleasant, friendly and involved way to consumers. In the case of flight attendants, Hochschild (1983) describes the specific training given to provide emotional labour, training which has the effect of commercialising human feelings. In a study of a Scottish restaurant Marshall (1986: 41) notes that staff were constantly encouraged to 'cater' for the customers: 'to smile, exchange pleasantries, and, if there was time, longer conversations'. However, this kind of emotional work tends to be difficult and demanding, often under-recognised and not well rewarded. It also tends to be carried out by women and may involve notions of 'sexual' servicing (see Adkins, 1995).

Indeed, research has shown how for many consumers what is actually consumed is the particular moment of delivery by the relatively low-level service deliverers. This causes problems for management, including the need to minimise friction with more highly paid (often male) workers backstage (see Whyte, 1948, for the classic examination of this in restaurants). Jan Carlzon (1987) (former President of the Scandinavian airline SAS) has termed the encounters between service producers and consumers 'moments of truth'. Because of their importance, it is necessary that organisations should be restructured with a flatter hierarchy. The actual service deliverers, the company's 'foot soldiers', need to be given more responsibility to respond effectively, quickly and courteously to the particular needs of the customers. The service deliverers should themselves be regarded as the 'managers' and be more consumer-oriented (see Poon, 1993 and see Chapter 8 this volume).

Crang (1993) pursued some of these issues in a study of a 'fun' restaurant in Cambridge. He noted how service encounters possess a performative character. One can think of this kind of workplace as a stage, involving a mix of mental, manual and emotional labour. Staff are chosen because they possess the right sort of cultural capital, they have to be informal, young, friendly, with the right sort of body and skills to produce appropriate emotional performances. The self is key since the performances have to be 'authentically' fun-loving, informal and sociable. Staff demonstrate various 'social and emotional' skills as they adjust their performances through the cultural readings and interactions with a wide variety of customers. The restaurant is described as a place of emotions, with staff talk of 'getting in the mood' at the beginning of the evening, to allow the emotions to flow. The staff, and especially the young female waitressing staff, operate under the gaze of customers and are expected to perform in accordance with gender specific notions (and see Desmond, 1999, on the prevalence within tourism of the bodily display of women dancers).

## Conclusion

There is now a sociology of tourism although there is no longer the sense that there is a single 'theory' that accounts for all such practices. Such a sociology has developed through a kind of parasitism upon broader debates and controversies within sociology and cultural studies, as hopefully this chapter has shown. Its future development is much to be encouraged, since otherwise the world's largest area of employment (and activity) will be seriously under-researched, especially as this area involves major reconfigurations of the very character of the social relations of hosts and guests (see Smith, 1989). The sociology of tourism is currently only just keeping up with tourism's awesome rate of economic and social development.

## Note

1. This chapter first appeared as 'The sociology of tourism' in Volume 1 of *Progress in Tourism, Recreation and Hospitality Management* (1989), pp. 48–57.

## References
Adkins, L. (1995) *Gendered Work*. Buckinghamshire: Open University Press.

Barthes, R. (1981) *Camera Lucida*. New York: Hill And Wang.

Boorstin, D. (1964) *The Image: A Guide to Pseudo-Events in America*. New York: Harper.

Brendon, P. (1991) *Thomas Cook: 150 Years of Popular Tourism*. London: Secker & Warburg.

Bruner, E. (1994) Abraham Lincoln as authentic reproduction: A critique of postmodernism. *American Anthropologist* 96, 397–415.

Bryman, A. (1995) *Disney and his Worlds*. London: Routledge.

Buzard, J. (1993) *The Beaten Track*. Oxford: Clarendon Press.

Campbell, C. (1987) *The Romantic Ethic and the Spirit of Modern Consumerism*. Oxford: Blackwell.

Carlzon, J., (1987) *Moments of Truth*. Cambridge, MA: Bollinger.

Cohen, E. (1972) Towards a sociology of international tourism, *Social Research* 39, 164–82.

Cohen, E. (1979) A phenomenology of tourist types. *Sociology* 13, 179–201.

Cohen, E. (1988) Traditions in the qualitative sociology of tourism. *Annals of Tourism Research* 15 (1), 29–46.

Crang, P. (1993) A new service economy: On the geographies of service employment. PhD thesis, University of Cambridge.

Crawshaw, C. and Urry, J. (1997) Tourism and the photographic eye. In C. Rojek and J. Urry (eds) *Touring Cultures*. London: Routledge.

Crick, M. (1988) Representations of international tourism in the social sciences: Sun, sex, sights, savings, and servility. *Annual Review of Anthropology* 18, 307–44.

Desmond, J. (1999) *Staging Tourism*. Chicago: University of Chicago Press.

Dicks, B. (2000) *Heritage, Place and Community*. Cardiff: University of Wales Press.

Duncan, J. (1978) The social construction of unreality: An interactionist approach to the tourist's cognition of environment. In D. Ley and M. Samuels (eds) *Humanistic Geography: Prospects and Problems*. London: Croom Helm.

Eade, J. and Sallnow, M. (1991) *Contesting The Sacred. The Anthropology of Christian Pilgrimage*. London: Routledge.

Eco, U. (1986) *Travels In Hyper-Reality*. London: Picador.

Edensor, T. (1998) *Tourists at the Taj*. London: Routledge.

Feifer, M. (1985) *Going Places*. London: Macmillan.

Fjellman, S. (1992) *Vinyl Leaves: Walt Disney World and America*. Boulder, CO: Westview Press.

Gregory, D. (1999) Scripting Egypt: Orientalism and the cultures of travel. In J. Duncan and D. Gregory (eds) *Writes of Passage*. London: Routledge.

Harvey, D. (1989) *The Condition of Postmodernity*. Oxford: Blackwell.

Hewison, R. (1987) *The Heritage Industry*. London: Methuen.

Hochschild, A. (1983) *The Managed Heart: Commercialization of Human Feeling*. Berkeley: University of California Press.

Holderness, G. (1988) Bardolatry: Or, the cultural materialist's guide to Stratford-upon-Avon. In G. Holderness (ed.) *The Shakespeare Myth*. Manchester: Manchester University Press.

Hollingshead, K. (2000) The tourist gaze and its games of truth. An elaboration of the governmentality of Foucault via Urry. Millennium Conference: Tourism 2000, Sheffield, September.

Home, D. (1984) *The Great Museum*. London: Pluto.

Judd, D. and Fainstein, S. (1999) *The Tourist City*. Yale University Press: Cornell.

Larsen, J. (2001) Tourism mobilities and the tourist glance: The 'tourist gaze' in motion. Mimeo. Dept of Sociology, Lancaster University.

Lash, S. and Urry, J. (1994) *Economies of Signs and Space*. London: Sage.

Lennon, J. and Foley, M. (2000) *Dark Tourism*. London: Continuum.

Lett, J. (1983) Ludic and liminoid aspects of charter yacht tourism in the Caribbean. *Annals of Tourism Research* 10 (1), 35–56.

Löfgren, O. (2000). *On Holiday: A History of Vacationing*. Berkeley: University of California Press.

Lumley, R., (1988) (ed.) *The Museum Time-Machine*, London: Routledge.

MacCannell, D. (1973) Staged authenticity: Arrangements of social space in tourist settings. *American Sociological Review* 79, 589–603.

MacCannell, D. (1989 [1976]) *The Tourist*. London: Macmillan.

MacCannell, D. (1992) *Empty Meeting Grounds*. New York: Routledge.

Macdonald, S. (1997) A people's story: Heritage, identity and authenticity. In C. Rojek and J. Urry (eds) *Touring Cultures*. London: Routledge.

Mars, G. and Nicod, M. (1984) *The World of Waiters*. London: Allen and Unwin.

Marshall, G., (1986) The workplace culture of a licensed restaurant. *Theory, Culture and Society* 3, 33–48.

McCrone, D. (1998) *The Sociology of Nationalism*. London: Routledge.

Osborne, P. (2000) *Travelling Light. Photography, Travel and Visual Culture*. Manchester: Manchester University Press.

Pearce, P. and Moscardo, G. (1986) The concept of authenticity in tourist experiences. *Australian and New Zealand Journal of Sociology* 22, 121–32.

Pearce, P. (1982) *The Social Psychology of Tourist Behaviour*. Oxford: Pergamon.

Perkins, H. and Thorns, D. (1998) Gazing or performing: Characterising the contemporary tourist experience: Work in progress. Paper given to World Congress of Sociology, Montreal, July–August.

Pine, R. (1987) *Management of Technological Change in the Catering Industry*. Aldershot: Avebury.

Poon, A. (1993) *Tourism, Technology and Competitive Strategies*. Wallingford: CAB International.

Roche, M. (2000) *Mega-Events and Modernity*. London: Routledge.

Rojek, C. and Urry, J. (eds) (1997) *Touring Cultures*. London: Routledge.

Samuel, R. (1994) *Theatres of Memory*. London: Verso.

Shields, R., (1991) *Places on the Margin*. London: Routledge.

Smith, V. (ed.) (1989) *Hosts and Guests. The Anthropology of Tourism*. Philadelphia: University of Pennsylvania Press.

Taylor, J. (1994) *A Dream of England. Landscape, Photography and the Tourist's Imagination*. Manchester: Manchester University Press.

Turner, C. and Manning, P. (1988) Placing authenticity – on being a tourist: A reply to Pearce and Manning. *Australian and New Zealand Journal of Sociology* 24, 136–8.

Turner, L. and Ash, J. (1975) *The Golden Hordes*. London: Constable.

Turner V. (1973) The center out there: Pilgrim's goal. *History of Religions* 12, 191–230.

Turner, V. (1974) *The Ritual Process,* Harmondsworth: Penguin.

Urry, J. (1992) The tourist gaze 'revisited'. *American Behavioral Scientist* 36, 172–86.

Urry, J. (1995) *Consuming Places.* London: Routledge.

Urry, J. (2002) *The Tourist Gaze.* 2nd edn. London: Sage.

Veijola, S. and Jokinen, E. (1994) The body in tourism. *Theory, Culture and Society* 6, 125–51.

Vergo, P. (ed.) (1989) *The New Museology.* London: Reaktion.

Ward, M. and Hardy, D. (1986) *Goodnight Campers! The History of the British Holiday Camp.* London: Mansell Publishing.

Whyte, W.F. (1948) *Human Relations in the Restaurant Industry.* New York: McGraw-Hill.

Wilson, A. (1992) *Culture of Nature.* Oxford: Blackwell.

Wouters, C. (1989) The sociology of emotions and flight attendants: Hochschild's 'Managed Heart'. *Theory, Culture and Society* 6, 95–124.

Chapter 3

# The Economics of Tourism

M. THEA SINCLAIR, ADAM BLAKE and GUNTUR SUGIYARTO

## Introduction

The economics of tourism is concerned with the allocation of scarce resources to satisfy consumers' demand for tourism and with the impact of
tourism at the macroeconomic and microeconomic levels. Tourism supply
is itself a composite of various goods and services, including accommodation, transport, agency services, food and souvenirs. While the existing
literature has treated the demand for tourism in depth, the literature on the
supply of tourism has tended to focus on certain sectors, mainly hotel accommodation, air transport and the tour operator sector, because of the
fragmented nature of supply. The literature on the demand for tourism has
examined the motivations for tourism, estimating the responsiveness of
demand to different determinants and providing forecasts of future levels
of demand. The supply-side literature has focused on the structure of tourism-related sectors, including vertical and horizontal integration within
and between hotels, airlines, tour operators and travel agents, as well as the
type of competition that occurs in each market.

The demand- and supply-side characteristics of tourism combine to
provide assessments of the wider impacts of tourism, ranging from measuring the size of tourism with input-output models, to quantifying the
impact of additional tourism demand through computable general equilibrium models and assessing the importance of tourism in economic
development. The environmental impact of tourism has been examined
from a variety of perspectives, extending from studies that provide
means of correcting environmental externalities to studies assessing the
importance of sustainable tourism development. All of these areas inter-
relate to provide policy recommendations on the appropriateness of
tourism taxation, regulation and controls, for the practical governance of
tourism.

## The Demand for Tourism

Analysis of tourism demand is useful for increasing our understanding of the relative importance of different economic determinants of demand, for forecasting and for related policy-formulation. Most of the past economic research on the demand for tourism has been based on two approaches, namely the single equation and the system of equations approaches. The former is a traditional approach, involving single equations which are specified on an a priori basis, while the latter is more recent, comprising a system of equations based on the theory of consumer demand. Both approaches permit the formulation and testing of hypotheses concerning the effects of particular variables on tourism demand, and permit the estimation of elasticity values that quantify the response of demand to a change in each explanatory variable. The elasticity values obtained from the two approaches are not strictly comparable in that those obtained from a system of equations refer to the changes in the shares of the tourism expenditure budget which are spent on tourism in different areas (or on different types, such as beach and city tourism), while the elasticity values obtained from the single equation approach refer to the change in tourism demand *per se*. Different forms of tourism display different elasticities. For example, business travel and visits to friends and relatives tend to be more price inelastic than general vacation demand, reflecting a degree of obligation rather than choice (Bull, 1995).

The early literature on tourism demand played a useful role in identifying the determinants of tourism demand, while more recent literature has made important contributions in terms of both the conceptual underpinnings of tourism demand analysis and econometric innovations in tourism demand modelling. This section will examine the contributions and the ways in which economic thinking about tourism demand has evolved over time. We will start by examining the contributions made by the early literature, based on single equation models of demand, and then discuss the increasing rigour that has been introduced by system of equations approaches. References to the innovations in the econometric techniques that can be used to model tourism demand will be made during the discussion. Tourism demand models have also been used for forecasting, using a range of modelling methods, including econometric approaches, statistical models and artificial intelligence techniques. They will not be discussed, as they merit more extensive consideration (see for example, Witt & Witt, 1995).

### The single equation approach and the economic determinants of tourism demand

Tourism demand can be examined for individual or groups of countries, states, regions, areas, for different types of visits or tourists, particular types of tourism products such as sports tourism and natural resources-based tourism, and for specific components of tourism products such as transportation, attractions and accommodation (Darnell *et al.*, 1990; Sinclair and Stabler, 1997; Crouch, 1994a, 1994b). The seasonality of tourism demand can also be considered (for example, Baron, 1975; Sutcliffe & Sinclair, 1980; Lim & McAleer, 2001). Noval (1975) classified six types of variables, namely the tendency to generate travel, tendency to receive/attract travel, impediments to travel, interaction between pairs of countries, interdependence factors and stochastic disturbances. Vanhove (1980) discussed market, destination, location and ties elements. Mikulicz (1983) further categorised three groups of independent variables that include market volume, costs of travel and image.

Much of the literature (reviewed by Archer, 1976; Johnson and Ashworth, 1990; Sheldon, 1990; Crouch, 1994a; Sinclair, 1991a) has focused on the demand for tourism at the national level, measuring demand as the number of tourist arrivals or departures, expenditure or receipts from tourism or the number of overnight stays (Jafari, 2000). Early studies were useful in identifying and discussing the main economic determinants of tourism demand: income, relative prices, exchange rates, and transport costs. In addition specific events may affect tourism demand. A single equation tourism demand function may, therefore, take the form:

$$D_{ij} = f(Y_i, P_{ij/c}, E_{ij/c}, T_{ij/c}, DE, \varepsilon)$$

where $D_{ij}$ is tourism demand by origin i for destination j; $Y_i$ is income of origin i; $P_{ij/c}$ is prices in origin i relative to destination j and competitor destinations c; $E_{ij/c}$ is exchange rates between origin i, destination j and competitor destinations c; $T_{ij/c}$ is the transport cost between origin i, destination j and competitor destinations c; DE is an event dummy variable to take account of special events, such as sporting events or political upheavals, and $\varepsilon$ is the disturbance term that captures all other factors which may influence the demand. All variables occur at time period $t$.

Income is generally considered to be a key determinant of tourism demand and commonly enters the demand function in per capita form (Artus, 1970, 1972; Askari, 1973; Barry and O'Hagan, 1971; Chadee and Mieczkowski, 1987; Diamond, 1977; Gray, 1966; Gunadhi and Boey, 1986; Kliman, 1981; Kwack, 1972; Little, 1980; Loeb, 1982; Martin and Witt, 1987, 1988; Papadopoulos and Witt, 1985; Smith and Toms, 1978; Summary, 1987; Syriopoulus, 1995; Uysal and Crompton, 1984; Witt and Martin, 1985, 1987). Total disposable income was included as an explanatory variable in some studies (Gray, 1966; Kwack, 1972; Oliver, 1971), while total national income (GNP) was included in others (Jud and Joseph, 1974; Kwack, 1972;

Papadopoulos and Witt, 1985; Tremblay, 1989). Results from empirical studies indicate that income is an important determinant of international tourism demand (see for example, Archer 1989; Crouch 1994a, b).

Relative prices are also a key determinant of demand, but the appropriate form of the prices to include in the demand function is by no means clear. The usual approach is to use the consumer price index as a proxy for the tourists' costs of living, due to the lack of a tourism price index measured over baskets of goods purchased by tourists (Witt & Witt, 1995). Kim and Uysal (1997) discuss the possibility that prices may not be independent but may, instead, change as tourism demand changes (endogeneity). The ratio of individual origin and destination country prices was included as an explanatory variable by Summary (1987) and of origin prices to weighted average destination prices by Oliver (1971). Loeb (1982) used the ratio of destination area prices to a weighted average of origin and alternative destination area prices.

Exchange rates are often viewed as determinants of tourism demand, as tourists may be more aware of exchange rates than of living costs in the destination country. Some studies have included the exchange rate between the tourist origin and individual destination currencies (Gray, 1966; Gunadhi & Boey, 1986; Loeb, 1982; Martin & Witt, 1987, 1988; Smith & Toms, 1978; Summary, 1987; Uysal & Crompton, 1984; Witt & Martin, 1985, 1987). Others have used the exchange rate between the tourist origin and a weighted average of destinations (Gunadhi & Boey, 1986; Little, 1980; Tremblay, 1989), or a composite relative prices (or tourism costs and exchange rate) variable (Artus, 1970; Barry & O'Hagan, 1971; Jud & Joseph, 1974; Kliman, 1981; Kwack, 1972; Martin & Witt, 1987, 1988; Papadopoulos & Witt, 1985; Stronge & Redman, 1982; Uysal & Crompton, 1984; Witt & Martin, 1985, 1987). There is a case for including both exchange rates and relative prices in the demand function, as a favourable exchange rate in the destination country could be offset by high inflation (Witt & Witt, 1995, Song & Witt, 2000). Empirical results suggest that exchange rates adjusted by consumer price indices may be a reasonable proxy for the cost of tourism (Martin & Witt, 1987), although further research is necessary.

Transport costs are sometimes included in the demand function (Askari, 1973; Bechdolt, 1973; Gray, 1966; Kliman, 1981; Little, 1980; Martin & Witt 1987, 1988; Papadopoulos & Witt, 1985; Smith & Toms, 1978; Stronge & Redman, 1982; Summary, 1987; Tremblay, 1989; Witt & Martin, 1985; 1987). However, there are problems of the appropriate measure to use, as well as of data availability, for such reasons as the complexity of fare structures. The increasing proportion of tourists joining package tours, which include airfares and accommodation, provides additional complications. Approximate measures such as airfares, petrol costs and distance are commonly used (Song & Witt, 2000). Hence, the incorporation of transport as a possible determinant of tourism demand should be treated with more caution and be the subject of more detailed theoretical and empirical investigation than has been the case to date (Sinclair & Stabler, 1997).

The use of dummy variables to account for specific or 'one off' events affecting tourism demand is also common. These include sporting events (Kliman, 1981; Little, 1980; Loeb, 1982) and political events including oil crises (Barry & O'Hagan, 1971; Gunadhi & Boey, 1986; Kliman, 1981; Little, 1980; Martin & Witt, 1987, 1988; Papadopoulos & Witt, 1985; Summary, 1987; Syriopoulos, 1989; Tremblay, 1989; Uysal & Crompton, 1984; Witt & Martin, 1985, 1987). Other variables that have been taken into account include foreign exchange restrictions (Barry & O'Hagan, 1971; Gunadhi & Boey, 1986; Martin & Witt, 1987, 1988) and marketing expenditure (Barry & O'Hagan, 1971; Papadopoulos & Witt, 1985; Uysal & Crompton, 1984).

Most of the studies estimating tourism demand using single equation models have used multivariate regression analysis at the aggregate or cross-country level. The single equation approach, unlike the system of equations approach, does not require the inclusion of the same explanatory variables for each area (or type of tourism) but allows tourism demand equations to include variables specific to different areas (or types). The most commonly used functional form is the log-linear model, due to its relatively good empirical performance (Crouch, 1994a; Witt and Witt, 1995; Lee *et al.*, 1996) and convenience in providing demand elasticities (Crouch, 1994a). However, there has been little rigorous discussion of why the model is superior for explaining variations in tourism demand; computational convenience and the ease of interpretation of parameters seem to guide the choice (Ong, 1995). Equations can be specified in dynamic form, permitting the estimation of both short and long run elasticities for tourism demand (Syriopoulos, 1995). Dynamic aspects can also enter the model through the incorporation of tourists' expectations, supply rigidities and habit-persistent or stable behavioural patterns (Witt & Moutinho, 1989; Seddighi & Shearing, 1997; Kim & Song, 1998; Morley, 1998; Song and Witt, 2000; Song *et al.*, 2000; Rodriguez *et al.*, 2001).

The quantitative approach to tourism demand enables the modelling of cause and effects and 'what if' forecasting, and provides statistical measures of accuracy and significance. The modelling form includes econometric models that focus on the variables influencing demand, gravity models that adopt a geographical perspective with emphasis on mass and distance considerations (recently estimated by Durbarry, 2001 using panel data rather than traditional single equation methods) and trip generation models (a mixed approach of the previous two). The models can be used to provide income elasticity values, which measure the responsiveness of demand to changes in income. The price and exchange rate elasticities can be used to classify destinations into those for which demand is sensitive or insensitive to price or exchange rate changes.

However, examination of the findings from many of the studies which have used the single equation approach is subject to a number of difficulties. Fujii *et al.* (1985) noted that single equation models are inefficient in their use of information and are deficient in their analysis of cross-price elasticities. The measures of incomes, prices and exchange rates that have been used vary between different studies, sometimes without the provision of an economic rationale for the choice of measure, and many single equation models lack the underpinning in economic reasoning that is incorporated in system of equations models.

## System of equations approaches to tourism demand modelling

Recent developments in research on tourism demand involve the provision of an explicit theoretical basis for tourism demand modelling by using consumer demand theory and relating tourism demand at an aggregate level to individual consumer behaviour. Systems of equations, based on consumer demand theory, can be derived using the Almost Ideal Demand System (AIDS) approach formulated by Deaton and Muellbauer (1980a, b). The Linear Expenditure System (LES) model has also been used, although it tends to produce less satisfactory results than the AIDS model (Fujii et al., 1987). According to Deaton and Muellbauer, consumer demand theory proposes that the consumer has a fixed amount of income (budget) which, by a procedure known as 'stage budgeting', is first allocated between major categories of commodities such as food, accommodation and tourism. The consumer then distributes the expenditure on each of the categories between the commodities included in it, such as tourism in different destinations. The application of consumer choice theory involves making a number of assumptions about consumer behaviour, such as consistency of choice, so that the shares of total expenditure allocated to tourism in different destinations are treated as the results of choices by rational individual consumers. The shares of total expenditure on tourism allocated to different areas (or tourism types) can be estimated by means of the AIDS model:

$$w_i = \alpha_i + \sum_i \gamma_{ij} \log p_j + \beta_i \log(x/P) \quad i, j = 1, \ldots, n$$

where $w_i$ is the share of the budget of residents of country j allocated to tourism in area i; $p_j$ is the price level in country j; x is the budget for tourism expenditure by residents of country j; P is the price index taking account of prices in the range of destination areas, and $\alpha_i$, $\gamma_{ij}$, $\beta_i$ are parameters.

The system of equations approach permits the calculation of expendi-

**Table 3.1** Expenditure and uncompensated price elasticities: UK tourism demand for France, Portugal and Spain

| Country | Expenditure elasticities | | Own-price elasticities | | Cross-price elasticities | | | | | |
|---------|------------|------------|------------|------------|------------|------------|------------|------------|------------|------------|
| | | | | | Price of France | | Price of Portugal | | Price of Spain | |
| | 1969–79 | 1980–97 | 1969–79 | 1980–97 | 1969–79 | 1980–97 | 1969–79 | 1980–97 | 1969–79 | 1980–97 |
| France | 0.63** | 0.81** | –2.04** | –1.90** | – | – | 0.03 | 0.02 | 1.38** | 1.08** |
| Portugal | 0.82** | 0.95** | –2.24** | –1.80** | 0.07 | 0.02 | – | – | 1.35* | 0.83* |
| Spain | 1.20** | 1.15** | –1.82** | –1.93** | 0.52** | 0.66** | 0.10* | 0.12* | – | – |

*Note*: * and ** respectively indicate significance at the 5% and 1% levels.

ture, own-price and cross-price elasticities of tourism demand (see, for example, the elasticity estimates presented in Table 3.1). The expenditure elasticities, expressed as percentages, give the percentage change in the tourism budget share of area $i$ resulting from a percentage change in the expenditure budget. The own-price elasticities, also expressed as percentages, give the percentage change in the tourism budget share of area $i$ resulting from a percentage change in its own prices, whereas cross-price elasticities give the percentage change in the budget share of area $i$ resulting from a percentage change in prices in another area $j$. Both compensated elasticities, based on constant real expenditure, and uncompensated elasticities taking account of the change in expenditure resulting from the relative price changes, can be calculated. The approach thus provides a large amount of information.

The AIDS model has been applied to expenditure by US tourists in different European countries by O'Hagan and Harrison (1984) and White (1985), and tourism from higher income European countries in various Mediterranean countries by Syriopoulos and Sinclair (1993), Papatheodorou (1999) and De Mello *et al.* (2002). A relatively high expenditure elasticity value ($e > 1$) indicates that the country's share of the tourism budget increases considerably as tourists' expenditure budget for the combined area rises (an outcome that policy-makers often wish to achieve), whereas a relatively low value ($0 < e < 1$) indicates that its share increases less than proportionately.

Own-price elasticities of less than unity demonstrate low sensitivity of demand (inelastic demand) with respect to own-price changes, while elasticity values of greater than unity indicate a high degree of sensitivity (elastic demand). The signs of the cross-price elasticities denote whether tourism destination areas are substitutes (positive) or complements (negative) and are useful in indicating the degree of competitiveness or complementarity between different tourist destinations. For example, in the case of the UK demand for tourism examined by De Mello *et al.* (2002), Spain was found to be an expenditure-elastic destination relative to France and Portugal for the period 1969–97, as shown in Table 3.1. The UK demand for all three destinations was highly sensitive to changes in their own prices, with the demand for Spain becoming more price sensitive over time. The cross-price elasticity values were positive and significant for Portugal and Spain, and France and Spain, indicating that for UK tourists, these destinations are substitutes.

The advantage of the AIDS model compared with the single equation approach to tourism demand modelling is that the former uses economic reasoning to justify the variables that are used to explain tourism demand and the form in which they are included in the model (i.e. the specification of the set of equations used to estimate the model). In contrast, the single equation approach is specified a priori and, in the absence of a rigorous economic underpinning, it is not possible to assess the accuracy of the results that it provides. However, although the AIDS model is based on an economic specification of the relevant set of equations, the results that it provides may still be problematic because of econometric problems due to trending or endogeneity. For example, some of the variables that are assumed to be determined by external forces, such as income, may in fact change as tourism demand changes (endogeneity). These issues may be resolved by using a further procedure, put forward by Sims (1980) and Johansen (1988) and involving a model known as vector autoregression (VAR), along with an econometric technique known as cointegration analysis.

The VAR model is useful in testing whether the AIDS specification of tourism demand is appropriate in that, if it provides results which are similar to those obtained from the AIDS model, the researcher can be confident that they are not spurious. In addition, the VAR model provides information about the dynamic adjustment of tourism demand over time and can be used for forecasting. Hence, the AIDS and VAR models are complementary. The former provides a model which is justifiable in terms of economic reasoning and the latter provides a means of testing whether the AIDS model is appropriate in the circumstances under consideration. Structural equation modelling (Turner *et al.*, 1998; Turner & Witt, 2001) provides an additional means of analysing tourism in a multi-equation setting, examining the causes and interrelationships between different types of tourism demand in an integrated framework.

Additional research on the demand for tourism, based on an explicit theoretical foundation, could be undertaken using, for example, discrete choice models such as those specified by McFadden (1973), Stopher and Meyburg (1976) and Hensher and Dalvi (1987) to estimate the probability that particular tourist destinations will be chosen by consumers. The estimation of discrete choice models has been limited, to date, by availability of the relevant disaggregated data. However, there are also some new developments in modelling based on the use of neural networks for forecasting tourism demand (see, for instance, Pattie & Snyder, 1996; Uysal & Roubi, 1999; Law, 2000). Further research that could be undertaken includes more detailed examination of the demand for tourism as a composite product, consisting of a variety of characteristics (Papatheodorou, 1999, 2001). Investigation of the reasons why the demand for particular destinations or tourism types is sensitive or insensitive to changes in key economic variables is a further research issue of practical policy relevance.

## The Supply of Tourism

The economics of tourism supply has received little attention relative to tourism demand. Limitations on data availability, in particular, have precluded much quantitative research on the determinants of tourism supply and related estimation of supply elasticities for tourism. Tourism is a composite product, involving transport, accommodation, catering, attractions and other services such as shops and banks. It differs from other products in that it cannot be examined prior to purchase, cannot be stored and involves an element of travel. It is useful to consider it not as an industry *per se* but as a collection of interrelated industries and markets. These industries sell products to tourists as well as to a range of other customers, such as private consumers, businesses and governments. Research on the supply of tourism has, therefore, involved examination of the supply of each of tourism's component parts.

### The structure of the tourism industry

One of the most striking characteristics of the tourism industry since the 1960s is the considerable increase in the market share of the largest enterprises in sectors such as hotels, tour operators and airlines. The economic and technical advantages of horizontal integration (between the same type of enterprises) and vertical integration (between firms and their input suppliers or output purchasers) were pointed out at an early stage by Hunziker (1969) and Baretje and Defert (1972). Technology has been important as a driver of change, increasing economies of scale (Morrell, 1998). Guibilato (1988) argued that horizontal integration was relatively important during the 1980s as major airlines withdrew investments from hotel chains. However, in 1986 there were at least 12 important European airline and domestic and international hotel linkages, in the form of total ownership or considerable equity participation (Randall, 1986). Other forms of linkages include inter-organisational relationships between hotels and travel agencies (Medina-Muñoz & García-Falcón, 2000) and alliances between hotels and fast-food businesses (Preble *et al.*, 2000). Crotts *et al.* (2000) consider a variety of case studies of alliances in tourism businesses.

Davies and Downward (1996, 1998) and Davis (1999) have used the structure, conduct, performance (SCP) model of industrial organisation and behaviour to examine the tourism sector and find that there is some evidence of oligopoly in the UK tour operator and hotel sectors. However, while there may be some oligopolistic behaviour by tour operators in domestic markets, internationally no single firm or group of companies is dominant (Sinclair & Stabler, 1997: 113). The contestability of markets through the possibility of new entrants is an important factor influencing the level of competitiveness in different tourism markets (Sinclair & Stabler, 1997; Davies & Downward, 1998). Moreover, tourism destinations can undertake strategies to counteract, at least in part, the market power of tour operators (Klemm & Parkinson, 2001).

*The accommodation sector*

There is evidence that some forms of accommodation can exploit economies of scale not only within individual establishments but also by the management of a large number of hotels (Horwath Consulting, 1994; Hickey, 1988; McGuffie, 1990a, b; Wardell, 1987). This partly explains market concentration in the accommodation sector (McVey, 1986; McGuffie, 1987; Go, 1988, 1989). Go noted the increasing importance of large hotel chains, contrasting the 4.7% of US hotels which belonged to a chain in 1948 with the 1988 figure of over 60%. In Europe, Canada and the United States, there were over 3,000 hotel chains with more than 10 hotels in each in 1986, and the 200 largest chains owned at least 20% of all rooms. The relatively high growth rates of the large chains are likely to lead to an increase in the degree of horizontal integration. Substantial increases in large chain ownership can occur over relatively short time periods; between 1994 and 1997 the share of hotel rooms in Germany owned by chains rose from 24% to 36% (Zimmermann, 1998). The location of hotels belonging to large chains is particularly concentrated in major cities (McVey, 1986), and investment in them comes from a variety of national sources.

Borooah (1999) used the Seemingly Unrelated Regression Equations method to analyse the relationships between the number of guest rooms in a hotel and the earnings per occupied room, room occupancy rates and other 'shift factors'. The supply of guest rooms was found to be strongly responsive to increases in earnings per occupied room and less so to the room occupancy rate. Borooah concludes that it is only when hotels reach near-to-full occupancy levels that they increase prices and invest in capacity expansion.

Jeffrey and Barden (2000, 2001) utilise monthly time-series data on hotel occupancy to determine the factors that tend to raise occupancy rates, contribute to high or low levels of seasonality and affect the length of seasonality effects over the period covered (1992–94 in the UK). Among their findings, having a good location relative to local competitors is the strongest factor affecting overall occupancy rates. Hotels in small towns and in countryside locations in business areas have lower occupancy rates. Hotels relying on leisure tourism have high levels of seasonality while business hotels have very low levels. Long-term trends in occupancy are dominated by investment (higher levels of investment are associated with an upward trend) and region (some regions experiencing upward trends and others downward trends). These studies indicate that there is scope for using occupancy data to guide hotel management and marketing – hotel occupancy rates should not be an endpoint of management and marketing policies, but can be used to develop targeted initiatives.

Along with studies demonstrating greater market concentration in the tourism sectors, there has been increased interest in the role of small and medium tourism enterprises. The majority of tourism establishments are small enterprises, with 96% of hotels and restaurants in the European Union (EU) having fewer than nine employees (Smeral, 1998: 371), so that consideration of small firms is important in any analysis of tourism. Wanhill (2000) showed that the performance of small and medium tourism enterprises, in a sample of 216 projects in Wales, was better than expected when the enterprises were founded. Becton and Graetz (2001) examine the skill needs of small tourism businesses in Australia and find that while small firms recognise the need for training, they are disinclined to use external training for their staff, preferring to conduct training internally. However, there is no comparison with large firms' training strategies. Lerner and Haber (2000) examine factors effecting the performance of small tourism businesses in Israel, finding that the entrepreneur's management skills are the single most important factor determining small business success. Other factors, such as previous employment and former entrepreneurial experience, were not correlated with business success.

*Airlines*

The degree of market concentration in charter airline operations varies between countries and even between locations within a country, but appears to be highly concentrated in key markets. In the late 1980s, for example, the five main charter airlines had a combined market share in terms of passenger miles of over 80% in Spain and approximately 70% in the UK (Bote Gómez and Sinclair, 1991). The dominance of main charter airlines is being challenged, however, by the emergence of low-cost airlines, whose pricing strategies represent a significant shift in the behaviour of the airline industry (Piga & Filippi, 2002) and by increased levels of price-based competition amongst major airlines (Milman, 1997; French, 1998).

Scheduled airline operations, in contrast, have been characterised by relatively low levels of concentration, partly because national airlines operate in each country and have received implicit protection through bilateral landing rights agreements. The 1990s have seen important changes in this structure, however, whereby alliances between airlines have led to a large increase in global market concentration over a very short period of time. The largest five airlines together accounted for around 30% of passenger traffic in 1998, but the five largest alliances in 1999 accounted for over two-thirds of passenger traffic (Evans, 2001: 232).

Kleymann and Seristo (2001) and Shabita (2001) examine the motives for the formation of airline alliances. Kleymann and Seristo balance the risks inherent in alliance formation against potential benefits, arguing that alliance-specific investments can be used both to increase efficiency and to facilitate trust between alliance members. Shabita concentrates on alliances between US and European airlines, where the US partner develops domestic links to international gateways and the European partner secures markets on international flights to and from these gateways, concluding that the popularity of these alliances is due to deregulation in both Europe and the US.

Gudmundsson and Rhoades (2001) analyse the factors that tend to increase the longevity of an airline alliance, showing that certain activities – pooling (joint purchasing systems), marketing, code-sharing (flying under another alliance member's flight designator) and blockspace (allowing alliance members to book seats on other members' flights) – tend to reduce the likelihood of early termination of alliances. In one version of their model, the overall complexity and resource commitments involved in some activities – joint service (offering the same flight services) and ground facilities (sharing baggage handling and maintenance facilities and staff) – tend to increase the risk of alliance termination. Li (2000) also considers the factors that increase airline alliance longevity, concluding that the joint operation of customer loyalty and operations integration are the main factors that increase longevity, while code-sharing and pooling are also significant features in lasting alliances. Alliances that include expansion into non-core activities tend to lead to early alliance termination, while alliances that engage solely in code-sharing, joint operations or joint marketing also tend to be short term.

Park *et al.* (2001) consider the effects of airline alliances on market outcome, showing that parallel alliances between airlines whose networks overlap are likely to decrease the output and profits of alliance members, while complementary alliances between airlines whose networks do not overlap are likely to increase output and profits. Pender (1999) discusses the implications of airline franchising in Europe. Lafferty and van Fossen (2001) address the differences between horizontal integration within tourism's component sectors and vertical integration across them. Problems arise with vertical integration when management strategies differ in sectors, particularly between 'Fordist' airlines and 'post-Fordist' hotels.

Other recent developments in the tourism industry include deregulation and privatisation of air transport. Al-Jazzaf (1999) shows that airline privatisation has led to overall positive effects on performance. Barrett (2000) finds that airport competition in the deregulated European aviation market has led to commercialisation and privatisation of airports, which are found to be attractive to passengers and low-cost airlines. The degree of regulation of routes affects airline performance, and Melville (1998) finds that a more competitive environment provides a smaller airline with some market power. Forsyth (2001) argues that while some moves have been made towards liberalising air transport, most countries are hesitant about moving to greater deregulation. Regional agreements that include other sectors have achieved air transport liberalisation but the potential for liberalisation is restricted by the bilateral system of air transport regulation.

### Tour operators and travel agents

The tour operator and travel agent segments are dominated by a small number of firms. Bote Gómez and Sinclair (1991) found that in the UK the top five travel agents had a combined market share of 47% in the late 1980s while the top five tour operators had a combined market share of 77%. This concentration of large firms exists in the presence of a large number of small firms (Sheldon, 1986; Liston, 1986; Evans & Stabler, 1995). The rate of small tour operator start-ups and failures is high (Sheldon, 1994). Technology such as computer reservation systems has led to increasing returns to scale in the tour operator segment, but may have mixed effects on travel agents as travel agents become more reliant on the tour operators' own computer systems (Bennett, 1993).

An additional aspect of tourism business operation that has been examined in recent years is corporate social responsibility. Miller (2001) and Tapper (2001) examine the role of UK tour operators in relation to corporate responsibility. Research reveals that while many tour operators see a strongly competitive industry structure as a constraining force, they also believe that they can benefit if they are perceived to be acting responsibly. The fear of negative publicity through being seen as an irresponsible company also influences company actions.

## The Wider Impacts of Tourism

Tourism also has wider impacts at the macroeconomic and microeconomic levels; for example, on income generation, wages and employment, and on issues predominantly related to economic development, such as the balance of payments, stability of export earnings and export diversification. These will now be considered. The wider impacts of tourism on the environment will be considered in the subsequent section.

### The economic impact

Measurement of the economic impact of tourism has, in the past, relied on input–output and income multiplier approaches (for example, Archer, 1973, 1977a, 1989; Sinclair & Sutcliffe, 1978, 1988; Johnson & Thomas, 1990; Fletcher & Archer, 1991). Input–output models can be used to measure, in a national accounting framework, the value added attributable to tourism (Archer, 1977b, 1995; Archer & Fletcher, 1996; Henry & Deane, 1997; Statistics New Zealand, 1999; Kweka *et al.*2001) and to examine the impact of tourism in a local setting (Andrew, 1997, Wagner, 1997, Schwer *et al.*, 2000; Strauss & Lord, 2001). Input–output modelling uses data on the industrial structure of an economy and the interrelationships between sectors provided in input–output tables. In the tourism field, final demands by tourists for goods and services are traced through these data, under the assumption of fixed input–output coefficients, to derive the value added and employment in each sector of the economy and the totals that are needed to satisfy final demand. The input–output approach relies on the assumption that prices and wages do not change and, therefore, that capacity is unconstrained by factor markets. Andrew (1997) includes a linear programming approach that, simultaneously with the 'normal' input–output relationships, limits the regional external balance, with the results that tourism is shown to have positive effects on most sectors but negative effects on more traditional export sectors.

It is apparent, however, that substantial increases in tourism receipts do lead to changes in prices and wages, that employment constraints are important and that external balance constraints have significant effects (Copeland, 1991; Janaki & Wiktor, 2000; Kulendran & Wilson, 2000). Computable general equilibrium models have, therefore, been used to evaluate the economic impact of increases or decreases in tourism demand (Adams

& Parmenter, 1991, 1994, 1995; Zhou *et al.*, 1997; Blake, 2000; Blake *et al.* 2001a, b). These models build upon input–output models by allowing prices and wages to vary so as to lead to equilibrium in all markets of the economy, including the market for foreign exchange and the external balance. Crucial to the impact of additional tourist expenditures is the real exchange rate appreciation that occurs when prices and wages rise relative to foreign prices, which erodes the competitive advantage of other industries. Adams and Parmenter (1995), for example, find that an increased rate of growth of tourism receipts would slow down the growth of traditional export sectors and may lead to welfare losses in regions that specialise in traditional exports. The effects that tourism has on an economy may depend on the macroeconomic environment under which tourism takes place (Dwyer *et al.*, 2000), as well as on taxation policies that exist (Blake, 2000).

## Employment and wages

Tourism generates considerable employment, both directly in the sectors in which tourist expenditure occurs and, more widely, via inter-industry linkages. Employment in tourism can be measured by the expenditure method, whereby data from input–output tables are used to match tourism expenditure by good and service and employment by sector (Statistics New Zealand, 1999; Heerschap, 1999). This approach is rather data-intensive. Hence, some authors have used an employment count method, which entails the summing of employment in sectors or job categories that are assumed to pertain to the tourism industry (Thomas & Townsend, 2001), although the selection of categories for inclusion is problematic (Johnson & Thomas, 1990). Tourism accounted for 4.1% of employment in New Zealand in 1995 (Statistics New Zealand, 1999) and 7% of employment in the UK in 1998 (Thomas & Townsend, 2001: 297).

Aggregate figures for employment in tourism hide a variety of structural characteristics of employment such as the ratio of full-time to part-time employment, of manual to skilled and female to male employees, and of ethnic minority to indigenous workers (Goodall, 1987; Williams & Shaw, 1988). Thomas and Townsend (2001) examine part-time and full-time employment in tourism in the UK, finding that while the 1980s saw a fall in the full- to part-time employment ratio in tourism sectors and in the economy as a whole, the 1990s saw increases in the full- to part-time employment ratio in tourism while the downward trend continued in the rest of the economy. Studies of the gender structure of employment in tourism (Bagguley, 1990; Kinnaird *et al.*, 1994; Adkins, 1995; Swain, 1995; Sinclair, 1991a, 1997) indicate both vertical segmentation, as most top jobs are carried out by men (Guerrier, 1986; Hicks, 1990; Purcell, 1997), and horizontal segmentation, as transport is dominated by male employment, while accommodation and catering are dominated by female employment (Purcell, 1997). Women undertake the majority of seasonal, part-time and low-paid tourism work in many areas (Breathnach et al., 1994; Hennessy, 1994).

Wages in the tourism industry tend to be lower than in other sectors of the economy (Lee & Kang, 1998; Szivas & Riley, 1999). However, as Lee and Kang show, there are other sectors of the economy that show an even larger gender wage gap, and the tourism sector has a more even distribution of income than some other sectors. Szivas and Riley (1999) examine the mobility of labour into tourism (hotels and restaurants) in Hungary during the period 1986–96. They found that new workers in tourism came from all sectors of the economy but the largest proportions came from jobs in the trade and manufacturing sectors, despite the fact that average wages in those industries were higher than in tourism.

## Tourism and economic development

Tourism is often seen as having great potential in developing countries which have substantial natural resources to attract tourists (Bird, 1992). For developing countries facing falling and erratic prices for their traditional exports, tourism can bring substantial benefits, increasing foreign exchange earnings and contributing to a diversification of earnings that may lessen the volatility of export earnings overall (Sinclair & Tsegaye, 1990; Sinclair, 1998, 1999; Durbarry, 2002; Lea, 1993). In many developing countries tourism is the main, or one of the most important, exports (Sinclair, 1991a; Dieke, 1993; Varley, 1978; Curry, 1992; Mudambi, 1994; Archer, 1995; Archer & Fletcher, 1996; Conlin & Baum, 1995 and see Chapter 7 this volume), providing a path towards development through the services sector (Sinclair & Bote Gómez, 1996) and growth enhancement (Kweka et al., 2001). However, the benefits from tourism for developing countries may be constrained by import leakages (Sinclair, 1991a; Telfer & Wall, 1996), the need for foreign investment in hotel development and hence the repatriation of earnings (Kusluvan & Karamustafa, 2001) as well as environmental damage (Faulkner, 1998). Tourism development may also require specific NGO and government institutional support (Dieke, 1995; Pryce, 1998; Holm-Petersen, 2000; de Villiers, 2000), training and education (Doswell, 2000) and regional co-operation (Teye, 2000)

## Tourism and the environment

The relationship between tourism and the environment has received considerable attention in recent years (for example, Pawson et al., 1984; Sindiyo & Pertet, 1984; Andronikou, 1987, Smith & Jenner, 1989; Romeril,

1989; Farrell & Runyan, 1991; Cater & Goodall, 1992; Eber, 1992). A key debate has concerned the extent to which tourism affects the environment adversely, thereby prejudicing the interests of future generations, or to which it serves as a force for environmental sustainability or enhancement. The effects that tourism has on the environment stem from the fact that many of the resources that are used by tourists are public goods that are freely available for unrestricted use, or are subject to prices that do not reflect the full social costs and benefits of their use (Sinclair & Stabler, 1997). The differences between the social and private costs and benefits are known as externalities, many relating to the physical environment, including natural resources, but some affecting socio-cultural characteristics (Saveriades, 2000). In practice, the un-priced externalities associated with tourism, such as congestion, occur through (largely unmeasured) inter-temporal effects. The common outcome of under-pricing is degradation of environmental resources, as large numbers of tourists use resources at a rate that does not allow for their full replacement. Thus, tourism may be inconsistent with environmental sustainability.

However, very few studies have specified the definition of environmental sustainability to which they refer. For example, different definitions refer to different types of capital – natural resource, human-made and human capital – in various combinations. Weak definitions of sustainability allow substitution between different types of capital (Cook *et al.*, 1992; Beioley, 1995) while strong assumptions do not allow substitution and very strong assumptions do not allow substitution between different types of natural resources. The underlying argument is that each generation should leave the next generation at least the same level of capital as it inherited, deriving from inter-generational equity concerns.

There is particular concern about the degree to which tourism development is consistent with environmental sustainability (Ioannides, 1995; Collins, 1999), how it can be achieved (Garrod & Fyall, 1998; Collins, 1999) and who should be responsible (Berry & Ladkin, 1997; Godfrey, 1998; Bramwell & Alletorp, 2001). It has been argued that externalities are associated with market failure and that market mechanisms can be used to correct them. Thus, price-based instruments in the form of taxes or subsidies can be used to correct for under- or over-pricing of resources (Mourmouras, 1993; Wanhill, 1980; Piga, forthcoming) and provide revenue to finance tourism-related expenditures (Bird, 1992). This requires the prior attribution of a social value to un-priced resources by means of such methods as hedonic pricing (Sinclair *et al.*, 1990, Garrod & Willis, 1991; Willis and Garrod, 1993a), the travel cost method (Smith *et al.*, 1991; Loomis *et al.*, 1991) and contingent valuation (Hanley & Ruffel, 1993; Lockwood *et al.*, 1993; Willis & Garrod, 1993a; 1993b; Bostedt & Mattsson, 1995; Garrod &

Fyall, 1998). The challenge is to ensure that the interests of future as well as current generations are taken into account when the social value of resources is estimated.

Other forms of intervention and policy strategies can be used to support environmental objectives (Stabler, 1997; Inskeep, 2000; Mahaliè, 2000), although agreement on the levels of acceptable environmental damage is difficult without knowing the value of resources (Davis, 1999). Collins (1999) argues that sustainability cannot be achieved using price-based measures and must be addressed through stronger quantitative restrictions. Mechanisms that can be used include limits on visitor numbers. The involvement of local communities in the tourism development process tends to decrease social problems (Sinclair & Pack, 2000) and enables the incorporation of local knowledge about the environment (Ioannides, 1995).

Aviation has a particular set of environmental concerns, ranging from noise pollution, accident risk and the emission of gases that contribute to the depletion of the ozone layer and global warming. Although aviation has been estimated to be responsible for only 1% of any future rise in global temperatures caused by artificial emissions (Janiæ, 1999), emissions from aviation may increase substantially over the next 50 years (Olsthoorn, 2001). However, increases in aviation also bring about positive outcomes. As the number and standard of airports and number and frequency of air connections are improved to meet tourist demand, a greater range of travel destinations becomes available.

Environmental quality management can improve the competitiveness of a destination (Mahaliè, 2000). Tourism provides countries with a return for their natural resources (Boo, 1990) and can replace other activities that may cause more harm to the environment (Forsyth, 1995a). Tourism activities also have the potential for positive externalities. The willingness of tourists to pay to see environmental resources provides incentives for governments as well as businesses to implement environmental protection or improvement programmes. Historical buildings and districts, as well as cultural activities and events can also be attractions to tourists, and there are incentives for governments and businesses to improve and protect them (Stabler, 1998). The ability to gain employment in the tourism sector and to earn foreign exchange from tourism takes resources away from other sectors, which may be environmentally 'dirty' activities.

Before leaving the debate about tourism and the environment, it is useful to note some ambiguities that have occurred in the literature. The term 'sustainable tourism' (see Clarke, 1997, for a review) has arisen in the context of concerns about short-term horizons in resource use and is particularly ambiguous. It has been used, on the one hand, to refer to tourism that is consistent with ongoing business profitability (Wight, 1993, 1994;

Forsyth, 1995b; Stabler & Goodall, 1996; Curtin & Busby, 1999) and, on the other, to tourism that is consistent with environmental sustainability. The former case encompasses the outcome that natural resources are degraded and human-made resources substituted for them, so that both tourism and business profits are sustainable over the long term even though environmental sustainability, in all but the weak definition, is not achieved. For example, businesses may cut prices and expand tourism in a destination for short-term profit motives, but the ensuing congestion and negative destination image reduce the long-term viability of the destination (Curtin & Busby, 1999). In the latter case, it is assumed that tourism is consistent with some (often unspecified) definition of environmental sustainability. As the term 'sustainable tourism' refers directly to tourism, and not to the environment, it is the former definition which is, literally, more accurate.

The term 'ecotourism' is also ambiguous. Weaver (1999: 793) argues that ecotourism meets three criteria: (i) being nature-based; (ii) with a cultural component; and (iii) with the tourism activity carried out so as to have no harmful effect on either the environment or culture at the destination. However, other authors' use of the term has involved only one or two of these criteria; for example, the cultural criterion is often ignored. The third criterion has also been ignored by businesses which market ecotourism as an activity that is nature-based but fail to ensure that it is organised so as to avoid degrading the environment and/or culture at the destination. The only criterion that is common to all use of the term is that ecotourism refers to tourism that is, in some way, nature-based. Hence, the use of the term without further explanation is problematic. In practice, the development of nature-based tourism involves a number of issues, including the degree to which it needs to be conducted on a small scale, its suitability for peripheral and developing areas and the extent to which it is consistent with environmental sustainability (Lawrence & Wickins, 1997; Lew, 1998; Campbell, 1999).

## Taxation, regulation and government policy

The recent literature on tourism economics includes a small but expanding body of research on the role of government in the tourism sector in addition to government policy relating to the environment and sustainable tourism, discussed above. Fayos-Solá (1996) describes three phases of tourism policy that have been apparent over the last half-century. In the first phase, the implicit or explicit objective of tourism policy was to increase tourist arrivals, encouraging mass tourism in order to contribute to the balance of payments. Following the recognition of a number of problems inherent with mass tourism, tourism policy entered a second phase of attempting to control the social, economic and environmental impacts of tourism. In the third phase, the objectives and methods of tourism policy changed to incorporate the marketing of tourism to a segmented market, and incorporated the understanding that government policy has a substantial impact on tourism competitiveness.

Bird (1992) considers fiscal policy in relation to tourism and argues that in addition to ensuring that appropriate fees are charged for the use of public infrastructure, tax revenue can be earmarked to provide tourism infrastructure and compensate local host populations. Specific tourism taxes can be charged where appropriate tax handles can be found, such as in accommodation, but it is important to examine the incidence of the taxes that are levied (Fish, 1982; Fujii *et al.*, 1985). Durbarry and Sinclair (2001) show that where the price elasticity of demand for tourism is high, reductions in tourism taxation may increase tourism receipts. Blake (2000) argues that taxes should only be raised where it is efficient to do so, and that the marginal welfare effect of raising additional revenue should be considered; in Spain, for example, the difficulty of finding appropriate tax handles compromises the ability to raise taxes efficiently. The effect of taxes on domestic tourists and the initial levels of taxes faced by domestic versus foreign tourists are both important issues in tourism taxation.

Competition policy also has implications for the tourism sector. The increased vigilance of competition authorities in the UK following the 1998 Competition Act, and the signalling of stricter competition rulings by the European Commission via its prohibition of Airtours' bid for First Choice in 1999, shows that tour operators are under pressure to operate under tighter competition rules (Sinclair, 2001). The air transportation sector has been characterised by a policy of liberalisation in the EU and many other countries. The 'Open Skies' policy in the US and deregulation in the EU have led to significant improvements in air transport services and also welfare gains (Button & Taylor, 2000; Forsyth, 2001; Al-Jazzaf, 1999; Barrett, 2000; Gillen & Hinsch, 2001). However, the liberalisation of air transport should be tempered with concern for environmental externalities (Abeyratne, 1999).

## Conclusions

Research on the economics of tourism is still dominated, to a large degree, by studies of tourism demand, although the nature of these studies has changed during recent years. In contrast to the majority of early studies of tourism demand, more recent research incorporates more advanced econometric methods and, where data are available, the estimation of system of equations models. The results provided by these studies are useful for policy-makers, indicating the degree of sensitivity of tourism demand to important economic determinants, notably changes in relative inflation rates, exchange rates and income in major origin markets. Policy-makers are provided with guidance, for example, concerning their tourism pricing policy or the degree to which they should prioritise different source markets.

Unlike the research on tourism demand, which is analytical and quantitatively orientated, much of the literature relating to tourism supply is relatively un-analytical. The quantitative research on the supply-side that does exist is fragmented, in part because services that are provided for tourists, such as catering and transportation, are also used to meet the ongoing needs of the local population. Hence, it is often difficult or impossible to distinguish between the supply that is provided for tourists and that which is provided for non-tourism purposes. For this reason, little research has been undertaken on the determinants of tourism supply. Even with respect to individual supply-side sectors, there has been little research on the substitutability or complementarity between factors of production used in tourism-related industries or supply elasticities for individual sectors. While some studies have examined horizontal and vertical integration in tourism, there are still many areas that remain virtually untouched, such as the causes and effects of different forms of domestic and international integration and the implications for public policy.

Research on the estimation of the wider impacts of tourism has largely been limited to the use of input–output models to estimate the size of tourism's impact on different sectors of the economy, although the use of computable general equilibrium models for impact evaluation is increasing. Few studies have estimated the impact that additional increases in tourism demand have on the whole economy, or the impact that tourism has on wages and employment. While there has been some work on the economics of tourism in developing countries, the literature is still some way from providing comprehensive responses to their development needs.

Considerable research has been conducted on the environmental impacts of tourism but, partly because of the specific characteristics of natural resources in different areas, this has been limited mainly to small-scale studies of particular environments. There has been some confusion between environmental externalities and sustainable development, with the result that few concrete policy implications have arisen. While there have been some developments in policy-related research, particularly concerning aviation liberalisation and regulation, large areas of taxation and regulatory policy remain relatively unresearched. The conclusion is that although the literature on the economics of tourism has progressed significantly in recent years, specific areas remain relatively unresearched, providing significant scope for new contributions.

## Note

1. This chapter first appeared as 'The economics of tourism' in Volume 1 of *Progress in Tourism, Recreation and Hospitality Management* (1989), pp. 1–27.

## Bibliography

Abeyratne, R.I.R. (1999) Management of the environmental impact of tourism and air transport on small island developing states. *Journal of Air Transport Management*. 5, 31–7.

Adams, P.D. and Parmenter, B.R. (1991) *The Medium-Term Significance of International Tourism for the Australian Economy* (Part I). Canberra: Bureau of Tourism Research.

Adams, P.D. and Parmenter, B.R. (1994) *The Medium-Term Significance of International Tourism for the Australian Economy* (Part II). Canberra: Bureau of Tourism Research.

Adams, P.D. and Parmenter, B.R. (1995) An applied general equilibrium analysis of the economic effects of tourism in a quite small, quite open economy *Applied Economics* 27, 985–94.

Adkins, L. (1995) *Gendered Work: Sexuality, Family and the Labour Market*. Buckingham and Philadelphia: Open University Press.

Al-Jazzaf, M.I. (1999) Impact of privatization on airlines performance: An empirical analysis. *Journal of Air Transport Management* 5, 45–52.

Andrew, B.P. (1997) Tourism and the economic development of Cornwall. *Annals of Tourism Research* 24 (3), 721–35.

Andronikou, A. (1987) Cyprus: Management of the tourist sector. *Tourism Management* 7 (2), 127–29.

Archer, B.H. (1973) *The Impact of Domestic Tourism*. Occasional Papers in Economics, No. 2. Bangor: University of Wales Press.

Archer, B.H. (1976) *Demand Forecasting in Tourism*. Occasional Papers in Economics, No. 9. Bangor: University of Wales Press.

Archer, B.H. (1977a) *Tourism Multipliers: The State of the Art*. Occasional Papers in Economics, No. 9. Bangor: University of Wales Press.

Archer, B.H. (1977b) *Tourism in the Bahamas and Bermuda: Two Case Studies*. Occasional Papers in Economics, No. 10. Bangor: University of Wales Press.

Archer, B.H. (1989) Tourism in island economies: Impact analysis. In C.P. Cooper (ed.) *Progress in Tourism, Recreation and Hospitality Management* (Vol. 1). London: Belhaven.

Archer, B.H. (1995) Importance of tourism for the economy of Bermuda. *Annals of Tourism Research* 22 (4), 918–30.

Archer, B.H. and Fletcher, J. (1996) The economic impact of tourism in the Seychelles. *Annals of Tourism Research* 23 (1), 32–47.

Artus, J.R. (1970) The effect of revaluation on the foreign travel balance of Germany. *IMF Staff Papers* 17, 602–19.

Artus, J.R. (1972) An econometric analysis of international travel. *IMF Staff Papers* 19, 579–614.

Askari, H. (1973) Demand for travel to Europe by American citizens. *Economia Internazionale* 26, 305–17.

Bagguley, P. (1990) Gender and labour flexibility in hotels and catering. *Services Industries Journal* 10, 737–47.

Baretje, R. and Defert, P. (1972) *Aspects Économiques du Tourism*. Paris: Berger, Levrault.

BarOn, R.R.V. (1975) Seasonality in tourism. Technical Series 2. *Economist* Intelligence Unit, London.

Barrett, S. D. (2000) Airport competition in the deregulated European aviation market. *Journal of Air Transport Management* 6, 13–27.

Barry, K. and O'Hagan, K. (1971) An econometric study of British tourist expenditure in Ireland. *Economic and Social Review* 3 (2), 143–61.

Bechdolt Jr, B.V. (1973) Cross-sectional travel demand function: US visitors to Hawaii, 1961–1970. *Quarterly Review of Economics and Business* 13, 37–47.

Becton, S. and Graetz, B. (2001) Small business – small minded? Training attitudes and needs of the tourism and hospitality industry. *International Journal of Tourism Research* 3, 105–13.

Beioley, S. (1995) Green tourism – soft or sustainable? *Insights* (May), B75–89.

Bennett, M.M. (1993) Information technology and travel agency: A customer service perspective. *Tourism Management* 14 (4), 259–66.

Berry, S. and Ladkin, A. (1997) Sustainable tourism: A general perspective. *Tourism Management* 18 (7), 433–40.

Bird, R.M. (1992) Taxing tourism in developing countries. *World Development* 20, 1145–58.

Blake, A. (2000) *The Economic Impact of Tourism in Spain*. TTRI Discussion Paper No. 2000/2.

Blake, A., Durbarry, R., Sinclair, M.T. and Sugiyarto, G. (2001a) *Modelling Tourism and Travel Using Tourism Satellite Accounts and Tourism Policy and Forecasting Models*. TTRI Discussion Paper No. 2001/4.

Blake, A., Sinclair, M.T. and Sugiyarto, G. (2001b) *The Economy-Wide Effects of Foot-and-Mouth Disease in the UK Economy*. TTRI Discussion Paper No. 2001/3.

Boo, E. (1990) *Ecotourism: The Potential and Pitfalls*. Washington: World Wildlife Fund.

Borooah, V.K. (1999) The supply of hotel rooms in Queensland, Australia. *Annals of Tourism Research* 26 (4), 985–1003.

Bostedt. G. and Mattsson. L. (1995) The value of forests for tourism in Sweden. *Annals of Tourism Research* 22 (3), 671–80.

Bote Gómez, V. and Sinclair, M.T. (1991) Integration in the tourism industry. In M.T. Sinclair and M.J. Stabler (eds) *The Tourism Industry: An International Analysis*. Wallingford: CAB International.

Bote Gomez, V., Sinclair, M.T, Sutcliffe, C.M.S. and Valenzuela Rubio, M. (1989) Vertical integration in the British/Spanish tourism industry. Leisure, labour and lifestyles: International comparisons. Tourism and leisure: Models and theories. *Proceedings of the Leisure Studies Association 2nd International Conference*. Conference Paper No. 39, 8 (1), Brighton: Leisure Studies Association.

Bramwell, B. and Alletorp, L. (2001) Attitudes in the Danish tourism industry to the roles of business and government in sustainable tourism. *International Journal of Tourism Research* 3, 91–103.

Breathnach, P., Henry, M., Drea, S. and O'Flaherty, M. (1994) Gender in Irish tourism employment. In V. Kinnaird and D. Hall (eds) *Gender: A Tourism Analysis*. Chichester: Wiley.

Bull, A. (1995) *The Economics of Travel and Tourism*. Harlow: Longman.

Button, K. and Taylor, S. (2000) International air transportation and economic development. *Journal of Air Transport Management* 6, 209–22.

Campbell, L.M. (1999) Ecotourism in rural developing communities. *Annals of Tourism Research* 26 (3), 534–53.

Cater, E. and Goodall, B. (1992) Must tourism destroy its resource base? In A.M. Mannion and S.R. Bowlby (eds) *Environmental Issues in the 1990s*. Chichester: Wiley.

Chadee, D. and Mieczkowski, Z., (1987) An empirical analysis of the effects of exchange rate on Canadian tourism. *Journal of Travel Research* 26 (1), 13–18.

Clarke, J. (1997) A framework of approaches to sustainable tourism. *Journal of Sustainable Tourism* 5, 224–33.

Collins, A. (1999) Tourism development and natural capital. *Annals of Tourism Research* 26 (1), 98–109.

Conlin, M.V. and Baum, T. (1995) *Island Tourism*. Chichester: Wiley.

Cook, S.D., Stewart, E. and Repass, K. (1992) *Discover America: Tourism and the Environment*. Washington: Travel Industry Association of America/London: Belhaven.

Copeland, B.R. (1991) Tourism, welfare and de-industrialization in a small open economy. *Economica* 58 (4), 515–29.

Crotts, J., Buhalis, D. and March, R. (eds) (2000) *Global Alliance in Tourism and Hospitality Management*. Haworth Hospitality Press, USA. Reviewed by A. Reichel *Annals of Tourism Research* 28 (4), 1084–86.

Crouch, G.I. (1994a) The study of international tourism demand: A survey of practice. *Journal of Travel Research* (Spring), 41–55.

Crouch, G.I. (1994b) The study of international tourism demand: A review of findings. *Journal of Travel Research* (Summer), 12–23.

Curry, S. (1992) Economic adjustment policies and the hotel sector in Jamaica. In P. Johnson and B. Thomas (eds) *Perspectives on Tourism Policy*. London: Mansell.

Curtin, S. and Busby, G. (1999) Sustainable destination development: The tour operator perspective. *International Journal of Travel Research* 1, 135–47.

Darnell, A., Johnson, P. and Thomas, B. (1990) Modelling museum visitor flows: A case study of Beamish Museum. *Regional Studies* 10 (3), 251–57.

Davies, B. (1999) Industrial organisation: The UK hotel sector. *Annals of Tourism Research* 25 (2), 294–311.

Davies, B. and Downward, P. (1996) The structure, conduct, performance paradigm as applied to the UK hotel industry. *Tourism Economics* 2, 151–58.

Davies, B. and Downward, P. (1998) Competition and contestability in the UK package tour industry. *Tourism Economics* 4 (3), 241–51.

Davis, P.B. (1999) Beyond guidelines: A model for Antarctic tourism. *Annals of Tourism Research* 26 (3), 516–33.

De Mello, M. Pack, A., Sinclair, M.T. (2002) A System of equations model of UK tourism demand in neighbouring countries. *Applied Economics*. Forthcoming.

De Villiers, N.N. (2000) Open Africa: An African NGO tourism initiative. In P.U.C. Dieke (ed.) *The Political Economy of Tourism Development in Africa*. New York, Sydney and Tokyo: Cognizant.

Deaton, A. and Meullbauer, J. (1980a) *Economics and Consumer Behaviour*. Cambridge: Cambridge University Press.

Deaton, A. and Meullbauer, J. (1980b) An almost ideal demand system. *American Economic Review* 70 (3), 312–26.

Diamond, J, (1977) Tourism's role in economic development: The case re-examined. *Economic Development and Cultural Change* 25 (3), 539–53.

Dieke, P.U.C. (1993) Tourism in the Gambia: Some issues in development policy. *World Development* 21 (2), 277–89.

Dieke, P.U.C. (1995) Tourism and structural adjustment programmes in the African economy. *Tourism Economics* 1, 71–93.

Doswell, R. (2000) African tourism training and education: Hits and misses. In P.U.C. Dieke (ed.) *The Political Economy of Tourism Development in Africa*. New York, Sydney and Tokyo: Cognizant.

Durbarry, R. (2001) *Tourism Expenditure in the UK: Analysis of Competitiveness Using Gravity-Based Model*. Christel Dehaan Tourism and Travel Research Institute Discussion Paper No. 2001/1, Business School, University of Nottingham.

Durbarry, R. (2002) The economic contribution of tourism in Mauritius. *Annals of Tourism Research* 29 (3), 862–65.

Durbarry, R. and Sinclair, M.T. (2001) Tourism taxation in the UK. Mimeo.

Dwyer, L., Forsyth, P., Madden, J. and Spurr, R. (2000) Economic impacts of inbound tourism under different assumptions regarding the macroeconomy. *Current Issues in Tourism* 3 (4), 325–63.

Eber, S. (ed.) (1992) *Beyond The Green Horizon. Principles for Sustainable Tourism*. Godalming: World Wide Fund For Nature.

Evans, N. (2001) Collaborative strategy: An analysis of the changing world of international airline alliances. *Tourism Management* 22 (2), 229–43.

Evans, N. and Stabler, M.J. (1995) A future for the package tour operator in the 21st century? *Tourism Economics* 1 (3), 245–63.

Farrell, B.H. and Runyan, D. (1991) Ecology and tourism. *Annals of Tourism Research* 18 (1), 26–40.

Faulkner, W. (1998) Tourism development. In E. Laws, W. Faulkner and G. Moscardo (eds) *Embracing and Managing Change in Tourism: International Case Studies*. London and New York: Routledge.

Fayos-Solá, E. (1996) Tourism policy: A midsummer might's dream? *Tourism Management* 17 (6), 405–12.

Fish, M. (1982) Taxing international tourism in West Africa. *Annals of Tourism Research* 9 (1), 91–103.

Fletcher, J. and Archer, B. (1991) The development and application of multiplier analysis. In C.P. Cooper (ed.) *Progress in Tourism, Recreation and Hospitality Management, 1*. London: Belhaven.

Forsyth, T.J. (1995a) Tourism and agricultural development in Thailand. *Annals of Tourism Research* 22 (4), 877–900.

Forsyth, T.J. (1995b) Business attitudes to sustainable tourism: Responsibility and self regulation in the UK outgoing tourism industry. Paper presented at the Sustainable Tourism World Conference, Lanzarote.

Forsyth, P. (2001) Promoting trade in airline services. *Journal of Air Transport Management* 7, 43–50.

French, T. (1998) Europe's regional airlines. *Travel and Tourism Analyst* 5, 1–18.

Fujii, E., Khaled, M. and Mak, J. (1985) The exportability of hotel occupancy and other tourist taxes. *National Tax Journal* 2, 169–77.

Fujii, E.T., Khaled, M. and Mak, J. (1987) An empirical comparison of systems of demand equations: An application to visitor expenditures in resort destinations. *Philippine Review of Business and Economics* 24 (1–2), 79–102.

Garrod, B. and Fyall, A. (1998) Beyond the rhetoric of sustainable tourism? *Tourism Management* 19 (3), 199–212.

Garrod, G. and Willis, K. (1991) The environmental economic impact of woodland: A two-stage hedonic price model of the amenity value of forestry in Britain. *Applied Economics* 24, 715–28.

Gillen, D. and Hinsch, H. (2001) Measuring the economic impact of liberalization of international aviation on Hamburg airport. *Journal of Air Transport Management* 7, 25–34.

Go, F. (1988) Key problems and prospects in the international hotel industry. *Travel and Tourism Analyst* 1, 27–49.

Go, F. (1989) International hotel industry – capitalizing on change. *Tourism Management* 10 (3), 195–200.

Godfrey, K.B. (1998) Attitudes towards 'sustainable tourism' in the UK: A view from local government. *Tourism Management* 19 (3), 213–24.

Goodall, B. (1987) Tourism policy and jobs in the United Kingdom. *Built Environment* 13 (2), 109–23.

Gray, H.P. (1966) The demand for international travel by United States and Canada. *International Economic Review* 7 (1), 83–92.

Gudmundsson, S.V. and Rhoades, D.W. (2001) Airline alliance survival analysis: Typology, strategy and duration. *Transport Policy* 8, 209–18.

Guerrier, Y. (1986) Hotel manager: An unsuitable job for a woman? *Service Industries Journal* 6 (2), 227–40.

Guibilato, G. (1988) Les évolutions récentes de l'économie hôtelière. *Teoros* 7 (3), 29–35.

Gunadhi, H. and Boey, C.K. (1986) Demand elasticities of tourism in Singapore. *Tourism Management* 7 (4), 239–53.

Hanley, N. and Ruffell, R. (1993) *The Contingent Valuation of Forest Characteristics.* *Journal of Agricultural Economics* 44, 218–44.

Heerschap, N.M. (1999) The employment module for the tourism satellite account of the OECD. *Tourism Economics* 5 (4), 383–413.

Hennessy, S. (1994) Female employment in tourism development in south-west England. In V. Kinnaird and D. Hall (eds) *Gender: A Tourism Analysis.* Chichester: Wiley.

Henry, E.W. and Deane, B. (1997) The contribution of tourism to the economy of Ireland in 1990 and 1995. *Tourism Management* 18 (8), 535–53.

Hensher, D.A. and Dalvi, Q. (eds) (1987) *Determinants of Travel Choices.* Aldershot: Saxon House.

Hickey, J. (1988) Hotel reservation systems and sources of business. *Travel and Tourism Analyst* 2, 23–36.

Hicks, L. (1990) Excluded women: How can this happen in the hotel world? *Service Industries Journal* 10 (2), 348–63.

Holm-Petersen, E. (2000) Institutional support for tourism development in Africa. In P.U.C. Dieke (ed.) *The Political Economy of Tourism Development in Africa.* New York, Sydney and Tokyo: Cognizant.

Horwath Consulting (1994) *The United Kingdom Hotel Industry (1994).* London: Horwath International.

Hunziker, W. (1969) Tendances concentrationistes dans le tourisme national et international. *Tourist Review* 4, 146–52.

Inskeep, E. (2000) Planning sustainable tourism in Ghana. In P.U.C. Dieke (ed.) *The Political Economy of Tourism Development in Africa*. New York, Sydney and Tokyo, Cognizant.

Ioannides, D. (1995) A flawed implementation of sustainable tourism. *Tourism Management* 16 (8), 583–92.

Jafari, J. (ed.) (2000) *Encyclopaedia of Tourism*. London: Routledge.

Janaki, R.R. and Wiktor, L. (2000) Tourism impact modelling for resource extraction regions. *Annals of Tourism Research* 27 (1), 188–202.

Janić, M. (1999) Aviation and externalities: The accomplishments and problems. *Transportation Research Part D* 4, 159–80.

Jeffrey, D. and Barden, R.R.D. (2000) Monitoring hotel performance using occupancy time-series analysis: The concept of occupancy performance space. *International Journal of Tourism Research* 2, 383–402.

Jeffrey, D. and Barden, R.R.D. (2001) Multivariate models of hotel occupancy performance and their implications for hotel marketing. *International Journal of Tourism Research* 3, 33–44.

Johansen, S. (1988) A statistical analysis of cointegration vectors. *Journal of Economic Dynamics and Control* 12, 231–54.

Johnson, P. and Ashworth, J. (1990) Modelling tourism demand: A summary review. *Leisure Studies* 9 (2), 145–60.

Johnson, P. and Thomas, B. (1990) Measuring the local employment impact of a tourist attraction: An empirical study. *Regional Studies* 24 (5), 395–403.

Jud, G.D. and Joseph, H. (1974) International demand for Latin American tourism. *Growth and Change* 5 (1), 25–31.

Kim, S. and Song, H. (1998) Analysis of inbound tourism demand in South Korea: A cointegration and error correction approach. *Tourism Analysis* 3, 25–41.

Kim, Y. and Uysal, M. (1997) The endogenous nature of price variables in tourism demand studies. *Tourism Analysis* 2, 9–16.

Kinnaird, V., Kothari, U. and Hall, D. (1994) Tourism: Gender perspectives. In V. Kinnaird and D. Hall (eds) *Tourism: A Gender Analysis*. Chichester: Wiley.

Klemm, M. and Parkinson, L. (2001) UK tour operator strategies: Causes and consequences. *International Journal of Tourism Research* 3, 367–75.

Kleymann, B. and Seristo, H. (2001) Levels of airline alliance membership: Balancing risks and benefits. *Journal of Air Transport Management* 7, 303–10.

Kliman, M.L. (1981) A quantitative analysis of Canadian overseas tourism. *Transportation Research* 15A (6), 487–97.

Kulendran, N. and Wilson, K. (2000) Is there a relationship between international trade and international travel? *Applied Economics* 32, 1001–09.

Kusluvan, S. and Karamustafa, K. (2001) Multinational hotel development in developing countries: An exploratory analysis of critical policy issues. *International Journal of Tourism Research* 3, 179–97.

Kwack, S.Y. (1972) Effects of income and prices on travel spending abroad (1960 III–1967 IV). *International Economic Review* 13 (2), 245–56.

Kweka, J., Morrissey, O. and Blake, A. (2001) *The Economic Significance of Tourism in Tanzania: Input-Output Multiplier Analysis*. TTRI Discussion Paper No. 2001/1.

Lafferty, G. and Van Fossen, A. (2001) Integrating the tourism industry: Problems and strategies. *Tourism Management* 22, 11–19.

Law, R. (2000) Back-propagation learning in improving the accuracy of neural network-based tourism demand forecasting. *Tourism Management* 21, 331–40.

Lawrence, T. B. and Wickins, D. (1997) Managing legitimacy in ecotourism. *Tourism Management* 18 (5), 307–16.

Lea, J. (1988) *Tourism and Development in the Third World*. London: Routledge.

Lee, C. and Kang, S. (1998) Measuring earnings inequality and median earnings in the tourism industry. *Tourism Management* 19 (4), 341–8.

Lee, C.K., Var, T. and Blaine, T.W. (1996) Determinants of inbound tourist expenditures. *Annals of Tourism Research* 23 (3), 527–42.

Lerner, M. and Haber, S. (2000) Performance factors of small tourism ventures: The interface of tourism, entrepreneurship and the environment. *Journal of Business Venturing* 16, 77–100.

Lew, A. (1998) Ecotourism trends. *Annals of Tourism Research* 25 (3), 742–6.

Li, M.Z.F. (2000) Distinct features of lasting and non-lasting airline alliances. *Journal of Air Transport Management* 6, 65–73.

Lim, C. and Mcaleer, M. (2001) Monthly seasonal variations: Asian tourism to Australia. *Annals of Tourism Research* 28 (1), 68–82.

Liston, K. (1986) David and Goliath. *Courier* (Nov/Dec), 19–21.

Little, J.S. (1980) International travel in the US balance of payments. *New England Economic Review* May, 42–55.

Lockwood, M., Loomis, J. and Delacy, T. (1993) A contingent valuation survey and benefit-cost analysis of forest preservation in East Gippsland, Australia. *Journal of Environmental Management* 38, 233–43.

Loeb, P.D. (1982) International travel to the United States: An econometric evaluation. *Annals of Tourism Research* 9 (1), 7–20.

Loomis, J.B, Creel, M. and Park, T. (1991) Comparing benefit estimates from travel cost and contingent valuation using confidence intervals from Hicksian welfare measures. *Applied Economics* 23, 1725–31.

Mahaliè, T. (2000) Environmental management of a tourist destination: A factor of tourism competitiveness. *Tourism Management* 21 (1), 65–78.

Martin, C.A. and Witt, S.F. (1987) Tourism demand forecasting models: Choice of appropriate variable to represent tourist's cost of living. *Tourism Management* 8 (3), 233–46.

Martin, C.A. and Witt, S.F. (1988) Substitute prices in models of tourism demand. *Annals of Tourism Research* 15 (2), 255–68.

McFadden, D. (1973) Conditional logit analysis of qualitative choice behaviour. In P. Zarembka (ed.) *Frontiers in Econometrics*. New York: Academic Press.

McGuffie, J. (1987) UK hotel industry: Revival for the chains at home and abroad. *Travel and Tourism Analyst* (September), 15–31.

McGuffie, J. (1990a) CRS Development and the hotel sector – Part I. *Travel and Tourism Analyst* 1, 29–41.

McGuffie, J. (1990b) CRS development and the hotel sector – Part II. *Travel and Tourism Analyst* 2, 18–36

McVey, M. (1986) International hotel chains in Europe: Survey of expansion plans as Europe is 'rediscovered'. *Travel and Tourism Analyst* (September), 3–23.

Medina-Muñoz, D. and Garcia-Falcón, J.M. (2000) Successful relationship between hotels and agencies. *Annals of Tourism Research* 27 (3), 737–62.

Melville, J.A. (1998) Identifying the regulatory effect of bilateral agreements on international aviation. *Journal of Air Transport Management* 4, 39–46.

Mikulicz, H. (1983) Determinants of tourism flow in Europe. *On the Importance of Research in the Tourism Industry* (pp. 7–16). Seminar, Helsinki, Finland, 8–11 June. European Society for Opinion and Marketing Research.

Miller, G. (2001) Corporate responsibility in the UK tourism industry. *Tourism Management* 22 (4), 589–98.

Milman, A. (1997) The US airline industry. *Travel and Tourism Analyst* 3, 4–21.

Morley, C. (1998) A dynamic international demand model. *Annals of Tourism Research* 25 (1), 70–84.

Morrell, P.S. (1998) Airline sales and distribution channels: The impact of new technology. *Tourism Economics* 4 (1), 5–19.

Mourmouras, A. (1993) Conservationist government policies and intergenerational equity in an overlapping generations model with renewable resources. *Journal of Public Economics* 51, 249–69.

Mudambi, R. (1994) A Ricardian excursion to Bermuda: An estimation of mixed strategy equilibrium. *Applied Economics* 26, 927–36.

Noval, S. (1975) The demand for international tourism and travel: Theory and measurement. PhD thesis, Princeton University.

O'Hagan, J.W. and Harisson, M.J. (1984) Market share of US tourist expenditure in Europe: An econometric analysis. *Applied Economics* 16 (6), 913–31.

Oliver, F.R. (1971) The effectiveness of UK travel allowances. *Applied Economics* 3 (3), 219–26.

Olsthoorn, X. (2001) Carbon dioxide emissions from international aviation: 1950–2050. *Journal of Air Transport Management* 7, 87–93.

Ong, C. (1995) Tourism demand models: A critique. *Mathematics and Computers in Simulations* 39, 367–72.

Papadopoulos, S.I. and Witt, S.F. (1985) A marketing analysis of foreign tourism in Greece. In S. Shaw, L. Sparks and E. Kaynak (eds) *Proceeding of Second World Marketing Congress* (pp. 682–93). University of Stirling.

Papatheodorou, A. (1999) The demand for international tourism in the Mediterranean region. *Applied Economics* 31, 19–30.

Papatheodorou, A. (2001) Why people travel to different places. *Annals of Tourism Research* 28 (1), 164–79.

Park, J., Zhang, A. and Zhang, Y. (2001) Analytical models of international alliances in the airline industry. *Transportation Research Part B* 35, 865–86.

Pattie, D.C. and Snyder, J. (1996) Using neural network to forecast visitor behaviour. *Annals of Tourism Research* 23 (1), 151–64.

Pawson, I.G., Stanford, D.D., Adams, V.A. and Nurbu, M. (1984) Growth of tourism in Nepal's Everest region: Impact on the physical environment and structure of human settlements. *Mountain Research and Development* 4 (3), 237–46.

Pender, L. (1999) European aviation: The emergence of franchised airline operations. *Tourism Management* 20 (4), 565–74.

Piga, C. (forthcoming) Pigouvian taxation in tourism. *Environmental and Resource Economics*.

Piga, C. and Filippi, N. (2002) Booking and flying with low cost airlines. *International Journal of Tourism Research* 4, 237–49.

Preble, J., Reichel, A. and Hoffman, R.C. (2000) Strategic alliances for competitive advantage: Evidence from Israel's hospitality and tourism industry. *Hospitality Management* 19, 327–41.

Pryce, A. (1998) The World Bank group and tourism. *Travel and Tourism Analyst* 5, 75–90.

Purcell, K. (1997) Women's employment in UK tourism: Gender roles and labour markets. In M.T. Sinclair (ed.) *Gender, Work and Tourism*. London and New York: Routledge.

Randall, J. (1986) European airlines move into hotels: Survey of the leading carriers' expanding hotel interests. *Travel and Tourism Analyst* (July), 45–54.

Rodriguez, F.J.L, Ibanez, M.N. and Rodriguez, J.V. (2001) Panel data and tourism: A case study of Tenerife. *Tourism Economics* 7 (1), 75–88.

Romeril, M. (1989) Tourism and the environment: Accord or discord? *Tourism Management* 10 (3), 204–8.

Saveriades, A. (2000) Establishing the social tourism carrying capacity for the tourist resorts of the east coast of the Republic of Cyprus. *Tourism Management* 21 (1), 147–56.

Schwer, R.K., Gazel, R. and Daneshvary, R. (2000) Air-tour impacts; the Grand Canyon case. *Annals of Tourism Research* 27 (3), 611–23.

Seddighi, H.R. and Shearing, D.F. (1997) The demand for tourism in north-east England with special reference to Northumbria: An empirical analysis. *Tourism Management* 18 (8), 499–511.

Sheldon, P.J. (1986) The tour operator industry: An analysis. *Annals of Tourism Research* 13 (3), 349–65.

Sheldon, P.J. (1990) A review of tourism expenditure rescarch. In C.P. Cooper (ed.) *Progress in Tourism, Recreation and Hospitality Management 2*. London: Belhaven.

Sheldon, P.J. (1994) Tour operators. In S.F. Witt and L. Moutinho (eds) *Tourism Management and Marketing Handbook* (2nd edn). Hemel Hempstead: Prentice Hall.

Sims, C. (1980) Macroeconomics and reality. *Econometrica* 48, 1–48.

Sinclair, M.T. (1991a) Women, work and skill: Economic theories and feminist perspectives. In N. Redclift and M.T. Sinclair (eds) *Working Women: International Perspectives on Labour and Gender Ideology*. London and New York: Routledge.

Sinclair, M.T. (1991b) The tourism industry and foreign exchange leakages in a developing country. In M.T. Sinclair and M.J. Stabler (eds) *The Tourism Industry: An International Analysis*. Wallingford: CAB International.

Sinclair, M.T. (1997) Issues and theories of gender and work in tourism. In M.T. Sinclair (ed.) *Gender, Work and Tourism*. London and New York: Routledge.

Sinclair, M.T. (1998) Tourism and economic development: A survey. *Journal of Development Studies* 34 (5), 1–51.

Sinclair. M.T. (1999) Portfolio models of tourism. In T. Baum and R. Mudambi (eds) *Economic and Management Methods for Tourism and Hospitality Research*. Chichester: Wiley.

Sinclair, M.T. (2001) Competition or collective dominance in tourism supply? Implication for Spanish firms. Mimeo.

Sinclair, M.T. and Bote Gómez, V. (1996) Tourism, the Spanish economy and the balance of payments. In M. Barke, M. Newton and J. Towner (eds) *Tourism in Spain: Critical Perspectives*. Wallingford: CAB International.

Sinclair, M.T. and Pack, A. (2000) Tourism and conservation: The application of economic policy instruments to wildlife tourism in Zimbabwe. In P.U.C. Dieke (ed.) *The Political Economy of Tourism Development in Africa*. New York, Sydney and Tokyo: Cognizant.

Sinclair, M. T. and Stabler, M. (1997) *The Economics of Tourism*. London, New York: Routledge

Sinclair, M.T. and Sutcliffe, C.M.S. (1978) The first round of the Keynesian income multiplier. *Scottish Journal of Political Economy* 25 (2), 177–86.

Sinclair, M.T. and Sutcliffe, C.M.S. (1988) The estimation of Keynesian income multipliers at the sub-national level. *Applied Economics* 20 (11), 1435–44.

Sinclair, M.T. and Tsegaye, A. (1990) International tourism and export instability. *The Journal of Development Studies* 26 (3), 487–504.

Sinclair, M.T., Clewer, A. and Pack, A. (1990) Hedonic prices and the marketing of package holidays. In G. Ashworth and B. Goodall (eds) *Marketing Tourism Policies*. London and New York: Routledge.

Sindiyo, D.M.and Pertet, F.N. (1984) Tourism and its impact on wildlife in Kenya. *Industry and Environment* 7 (1), 14–19.

Smeral, E. (1998) The impact of globalization on small and medium enterprises: New challenges for tourism policies in European countries. *Tourism Management* 19 (4), 371–80.

Smith, A.B. and Toms, J.N. (1978) *Factors Affecting Demand for International Travel to and from Australia*. Occasional Paper No. 11. Canberra: Bureau of Transport Economics, Australian Government Publishing Service.

Smith, C. and Jenner, P. (1989) Tourism and the environment. *Travel and Tourism Analyst* 5, 66–86.

Smith, V.K, Palmquist, R.B. and Jakus, P. (1991) Combining Farrel frontier and hedonic travel cost models for valuing estuarine quality. *Review of Economic and Statistics* 63 (4), 694–9.

Song, H., Romilly, P. and Liu, X. (2000) An empirical study of outbound tourism demand in the UK. *Applied Economics* 32, 611–24.

Song, H. and Witt, S.F. (2000) *Tourism Demand Modelling and Forecasting: Modern Econometric Approaches*. Amsterdam: Pergamon.

Stabler. M.J. (1997) *Tourism and Sustainability: Principles and Practice*. Wallingford: CAB International.

Stabler, M.J. (1998) The economic evaluation of the role of conservation and tourism in the regeneration of historic urban destinations. In E. Laws, B. Faulkner and G. Moscardo (eds) *Embracing and Managing Change In Tourism: International Case Studies*. London and New York, Routledge.

Stabler, M.J. and Goodall, B. (1996) Environmental auditing in planning for sustainable island tourism. In L. Briguglio, B. Archer, J. Jafari and G. Wall (eds) *Sustainable Tourism in Small States: Issues and Policies*. London: Pinter (Cassell).

Statistics New Zealand (1999) *Tourism Satellite Account (1995)*. Statistics New Zealand, Wellington, New Zealand.

Stopher, P.R and Meyburg, A.H (eds) (1976) *Behavioural Travel-Demand Model*. Lexington, MA: D.C. Heath.

Strauss, C.H. and Lord, B.E. (2001) Economic impacts of a heritage tourism system. *Journal of Retailing and Consumer Services* 8, 199–204.

Stronge, W.B. and Redman, M. (1982) US tourism in Mexico: An empirical analysis. *Annals of Tourism Research* 9 (1), 21–35.

Summary, R. (1987) Estimation of tourism demand by multiple regression analysis: Evidence from Kenya. *Tourism Management* 8 (1), 317–22.

Sutcliffe, C.M.S. and Sinclair, M.T. (1980) The measurement of seasonality within tourist industry: An application to tourist arrival in Spain. *Applied Economics* 12 (4), 429–41.

Swain, M.B. (1995) Gender in tourism. Special Issue. *Annals of Tourism Research* 22 (2).

Syriopoulos, T. (1989) *Dynamic Modelling of Tourism Demand in Mediterranean*. *Studies in Economics*. No. 89/12. Canterbury: University of Kent.

Syriopoulos, T. (1995) A dynamic model of tourism demand in Mediterranean tourism. *International Review of Applied Economics* 9 (3), 318–36.

Syriopoulos, T. and Sinclair, M.T. (1993) An econometric study of tourism demand: The AIDS model of US and European tourism in Mediterranean countries. *Applied Economics* 25 (12), 1541–52.

Szivas, E. and Riley, M. (1999) Tourism employment during economic transition. *Annals of Tourism Research* 26 (4), 747–71.

Tapper, R. (2001) Tourism and socio-economic development: UK tour operators' business approaches in the context of the new international agenda. *International Journal of Tourism Research* 3, 351–66.

Telfer, D.J. and Wall, G. (1996) Linkages between tourism and food production. *Annals of Tourism Research* 23 (3), 635–53.

Teye, V.B. (2000) Regional co-operation and tourism development in Africa. In P.U.C. Dieke (ed.) *The Political Economy of Tourism Development in Africa*. New York, Sydney and Tokyo, Cognizant.

Thomas, B. and Townsend, A. (2001) New trends in the growth of tourism employment in the UK in the 1990s. *Tourism Economics* 7 (3), 295–310.

Tremblay, P. (1989) Pooling international tourism in Western Europe. *Annals of Tourism Research* 16, 477–91.

Turner, L.W., Reisinger, Y. and Witt, S. F. (1998) Tourism demand analysis using structural equation modelling. *Tourism Economics* 4 (4), 301–23.

Turner, L.W and Witt, S.F. (2001) Factors influencing demand for international tourism: Tourism demand analysis using structural equation modelling, revisited. *Tourism Economics* 7 (1), 21–38.

Uysal, M. and Crompton, J.L. (1984) Determinant of demand for international tourist flows to Turkey. *Tourism Management* 5 (4), 288–97.

Uysal, M. and Roubi, M.S.E. (1999) Artificial neural networks versus multiple regression in tourism demand analysis. *Journal of Travel Research* 38, 111–18.

Vanhove, N. (1980) Forecasting in tourism. *The Tourist Review* 3, 2–7.

Varley, R.C.G. (1978) *Tourism in Fiji: Some Economic and Social Problems*. Occasional Papers in Economics, No. 12. Bangor: University of Wales Press.

Wagner, J.E. (1997) Estimating the economic impacts of tourism. *Annals of Tourism Research* 24 (3), 592–608.

Wanhill, S.R.C. (1980) Charging for congestion at tourist attractions. *International Journal of Tourism Management* 1 (3), 168–74.

Wanhill, S. (2000) Small and medium tourism enterprises. *Annals of Tourism Research* 27 (1), 132–47.

Wardell, D. (1987) Hotel technology and reservation systems: Challenges facing the lodging industry. *Travel and Tourism Analyst*, June, 33–47.

Weaver, D.B. (1999) Magnitude of ecotourism in Costa Rica and Kenya. *Annals of Tourism Research* 26 (4), 792–816.

White, K.J. (1985) An international travel demand model. *Annals of Tourism Research* 12 (4), 529–45.

Wight, P. (1993) Ecotourism: Ethics or eco-sell? *Journal of Travel Research* 31, 3–9.

Wight, P. (1994) The greening of the hospitality industry: Economic and environmental good sense. In A.V. Seaton (ed.) *Tourism: The State of the Art*. Chichester: Wiley.

Williams, A.M., Shaw, G. (1988) Tourism: Candy floss industry or job generator?. *Town Planning Review* 59, 81–103.

Willis, L. and Garrod, G. (1993a) The value of waterside properties: Estimating the impact of waterways and canals on property values through hedonic price models and contingent valuation methods. *Countryside Change Unit Working Paper 44*. Newcastle: University of Newcastle.

Willis, L. and Garrod, G. (1993b) Valuing wildlife: The benefits of wildlife trusts. *Countryside Change Unit Working Paper 46*. Newcastle: University of Newcastle.

Witt, C.A. and Witt, S.F. (1995) Forecasting tourism demand: A review of empirical research. *International Journal of Forecasting* 11, 447–75.

Witt, S.F. and Martin, C.A. (1985) Forecasting future trends in European tourist demand. *The Tourist Review* 4, 12–20.

Witt, S.F. and Martin, C.A. (1987) International tourism demand models – inclusion of marketing variables. *Tourism Management* 8 (1), 33–40.

Witt, S.F. and Moutinho, L. (1989) *Tourism Marketing and Management Handbook*. New York: Prentice Hall.

Zhou, D., Yanagida, J.F., Chakravorty, U. and Ping Sun, L. (1997) Estimating economic impacts from tourism. *Annals of Tourism Research* 24 (1), 76–89.

Zimmermann, R. (1998) Hotels in Germany. *Travel and Tourism Analyst* 5, 57–74.

*Chapter 4*

# The Statistical Measurement of Tourism

JOHN LATHAM and CHRIS EDWARDS

## Introduction

Tourism is a complex process comprising many parts and interconnections, involving not only visitors and their movements but also the destination and host community. It is not surprising therefore that it is increasingly being seen as an important area of study in its own right with ongoing debate as to whether it can be considered as a scientific discipline with its own theoretical development and methodologies (Dann *et al.*, 1988; Tribe, 1997). Faulkner and Goeldner (1998) raise the question of whether tourism is destined to remain a loosely connected multidisciplinary field of study given that there is 'currently no coherent body of theory that suggests the existence of a common research paradigm (or that might be synthesised to provide a unifying theme)'.

For discussions of the conceptual framework of tourism and its evolution as a discipline, see Leiper (1979); Goeldner (1988); Echtner and Jamal (1997); and Cooper *et al.* (1998). The realm of measurement is particularly important in this context.

> An important part of the maturing process for any science is the development or adaptation of consistent and well-tested measurement techniques and methodologies which are well-suited to the types of problems encountered in practice. (Ritchie, 1975)

Without a reliable historical and ongoing quantitative account of tourism, its development as an area of study would be severely hampered.

The statistical measurement of tourism is a relatively recent activity – its historical development is described in some detail by Burkart and Medlik (1981) and Lickorish (1997). Lickorish describes the roles of major national and international organisations in developing the methodologies for collecting tourism data. He singles out the work of the World Tourism Organization (WTO) as 'the most significant and praiseworthy' from the long-term point of view – for example, the WTO is the driving force behind the creation of the Tourism Satellite Account (TSA). Tourism statistics are typically measurements of arrivals, trips, tourist nights and expenditure, and these often appear in total or split into categories such as business and leisure travel. They are normally estimates, often based on sample surveys with grossing-up procedures, and are liable to large errors. Much of the methodology used to compile tourism statistics centres on standard social survey work involving questionnaires, interviewers, observers, etc. and is well documented. Nevertheless, within a general framework of research methodology that is applicable in numerous areas of study, the statistical measurement of tourism does have its own peculiarities.

Problems arise because of the very nature of the populations under study. Tourists are by definition highly mobile individuals, thus making it difficult to ensure in any sampling procedures representative or probabilistic samples. Further, a mobile subject can be difficult to isolate for a period of time and the interviewing of tourists often takes place in unfamiliar surroundings, sometimes in locations where there are crowds or high levels of noise. There are other variable influences such as the weather: when interviews are conducted out of doors, for example, periods of heavy rain can reduce response rates as well as affect the quality of information gained.

Even if the theoretical problems of sampling and its practical aspects can be overcome, serious doubts can still be cast on the reliability of tourism data. It is recognised that 'intentions studies' (where measurement is taken before travel) are likely to produce information that is at variance with the reality that occurs at a later date. Data collected during travel represent a mixture of actual and intended behaviour, and post-travel measures involve problems of identifying and locating respondents as well as those associated with individuals finding difficulty in accurate recall. There are, therefore, methodological problems that may be present in survey research in general, but which are particularly acute in the measurement of tourism. For a fuller account of the unique nature of travel and tourism research, see McIntosh and Goeldner (1986), Lim (1997), Walle (1997) and Latham (1998).

It is the aim of this chapter to describe the current position and review the progress made in recent years in the collection and organisation of tourism statistics; a discussion of methodological issues is included. For convenience, international tourism statistics and domestic tourism statistics are treated separately, although it is recognised that international and domestic tourist movements may be considered as different aspects of the same activity, with the result that there is much commonality.

## Statistics of International Tourism

### Sources

In 1998 the number of international tourist arrivals worldwide was estimated to be 636 million, generating US$442 billion in international tourist receipts (BTA, 2001). These figures are the sum of estimates for regions which are themselves totals for individual countries. Such impressive values are in fact one point in an increasing, long-term trend. Individual countries produce their own statistics; the two main compilations of international tourism statistics, both published annually, are:

(1) The World Tourism Organization (WTO) *Yearbook of Tourism Statistics*, which has been published since 1947 under the titles *International Travel Statistics*; *World Travel Statistics*; *World Travel and Tourism Statistics* and its present title.

(2) The Organisation for Economic Co-operation and Development (OECD) *Tourism Policy and International Tourism in OECD Member Countries*, sometimes referred to as the 'Blue Book'.

*The Yearbook of Tourism Statistics* (two volumes) provides a summary of the most important tourism statistics for about 190 countries and territories, and can be supplemented by the WTO's *Compendium of Tourism Statistics* (since 1985 published annually), a pocket-book designed to provide a condensed and quick reference guide on the major tourism statistical indicators. The OECD 'Blue Book' is more restrictive in the sense that its coverage is for OECD member countries only, although these do include the main generating and receiving countries. As its name suggests, it is not merely a statistical compilation and is much concerned with an examination of government policy and planning and of the obstacles to international tourism. There are, however, areas in the 'Blue Book' which act to expand on the WTO publication. For a fuller analysis of sources, see Lickorish (1997).

### Why measure international tourism?

Governments are keen to evaluate the dimensions and assess the significance of international tourism in terms of movements into and out of their own countries mainly to determine its effect on their balance of payments. The balance on the 'travel account', the difference between earnings from overseas visitors and spending by residents travelling abroad, reflects the contribution of international tourism to a nation's economy. In Europe, nine major countries have consistently recorded deficits on their travel account. These countries have severe winter weather. In 1995, according to the OECD, Germany had a travel account deficit of $34.5 billion. The travel account of Japan recorded a deficit of $33.6 billion and the UK recorded a deficit of $5.7 billion. On the other hand, Spain recorded a surplus of $20 billion, followed by the USA ($1.5 billion), France ($15 billion) and Austria ($3 billion).

However, governments' interest in tourism statistics is not merely in terms of the effect of tourism on balance of payments. Trends in movements can be monitored and information collected for official records. Statistics are used for planning purposes – a main aim of the WTO's *Yearbook of Tourism Statistics* is to present a comprehensive compendium of comparable data for the analysis of tourism developed at world, regional and national levels. The marketing arm of government is also likely to make use of information collected, such as origins of international visitors. Tourism organisations at regional and local levels also make use of international tourism statistics as they seek information on which to base development programmes and marketing activities.

Finally, although commercial organisations within the tourism industry that use international tourism statistics are in a minority, nevertheless there are many for whom information provided can be of help, again mainly in the areas of planning and marketing. For example, an incoming tour operator needs to be aware of current trends so that programmes can be adjusted accordingly. An inadequate system of measuring tourism can deprive

> both tourism authorities and tourism companies of the information essential for formulating public policy or developing business strategies. At the same time it contributes to a regrettable lack of social awareness of the importance of tourism as a factor promoting economic growth and as a source of employment (Paci, 1998)

Shackleford (1980) considers that the collection of tourism statistics as an element of state responsibility to be both necessary and desirable, beyond economic and commercial considerations. Although most states do now accept this responsibility, the WTO records that 159 of the world's 175 sovereign nations collect data on the expenditures of inbound international visitors (WTO, 1997), the collection and analysis of detailed statistics requires commitment in terms of resources. It can be argued that the benefits of collecting tourism statistics are increasingly being recognised as indicated by the development of the tourism satellite account (TSA). The WTO, World Travel and Tourism Council (WTTC) and the OECD are all working on TSAs in an attempt to provide a comprehensive and internationally uniform information base on the economic impacts of tourism. In March 2000, the United Nations Statistical Commission approved the international standards contained in the TSA, which sets a series of global standards and definitions that measure tourism's contribution to national economies in terms of percentage of Gross Domestic Product (GDP), jobs and capital investment. It is only when the benefits, both economic and otherwise, are recognised that there will be a desire to compile statistical information in line with international standards.

## What is measured?

Having outlined in broad terms some of the reasons for measuring international tourism, it is necessary to match what is measured against the purpose of measurement. An initial problem is the lack of comparability of data, not only in terms of the measures themselves (for example, visitor days or visitor nights) but also in terms of the procedures and methodology used (for example, different sampling procedures). This makes comparison between countries difficult although the OECD and WTO in particular attempt to make clear any obvious differences in data collection procedures and group countries accordingly. Further, the WTO has organised various activities and has published much material with the aim of reducing differences in practice and terminology, in particular *Recommendations on Tourism Statistics* (1994a) and *General Guidelines for Developing the Tourism Satellite Account* (2001).

Frechtling (1976), following an examination of the approaches taken by national and international bodies, including the WTO, concluded that the travel industry was converging on definitions of trip, travel and traveller. He also identified three principles which need to be observed in the formation of definitions and terminology:

(1) Definitions should be discrete and unambiguous.
(2) Definitions should facilitate measurement as much as is consistent with other objectives.
(3) Definitions should follow established usage as much as possible.

Although these principles remain sound, it should be noted that in 'normal' usage the term 'tourism' itself would refer to pleasure travel and exclude business travel. This is not in line with what has become accepted as standard, as it is usual to include, as a tourist, a person travelling not only for pleasure but also on business, visiting friends and relatives and for other personal business such as shopping. This makes sense since business tourism significantly impacts on the tourism industry – a typical business trip might involve a flight, a car hire, a stay in a hotel, shopping, visit to an attraction and the general use of tourism facilities. People visiting friends and relatives often engage in 'tourism activities' during their stay. It is interesting that Americans prefer to talk about travel, rather than tourism.

The following definitions are based on the WTO (1995) definitions and classifications and explain the various types of visitors:

| | |
|---|---|
| 'Tourism' | The activities of persons travelling to and staying in places outside their usual environment for not more than one consecutive year for leisure, business and other purposes. |
| 'Tourist (overnight visitor)' | Visitor staying at least one night in a collective or private accommodation in the place visited. |
| 'Same Day Visitor (excursionist)' | Visitor who does not spend the night in a collective or private accommodation in the place visited. |
| 'Visitor' | Any person travelling to a place other than that of his/her usual environment for less than 12 consecutive months and whose main purpose of travel is not to work for pay in the place visited. |
| 'Traveller' | Any person on a trip between two or more locations. |

There are three main categories of statistics: of volume, of expenditure and statistics relating to the profile of the tourist and his trip.

## Volume statistics

The most obvious measure of volume is that of the total number of international tourist arrivals/departures in the given time period. Such a measure relates to trips and not individuals in the sense that, for example, a businessman who makes 10 trips in a year is counted 10 times. A disadvantage of using this particular measure is that it does not take account of the length of stay, which is important to most suppliers of the tourism product such as accommodation establishments, though not for passenger transport carriers. A more satisfactory measure of volume for some purposes is that of total tourist nights as it is a measure of overall demand, but also acts as a measure of the likely impact on a destination in physical terms. It can be calculated as the product of tourist arrivals/departures and average length of stay. The implied equation here is exact, though of course errors in the values of the two terms of the product combine in the normal way.

## Expenditure statistics

The basic statistics of monetary flows are naturally compiled under the headings of income and expenditure. Total visitor expenditure is a simple measure of the economic value of tourism to a nation, though it must be tempered by the expenditure of outgoing tourists. Incoming visitors can be considered to be purchasing exports in view of the effect of their spending on the balance of payments. Tourist expenditure normally covers spending within a country and excludes payments made to passenger transport carriers for travel to and from the destination country. It can be classified under the headings of accommodation, meals, entertainment, shopping and travel within the host country.

The WTO (1994b, 2001) has published guidelines for the measurement of travel and tourism in the form of a comprehensive analysis of the items of expenditure as well as practical methods for obtaining statistics. The objective of its methods is to make available to member states, the developing countries in particular, operational tools to facilitate the collection, processing and publication of data, thus leading to greater precision in the evaluation of the economic impact of tourism. The WTO's *Yearbook of Tourism Statistics* provides statistics of international tourism receipts and expenditure.

The OECD is an organisation with the objectives of promoting high rates of growth in member countries and sees tourism expenditure as an important catalyst of growth. The OECD 'Blue Book' therefore provides a detailed coverage of the economic importance of international tourism in member countries, in terms of receipts and expenditure, and the travel account in the balance of payments. *Measuring the Role of Tourism in OECD Economies* (OECD, 2000) describes the application of 'tourism accounts' in 16 OECD countries and provides a methodology for the implementation of tools to measure the impact of tourism.

### Profile statistics

Statistics relating to the profile of the tourist typically include details of age, sex, occupation, income, nationality or country of residence and group type. The profile of the visit or trip covers origin, destination, timing of visit, purpose of visit, mode of transport, type of accommodation, details of activities engaged in and places visited and whether the visit is part of a tour or is independently organised. Goeldner *et al.* (2000) give a description of trip characteristics used in North America.

The British Tourist Authority concentrates its marketing activities on segments or groups of customers around the world which have demonstrated, through research, that they will generate the greatest financial return. A considerable amount of research has been carried out over recent years to identify specific market segments by lifestyle or psychographics. The level of sophistication is such that between 50 and 100 lifestyle segments have been identified for countries where the BTA has a presence.

Mode of transport for international tourism refers to the transport used to enter the country visited. It is interesting to note that a tourist who enters a country by plane and then hires a car may appear to be an arrival by road. The usual classifications of transport are air, sea, rail and road. Type of accommodation used covers a wide range of possibilities with much variation by country.

## Methods used

In view of the difficulties involved in measuring the movement of people and associated variables, it is not possible to produce exact values. Most statistics of tourism are in reality estimates. Even though there are controls at boundaries between countries and currency controls and restrictions, these do not always work to provide accurate, relevant information.

Volume statistics can be the result of counting procedures either at entry/exit points or at accommodation establishments using registration forms. These are supplemented by records kept by passenger transport carriers. In addition, household and destination surveys will elicit information on international travel even though they are not intended solely for this purpose.

Expenditure statistics can be derived indirectly using foreign currency estimates from bank records or from providers of tourist services and facilities supplying estimates of receipts. Increasingly, information is obtained directly from a sample of tourists who are asked to provide details of their expenditure on leaving or, in the case of outgoing tourists, on return.

Satellite accounting requires the measurement of both demand (the expenditure of visitors or on their behalf) and supply which focuses on goods and services consumed by visitors. Paci (1998) argues that the reconciliation of these two approaches gives the TSA system several distinct benefits when compared to traditional systems of measuring the economic importance of tourism. These include a greater use of common definitions and enhanced credibility of the analysis.

## Some examples

*Canada*  Canada has, for some time, been a country that has taken a lead role in the collection and use of international tourism statistics. Historically, methodologies were patterned on the preponderance of travel between Canada and the United States (Baille, 1985), though existing and potential markets worldwide have been identified. Taylor (1987) describes a number of research initiatives taken in the 1980s in Canada as a response to a review of data needs and availability.

Initiatives in the 1990s have centred on the formation in 1994 of the Canadian Tourism Commission (CTC), replacing Tourism Canada as the national tourism organisation. Previously, research needs had not been directly influenced by external users or the industry; research tended to emphasise international market profiles, travel trends and economic impacts, thus meeting some but not all of industry needs. The Board of Directors of CTC is dominated by representatives from industry and a significant proportion of its budget is derived from the private sector. Smith (1999) describes in some detail the move towards a national tourism research agenda in Canada.

According to Smith, a Research Committee was formed to develop and disseminate the best possible data and information to support decision making in the industry. Improvements were made in the major surveys such as the Canadian Travel Survey, and analytical tools developed including the world's first satellite account (Smith & Wilton, 1997). Research continues on international markets and on advertising effectiveness.

*The United Kingdom* The UK has one single survey, the International Passenger Survey (IPS) which measures both incoming and outgoing international tourism flows in a consistent manner. It started in 1961 by covering only major routes but has since developed so that all the ports of exit/entry are covered. The survey is based on a stratified random sample of passengers entering and leaving the UK, sampling being carried out separately for air, sea and tunnel. For further details of the sample design, see the British Tourist Authority website. The aims of the IPS are:

(1) To collect data for the travel account (which acts to compare expenditure by overseas visitors to the UK with expenditure overseas by visitors from the UK) of the balance of payments.
(2) To provide detailed information on foreign visitors to the UK, and on outgoing visitors travelling overseas.
(3) To provide data on international migration.
(4) To provide information on routes used by passengers as an aid to aviation and shipping authorities.

*Developing countries* Traditionally, there has been a serious lack of reliable and uniform statistical information in developing countries. The World Tourism Conference in Manila (WTO, 1980) commented on the frequent duplication of tourist market information and called on the WTO 'to continue its efforts to facilitate the exchange of technical tourist information, specifically by considering the possibility of establishing a worldwide tourist information system'.

There have been slow but significant developments since then which have ensured that countries such as Dominica are now receiving WTO support in establishing a TSA. See Lickorish (1997) for a description of developments over the last few decades. It can be argued, therefore, that the adoption of the tourism satellite accounting system by developing countries will increase reliability and uniformity in statistical information.

## Statistics of Domestic Tourism

### Why measure domestic tourism?

The main difference between domestic and international tourism from the statistical point of view is that with the latter a frontier has to be crossed – this provides an easy opportunity to observe and record such a movement. Demand for accommodation and other services and facilities by domestic tourists may complement or compete with that by tourists from abroad. It is therefore desirable to analyse the two types of demand together, though in practice this is not as yet normally the case owing to the higher priority given to the collection of international tourism statistics and the greater difficulties of measuring domestic tourism.

Domestic tourism worldwide is in terms of volume and value much more important than international tourism. Latham (1998) estimates that expenditure worldwide on domestic tourism may be worth up to 10 times that on international tourism. Certainly the majority of trips do not involve the crossing of international boundaries. However, compared to the statistics available for international tourism movements, those for domestic tourism are extremely poor both in terms of quality and quantity. The main reasons for this are the relative difficulty of obtaining information from domestic tourists, and, due to the fact that domestic movements have no direct impact on a country's balance of payments or foreign exchange earnings, less effort is made.

Generally figures underestimate true domestic movements, as visits to friends and relatives, the use of forms of accommodation other than hotels (for example, second homes, camp and caravan sites) and travel by large segments of a population from towns to the countryside are for the most part not included.

The WTO (1984) reported that 'there are relatively few countries that collect domestic travel and tourism statistics'. There have since then been gains, through some increase in the number of countries that collect domestic data, greater attention paid to methodology and consistency, and the development of the TSA which recognises the significance of domestic tourism. Nevertheless, some countries rely exclusively on the traditional hotel sector, thereby leaving out of account the many travellers staying in supplementary accommodation establishments or with friends and relatives. A full coverage of domestic tourism clearly requires the use of methods of collection other than the traditional use of hotel records, which may nevertheless still provide valuable information.

The WTO (1981) identifies four main uses of domestic tourism statistics.

(1) *To measure the contribution of tourism to the overall economy.* The authorities responsible for tourism wish to know its contribution to the Gross Domestic Product. Because of the complex nature of the tourism sector, there are enormous problems involved in this calculation – nevertheless estimates are produced.
(2) *For promotion and marketing policies.* Increasingly countries are aware of the need to encourage nationals to spend holidays within their country rather than abroad, and develop campaigns to this end.
(3) *To assist area development policies.* Many governments assume responsibility for the geographical distribution of domestic tourism with the dual aim of ensuring a better quality of the environment in the principal tourism areas, and to promote underdeveloped areas and relieve congested areas.
(4) *To aid social policies.* A small but increasing number of authorities provide aid for the underprivileged, either directly for holidays or in the form of subsidies for the construction and operation of socially orientated tourist reception plants. Because of the financial implications, a statistical knowledge of holiday-taking habits and trends by nationals is required for the formation of policies.

In addition to the above, use is made of domestic tourism statistics by regional and local tourist organisations in order to market and develop their own destinations; and by individual businesses within the tourist industry.

### Definitions

Domestic tourism refers to trips undertaken by residents of a country within the national territory of that country. On closer examination, definitions do vary considerably:

- *Purpose of visit* – all countries using this concept define a domestic tourist as one who travels for a purpose other than the exercise of a remunerated activity.
- *Length of trip and/or distance travelled* – certain definitions state that the traveller should, for example, be involved in an overnight stay and/ or travel a prescribed minimum distance.

- *Type of accommodation* – for practical reasons, some countries restrict the concept of domestic tourism to cover only those persons using commercial accommodation facilities.

The WTO (1994a) recommends the following definition of domestic visitors:

> The term 'domestic visitor' describes any person residing in a country, who travels to a place within the country, outside his/her usual environment for a period not exceeding 12 months, and whose main purpose of visit is other than the exercise of an activity remunerated from within the place visited.

This definition covers 'domestic tourists', where an overnight stay is involved, and 'domestic excursionists' where the stay in the place visited is less than 24 hours and no overnight stay is involved.

## What is measured?

Although measures of domestic tourism are often presented for a country as a whole, they are often more useful if they are broken down to provide reliable information for specific destination areas. Individual destinations or attractions may well conduct their own research and make use of national data either to provide context or supplementary information (Cooper *et al.*, 1998).

Baseline requirements might be considered to be domestic tourism arrivals and nights classified by:

- the month concerned;
- the type and class of accommodation establishment;
- the location of the accommodation establishment; and
- overall expenditure on domestic tourism.

Certain other variables such as length of stay, occupancy rate and average expenditure may be derived from these basic statistics. Data supplementary to such basic minimum requirements are in fact gathered by many countries and information concerning socio-economic characteristics (age, sex, social group), mode of transport and purpose of visit are clearly of use in promoting domestic tourism. It should be remembered that resources in many of the developing countries are often limited and restrict data collection.

The development of the TSA has given greater prominence to the collection and use of domestic tourism data, and a review of what is measured, particularly for economic purposes.

## Methods used

As with international tourism statistics, those of domestic tourism are in reality estimates, subject to various forms of error and are produced with differing levels of accuracy. In recent years methods other than those based on the use of hotel records have been developed and involve eliciting information from the tourists themselves via sample surveys. For example, there are two surveys covering domestic tourism in the United Kingdom, the results of which together provide a comprehensive statistical analysis. Table 4.1 provides details of their history, coverage and survey design.

The main methods of collection of statistics of domestic tourism are detailed below.

**Table 4.1** Surveys covering domestic tourism in the United Kingdom

---

**United Kingdom Tourism Survey – (UKTS)**

**Commencing**
1972 as the British Home Tourism Survey. Annual and monthly reporting. Became British Tourism Survey Monthly (BTSM) in 1985. Monthly, annual and trend reports (6 per annum). Replaced by UKTS in 1989.

**Coverage**
All tourism by UK residents of 1+ nights at home and abroad.

**Design**
75000 random in-home interviews of adults 15+ undertaken each month. Trip recall period is the previous two months. Survey adopted 'CAPI' (computer assisted personal interviewing) in 1994.

**British National Travel Survey (BNTS)**

**Commencing**
1961 as the British National Travel Survey. Annual since 1961. Became British Tourism Survey Yearly (BTSY) in 1985. Annual reporting. Became British National Travel Survey in 1988. Annual reporting.

**Coverage**
All holidays by UK residents.

**Design**
3000 random in-home interviews.

*Source*: http://www.statistics.gov.uk

---

*Household surveys*

'Household surveys' are suitable for recording the tourism of large numbers of people, and residents of a country, whether they travel within the country, or abroad, can be contacted in their home. Such surveys are based on a knowledge of the profile of the resident population and provide a balanced view of domestic tourism for pleasure purposes. Further, in theory, international comparisons can be made.

An example of the use of a household survey, given by Goeldner *et al.* (2000), is the Canadian Travel Survey. The mainstay of Canada's tourism industry is domestic travel and there was a management stipulation that studies be carried out to measure the value, volume and characteristics of Canadian domestic tourism by the most cost efficient method possible, and in conjunction with the central statistical agency, Statistics Canada. Statistics Canada runs a monthly household survey and government departments can purchase supplementary questions in units of 10,000 households. Since 1982, the survey has been conducted twice a year, instead of four times, as a result of the evidence of stability of travel patterns prior to this date. Further details of the methods used for the Canadian Travel Survey can be found on www.statcan.ca.

Most countries nowadays conduct national travel surveys which cover domestic travel and travel made by their residents to foreign destinations. In addition to providing profiles of those who travel, they interestingly provide information relating to those who do not. A national holiday survey is one which concentrates solely on holiday tourism, normally dealing with the previous year's holidays, although in some cases interviewing takes place at regular intervals throughout a year in order to minimise recall problems. Less common is the all-tourism survey which provides a more comprehensive profile and an example of which is the United States National Travel Survey.

Although trends can be monitored within a country on an annual basis, it is dangerous to make firm comparisons between countries because of the differing definitions and methodologies used. In 1967, the OECD Tourism Committee published details of common data that it recommended be obtained through national holiday surveys undertaken by its members (see, for example, the OECD 'Blue Book'). In 1995 the Council of the European Union adopted a directive 'On the Collection of Statistical Information in the Field of Tourism', which places a requirement on national governments of member states of the EU to provide a regular set of specific tourism statistics. Maintained by Eurostat, specific guidance is given regarding terminology and methodology. The system represents an attempt to generate a set of reliable and comparable statistics for EU states and other countries participating on a voluntary basis. Both domestic and international tourism are covered by this directive.

### Destination surveys

'Destination surveys' are normally limited to areas with high levels of tourist activity and can provide information outside the scope of a household survey on the volume, value and characteristics of tourism to individual destinations within a country, such as a region or a resort. Information is drawn from surveys of accommodation establishments (using registration forms) and sample surveys of visitors at the destination, and can build on details from a national travel survey which might provide data for trips to the regions of a country.

### Enroute surveys

'Enroute surveys', or surveys of travellers during the course of their journey, are similar to frontier surveys in the sense that a strategic point is selected for interviewing. The way the survey is conducted depends on the transport used. Its main advantages are that all forms of tourism can be covered and many interviews can be conducted in a day. However, the representativeness of the sample is in doubt, making errors difficult to estimate because of an incomplete knowledge of traffic movement within a country. A further problem, as in most survey work, concerns non-response, particularly if the potential respondent is asked to complete the questionnaire in his own time and then to post it. Enroute survey response rates are optimised by selecting the respondent at a propitious point in his trip and collecting the information 'in situ' – response rates of over 90% are then possible (Hurst, 1987). Hurst reviews the use of enroute survey methods and provides guidance in assessing their value with regard to cost per interview, sampling error and control.

### Surveys of the suppliers of tourism services

In addition, 'surveys of the suppliers of tourism services' can be undertaken in order to elicit information such as occupancy rates, numbers of overnight stays and visitor numbers. The Tourism Satellite Account tackles the problems associated with definitions of the supply side of tourism. The purpose of the TSA is to measure the economic activity generated by tourism not only in terms of demand for commodities but also through an analysis of production required to meet that demand (Sonpal, 1998).

## Methodological issues

General coverage of the basic concepts of sampling and sampling design can be found within a number of standard business texts, for example see Aaker *et al.* (2000). Witt and Moutinho (1995) place these within the context of tourism. Aaker *et al.* explain simple random sampling, systematic sampling, stratified random sampling, cluster sampling and quota sampling, together with their advantages and disadvantages. In large surveys, methods are normally combined. They also provide a more detailed descriptive account of the different sources of error that may be present and the measurement of error during the different stages of a research process.

Over many years, the WTO (1979, 1981, 1984, 1994b, 1998) has produced a number of methodological publications relating to the collection, analysis and presentation of tourism statistics. It has played a leading role in attempts to create consistency worldwide, notably in terms of definitions, measurement and methodology. During the 1990s, the OECD, the European Union (through Eurostat, its statistical agency) and other regional organisations, have also given serious consideration to definitions and methodological issues. Middleton (1994), Proctor (1997) and Woodside *et al.* (2000) describe and analyse different means by which tourism data are collected. Some methodological points relating to the main methods in use in the collection of tourism statistics are outlined below.

*Data collected at international borders*

The majority of states collect data at borders, and for a variety of purposes, including tourism. Many states, for example India, undertake what they consider to be a census, making use of data collected to compile counts of different tourist types. Others, such as the United Kingdom, utilise complex sampling procedures to interview a selection of tourists to capture data on visits, expenditure, places visited and so on. Grossing up is then undertaken with appropriate weightings to arrive at estimates of values. The procedures used at frontiers are often not satisfactory in that they do not always have tourism purposes in mind but are for administrative controls. Further, counting at entry/exit points does not provide an effective measure if no information is available on length of stay.

*Data collected at accommodation establishments*

Countries often make use of data and information collected through registration at accommodation establishments. In some cases, this is the main means of collecting tourism data, with the drawback that international tourists visiting friends and relatives are not counted and domestic tourism may be ignored altogether. Occupancy surveys may be used to construct measures of demand.

## Data collected by passenger carriers

All passenger carriers naturally collect travel data as part of their own business operations, and these may be used by national tourist offices to supplement other data that is available to them.

## Visitor surveys

Surveys of visitors are conducted in a variety of contexts, ranging from those within regions of a country or towns/cities, to those conducted at individual sites or tourist attractions. Sampling procedures are used to select specific visitors, normally for personal interview. Sampling, in the context of visitors moving freely at a location, is normally non-scientific and so it is not possible to have great confidence in findings. In addition to producing measurements of volume, value and visitor type, visitor surveys are utilised to gauge opinions on the experience offered and other information for marketing purposes.

## Diary questionnaires

Diary questionnaires can be used in surveys of visitors to an area. The methodology involves giving visitors a questionnaire to be completed during their visit and returned by post after they leave. Although such data collected may sometimes be superior to that produced by visitor surveys, the low response rate is normally considered a major limitation.

## Unobtrusive observation

Unobtrusive observation of visitors and their behaviour is a relatively inexpensive and reliable method of collecting data about visitors in a variety of settings. The method is best used to collect qualitative information, as it provides insight into behaviour that may supplement quantitative information.

## Intention studies and satisfaction studies

Tourists and visitors can be questioned before, during or following a trip or visit. The results of intention studies will obviously contain a degree of inaccuracy for reasons of changes of mind or plan prior to the actual trip taking place, or merely because the information given represents a wish, desire or a lie. Nevertheless, they can be valuable in the short term to gauge likely demand, and can influence pricing or approaches to marketing. Satisfaction surveys are conducted following the tourism experience. Generally, these are best completed immediately following the experience using a fresh memory. A common example is that of airlines associated with tour operators distributing questionnaires for completion during the return flight.

## Social and Environmental Impacts

It has increasingly been recognised that the impact of tourism to a destination should not solely be measured in economic terms. Indeed, social and environmental impacts now represent key dimensions of tourism research (Faulkner & Goeldner, 1998), although their measurement can be somewhat problematic (see for example, Coccossis & Parpairis, 2000; Wall, 1999). According to Briassoulis (2000), the study of carrying capacity, driven by a growing awareness of the need for sustainability, can be identified as the most thoroughly studied issue relating to the environmental impact of tourism. Cleverdon (2000) argues that development of the Tourism Satellite Account (TSA) has the principal drawback that it has been driven solely from an economic perspective, and that its inherent detail could lead to the risk that planners and administrators pay inadequate attention to the less readily quantifiable concerns and impacts from other perspectives.

## The Future

In recent years there have been moves towards a greater coverage of tourism statistics, together with the use of more sophisticated research techniques mainly by the developed countries. There has been convergence in the area of definition, though research designs do vary considerably, often of necessity, but even in the collection of similar data on domestic as well as international tourism. According to Frechtling (1999), this has prevented valid comparisons among nations, or even for the same nation over different periods of time, and has frustrated business and government attempts to draw valid conclusions about the nature and course of tourism demand in national economies. There is also concern about the reliability of estimates, particularly relating to data collected at a local level, and analyses show that error bounds (which are in any case not normally calculated) are not always within acceptable limits. The future is likely to see further refinements of methodologies used in different countries, together with further attempts to ensure comparability of data on domestic as well as international tourism. Given that data are collected at a cost, there may be developments in some countries in terms of the ways in which the public and private sectors work together to produce statistics that are reliable and usable by a number of stakeholders.

Modern technology is such that a global tourism database, perhaps under the auspices of the WTO, could be set up to meet information needs of countries all over the world. Certainly, in the case of the developing countries with their greater resource constraints in collecting statistics, this would be of great benefit, supplementing data that could be collected at a more reasonable cost, say, in the form of a destination survey.

The growing use of the Internet by tourism researchers and managers has been achieved by significant advances in user-friendliness of the search systems available and the rapidly expanding, inexpensive and accessible array of information sources it can provide (William *et al.*, 1996). The Internet facilitates rapid dissemination of statistical information worldwide. Both tourism industry associations and government-sponsored organisations have comprehensive websites containing tourism statistics and their interpretation. Goeldner *et al.* (2000) believe the Travel Industry Association of America to be the most authoritative source of information on the US travel industry and advises a visit to its website. Using the Web as a research tool is still in its infancy, though many software companies now offer reliable Internet survey tools (Robson, 1999). Web questionnaires may offer a fast and cheap way of gathering tourism statistics. (See William *et al.* (1996) for a discussion on using the Internet for tourism research.)

Recent years have seen the introduction of a new concept, the Tourism Satellite Account (TSA), for measuring the economic impact of tourism. This development can be considered a major innovation as it has seriously questioned the approaches and their limitations of previous decades. Frechtling (1999) explores the major issues under debate in developing the TSA concepts and measurement techniques. It is worthy of note that the economic consequences of both domestic and international tourism come within the consideration of the TSA. There is still much work to be done in this area before its full potential can be realised, and it will be interesting to see how TSAs relate to the WTO and OECD development of multi-national standards and other new initiatives worldwide.

## Note
1. This chapter first appeared as 'The statistical measurement of tourism' in Volume 1 of *Progress in Tourism, Recreation and Hospitality Management* (1989), pp. 55–76.

## References
Aaker, D.A., Kumar, V. and Day, G.S. (2000) *Marketing Research*. New York: John Wiley.

Baille, J.G. (1985) The evolution of Canadian international travel documentation. *Annals of Tourism Research* 12 (4), 563–79.

Briassoulis, H. (2000) Environmental impacts of tourism: A framework for analysis and evaluation. In H. Briassoulis and J. Van Der Straatten (eds) *Tourism and the Environment* (2nd edn) (pp. 21–37). Dordrecht: Kluwer.

British Tourist Authority (2001) *Tourism Intelligence Quarterly* 22 (4).

Burkart, A.J. and Medlik, S. (1981) *Tourism – Past, Present and Future.* London: Heinemann.

Cleverdon, R. (2000) The problem with tourism satellite account. *Tourism Trendspotter* 2 (6), 16–18.

Coccossis, H. and Parpairis, A. (2000) Tourism and the environment: Some observations on the concept of carrying capacity. In H. Briassoulis and J. Van Der Straatten (eds) *Tourism and the Environmen* (2nd edn) (pp. 91–105). Dordrecht: Kluwer.

Cooper, C., Fletcher, J., Gilbert, D. and Wanhill, W. with Shepherd, R. (ed.) (1998) *Tourism Principles and Practice.* New York: Addison Wesley Longman.

Dann, G., Nash, D. and Pearce, P. (1988) Methodology in tourism research. *Annals of Tourism Research* 15 (1), 1–28.

Echtner, C.M. and Jamal, T.B. (1997) The disciplinary dilemma of tourism studies. *Annals of Tourism Research* 24 (4), 868–83.

Faulkner, B. and Goeldner, C.R. (1998) Progress in tourism and hospitality research. *Journal of Travel Research* 37 (5), 76.

Frechtling, D.C. (1976) Proposed standard definitions and classifications for travel research. *Marketing Travel and Tourism, Seventh Annual Conference Proceedings* (pp. 59–74). Boca Raton: Travel Research Association.

Frechtling, D.C. (1999) The tourism satellite account: Foundations, progress and issues. *Tourism Management* 20, 163–70.

Goeldner, C.R. (1988) The evolution of the discipline of tourism. Paper presented to teaching tourism into the 1990s, International Conference for Tourism Educators. Guildford: University of Surrey.

Goeldner, C.R., Brent Ritchie, J.R. and Mcintosh, R.W. (2000) *Tourism, Principles, Practices, Philosophies* (8th edn). New York: John Wiley.

Hurst, F. (1987) Enroute surveys. In J.R.B. Ritchie and C.R. Goeldner (eds) *Travel, Tourism and Hospitality Research: A Handbook for Managers and Researchers* (pp. 401–16). New York: John Wiley.

Latham, J. (1998) Patterns of international tourism. *Progress in Tourism and Hospitality Research,* 4 (1), 45–52.

Leiper, N. (1979) The framework of tourism. *Annals of Tourism Research* 6 (4), 390–407.

Lickorish, L.J. (1997) Travel statistics – the slow move forward. *Tourism Management* 18 (8), 491–7.

Lim, C. (1997) An econometric classification and review of international tourism demand models. *Tourism Economics* 3 (1), 69–81.

Mcintosh, R.W. and Goeldner, C.R. (1986) *Tourism Principles, Practices, Philosophies.* New York: John Wiley.

Middleton, V.T.C. (1994) *Marketing in Travel and Tourism.* Oxford: Butterworth-Heinemann.

Organisation for Economic Co-Operation and Development (Annual) *Tourism Policy and International Tourism in OECD Member Countries.* Paris: OECD.

Organisation for Economic Co-Operation and Development (2000) *Measuring the Role of Tourism in OECD Economies.* Paris: OECD.

Paci, E. (1998) The World Tourism Organisation's efforts in the development of a tourism satellite account. *Tourism Economics* 4 (3), 279–81.

Proctor, T. (1997) *Essentials of Marketing Research.* London: Pitman.

Ritchie, J.R.B. (1975) Some critical aspects of measurement theory and practice in travel research. In R.W. McIntosh and C.R. Goeldner (1986) *Tourism Principles, Practices, Philosophies* (pp. 437–51). New York: John Wiley.

Robson, J. (1999) Using technology for research. *Tourism Trendspotter* 2 (1), 12.

Shackleford, P. (1980) Keeping tabs on rourism: A manager's guide to statistics. *International Journal of Tourism Management* 1 (3), 148–57.

Smith, S.L.J. (1999) Toward a national tourism research agenda for Canada. *Tourism Management* 20, 297–304.

Smith, S.L.J. and Wilton, D. (1997) TSAs and the WTTC/WEFA methodology: Different satellites or different planets? *Tourism Economics* 3 (3), 249–63.

Sonpal, C. (1998) Balance of payments and travel account – surplus of deficit. *Insights* (March), A–143. London: BTA,.

Taylor, G.D. (1987) Research in national tourist organisations. In J.R.B. Ritchie and C.R. Goeldner (eds) *Travel, Tourism and Hospitality Research: A Handbook for Managers and Researchers* (pp. 117–28) New York: John Wiley.

Tribe, J. (1997) The indiscipline of tourism. *Annals of Tourism Research* 24 (3), 638–57.

Wall, G. (1999) Rethinking impacts of tourism. *Progress in Tourism and Hospitality Research* 2 (3–4), 207–15.

Walle, A.H. (1997) Quantitative versus qualitative tourism research. *Annals of Tourism Research* 24 (3), 524–36.

William, P.W., Bascombe, P., Brenner, N. and Green, D. (1996) Using the internet for tourism research: 'Information Highway' or 'Dirt Road'? *Journal of Travel Research* 34 (3), 63.

Witt, S.F. and Moutinho, L. (eds) (1995) *Tourism Marketing and Management Handbook*. Hemel Hempstead, UK: Prentice Hall Europe.

Woodside, A.G., Crouch, G.I., Mazanek, J.A., Oppermann, M. and Sakai, M.Y. (eds) (2000) *Consumer Psychology in Tourism, Hospitality and Leisure*. Wallingford: CABI Publishing.

World Tourism Organization (Annual) *Yearbook of Tourism Statistics* (2 vols). Madrid: WTO.

World Tourism Organization (Annual) *Compendium of Tourism Statistics*. Madrid: WTO.

World Tourism Organization (1979) *Survey of Surveys and Research in the Field of Tourism*. Madrid: WTO.

World Tourism Organization (1980) *Manila Declaration on World Tourism*. Madrid: WTO.

World Tourism Organization (1981) *Technical Handbook on the Collection and Presentation of Domestic and International Tourism Statistics*. Madrid: WTO.

World Tourism Organization (1984a) *Domestic Tourism Statistics*. Madrid: WTO.

World Tourism Organization (1998) *Tourism Satellite Account (TSA)*. Madrid: WTO.

World Tourism Organization (1994a) *Recommendations on Tourism Statistics*. Madrid: WTO.

World Tourism Organization (1994b) *Tourism to the Year 2000 and Recommendations on Tourism Statistics*. Madrid: WTO,.

World Tourism Organization (1995) *Concepts, Definitions and Classifications for Tourism Statistics*. Madrid: WTO.

World Tourism Organization (1997) *Yearbook of Tourism Statistics*. Madrid: WTO.

World Tourism Organization (2001) *General Guidelines for Developing the Tourism Satellite Account*. Madrid: WTO.

**Websites consulted**
British Tourist Authority – http://www.britishtouristauthority.org
Canadian Government Statistics – http://www.statcan.ca
Surveys covering UK tourism – http://www.statistics.gov.uk

## Chapter 5

# Perspectives on Temporal Change and the History of Tourism and Recreation

GEOFF WALL

Investigations of the history of recreation, be they studies of activities, events, places or participants, may be undertaken for many reasons. Curiosity and the intrinsic interest of the subject combine to encourage some to study the history of recreation for its own sake, and such researchers may require no further justification for their activities. However, if such studies are not placed within a broader context, there is a danger that they will be merely antiquarian and fail to make the full contribution to the understanding of society they have the potential to make. Activities undertaken in leisure, while not free of constraints, by definition involve a large element of choice. In consequence, their investigation may reveal different and complementary insights into the workings of a society when compared with other areas of life where choices may be more constrained.

For too long it has been common, almost fashionable, to begin academic papers on outdoor recreation with references to growing population, expanded leisure, rising incomes, improved transportation and greater urbanisation, and to attribute rapid rates of growth in participation in outdoor recreation and tourism to expansion of these causal factors. Attention is drawn to growth, to the relative neglect of activities or areas which are stagnant or in decline. Such perspectives ignore many recent trends in Western societies that have implications for both supply and demand – such as declining birth rates and greater longevity, increased unemployment, economic vagaries, traffic congestion and changes in the structure of metropolitan areas, making such assertions both simplistic and dated. There is also every reason to believe that even the recent past was much more complex than these generalisations imply. Such statements gloss over the real importance of fluctuations in such variables and imply that the nature of their influence upon leisure, recreation and tourism are well understood when, in fact, such relationships continue to be fruitful areas of research. Furthermore, the emphasis on the rapidity of change, which often accompanies such assertions, suggests a break with the past rather than the considerable continuities that more careful analyses reveal. Thus, it is argued that recreation and tourism researchers should be much more cognisant than they frequently have been of the temporal contexts of their studies.

There are also sound practical reasons why recreation and tourism researchers should understand the temporal dimensions of their topics. Processes of change may be best understood through studies that are more than cross-sections in time, and policy recommendations must acknowledge the existence of preceding situations that place limitations on options. The world is not a *tabula rasa* and possible futures are very much constrained by decisions which have been made in the past. An understanding of past patterns of recreation and the evolution of recreational and tourism activities and areas can also lead to the development of interpretive materials to cater to the considerable interest in heritage. Thus, the history of recreation need not be a purely academic enterprise for it also has its applied aspects.

Heritage tourism is one topic that has seen a substantial increase in attention from both academics and practitioners, heritage being defined simply as 'the contemporary use of the past' (Graham *et al.*, 2000: 2). Both historians and heritage devotees are selective in their recollections, but the recognition of heritage implies a conscious choice to value some manifestations of the past above others and often to create tourism products rooted in selected representations of the past. What is deemed to be heritage, how it is treated (preserved, restored, renovated or sometimes totally reconstructed), and the stories that are told about it (interpretation) raise questions concerning authenticity of experience and commodification of culture, usually reflecting access to power and the perspectives of dominant ideologies. These are complex issues that engross many researchers. The writings of Lowenthal (1985, 1996) provide an erudite perspective on time, and the uses of the past in the present. Building on initial work on the tourist-historic city (Ashworth & Tunbridge, 1990), Ashworth and his colleagues provide insightful discussion and numerous examples of the contentious issues surrounding heritage and its management (Ashworth & Tunbridge; 2000, Tunbridge & Ashworth, 1996). These publications provide a readily accessible introduction to what has become a large and rapidly expanding literature (see Chapter 9 this volume).

While it is suggested that many tourism, recreation and leisure studies should be more firmly placed in their temporal contexts, there is also a need for researchers with a predominantly historical focus to look beyond the narrow bounds of their subject matter. Heritage, with its complexities and contentious issues, requires that one does this and this is one reason why it has captured the imagination of a diverse audience. Furthermore, if the anti-quarian trap is to be avoided then researchers must strive to move beyond the case study. There is evidence that this is starting to occur. For example Travis (1993) has chronicled the development of a number of resorts in Devon in the United Kingdom. In being critical of case studies, it is not this author's intention to suggest that good case studies are not needed, for accurate factual information must be acquired, and examples must be developed to test hypotheses and to illuminate and illustrate generalisations. The point is that case studies will be most useful if they are linked to broader themes and serve a higher purpose rather than being ends in themselves.

Although some investigations attempt to present a national perspective, such as those of Richardson (1999) on Australia and MacDowall (1999) on the much smaller island of Bermuda, a number of studies reach beyond national boundaries and are all the more important because of this. Jakle's (1985) study of travel in North America is largely confined to the United States as is Belasco's (1979) on travel and accommodation. On the other hand, and of particular importance in consequence, is Towner's (1996) study of the historical geography of recreation and tourism in the Western world. This is a seminal work that encompasses not only the tourists and the places they visited, but also the people that catered to their needs. Another important work with an international perspective is that of Tissot (2000) on Switzerland. Put somewhat simplistically, this book is concerned essentially with the English as tourists and the Swiss as suppliers of tourism opportunities. In other words, it sees the Swiss as pioneers in catering to tourists, responding to novel demands emanating from England as the industrial revolution also precipitated a revolution in leisure and recreation: new forms of tourism evolved and tourism technologies were developed in England and exported to Switzerland. However, almost all of the studies of the history of tourism and recreation have been undertaken in the Western world and historical studies of tourism and recreation in the developing world are only slowly beginning to emerge (Smith, 1992; Douglas, 1997).

If progress is to be made and studies are to be cumulative in their contribution to knowledge, then it is necessary to impose a structure upon information. Of course, many such structures are possible; no one single structure will suit all needs, and the utility of different structures will vary with the objectives of the study. One relatively straightforward means of categorising information is by topic (Marsh & Wall, 1982; Butler & Wall, 1985). Thus, one might be interested in spas or seaside resorts, in urban or rural recreation, in public or private provision, in recreations of the elite or the experiences of the proletariat, in the evolution of particular activities or in a multitude of other topics. Perhaps not surprisingly, topical coverage is very uneven. For example, there is excellent documentation on seaside resorts (Walvin, 1978; Walton, 1983, 2000, Soane 1993, Morgan & Pritchard, 1999) but, in spite of existence of a substantial literature, the definitive work on spas has yet to be written. Similarly, there is a vast academic and popular literature on national parks in many parts of the world (Bella, 1987; MacEwen & MacEwen, 1982; Runte, 1979; Forest, 1984; Wirth, 1980, Marsh & Hodgins 1997), but much less extensive documentation of parks and tourism at regional, provincial (although see Jasen, 1995) and state levels, or of the evolution of urban park systems, although documentation of the latter is beginning to emerge (Cranz, 1982; Schuyler, 1986). The evolution of tourism in a number of national parks, such as Yosemite (Demars, 1991), have received attention, as have other prominent tourism destinations (Sears, 1989), including Niagara Falls (McGreevy, 1994). The histories of sports and recreation usually concentrate upon the elite performers, winners and professional athletes to the relative neglect of the recreational participant; but, again, this is beginning to change (Bailey, 1978; Lowerson & Myerscough, 1977; Malcolmson, 1973).

If the history of recreation is to be more than a collection of disparate topics then a means of integrating the topics must be found. One such means is the application of themes that cut across the various topics. Examples of such themes include the roles of health, religion, technological change, socioeconomic influences, landscape evaluation and cultural transfer. Regardless of the topics, it is likely that one or more of these themes will be relevant to most historical studies of outdoor recreation.

History is the study of change through time. A considerable and growing body of literature is concerned with understanding such changes, although only a limited proportion of this work has been contributed by professional historians. The time-scales of such investigations vary greatly and the nature and availability of data also vary with time (Towner, 1984, 1988). Considerable attention has been given to seasonality and the various problems associated with it (Baum & Lundtorp, 2001), and weekly and diurnal patterns of recreation have also received consideration (Murphy, 1982). Zuzanek *et al.* (1998) have examined trends in the use of time over two decades in two countries, Canada and the Netherlands. Rapoport and Rapoport (1975) have found the family life-cycle to be a useful concept for understanding changes in individual recreational behaviour and associated changes in society and demands upon facilities and resources. Other authors have considered the possibility of displacement and succession as initial users of a site elect to go elsewhere and are replaced by newcomers with different expectations as the experiences available at that site are modified (Schreyer, 1979; Roggenbuck *et al.* 1980). Similarly, authors interested in the ecological impacts of recreation have been concerned with changes in the numbers of users, the extent to which they modify the resources, and the potential for their recovery. They conclude that most impact takes place at relatively low levels of use, successive increments of use generally being associated with diminishing marginal rates of change, but that periods required for recovery are much longer than those for impact, and may number in hundreds of years in some fragile environments (Hammitt & Cole, 1987). Thus, temporal frames of reference employed by researchers vary widely.

While the studies that have been mentioned in the preceding paragraph are all concerned with change through time, because of the short periods investigated and the recency of the times under consideration, some, with justification, may not consider them to be historical. This doubt should not exist in the case of resort cycles that are concerned with changes over decades and even centuries. Butler (1980) has suggested that the history of resorts exhibits considerable similarities to the S-shaped product life-cycle. Numbers of visitors change over time as resorts go through successive stages which Butler has called exploration, involvement, development, consolidation, stagnation and decline or rejuvenation, the latter depending upon the availability of previously untapped resources. One great value of the resort cycle is that it succeeds in incorporating a number of other concepts and ideas. Thus, it encompasses changes in the numbers and types of visitors (Plog, 1974), modifications in sources of investment and control over development (Brown, 1985), alterations in resident attitudes (Doxey, 1976) and it could, potentially, include notions of landscape change.

Although instant resorts, such as Cancun, and some resorts in developing countries which were pioneered by colonial elites, do not fit the model, the resort cycle has great intuitive appeal and, as a descriptive model, it appears to fit a large number of cases more than superficially. It would be unwise to employ the model for predictive purposes but it does have some applied utility in that it encourages one to question the inevitability of the cycle and to search for strategies that might arrest the cycle at a desirable stage.

The resort cycle has spawned a rapidly growing body of literature that is too voluminous to be reviewed here. The writings of Agarwal (1994, 1997, 2002) provide convenient points of access to much of this literature. Some researchers have questioned the validity and utility of the model, are concerned about the data with which it might be tested, and question if it can be proved or disproved (Haywood, 1986). Others have found it to provide a useful organising framework for their studies and have attempted to test it in particular situations (Stansfield, 1978; Hovinen, 1981). There is potential to incorporate additional concepts into the model. For example, Meyer-Arendt (1985), using a series of studies in the Gulf of Mexico, associated changes in resort morphology and environmental modification with different stages of the model. The reconciliation and linking of seemingly disparate concepts may be a fruitful path to follow in the search for more broadly based understanding.

While Butler's cycle has received most attention in the literature there are others that are less widely known. In fact, Weaver (2000) has suggested that Butler has described only one among a number of possible trajectories of change. Krakover (1985), drawing upon the experiences of arid areas in Israel, has suggested a different series of situations which may be common to evolving resorts in remote areas. In contrast to Butler, he stresses the importance of government investment in the early stages of development when infrastructure must be constructed. Government involvement changes to a regulatory role in later stages when business opportunities may be more attractive to private investors.

There may also be other cycles which operate at different time-scales and have yet to be documented. Investment in many forms of recreation is lumpy. For example, the sizes of hotels are now such that the construction of a large new hotel may change the accommodation situation of under-supply to over-supply with resulting implications for occupancy rates, pricing and visitor behaviour. Demand may have to rise considerably to increase occupancy rates to a level at which there is excess demand and sufficiently high prices to merit the installation of new supply when the cycle may start again. Such speculation awaits empirical verification.

Investigations of changes through time in recreation have been both cause and effect of increased interest in the history of recreation and have been associated with the integration of concepts and the development of generalisations. However, if historians of recreation are to make a major contribution to knowledge it is necessary that they not only strive to link concepts and generalise, but they must also address issues which are of interest to other disciplines. Examples of such issues abound. They include evolving class structures, economic cycles, technological change (for example, changes in transportation technology as examined by Brent, 1997), quality of life, people-environment interaction, gender roles and national identity. Examples of the latter can be found in the recent growing interest in the activities and opinion of early women travellers noted in the contribution on gender in this volume (Chapter 13) and which is one of a number of themes, such as colonialism and landscape evaluation, evident in the interpretation and deconstruction of travel narratives (Gruffudd *et al.*, 2000).

The evolution of leisure and recreation is itself a phenomenon with implications for many other areas. The growing literature on recreation as a means of social control, though controversial, is a good example of the kind of approach that is needed (Cunningham, 1980; Clarke and Crichter, 1985; Golby and Purdue, 1984). Although the concept has received only limited attention in North America, it has generated considerable debate in Britain and encouraged re-assessment of the significance of leisure with implications for a number of the issues mentioned above. If historians of recreation are to do justice to their subject matter they must set themselves lofty goals, reach out beyond the narrow confines of their sub-discipline and relate their findings to major themes which challenge intellects across disciplines. Wadsworth (1975) suggested that: 'As the prevailing culture and attitudes of a society change, so also do its leisure pursuits; by studying the pursuits it is possible to increase our understanding of the progress and development of that society.' His ideas are not new for Josiah Strutt, writing in 1801, indicated that:

> In order to form a just estimation of the character of any particular people, it is absolutely necessary to investigate the sports and pastimes most generally prevalent among them . . . When we follow them to their retirements, where no disguise is necessary, we are most likely to see them in their true state, and may best judge of their natural dispositions.

There are signs that the challenges of such demanding, but far-reaching, questions are being taken up. However, should recreational historians shy away from using their expertise to illuminate the broader questions of society, there is a danger that they will fail to make the contributions to knowledge of which they are capable, and that they will end up merely talking to themselves.

## Note
1. This chapter first appeared as 'Perspectives on temporal change and the history of recreation' in Volume 1 of *Progress in Tourism, Recreation and Hospitality Management* (1989), pp. 154–60.

## Bibliography
Agarwal, S. (1994) The resort cycle revisited: Implications for resorts. *Progress in Tourism, Recreation and Hospitality Management* 5, 191–208.

Agarwal, S. (1997) The resort cycle and seaside tourism: An assessment of its application. *Tourism Management* 18, 65–73.

Agarwal, S. (2002) Restructuring seaside tourism: The resort lifecycle. *Annals of Tourism Research* 29 (1), 25–55.

Ashworth, G.J. and Tunbridge, J.E. (1990) *The Tourist-Historic City*. London: Belhaven Press.

Ashworth, G.J. and Tunbridge, J.E. (2000) *The Tourist-Historic City: Retrospect and Prospect of Managing the Heritage City*. Kidlington: Pergamon.

Bailey, P. (1978) *Leisure and Class in Victorian England: Rational Recreation and the Contest for Control, 1830–1885*. London: Routledge & Kegan Paul.

Baum, T. and Lundtorp, S. (eds) (2001) *Seasonality in Tourism*. Kidlington: Pergamon.

Belasco, W.J. (1979) *Americans on the Road: From Autocamp to Motel, 1910–1945*. Cambridge, MA: MIT Press.

Bella, L. (1987) *Parks for Profit*. Montreal: Harvest House.

Brent, M., (1997) Coastal resort morphology as a response to transportation technology. Unpublished PhD thesis, University of Waterloo.

Brown, B.J.H. (1985) Personal perception and community speculation: A British resort in the 19th century. *Annals of Tourism Research* 12 (3), 355–69.

Butler, R. (1980) The concept of a tourist area cycle of evolution: Implications for the management of resources. *Canadian Geographer* 24 (1), 5–12.

Butler, R. and Wall, G. (1985) Introduction: Themes in research on the evolution of tourism. *Annals of Tourism Research* 12 (3), 287–96.

Clarke, J. and Chrichter, C. (1985) *The Devil Makes Work: Leisure in Capitalist Britain*. London: Macmillan.

Cohen, E. (1985) Towards a sociology of tourism. *Annals of Tourism Research* 39 (1), 104–22.

Cranz, G. (1982) *The Politics of Park Design: A History of Urban Parks in America*. Cambridge, MA: MIT Press.

Cunningham, H. (1980) *Leisure in the Industrial Revolution*. London: Croom Helm.

Demars, S.E. (1991) *The Tourist in Yosemite 1855–1985*. Salt Lake City: University of Utah Press.

Douglas, N. (1997) The fearful and the fanciful: Early tourists' perceptions of Western Melanesia. *Journal of Tourism Studies* 8 (1), 52–61.

Doxey, G. (1976) When enough's enough: The natives are restless on Old Niagara. *Heritage Canada* 2 (2), 26–7.

Forest, R.A. (1984) *America's National Parks and Their Keepers*. Washington, DC: Resources for the Future.

Golby, J.M. and Purdue, A.W. (1984) *The Civilisation of the Crowd: Popular Culture in England 1750–1900*. London: Batsford.

Graham, B. and Ashworth, G.J. and Tunbridge, J.E. (2000) *A Geography of Heritage: Power, Culture and Economy*. London: Arnold.

Gruffudd, P., Herber, D.T. and Piccini, A. (2000) In search of Wales: Travel writing and narratives of difference, 1918–1950. *Journal of Historical Geography* 26 (4), 589–604.

Hammitt, W.E. and Cole, D.N. (1987) *Wildland Recreation: Ecology and Management*. New York: Wiley.

Haywood, K.M. (1986) Can the tourist-area life cycle be made operational? *Tourism Management* 7 (3), 154–67.

Hovinen, G. (1981) A tourist cycle in Lancaster County, Pennsylvania. *Canadian Geographer* 25 (3), 283–5.

Jakle, J.A. (1985) *The Tourist: Travel in Twentieth-Century North America.* Lincoln: University of Nebraska Press.

Jasen, P. (1995) *Wild Things: Nature, Culture and Tourism in Ontario 1790–1914.* Toronto: University of Toronto Press.

Krakover, S. (1985) Development of tourism resort areas in arid regions. In Y. Gradus (ed.) *Desert Development: Man and Technology in Sparse-Lands* (pp. 271–284). Dordrecht: D. Reidel.

Lowenthal, D. (1985) *The Past is a Foreign Country.* Cambridge: Cambridge University Press.

Lowenthal, D. (1996) *The Heritage Crusade and the Spoils of History.* Cambridge: Cambridge University Press.

Lowerson, J. and Myerscough, J. (1977) *Time to Spare in Victorian England.* Hassocks, Sussex: Harvester.

MacDowall, D. (1999) *Another World: Bermuda and the Rise of Modern Tourism.* Basingstoke: Macmillan.

MacEwen, S. and MacEwen, M. (1982) *National Parks: Conservation or Cosmetic?* Hemel Hempstead: George Allen and Unwin.

Malcolmson, R.W. (1973) *Popular Recreations in English Society 1700–1850.* Cambridge: Cambridge University Press.

Marsh, J. and Hodgins, B. (eds) (1997) *Changing Parks: The History, Future and Cultural Context of Parks and Heritage Landscapes.* Toronto: Natural Heritage / Natural History.

Marsh, J. and Wall, G. (1982) Themes in the investigation of the evolution of outdoor recreation. In G. Wall and J. Marsh (eds) *Recreational Land Use: Perspectives on its Evolution in Canada.* Carleton Library Series 126. Ottawa: Carleton University.

McGreevy, P. (1994) *Imagining Niagara: The Meaning and Making of Niagara Falls.* Amherst: University of Masssachusetts Press.

Meyer-Arendt, K.J. (1985) The Grand Isle, Louisiana resort cycle. *Annals of Tourism Research* 12 (3), 449–65.

Morgan, N.J. and Pritchard, A. (1999) *Power and Politics at the Seaside: The Development of Devon's Resorts in the Twentieth Century.* Exeter: University of Exeter Press.

Murphy, P. (1982) Tourism planning in London: An exercise in spatial and seasonal management. *Tourist Review* 1, 19–23.

Plog, S.C. (1974) Why destination areas rise and fall in popularity. *Cornell Hotel and Restaurant Association Quarterly* 14 (4), 55–8.

Rapoport, R. and Rapoport, R.N. (1975) *Leisure and the Family Life Cycle.* London: Routledge & Kegan Paul.

Richardson, J. (1999) *A History of Australian Travel and Tourism.* Elsternwick: Hospitality Press.

Roggenbuck, J.W., Smith, A.C. and Wellman, A.D. (1980) *Specialization, Displacement and Definition of Depreciative Behaviour Among Virginia Canoeists.* St Paul, MN: North Central Forest Experiment Station, US Department of Agriculture.

Runte, A. (1979) *National Parks: The American Experience.* Lincoln: University of Nebraska Press.

Schreyer, R. (1979) *Succession and Displacement in River Recreation: Problem Definition and Analysis.* St Paul, MN: North Central Forest Experiment Station, US Department of Agriculture.

Schuyler, D. (1986) *New Urban Landscape: The Redefinition of City Form in Nineteenth-Century America.* Baltimore: Johns Hopkins University Press.

Sears, J.F. (1989) *Sacred Places: American Tourist Attractions in the Nineteenth Century*. Oxford: Oxford University Press.

Smith, R. (1992) Beach resort evolution: Implications for planning. *Annals of Tourism Research* 19 (2), 304–22.

Soane, J. (1993) *Fashionable Resort Regions: Their Evolution and Transformation*. Oxford: CAB International.

Stansfield, C. (1978) Atlantic City and the resort cycle: Background to the legalization of gambling. *Annals of Tourism Research* 5 (2), 238–51.

Strutt, J. (1801) *The Sports and Pastimes of the People of England*. London: William Tegg.

Tissot, L. (2000) *Naissance d'une Industrie Touristique: Les Anglais et la Suisse au 19e Siecle*. Lausanne: Payot Lausanne.

Towner, J. (1984) The grand tour: Sources and a methodology for an historical study of tourism. *Tourism Management* 5 (3), 215–22.

Towner, J. (1988) Approaches to tourism history. *Annals of Tourism Research* 15 (1), 47–62.

Towner, J. (1996) *An Historical Geography of Recreation and Tourism in the Western World 1540–1940*. Chichester: John Wiley.

Travis, J. (1993) *The Rise of the Devon Seaside Resorts 1750–1900*. Exeter Maritime Studies No. 8. Exeter: University of Exeter Press.

Tunbridge, J.E. and Ashworth, G.J. (1996) *Dissonant Heritage: The Management of the Past as a Resource in Conflict*. London: Wiley.

Wadsworth, P.M. (1975) Leisure pursuits in nineteenth-century Bath. Unpublished MA thesis, University of Kent.

Walton, J.K. (1983) *The English Seaside Resort: A Social History 1750–1914*. Leicester: Leicester University Press.

Walton, J.K. (2000) The *British Seaside: Holidays and Resorts in the Twentieth Century*. Manchester: Manchester University Press.

Walvin, J. (1978) *Beside the Seaside: A Social History of the Popular Seaside Holiday*. London: Allen Lane.

Weaver, D. (2000) A broad context model of destination development scenarios. *Tourism Management* 21 (3), 217–24.

Wirth, C.L. (1980) *Parks, Politics and the People*. Oklahoma: University of Oklahoma Press.

Zuzanek, J., Beckers, T. and Peters, P. (1998) The 'harried leisure class' revisited: Dutch and Canadian trends in the use of time from the 1970s to the 1990s. *Leisure Studies* 17 (1), 1–19.

## Chapter 6

# Marketing of the Service Process: State of the Art in the Tourism, Recreation and Hospitality Industries

FRANK GO and MICHAEL HAYWOOD

## Introduction

Marketing as applied to hospitality and tourism has generated a large literature, and to a lesser extent in recreation. The interest, growth and competition in these three leisure-driven service industries evolved from the old labour-intensive economy and has shifted to the information society. In this context, the advocates of the information-based society (Bell, 1973; Piore & Sabel, 1984; Castells, 1989), are positioned *vis-à-vis* those writers who 'place emphasis on continuities' (Webster, 1999: 139). The information technology and communication (ICT) revolution has dramatic consequences for the way we approach tourism (Wahab & Cooper, 2001), but also, recreation and hospitality marketing processes, as organising concepts. Information is the key to the omnipresence of global brands, computer reservation systems, transnational benchmarking and the need to view competition both from international and local perspectives. The latter perspective is intertwined with those thinkers who argue that information, both in terms of 'form and function', is subject to 'long established principles and practices' (Webster, 1999). This chapter tries to give some insights, through a literary review, of the changes and opportunities that have occurred over the past decades and especially as the result of information technology and communication. It is important to note that it is not the technologies themselves that drive change, but the way in which they are organised to fit successfully the tourism, recreation and hospitality marketing processes (Go & Appelman, 2001). In this respect, 'globalisation' has become an issue that rivals sustainability (Wahab & Cooper (2001). It is important to note that while ICT can influence human behaviour, it can only do this to the extent that ICT is able to 'fit' the desires of people. Translated into the tourism, recreation and hospitality marketing context, ICT may have enabled the rise of global brand marketing, computer reservation systems, and transnational benchmarking. However, there are growing, widespread concerns, for instance by the anti-globalist movement, about the deleterious effects attributed to by distance-abolishing technologies of social, cultural and economic events and global free trade. In the information-based society it is essential to determine the extent to which marketing thought – particularly in the areas of tourism, recreation and hospitality – is responding to these concerns and providing evidence of progress. For example, Klein (2000) and Rifkin (2000) are both emerging vanguards who raise thought-provoking issues concerning the significance of traditional social relations in future society.

In assessing the state of the art of marketing, therefore, we feel obliged to examine a number of issues. These include how academics and practitioners deal with changes and opportunities that come about through the impact of ICT; the organisation of marketing; the changes in the organisation of marketing and production and their societal impacts. Here it is important that both levels of analysis are of the same logical order and constitute a duality. Although the systematic bias towards the applied technology direction is acknowledged, it is recognised that marketing has micro/macro, profit/non-profit, public/private, as well as positive/normative perspectives (Hunt, 1975). With the emergence of a service marketing paradigm we furthermore recognize how the hospitality, tourism and recreation fields shifted from a technical to a wider strategic perspective. Currently the hospitality, tourism and recreation fields continue to evolve from the geographic confines of the marketplace (Jansen-Verbeke & Dietvorst, 1987) to the temporal realm of cyberspace, causing a rethinking of human relationships, the relation between commercial and public domains whereby lifestyle and experiential marketing, within the hospitality, tourism and recreation contexts is likely to take central stage. As a result of advances in information and communication technology, tourism, hospitality and recreation are becoming increasingly integrated within the experience-economy context.

In the past decade there has been a move towards the integration of hospitality and tourism research (Khan *et al.*, 1993). However, marketing in each of the three domains developed almost entirely separately and outside the emerging study of services marketing, the precursor of lifestyle and experiential marketing. Therefore, each will be first discussed individually.

## Hospitality Marketing

In commercial terms, hospitality includes accommodation and food-service businesses (profit and non-profit) that cater to people who are away from home. Most of the early marketing literature was written to assist independent and invariably smaller mom and pop businesses to attract and hold customers or guests. Based on industry need, and borrowing somewhat from the retail industry, early emphasis was placed on merchandising and sales promotion.

In fact, it is virtually impossible to pick up an industry trade journal published during the 1960s and 1970s that is not replete with articles on how to attract customers or make more effective use of the media. The popular texts of the period have a similar focus. For the foodservice industry, the discussion focuses on food or the menu (Kotschevar, 1975; Seaburg, 1973), while in the hotel sector the emphasis is on how to effectively sell rooms. Books by Stein (1971) and the consummate marketing professional, Dewitt Coffman (1970, 1980), became the standard marketing texts for the 1970s. So strong was their practical approach that attempts by marketing academics to break into the field were thwarted. Breaking free from this mould was the conceptually original and landmark, *Marketing of the Meal Experience* by Campbell-Smith (1967). Though largely unheralded, particularly in North America, it is fair to say that this consumer-oriented book was far ahead of its time. Recently, there has been a renewed interest in the experiences of customers (Bitner *et al.*, 1985; Pine & Gilmore, 1998; Wolf, 1999; Rifkin, 2000).

With the exception of two conceptually sound and well-written texts (Buttle, 1986; Lewis & Chambers, 1989), the books on marketing have been unspectacular and burdened with heavy doses of advertising and promotional ideas (Laine and Laine, 1972; Taylor, 1981; Gottlieb, 1982; Feltenstein, 1983; Abbey, 1989). Attempts at writing more inclusive marketing texts have been made (Kotas, 1975; Astroff & Abbey, 1978; Eisen, 1980; Summer, 1982; Nykiel, 1983; Reid, 1983; Lewis *et al.*, 1986) but by and large they provide superficial and unsatisfactory coverage of many complex marketing issues. At a time when hospitality businesses were expanding and the complexity of managing chain organizations (Wyckoff & Sasser, 1978), fast-food corporations (Emerson, 1979) and hotel conglomerates, such as Holiday Inn (Pearce & Robinson, 1982), was intensifiying, marketers, academics and students at the university level were inevitably drawn towards the more rigorous and thorough general marketing texts written by authors such as Kotler (1980).

Upset by the formidable ignorance of marketing within the industry and the lack of empirically defensible marketing research, several marketing professionals and academics moved into the vacuum. The prodigious output of authors such as Peter Yesawich and Robert Lewis is especially noticeable. Their contributions have been major; almost single-handedly they have pulled the field of hospitality marketing into the mainstream of marketing thought. As a consequence, hospitality marketing took on a more strategic focus (Sasser & Morgan, 1977; Blomstrom, 1983) with increasing attention being given to such topics as:

- market segmentation (Lewis, 1980; Moller *et al.*, 1985; Swinyard & Struman, 1986; Garvey, 1986);
- positioning (McNaughton, 1981; Lewis, 1982; Lewis, 1985);
- a new marketing mix (Renaghan, 1981; Booms & Bitner, 1982; Goffe, 1986);
- marketing planning (Yesawich, 1979; Doswell & Gamble, 1979);
- research techniques (Welch, 1985; Lewis, 1985; Ritchie and Goeldner, 1987; Yesawich, 1987);
- environment (Booms & Bitner, 1982);
- demand and capacity management (Hart & Lawless, 1983; Yesawich, 1984; Jeffrey & Hubbard, 1986);
- consumer buying behaviour (Swinyard, 1977; Lewis, 1984; Lewis & Klein, 1985; Dhir, 1987; Wilensky & Buttle, 1988);
- life cycles (Hart *et al.*, 1984; Leven, 1985; Haywood, 1985);
- new product development (Withiam, 1985; Haywood, 1985; Feltenstein,1986);
- pricing and discounting (Kreul, 1982; Abbey, 1983; Miller, 1987; Greenburg, 1985; Carroll, 1986; Lewis, 1986; Lefever & Morrison, 1988; Lewis & Roan, 1986);
- competition (Akehurst, 1986; Haywood, 1986);
- promotional strategies (Lewis, 1987; Renaghan & Kaye, 1987; Morrison, 1989);
- consumer feedback and complaint handling (Lewis, 1983; Lewis & Morris, 1987; Davis & Horney, 1988);
- customer satisfaction (Lewis, 1987; Renaghan & Kaye, 1987; Cadotte & Turgeon, 1988);
- service delivery systems (Levitt, 1972; Pickworth, 1988).

In addition, consumer omnibus studies on eating-out behaviour were commissioned by the major foodservice, catering and lodging associations (such as the National Restaurant Association and the American Hotel and Motel Association), advancing our market knowledge tremendously. However, we are still largely ignorant about the marketing behaviour of hotel and restaurant companies. A few attempts have been made to determine how the hospitality marketing function is pursued or managed (Haywood, 1975), and a growing body of well-researched case studies developed at both Harvard and the University of Guelph identify important marketing issues.

With the burgeoning of services in general, it was interesting to note that more marketing researchers are including hospitality services in their surveys. The following list is a way of highlighting topics of interest and sources in the more general business marketing literature:

- Consumer decision-making processes (Lewis, 1981; Meryer, 1981; Wolf & Latane, 1983; Louviere & Woodsworth, 1983; Filiatrault & Ritchie, 1983; Bon & Pras, 1984; McDougall, 1986; June & Smith, 1987);
- Customer satisfaction (Swan *et al.*, 1981; Cadotte *et al.*, 1987);
- Business location analysis (Arbel & Pizam, 1977; Smith, 1985, 1986; Wall *et al.*, 1985; Pillsbury, 1987);
- Market segmentation (Boote, 1981);
- Risk-taking and development (Bartram *et al.*, 1980).

In this review it is evident that a lack of attention has been given to the marketing of institutional foodservice. Clearly this is a growth area in many companies (Camacho, 1988) and interest in marketing is evident. For example, there are bibliographies on school foodservice marketing (Shanklin *et al.*, 1987) and dietetics (Pickworth & Pickworth; 1981); the marketing of nutrition has become a topic of interest (Carlson, 1986; Regan, 1987); and, the state of the art in marketing hospital foodservice departments has been studied (Pickens & Shanklin, 1985). Particular note should be made of the interest in health care marketing (Berkowitz & Flexner, 1978; Rice *et al.*, 1981; Rubright & MacDonald, 1981).

With the rapid expansion of other service industries, the similarity between hospitality management and the management of other service businesses has not gone unnoticed (Haywood, 1987; Barrington & Olsen, 1987; Teare *et al.*, 1990). While there is still a tendency to borrow heavily from the marketing literature flowing from the consumer goods industries, service marketing literature in the 1980s and 1990s boomed. For obvious reasons that stem from the unique characteristics of services, a new set of ideas concerning the hospitality marketing process has been suggested. For example, the involvement of the customer in the simultaneous production and consumption of services has raised concern over the issue of service quality, particularly as it relates to its management and measurement (Haywood, 1983; Wyckoff, 1984; King, 1984; Hart & Casserly, 1985; Moores, 1986), the development of food products and the links with capacity, productivity and service delivery systems (Pickworth, 1988; Jones, 1988).

More recently, customer retention, including finding out what service customers really want and how they evaluate services, became the top priority issue (Teare *et al.*, 1998). The call for the development of the area of customer-relations or relationship marketing (Stringer, 1981; Lockwood & Jones, 1989) was right on the mark. In essence, the service management, marketing models show that hospitality marketing is inextricably tied to aspects of human resource management, training and operations management and the research of these areas (Brotherton, 1999). In a period of rapid change and diversity, hospitality companies will need to deliver their products with greater flexibility to compete effectively. It implies that both a more multicultural (Shames & Glover, 1989) and international focus (Teare *et al.*, 1998) as well as a devolution of 'decisionmaking authority and responsibility for control and enhancement of product and or service quality to the point of production' (Klidas, 2001: 27) shall be required in future.

## Tourism Marketing

As in the hospitality field, societal and economic changes since the 1980s resulted in rapid expansion and growth of domestic and international tourism in many countries. Competition among destination, economic instabilities, oil crises and political events have demonstrated the vital significance of marketing in the development and operation of a whole range of tourism services. For example, transportation and lodging businesses, tour operators, travel agencies, as well as towns, cities, regions and nation-states are all actively involved in encouraging tourists. The scope of tourism marketing, therefore, is enormous and extends into both the public and private sectors of the economy. Large amounts of money are being allocated to tourism marketing research (though the amounts are still viewed as inadequate at the corporate level (Rovelstad & Blazer, 1983), so a rich empirical base is being established.

Among the earliest publications relating to tourism marketing were market studies (Bjorkman, 1963); analyses of tourist markets (Schmidhauser, 1962; Crampton, 1966); and demand-forecasting studies and econometric modelling (Lickorish, 1972; Archer, 1976; Baron, 1979). Mention should be made of the studies and reports published by the IUOTO (International Union of Travel Organisations) later to become the WTO (World Tourism Organization). Since the 1970s, information on marketing has also been disseminated through many national and international tourism seminars sponsored by such organisations as the Pacific

Area Tourist Association (PATA), and the Travel and Tourism Research Association (TTRA) and its various chapter organisations. Furthermore, researchers or research institutes at numerous universities (Colorado, Texas A&M, Utah, George Washington, Hawaii and Surrey, to name a few) have provided a wealth of marketing knowledge. The *Journal of Travel Research* has become the world's leading research journal, publishing many articles relating to the subject area. A brief retrospective of the existing literature in marketing reveals that research interest seems to be focused on the following topics:

- developing marketing programmes (McCleary, 1987; Frechtling, 1987);
- identifying the tourist or segmenting the market (Crask, 1981; Calatone & Johar, 1984; Woodside & Jacobs, 1985; McQueen & Miller, 1985; Pearce, 1985; Kaynak, 1985; Davis & Sternquist, 1987; Weaver & McCleary, 1984; Dybka, 1987; Woodside *et al.*, 1987; Snepenger, 1987; McCleary, 1987; McGuire *et al.*, 1988);
- understanding consumer behaviour and tourists' decision-making processes (Woodside & Sherrell, 1977; Gittelson & Crompton, 1983; Bronner & de Hoog, 1984; Moutinho, 1987; Nickels & Snepenger, 1988);
- measuring tourist demand and improving forecasting procedures (Merlo, 1985; Hess & Voink, 1986; Witt & Martin, 1987; Uysal & Crompton, 1985; Ritchie & Sheridan, 1988; Calatone *et al.*, 1987);
- advertising/communications and conversion studies (Woodside & Motes, 1981; Pritchard, 1982; Bellman *et al.*, 1984; Silberman & Klock, 1986; Mazanec, 1986);
- understanding images of destinations (Hunt, 1975; Haati & Yayas, 1982; Wee *et al.*, 1986; Phelps, 1986; Gartner & Hunt, 1987; Gartner, 1989; Gartner, 1997):
- attractiveness of tourist areas (Gearing *et al.*, 1974; Var *et al.*, 1977; Husbands, 1983; Squire, 1988);
- evaluating tourist satisfaction (Pizam *et al.*, 1978; Hannigan, 1980; Pearce, 1980; Pearce & Moscardo, 1985);
- issues in product development, attractions and life cycles (Ritchie & Beliveau, 1974; Ritchie & Zins, 1978; Butler, 1980; Go, 1981; Riley, 1983; Mercer, 1985; Haywood, 1986; Patton, 1986; Makens, 1987; Hall, 1987; Lew, 1987);
- marketing of package tours and tour operators (Allen, 1985; Sheldon & Mak, 1987; Kent *et al.*, 1987; Kale *et al.*, 1985).

Tourism marketing activities have not gone unnoticed by academics in other disciplines. Studies published deserve separate mention here because of the criticism or fresh perspective they provide. Of particular note are articles by Thurot and Thurot (1983), Uzzell (1984), Dilley (1986) and Nord (1986); their attention to tourism advertising is especially enlightening. Urban geographers and planners are paying attention to the marketing of cities as it pertains to tourism (Jansen-Verbeke, 1988; Ashworth & Voorgd, 1988 and see also Chapter 9 in this volume) focusing on a much neglected topic – the dynamics of location (the place component in the marketing mix). The literature on recreational geography (Smith, 1983) social and economic geography (Kamann *et al.*, 1998) and service-scape marketing (Bitner, 1992) provide useful insights here.

With regard to product development, tourism marketers should pay particular attention to the important relationship between marketing and tourism planning (Cooper *et al.*, 1993; Gunn, 1988; Dodd & Hemel 1999). Also linked to the area of product development is recognition of recent studies made in the implementation of information and communication technologies in tourism (Moutinho *et al.*, 1996; Klein *et al.*, 1996; Fesenmaier *et al.*, 2000; Buhalis & Schertler, 1999) and 'the deployment of change management' (Baker *et al.*, 1999: 407). Not only are new links among the various component businesses of tourism being created, but there are also tremendous opportunities for marketing to combine multiple shopping purposes and destinations (Dellaert *et al.*, 1998), evaluating national and city tourism destination marketing programmes (Faulkner, 1997; Go & Zhang, 1997) and the interfacing between national and regional tourism offices in the provision and distribution of destination information (Sheldon, 1993).

There are other oversights in the tourism marketing literature. The spate of tourism studies dealing with tourism impacts, whether upon citizens living in a tourist destination community, on tourists themselves as victims of crime or disease, or upon the quality of tourism's physical and natural resources, suggest problems inherent in marketing activities. Other than in studies written by critics of marketing (see Nord, 1986), the literature has inadequately addressed such concerns as the creation of false perceptions, the problems of overcrowding and difficulties involved in host/guest encounters. With the recent interest in business ethics, the ethical questions inherent in tourism marketing demand attention, especially as they relate to destinations in developing countries. A revision of the marketing concept as it applies to tourism may be in order (Haywood, 1990).

Part of the problem is that the whole issue of what is meant by tourism marketing is unclear. The texts and manuals on the subject are not much help. Many have been prepared primarily for tour operators or travel agencies (Reilly, 1980; Bishop, 1981; Davidoff & Davidoff, 1983; Mahoney & Warnell, 1986; Harris & Katz, 1987; NTA, 1987). Wahab's Tourism Marketing (1976) is based on a consumer-goods marketing model and is out of date, while Schmoll's Tourism Promotion (1977) is too narrowly focused. Only a few books stand out. One is Ritchie and Goeldner's *Travel, Tourism and Hospitality Research* (1987), which offers an excellent compendium of articles on research techniques written by experts in their field. Another useful book, although it is classified as a handbook, is *Tourism Marketing and Management* (Witt & Moutinho, 1989). It contains a wealth of interesting articles by practitioners and academics from many parts of the world. Recently, several authors have responded to the need to define the field of tourism marketing. Jefferson and Lickorish (1988) provide a practical guide with a destination emphasis, and Mill (1989), Mill and Morrison (1985), Middleton (1988), Crotts and Van Raaij (1994), Wahab and Cooper (2001) have produced tourism texts which will serve as models for further development. Last but not least, Uysal and Fesenmaier (1996) co-edited *Communication and Channel Systems in Tourism Marketing* an edited volume incorporating 'communication and channel systems of marketing as an integral component,' and Ritchie (1996) developed an insightful 'Assessment of the State of the Art in Tourism Marketing/Marketing Research.'

## Recreation Marketing

Most experts in the recreation, parks and arts fields will readily admit that marketing has yet to be embraced as a vitally important management function – particularly in the not-for-profit sector. Marketing has, however, found its way into some of the major texts in the field (Speelman, 1992) and is being actively discussed at conferences.

A spattering of articles that have appeared over the years argue for the adoption of a marketing approach (Vellas & Becherel, 1999; Torkildsen, 1999; Teare & Calder, 1996; Hodgson, 1991), a greater role for market research (Brunt, 1997) and a marketing role in developing new programmes (Fesenmaier & O'Leary, 1996). Recent advances in tourism marketing research have also been published as *Journal of Travel & Tourism Marketing*, Volume 5, numbers 1/2 & 3 1996. A growing number of papers have been written on marketing-related topics such as user fees (More & Stevens, 2000); target markets (Crompton, 1983); marketing audits (Ding & Pigram, 1995; Woodside & Sakai, 2001) and leisure activities (Hemingway, 1999). In the recreation/leisure literature at large there are, of course, a variety of articles on motivation and satisfaction levels (Tinsley & Kass, 1977; Lee, 1999; Chadee & Mattson, 1996; Beard & Ragheb, 1983; Cato, 1986); and even in the tourism literature, recreation articles are now making an appearance. For example, specific visitor management techniques are being discussed

(Graham *et al.*, 1988). It is interesting to note that an interest in 'quality' is also emerging in the recreation marketing literature (Baker & Crompton, 2000). The design of a quality plan which should result in considerable quality improvement of the tourism product is a possibility. The importance of quality improvement in tourism is paramount (Augustyn & Ho, 1998). Total quality management can facilitate this process to assist organisations in tourism-related areas in adopting quality into their strategy (Witt & Muhlemann, 1994).

The involvement of marketing with the arts should be mentioned. Its history can be traced to Baumol and Bowen (1966), who identified economic problems in the performing arts. Since then marketers have embraced this area in the marketing of non-profit organisations (Riley, 2000). Partnerships and collaboration have come of age in the tourism and recreational field. However, our understanding of how partnerships form and how to build the capacity of appropriate collaborative ventures has lagged behind developments in the field. Partnerships are contributing to sustainable tourism development (Selin, 2000; Hughes, 2000). Also worth mentioning is Gilbert and Lizotte (1998), who have been active advocates of a partnership between arts and tourism. All in all, the expanding body of information on the marketing of cultural industries is fascinating, as it embraces quality-of-life issues, which are of growing importance to marketers in tourism and recreation (Otto & Ritchie, 1996). Managing environments is a crucial point in successful recreational management (Broadhust, 2001; Tribe, 2000).

Finally, recreation marketers are being attracted to the concepts of service marketing (Gronroos, 2000). Ross's work (1993) on 'service quality and management', is also of particular relevance here. He suggests a fresh approach to marketing based upon the shifting focus to employee expectations of management; and he has investigated a set of service quality elements deemed significant by hospitality industry. Experience is also becoming more and more a topic of today's recreation management (Ryan, 1997), in which trends and prospects are extremely important (Kelly, 1999; Gartner, 2000; Jackson & Burton, 1999).

## Emerging Marketing Paradigms

The emergence of information technology and redrawing of both geographical and functional boundaries has resulted in network marketing. It has had far-reaching consequences and prompted outsourcing towards suppliers, the need for a new vision on the boundaries of the organisation and a re-thinking of the marketing discipline. The impact of this re-architecting is giving rise to the 'extended enterprise'. Unfortunately, the need for 're-tooling' has not yet been felt with full force in the hospitality, tourism and recreation industries. In this final section, four emerging and mutually supportive paradigms of importance to hospitality / tourism / recreation marketing are identified. Application of service marketing in a strategic marketing context, implemented with a social marketing conscience and viewed in a global context, can have profound implications for the field. It could help restructure the concept of marketing and help set new research agendas.

Throughout this paper, the extent to which the service marketing concept has made inroads into the literature has been noted. The pioneering efforts of such people as Levitt (1972), Rathmell (1974), George and Barksdale (1974), Donnelly (1976), Shostak (1977), Thomas (1978) and many others have been overwhelming. To summarise:

- Services are performances which tend to be produced in real time, often in the presence of the customer.
- The creation and delivery of a performance is unlike that of a manufactured good; more attention needs to be given to developing, testing and introducing new services.
- Customers may be actively involved in creating the service product.
- The intangibility of services makes their pricing difficult, particularly with respect to the perception of risk, search costs and prices for similar services.
- Capacity and demand management require special attention.
- Quality assurance is a persistent problem and needs to be better understood, measured and managed.
- Distribution channels will be controlled increasingly through information and communications technologies.
- Tourism services need to be more effectively bundled.

All of these concerns need to be addressed more thoroughly, but the concern which is of utmost importance is the service encounter. Not only does this affect how a service can be best marketed (Czepiel *et al.*, 1985; Lovelock, 1988), but how a service business should be organised and operated (Mills, 1986). For anyone who has tried to keep up on just this area of service marketing, the information available is overwhelming; and a whole new approach to marketing is being dictated (Lehtinen, 1986). Given this interest in encounters, marketing researchers would be wise to study the problems associated with cross-cultural marketing or the role of marketing intermediaries (Maister & Lovelock, 1982; Rao & Ovmlil, 1988; Shames & Glover, 1989) and learning from dramaturgy, because the service experience can be increasingly likened to theatre (Grove & Fisk, 1992).

Service marketing, however, does not happen in a vacuum; serious issues regarding the effective management of service organisations need to be addressed (Haywood, 1987). The slew of service management texts provides a useful start (Normann, 1984; Albrecht & Zemke, 1985; Heskett, 1986; Albrecht, 1988). The unique characteristics of services and the intensely competitive environment of hospitality, tourism and recreation organisations demand a more strategic approach. As Allen (1988) points out, five critical aspects to managing a service business have a strategic orientation:

(1) renewing the service offering;
(2) localising the point of service system;
(3) leveraging the service contract;
(4) using information power strategically; and
(5) determining the strategic value of a service business.

Evidence also suggests that positioning strategies (Shostak, 1987) and competitive strategies (Wilson, 1988) may be quite different for service businesses.

While there is no denying that hospitality, tourism and recreation organisations operate in an increasingly competitive world, the results orientation can be problematic. Fixation with results can focus the marketer and other managers on achieving the results to the near exclusion of recognising other benefits and problems derived from the process itself. To the extent that we believe tourism and recreation are community-based and community-driven activities (Murphy, 1985), there is a need to be concerned with longer-term results. As Kotler (1980) says, 'The sensitive marketer has to take responsibility for the totality of outputs (and outcomes) created'. The propensity for marketing to displace or even consume human values along with exchange values needs rectifying. Witt and Moutinho's *Tourism Marketing and Management Handbook* (1989) identifies a range of 'the most crucial issues in tourism marketing and management' likely to be of concern to us well into the twenty-first century.

The advent of information technology has caused a paradox of disintermediation and re-intermediation that impacts the access and use of high quality content. From a virtual network perspective a critical success factor is the existence of at least one partner who will take the lead in formulating and communicating the opportunity, identifying compatible partners, setting the agenda, and facilitating the process of formulating the brand strategy and operational plans. In the future, eContent cybermediaries, are likely to become the engine behind marketing partnership dynamics due to their ability to:

- handle large volumes of information;
- conduct business on the internet in an effective manner;
- operate in a 'boundaryless' manner by building relationships and increasing collaboration between different types of players;
- exploit cross-border opportunities; and
- collaborate with partners with the competency to turn information about customer-profiles into quality service delivery.

Such local operators will be sensitive to societal needs by fitting into the fabric of the host community (Go, 1982) and a diversity of cultures (Hirschman, 1985).

Consequently, we expect that in the twenty-first century the 'globalisation' phenomenon will drive 'experiential products' (Cooper-Martin, 1991) such as tourism, recreation and hospitality developments. Cooper-Martin (1991) described experiential products as 'All goods and services for which the consumption experience is an end in itself'. The expansion of the European Economic Community with former Eastern and Central European states and the growth of international franchising (Go & Christensen, 1989) are but two examples that will spell both upheaval and opportunity in global markets. Simultaneously, the re-emergence of regionalism coupled with the potential of economic growth through the clustering of small and medium-sized enterprises (SMEs) and public–private sector partnerships will require marketing professionals to have a much better grasp of the crucial role that locality plays when translating digital data into 'face-to-face' encounters.

In summary, the main challenge for the future will be to develop managers who will be able to deal with constant, rapid change and a multitude of issues. If creativity, commitment, consistency and innovation can be successfully applied to the challenge of translating digital data into 'face-to-face' encounters in the tourism, recreation and hospitality domains, in a sustainable manner, there is no reason why experiential marketing should not ascend to new heights.

## Note
1. This chapter first appeared as 'Marketing of the service process: State of the art in tourism, recreation and hospitality Industries' in Volume 2 of *Progress in Tourism, Recreation and Hospitality Management* (1990), pp. 129–50.

## Bibliography
Abbey, J. (1983) Is discounting the answer to declining cccupancies? *International Journal of Hospitality Management* 2 (2), 77–82.
Abbey, J. (1989) *Hospitality Sales and Advertising*. East Lansing, MI: Educational Institute.

Akehurst, G. (1986) Identification of the reactions of hotel managers to new competition. *International Journal of Hospitality Management* 5 (4), 189.

Albrecht, K. (1988) *At America's Service: How Corporations Can Revolutionize The Way They Treat Their Customers.* Homewood, IL: Dow Jones-Irwin.

Albrecht, K. and Zemke, R. (1985) *Service America: Doing Business in the New Economy.* Homewood, IL: Dow Jones-Irwin.

Allen, M. (1988) Strategic management of consumer services. *Long Range Planning* 21 (6), 20–5.

Allen, T. (1985) Marketing by a small tour operator in a market dominated by big operators. *European Journal of Marketing* 19 (5), 83–90.

Arbel, A. and Pizam, A. (1977) Some determinants of urban hotel location: The tourists' inclinations. *Journal of Travel Research* 15 (3), 18–22.

Archer, B.H. (1976) *Demand Forecasting in Tourism.* Bangor Occasional Papers in Economics, No. 9. Cardiff: University of Wales Press.

Ashworth, G.J. and Dietvorst, A.G.J. (eds) (1995) *Tourism and Spatial Transformations Implications for Policy and Planning.* Wallingford: CAB International.

Ashworth, G.J. and Voorgd, H. (1988) Marketing the city: Concepts, processes and Dutch applications. *Town Planning Review* 59 (1), 65–79.

Askari, H. (1971) Demand for package tours. *Journal of Transport Economics and Policy* 5 (1), 40–51.

Astroff, M.T. and Abbey, J.R. (1978) *Convention Sales and Service.* Dubuque, IA: Wm. C. Brown.

Augustyn, M. and S.K. Ho (1998) Service quality and tourism. *Journal of Travel Research* 37 (1), 71–5.

Baker, D.A and J.L. Crompton (2000) Quality, satisfaction and behavioral intensions. *Annals of Tourism Research* 27 (3), 785–804.

Baker, M., Sussman, S. and Welch, S. (1999) Information technology management. In Bob Brotherton (ed.) *The Handbook of Contemporary Hospitality Management Research* (pp. 397–414). Chicester: Wiley.

Baron, R. (1979) Forecasting tourism: Theory and practice. In *TTRA-A Decade of Achievement.* Tenth Annual Conference Proceedings, Bureau of Economic and Business Research. Salt Lake City: University of Utah.

Barrington, M.N. and Olsen, M.O. (1987) Concept of service in the hospitality industry. *Internaitonal Journal of Hospitality Management* 6 (3), 131–8.

Bartram, M. *et al.* (1980) Researching future developments in hotels. *The Market Research Society Conference* (pp. 101–11). March.

Beard, J. and Ragheb, M. (1983) Measuring leisure motivation. *Journal of Leisure Research* 15 (3), 219–28.

Becker, R.H., Berrier, D. and Barker G.D. (1985) Entrance fees and visitation levels. *Journal of Park and Recreation Management* 3 (1), 28–32.

Bell, D. (1973) *The Coming of the Post-Industrial Society: A Venture into Social Forecasting.* Harmondsworth: Penguin.

Bellman, G. *et al.* (1984) Toward higher quality conversion studies: Refining the numbers game. *Journal of Travel Research* 22 (4), 28–33.

Bishop, J. (1981) *Travel Marketing.* Folkestone: Bailey and Seinfen.

Bitner, M. (1992) Servicescapes: The impact of physical surroundings on customers and employees. *Journal of Marketing* 56 (April), 57–71.

Bitner, M., Nyquist, B. and Booms, B. (1985) The critical incident as a technique for analyzing the service encounter. In T. Block *et al. Services Marketing in a Changing Environment* (pp. 48–51). Chicago: AMA Marketing Association.

Bjorkman, B. (1963) Market studies in the field of international tourist traffic. *Tourist Review* 18 (4), 142–9.

Blackwell, J. (1970) Tourist traffic and the demand for accommodation: Some projections. *Economic and Social Review* 1 (3), 323–43.

Blomstrom (1983) Strategic market planning in the hospitality industry. Educational Institute for the American Hotel and Motel Association, Michigan.

Bon, J. and Pras, B. (1984) Dissociation of the roles of buyer, payer, and consumer. *International Journal of Research in Marketing* 1 (1), 7–16.

Booms, B.H. and Bitner, M.J. (1982) Marketing services by managing the environment. *Cornwell HRA Quarterly* (May), 35–9.

Boote, A.S. (1981) Market segmentation by personal values and salient product attributes. *Journal of Advertising Research,* 21 (1), 29–35.

Broadhust, R. (2001) *Managing Environments for Leisure and Recreation.* London: Routledge .

Bronner, A.A. and De Hoog, R. (1984) Computer assisted decision-making: A new tool for market research. *Esomar Congress* (pp. 171–91), Rome.

Brotherton, R. (ed.) (1999) *The Handbook of Contemporary Hospitality Management Research.* Chichester: Wiley.

Brunt, Paul (1997) *Market Research in Travel and Tourism.* Oxford: Butterworth-Heinemann.

Buhalis, D. and Schertler, W. (eds) (1999) *Information and Communication Technologies in Tourism.* Vienna/New York: Springer.

Bullaro, J.J., and Edginton, C.R. (1986) *Commercial Leisure Services: Managing for Profit, Service and Personal Satisfaction,* New York: Macmillan.

Buttle, F. (1986) *Hotel and Food Service Marketing: A Managerial Approach.* London: Holt, Rinehart and Winston.

Cadotte, E.R. *et al.* (1987) Expectations and norms in models of consumer satisfaction. *Journal of Marketing Research,* August, 305–14.

Calatone, R. and Johar, J.S. (1984) Seasonal segmentation of the tourism market using a benefit segmentation framework. *Journal of Travel Research* 23 (2), 14–24.

Calatone, R. *et al.* (1987) A comprehensive review of the tourism forecasting literature. *Journal of Travel Research* 26 (2), 28–39.

Camacho, F.E. (1988) Meeting the needs of senior citizens through lifecare communities: Marriott's approach to the development of a new business. *The Journal of Services Marketing* 2 (1), 49–53.

Campbell-Smith, G. (1967) *Marketing of the Meal Experience.* London: University of Surrey.

Carlson, B. (1986) Meeting consumer needs: The basis for successful marketing of nutrition in foodservice. *International Journal of Hospitality Management* 5 (4), 163.

Carroll, J.O. (1986) Focusing on discounting hotel rack rates. *Cornell H.R.A. Quarterly* (August), 13.

Castells, M. (1989) *The Informational City: Information Technology, Economic Restructuring and the Urban-Regional Process.* Oxford: Blackwell.

Cato, B. (1986) Happiness: The missing link of marketing in a technological society. *Visions in Leisure and Business* 5 (1 and 2), 64–73.

Cato, B. and Kunstler, R. (1988) Preferred leisure activities and reasons for participation: A comparison study with implications for marketing leisure services. *Journal of Park and Recreation Management* 6 (1), 54–65.

Chadee, D. and Mattson, J. (1996) An empirical assessment of customer satisfaction with tourism. *Service Industries Journal* 16 (3), 305–20.

Coffman, D. (1970) *Marketing for a Full House*. Ithaca, NY: Cornell University.

Coffman, D. (1980) *Hospitality for Sale*. Ithaca, NY: Cornell University.

Cooper, C., Fletcher, J., Gilbert, D. and Wanhill, S. (1993) *Tourism Principles and Practice*. Pitman: London.

Cooper, C.P. and Ozdil, I. (1992) From mass to 'responsible' tourism: The Turkish experience. *Tourism Management* 13 (4), 377–86.

Cooper-Martin, E. (1991) Consumers and movies: Some findings on experiential products. *Advances in Consumer Research* 18, 367–73.

Cowell, D. (1981) The role of market research in the development of public policy in the field of recreation and leisure. *Journal of the Market Research Society* 23 (3), 72–83.

Cowell, D. (1984) *The Marketing of Services*. London: Heinemann.

Crampton, L.J. (1966) A new technique to analyze tourist markets. *Journal of Marketing* 30 (2), 27–31.

Crask, M.R. (1981) Segmenting the vacationer market: Identifying the vacation preferences, demographics and magazine readership of each group. *Journal of Travel Research* 20 (1), 29–34.

Crompton, J.L. (1983) Developing new recreation and parks programs. *Recreation Canada* (July), 27–33.

Crompton, J.L. (1983) Selecting target markets: A key to effective marketing. *Journal of Park and Recreation Management* 1 (1), 7–26.

Crompton, J.L. and Lamb, C.W. (1986) The marketing audit: A starting point for strategic management. *Journal of Park and Recreation Management* 4 (1), 19–34.

Czepiel, J.A., Solomon, M.R. and Surprenant, C.F. (eds) (1985) *The Service Encountermanaging Employee/Customer Interaction in Service Businesses*. Lexington, MA: Lexington Books.

Davidoff, P.G. and Davidoff, D.S. (1983) *Sales and Marketing for Travel and Tourism*. Rapid City, SD: National Publishers of the Black Hills.

Davis, B.D. and Sternquist, B. (1987) Appealing to the elusive tourist: An attribute cluster strategy. *Journal of Travel Research* 25 (4), 25–31.

Davis, L. (1983) Recreation marketing: A common sense approach to program planning. *Recreation Canada* (September), 6–11.

Davis, R.V. and Horney, N. (1988) Guest feedback and complaint handling in the hospitality industry. *International Conference on Services Marketing* (Vol. 5). Cleveland, OH: Cleveland State University.

Dellaert, B.G.C., Arentze, T.A., Bierlaire, M., Borgers, A.W.J. and Timmermans, H.J.P. (1998). Investigating Consumers' tendency to combine multiple shopping purposes and destinations. *Journal of Marketing Research* 35 (May), 177–88.

Dhir, K.S. (1987) Analysis of consumer behaviour in the hospitality industry: An application of social judgement theory. *International Journal of Hospitality Management* 6 (3), 149–61.

Dilley, R.S. (1986) Tourist brochures and tourist images. *Canadian Geographer* 30 (1), 59–65.

Ding, P. and J. Pigram (1995) Environmental audits: An emerging concept in sustainable tourism development. *Journal of Tourism Studies* 6 (2) 2–10.

Dodd, D. and Hemel, A. Van (1999) *Planning Cultural Tourism in Europe: A Presentation of Theories and Cases*. Amsterdam: Boekman Foundation.

Donnelly, J.H. Jr (1976) Marketing intermediaries in channels of distribution for services. *Journal of Marketing* 40, 55–70.

Doswell, R. and Gamble, P.R. (1979) *Marketing and Planning Hotels and Tourism Projects*. London: Barrie and Jenkins.

Drinkwater, R. and Davies, I. (1987) Leisure marketing in action: Selling; sponsorship. *Leisure Management* 7 (11), 42–3, 49–50.

Dybka, J.M. (1987) A look at the American traveller: The US pleasure travel market study. *Journal of Travel Research* 25 (3), 2–4.

Eisen, I. (1988) *Strategic Marketing in Food Service: Planning for Change*. New York Lebhar Friedman Books.

Emerson, R.L. (1979) *Fast Food: The Endless Shakeout*. New York: Lebhar Friedman Books.

Faulkner, W. (1997) A model for the evaluation of national tourism destination marketing programs. *Journal of Travel Research* 35 (3), 23–32.

Feltenstein, T. (1983) *Restaurant Profits Through Advertising and Promotion: The Indispensable Plan*. Boston: CBI Publishing.

Fennell, G. (1987) A aadical agenda for marketing science: Represent thc marketing concept. In A.F. Firat *et al.* (eds) *Philosophical and Radical Thought in Marketing* (pp. 289–306). Lexington, MA: Lexington Books.

Ferguson, J.M. and Malone, K.M. (1988) Quality service in health clubs: Do employees know what customers want?. International Conference *On Services Marketing, Tool 5*. Cleveland, OH: Cleveland State University.

Ferraro, F.F. (1979) The evaluation of tourist resources: An applied methodology. *Journal of Travel Research* 17 (4), 24–32.

Fesenmaier, D.R., Klein, S. and Buhalis, D. (eds) (2000), *Information and Communication Technologies in Tourism*. Vienna / New York: Springer .

Fesenmaier, D.R. and O'Leary, J.T. (1996) *Recent Advances in Tourism Marketing Research*. Muzaffer Uysal, NY: Haworth Press.

Filiatrault, P. and Ritchie, J.J.R.B. (1980) Joint purchasing decisions: A comparison of influence structure in family and couple decision-making units. *Journal of Consumer Research* 7 (2), 131–40.

Fisk, G. (ed.) (1986) *Marketing Management Technology as a Social Process*. New York: Praegar.

Frechtling, D.C. (1987) Five issues in tourism marketing in the 1990s. *Tourism Management* 8 (2), 177–8.

Gartner, W.C. (1989) Tourism image: Attribute measurement of state tourism product using multi-dimensional scaling techniques. *Journal of Travel Research* 28 (2), 16–20.

Gartner, W.C. (1997) Image and sustainable tourism systems. In S. Wahab and J.J. Pigram (eds) *Tourism Development: A Challenge of Sustainability* (pp. 177–98), London: Routledge.

Gartner, W.C. (2000) *Trends in Outdoor Recreation, Leisure and Tourism*. Wallingford: CABI.

Gartner, W.C. and Hunt, J.D. (1987) An analysis of state image change over a twelve-year period, 1971–1983. *Journal of Travel Research* 26 (2), 15–9.

Garvey, J. (1986) Outlook and opportunities in market segmentation. In R. Lewis *et al.* (eds) *The Practice of Hospitality Management* 2. Westport, CT: AVI.

Gearing, C.E. *et al.* (1974) Establishing a measure of touristic attractiveness. *Journal of Travel Research* 12 (4), 1–8.

George, W.R. and Barksdale, H.C. (1974) Marketing activities in the service industry. *Journal of Marketing* 38, 65–70.

Gilbert, D. and M. Lizotte (1998) Tourism and the performing arts. *Travel and Tourism Analyst* 1, 82–96.

Gittelson, R.J. and Crompton, J.L. (1983) The planning horizons and sources of information used by pleasure vacationers. *Journal of Travel Research* 21 (3), 2–7.

Go, F.M. (1981) Development of new service products for the leisure travel market: A system's view. *Revue de Tourisme* 36 (2), 9–18.

Go, F.M. (1982) Hospitality and heritage: A profitable partnership. In A. Pizam *et al.* (eds) *The Practice of Hospitality Management* (pp. 173–82). Westport, CT: AVI.

Go, F.M. (1988) Appropriate marketing for travel destinations in developing nations. In Tej Vir Singh, H.L. Theuns and F.M. Go (eds) *Towards Appropriate Tourism: The Case of Developing Countries* (pp 159–80). Frankfurt: Verlag Peter Lang Gmbh.

Go, F.M. (1999) Internationalisation. In R. Brotherton (ed.) *The Handbook of Contemporary Hospitality Management Research* (pp. 477–96). Chicester: Wiley.

Go, F.M. and Christensen, J. (1989) Going global. *Cornell HRA Quarterly* 30 (3), 72–9.

Go, F.M. and Pine, R. (1995) *Globalization Strategy in the Hotel Industry*. London: Routledge.

Go, F.M. and Ritchie, J.R.B. (1990) Introduction to transnationalism and tourism. *Tourism Management* 11 (4), 287–90.

Go, F. and Welch, P. (1991) *Competitive Strategies for the International Hotel Industry*. Special Report No. 1180 (March). London: Economist Intelligence Unit.

Go, F.M. and Zhang Wei (1997) Applying importance-performance analysis to Beijing as an international meeting destination. *Journal of Travel Research* 35 (4) 42–9.

Go, F.M., Chan, A. and Pine, R. (1996) *Service Innovation in Hong Kong: Attitudes and Practice*. Hong Kong: Hong Kong Polytechnic University.

Go, F.M., Milne, D. and Whittles, L. (1991) Communities as destinations: A marketing taxonomy for the effective implementation of the tourism action plan. *Journal of Travel Research* 30 (4), 31–7.

Go, F.M., Govers, R. and Heuvel, M. Van Den (1999) Towards interactive tourism: Capitalising on virtual and physical value chains. In D. Buhalis and W. Schertler (eds) *Information and Communication Technologies in Tourism* (pp. 11–24). Vienna / New York: Springer.

Go, F.M.R. Govers and van den Heuvel, M. (1999) Towards interactive tourism: Capitalising on virtual and physical value chains. In D. Buhalis and W. Schertler (eds) *Information and Communication Technologies in Tourism Management* (pp. 11–24). Vienna / New York: Springer.

Goffe, P. (1986) Replacing place in the marketing mix strategy for hospitality services. *Florida University Hospitality Review* Spring 24.

Gottlieb, L. (1982) *Foodservice/Hospitality Advertising and Promotion*. Indianapolis, IN: Bobbs Merrill Educational Publishing.

Graham, R. *et al.* (1988) Visitor management in Canadian national parks. *Tourism Management* 9 (1), 44–62.

Greenberg, C. (1985) Room rates and lodging demand. *Cornell HRA Quarterly*, November, 10–11.

Greenley, G.E. and Matcham, A.S. (1986) Marketing orientation in the service of incoming tourism. *European Journal of Marketing* 20 (7), 64–73.

Gronroos, C. (1980) Designing a long range marketing strategy for services. *Long Range Planning* 13 (4), 36–42.

Gronroos, C. (2000) *Service Management and Marketing: A Customer Relationships Management Approach*. Toronto: Lexington Books.

Gunn, C.A. (1988) *Tourism Planning* (2nd edn). New York: Taylor and Francis.

Haati, A. and Yayas, U. (1982) Tourists' perception of Finland and selected European countries as travel destinations. *European Journal of Marketing* 17 (2), 34–42.

Hall, C.M. (1987) The effects of hallmark events on cities. *Journal of Travel Research* 26 (2), 44–5.

Hannigan, J.A. (1980) Reservations cancelled: Consumer complaints in the tourist industry. *Annals of Tourism Research* 7 (3), 366–84.

Harris, G. and Katz, K.M. (1987) *Promoting International Tourism*. Los Angeles, CA: Americas Group.

Hart, C.W.L. and Casserly, G.D. (1985) Quality: A brand-new, time-tested strategy. *Cornell HRA Quarterly* November 52–63.

Hart, C.W.L. and Lawless, M.J. (1983) Forces that shape restaurant demand. *Cornell HRA Quarterly* (November), 7–17.

Hart, C.W.L., Casserly, G.D. and Lawless, M.J. (1984) The product life cycle: How useful? *Cornell HRA Quarterly* 58 (November), 61–3.

Hawes, D. (1978) Satisfaction derived from leisure-time pursuits: An exploratory nationwide survey. *Journal of Leisure Research* 10 (4), 247–64.

Haywood, K.M. (1975a) *Marketing and Merchandizing Practices in the Canadian Hospitality industry, Volume 1, The Accommodation Sector*. Guelph, Ontario: University of Guelph.

Haywood, K.M. (1975b) *Management and Merchandizing Practices in the Canadian Hospitality Industry, Volume 2, The Foodservice Sector*. Guelph, Ontario: University of Guelph.

Haywood, K.M. (1983) Assessing the quality of hospitality services. *International Journal of Hospitality Management* 3 (4), 164–77.

Haywood, K.M. (1985a) Overcoming the impotency of marketing. *FLU Hospitality Review* (Fall), 30.

Haywood, K.M. (1985b) The Go system: Generating opportunities for hospitality. *International Journal of Hospitality Managment* 4 (1), 15–26.

Haywood, K.M. (1986) Scouting for competition for survival and success. *Cornell HRA Quarterly* (November), 80–7.

Haywood, K.M. (1986) Can the tourist-area life cycle be made operational? *Tourism Management* 7 (3), 154–67.

Haywood, K.M. (1987) Service management concepts: Implications for hospitality. *FIU Hospitality Review* 5 (2), 43–60.

Haywood, K.M. (1990) Revising and implementing the marketing concept as it applies to tourism. *Tourism Management* 11 (2), 195–205.

Hemingway, J.L. (1999) Leisure, social capital, and democratic citizenship. *Journal of Leisure Research* 31 (2) 150–65.

Heskett, J.L. (1986) *Managing in the Service Economy*. Boston: Harvard Business School Press.

Hess, T. and Voink, T. (1986) The uncommitted tourist. *Proceedings of the Esomar Congress* (pp. 69–84). Monte Carlo.

Hirschman, E. (1985) Marketing as an agent of change in subsistence cultures: Some dysfunctional consumption consequences. In R.J. Lutz (ed.) *Advances in Consumer Research* (Vol. 13) (pp. 99–104). Provo, UT: Association for Consumer Research.

Hodgson, A. (ed.) (1981) *The Travel and Tourism Industry: Strategies for the Future.* Oxford: Pergamon Press.

Hodgson, P. (1991) Market research in tourism: How important is it? *Tourism Management* 12 (4) 274–79.

Howard, D.R. and Crompton, J.L. (1986) *Financing, Managing and Marketing Recreation and Park Resources.* Dubuque, IA: William C. Brown Publishers.

Howard, D.R. (1985) An analysis of market potential for public leisure services. *Journal of Park and Recreation Management* 3 (1), 33–40.

Hughes, H. (2000) *Arts, Entertainment and Tourism.* Oxford: Butterworth-Heinemann.

Hunt, J.D. (1975) Image as a factor in tourism development. *Journal of Travel Research* 13 (3), 1–7.

Hunt, S.D. (1975) The nature and scope of marketing. *Journal of Marketing* 40, July, 17–28.

Husbands, W.C. (1983) Tourist space and tourist attraction: An analysis of the destination choices of European travelers. *Leisure Sciences* 5 (4), 289–307.

Jackson, E.L. and T.L. Burton (1999) *Leisure Studies: Prospects for the Twenty-First Century.* State College PA.

Jansen-Verbeke, M. (1988) *Leisure, Recreation and Tourism in Inner Cities: Explorative Case Studies.* Amsterdam: Nijmegen.

Jansen-Verbeke, M. and Dietvorst, A. (1987) Leisure, recreation and tourism: A geographic view on integration. *Annals of Tourism Research* 14 (2), 361–75.

Jefferson, A. and Lickorish, L. (1988) *Marketing Tourism – A Practical Guide.* Harlow: Longman.

Jeffrey, D. and Hubbard, N. (1986) Weekly occupancy fluctuations in Yorkshire and Humberside hotels, 1980–1984: Patterns and prescriptions. *International Journal of Hospitality Management* 5 (4), 177.

Jones, P. (1988) Quality, capacity and productivity in service industries. *International Journal of Hospitality Management* 7 (2), 104–12.

Joseph, W.B. *et al.* (eds) (1986) *Tourism Services Marketing: Advances in Theory and Practice.* Special Conference Series, Vol. 2. Cleveland, OH: Cleveland State University.

June, L. and Smith, S.L.J. (1987) Service attributes and situational effects on customer preferences for restaurant dining. *Journal of Travel Research* 26 (2), 20–7.

Kale, S.H. *et al.* (1987) Marketing overseas tour packages to the youth segment. *Journal of Travel Research* 25 (4), 20–4.

Kamann, D.J.F., Strijker, D. and Sijtsma, F.J. (1998) A reverse network engineering framework to develop tourism using a lifestyle approach. *Journal for Economic and Social Geography* 89 (3), 310–19.

Kaynak, E. (1985) Developing marketing strategy for a resource-based industry. *Tourism Management* 6 (3), 184–93.

Kelly, J.R. (1999) *Recreation Trends and Markets: The Twenty-First Century.* Champaign Sagamore Publishing.

Kent, W.E. *et al.* (1987) Reassessing wholesaler marketing strategies: The role of travel research. *Journal of Travel Research* 25 (3), 31–3.

Khan, M., Olsen, M. and Var, T. (1993) *VNR Encyclopedia of Hospitality and Tourism.* New York: Van Nostrand Reinhold.

King, C.A. (1984) Service-oriented quality control. *Cornell HRA Quarterly* (November), 92–8.

Klein, S., Schmid, B., Tjoa, A.M. and Werthner, H. (eds) (1996) *Information and Communication Technologies in Tourism.* Vienna / New York: Springer .

Kotas, R. (ed.) (1975) *Market Orientation in the Hotel and Catering Industry.* London: Surrey University Press.

Kotler, P. (1980) *Marketing Management – Analysis, Planning and Control.* Englewood Cliffs, NJ: Prentice Hall.

Kotler, P. (1987) Humanistic marketing: Beyond the marketing concept. In A.F. Firat *et al.* (eds) *Philosophical and Radical Thought in Marketing* (pp. 271–88). Lexington, MA: Lexington Books.

Kotler, P. and Levy, S.J. (1969) Broadening the concept of marketing. *Journal of Marketing* 33 (1), 10–15.

Kotschevar, L.H. (1975) *Management by Menu.* Chicago: National Institute for the Food Service Industry.

Kreul, L.M. (1982) Magic numbers: Psychological aspects of menu pricing. *Cornell HRA Quarterly* (August), 70–5.

Krippendorf, J. (1987) *The Holiday Makers: Understanding the Impact of Leisure and Travel.* Oxford: Heinemann.

Laine, S. and Laine, I. (1972) *Promotion in Foodservice.* New York: Mcgraw-Hill.

Lee, Y. (1999) How do individuals experience leisure? *Parks and Recreation* 34 (2), 40–6.

Lefever, M. and Morrison, A. (1988) Couponing for profit. *Cornell HRA Quarterly* (February), 57–63.

Lehtinen, J.R. (1986) *Quality Oriented Services Marketing.* Finland: University of Tampere.

Leven, M.A. (1985) Hotel life cycle. *Cornell HRA Quarterly* February, 10.

Levitt, T. (1972) The production line approach to service. *Harvard Business Review* (Sept–Oct), 41–52.

Lew, A.A. (1987) A framework of tourist attraction research. *Annals of Tourism Research* 14 (4), 553–75.

Lewis, R.C. (1980) Benefit segmentation for restaurant advertising. *Cornell HRA Quarterly* (November), 6–12.

Lewis, R.C. (1981) Restaurant advertising: Appeals and consumers' intentions. *Journal af Advertising Research* 21 (5), 69–74.

Lewis, R.C. (1982) Positioning analysis for hospitality firms. *International Journal of Hospitality Management* (Fall), 115–18.

Lewis, R.C. (1983) When guests complain. *Cornell HRA Quarterly* (August), 23–32.

Lewis, R.C. (1984a) Theoretical and practical considerations in research design. *Cornell HRA Quarterly* (February), 25–35.

Lewis, R.C. (1984b) Isolating differences in hotel attributes. *Cornell HRA Quarterly* (November), 64–77.

Lewis, R.C. (1984c) The basis of hotel selection. *Cornell HRA Quarterly* (May), 54–69.

Lewis, R.C. (1985) The market position: Mapping guests' perceptions of hotel operations. *Cornell HRA Quarterly* (August), 86.

Lewis, R.C. (1986) Customer-based hotel pricing: Many of the hotel industry's pricing policies run counter to economic wisdom and market realities. *Cornell HRA Quarterly* (August), 18.

Lewis, R.C. (1987) The measurement of gaps in the quality of hotel services. *International Journal of Hospitality Management* 6 (2), 83–8.

Lewis, R.C. *et al.* (eds) (1984) *The Practice of Hospitality Management II.* World Hospitality Conference. Westport, CT: AVI Publishing.

Lewis, R.C. and Chambers, R.E. (1989) *Marketing Leadership in Hospitality – Foundation and Practices.* New York: Van Nostrand Reinhold.

Lewis, R.C. and Klein, D.M. (1985) Personal constructs: Their use in marketing of intangible services. *Psychology and Marketing* 2 (3), 201–16.

Lewis, R.C. and Morris, S.V. (1987) The positive side of guest complaints. *Cornell HRA Quarterly* (February), 13–15.

Lewis, R.C. and Roan, C. (1986) Selling what you promote. *Cornell HRA Quarterly* (May), 13–15.

Lickorish, L.J. (1972) Forecasting in tourism. *Tourist Review* 27 (1), 28–30.

Lockwood, A. and Jones, P. (1989) Creating positive service encounters. *Cornell HRA Quarterly* (February), 44–50.

Lovelock, C.H. (1988) *Managing Services – Marketing, Operations and Human Resources*. Englewood Cliffs, NJ: Prentice Hall.

Louviere, J.J. and Woodsworth, G. (1983) Design and analysis of simulated consumer choice or allocation experiments. *Journal of Marketing Research* 20 (4), 350–67.

MacCannell, D. (1992) *Empty Meeting Grounds: The Tourist Papers*. London: Routledge.

Mackay, K.J. and Crompton, J.L. (1988) A conception model of consumer evaluation of recreation service quality. *Leisure Studies* 7 (1), 41–9.

Mahoney, E.M. and Warnell, G.R. (1986) *Tourism Marketing*. Extension Bulletin, Cooperative Extension Service, Michigan State University.

Maister, D.H. and Lovelock, C.H. (1982) Managing facilitator services. *Sloan Management Review* (Summer), 19–31.

Makens, J.C. (1987) The importance of US historic sites as visitor attractions. *Journal of Travel Research* 25 (3), 8–12.

Mann, G. (1981) Tourist motivation: An appraisal. *Annals of Tourism Research* 8 (2), 187–219.

Mathieson, A. and Wall, G. (1982) *Tourism – Economic, Physical and Social Impacts*. London: Longman.

Mazanec, J.A. (1986) Allocating an advertising budget to international travel markets. *Annals of Tourism Research* 14 (4), 609–34.

McCleary, K.W. (1987) A framework for national tourism marketing. *International Journal of Hospitality Management* 6 (3), 169–75.

McCleary, K.W. (1987) Marketing the United States to foreign tourists: America's greatest challenge. *Hospitality Education and Research Journal* 11 (2), 223–31.

McDougall, G.H.G. (1986) Products and services: Some insights into consumer decision making. *ASAC Conference* (pp. 212–21). British Columbia: Whistler.

McGuire, F. *et al.* (1988) Attracting the older traveler. *Tourism Management* 9 (2), 161–4.

McNaughton, R.W. (1981) How to develop a positioning strategy on a small restaurant's budget. *Cornell HRA Quarterly* (February), 10–14.

McNulty, R. and Penne, L. (1984) *Economics of Amenity*. Washington, DC: Partners for Livable Places.

McQueen, I. and Miller, K.E. (1985) Target market selection of tourists: A comparison of approaches. *Journal of Travel Research* 24 (1), 2–6.

Medlik, S. (1991) *Managing Tourism*. Oxford: Butterworth-Heinemann.

Mercer, J.A.T. (1985) Product life cycles of the windsurfer market. *European Journal of Marketing* 19 (4), 13–22.

Merlo, L. (1985) Marketing adaptation to the changing trends in tourist behaviour. *Trends of Tourism Demand* 35, 103–7. (The AIEST Conference.)

Meryer, R.J. (1981) A model of multiattribute judgements under attribute uncertainty and informational constraint. *Journal of Marketing Research* 28 (4), 428–41.

Middleton, V. (1988) *Marketing in Travel and Tourism*. Oxford: Butterworth-Heinemann.

Mill, R.C. and Morrison, A.M. (1985) *The Tourism System: An Introductory Text*. New York: Prentice Hall.

Miller, J. (1987) *Menu Pricing and Strategy* (2nd edn). New York: Van Nostrand.

Mills, P.K. (1986) *Managing Service Industries: Organizational Practices in a Post-Industrial Economy*. Cambridge, MA: Balinger.

Moller, K.E.K. *et al.* (1985) Segmenting hotel business customers: A benefit clustering approach. In T. Blah *et al.* (eds) *Services Marketing in a Changing Environment*. Chicago: American Marketing Association.

Moores, B. (ed.) (1986) *Are They Being Served? Quality Consciousness in Service Industries*. Oxford: Philip Allan.

Morrison, A.M. (1989) *Hospitality and Travel Marketing*. Albany, New York: Delmar Publishers Inc.

Moutinho, L. (1987) Consumer behaviour in tourism. *European Journal of Marketing* 21 (10), Whole Issue.

Moutinho, L. (ed.) (2000) *Strategic Management in Tourism*. Wallingford: CAB International.

Moutinho, L., Rita, P. and Curry, B. (1996) *Expert Systems in Tourism Marketing*. London: Routledge.

Murphy, P.E. (1985) *Tourism – A Community Approach*. New York: Methuen.

Nickels, C.M. and Snepenger, D. J. (1988) Family decision making and tourism behaviour and attitudes. *Journal of Travel Research* 26 (4), 29–37.

Nord, D.C. (1986) Canada perceived: The impact of Canadian tourism advertising in the United States. *Journal of American Culture* 9 (1), 23–30.

Normann, R. (1984) *Service Management: Strategy and Leadership in Service Businesses*. Chichester: John Wiley and Sons.

NTA (National Tour Association) (1987) *Partners in Profit: An Introduction to Group Travel Marketing*. Kentucky: Lexington.

Nykiel, R.A. (1983) *Marketing in the Hospitality Industry*. Boston CBI Publishing.

Orenstein, E. and Nunn, A. (1980) *The Marketing of Leisure*. London: Associated Business Press.

Otto, J.E. and Ritchie, Brent J.R. (1996) The service experience in tourism. *Tourism Management* 17 (3), 165–74.

Patten, S.G. (1986) Factory outlets and travel industry development: The case of Reading, Pennsylvania. *Journal of Travel Research* 25 (1), 10–17.

Pearce, J.A. and Robinson, R.B. (1982) *Strategic Management: Strategy Formulation and Implementation*. Homewood, IL: Richard D. Irwin.

Pearce, P. (1980) A favorability-satisfaction model of tourists' evaluations. *Journal of Travel Research* 19 (1), 13–17.

Phelps, A. (1986) Holiday destination image – the problem of assessment. An example developed on Menorca. *Tourism Management* 7 (3), 163–80.

Pickens, C. W. and Shanklin, C.W. (1985) State of the art in marketing hospital foodservice departments. *Journal of the American Dietetic Association* 85 (11), 1474–8.

Pickworth, J. (1988) Service delivery systems in the food service industry. *International Journal of Hospitality Management* 7 (1), 43–62.

Pickworth, J. and Pickworth, B. (1984) *An Annotated Bibliography of Food Service Articles in the Journal of American Dietetic Association from 1965–1983*. Chicago: American Dietetic Association.

Pillsbury, R. (1987) From Hamburger Alley yo Hedgerose Heights: Toward a model of restaurant location dynamics. *The Canadian Geographer* 39 (3), 326–44.

Pine, B.J. and Gilmore, J.H. (1998) *The Experience Economy*. Boston: Harvard Business School Press.

Piore, M. and Sabel, C. (1984) *The Second Industrial Divide*. New York: Basic Books.

Pizam, A. *et al.* (1978) Dimensions of tourist satisfaction with a destination area. *Journal of Tourism Research* 5 (3), 314–22.

Pritchard, G. (1982) Tourism promotion: Big business for the States. *Cornell HRA Quarterly* 23 (2), 48–52.

Raaij, W.F. Van and Crotts, A. (1994) Introduction: The economic psychology of travel and tourism. *The Economic Psychology of Travel and Tourism*. New York: Haworth.

Rao, C.P. and Ovmlil, A.B. (1988) Some critical distribution problems in services marketing. *International Conference on Services Marketing* (Vol. 5). Cleveland, OH: Cleveland State University.

Rathmell, J.M. (1974) *Marketing in the Service Sector*. Cambridge, MA: Winthrop Publishers.

Regan, C. (1987) Promoting nutrition in commercial foodservice establishments: A realistic approach. *Journal of the American Dietetic Association* 87 (4), 486–8.

Reid, R.D. (1983) *Foodservice and Restaurant Marketing*. Boston: CBI Publishing.

Reilley, R.T. (1980) *Travel and Tourism, Marketing Techniques*. Wheaton, IL: Merton House Publishing.

Renaghan, L.M. (1981) New marketing mix for the hospitality industry. *Cornell HRA Quarterly* (August), 30–5.

Renaghan, L.M. and Kaye, M. (1987) What meeting planners want: The conjoint analysis approach. *Cornell HRA Quarterly* (May), 67–76.

Rifkin, J. (2000) The age of access. *The New Culture of Hypercapitalism Where All of Life is a Paid-For Experience*. New York: Putnam.

Richards, G. (1996) The policy context of cultural tourism. In G. Richards (ed.) *Cultural Tourism in Europe* (p. 103). Oxon: CAB International.

Riley, C. (1983) The contribution of research to new product development in package tour operating. In *Seminar on the Importance of Research in the Tourism Industry* (pp. 135–47). Esomar.

Ritchie, J.R.B. (1987) Tourism marketing and the quality-of-life. In A.C. Samli (ed.) *Marketing and the Quality-of-Life Interface*. New York: Quorum Books.

Ritchie, J.R.B. (1988) Consensus policy in tourism: Measuring residence views via survey research. *Tourism Management* 9 (3), 119–22.

Ritchie, J.R.B. (1991) Global tourism policy issues: An agenda for the 1990s. In D.E. Hawkins, J.R.B. Ritchie, F. Go and D. Frechtling (eds) *World Travel and Tourism Review: Indicators, Trends and Forecasts* (Vol. 1) (pp. 149–58). Oxon: CAB International.

Ritchie, J.R.B. (1996) Beacons of light in an expanding universe: An assessment of the state of the art in tourism marketing / marketing research. *Journal of Travel & Tourism Marketing* 5 (4), 49–84.

Ritchie, J.R.B. and Goeldner, C.R. (1987) *Travel Tourism and Hospitality Research: A Handbook for Managers and Researchers*. New York: Wiley.

Ritchie, J.R.B. and Sheridan, M. (1988) Developing an integrated framework for tourism demand data in Canada. *Journal of Travel Research* 27 (1), 3–9.

Ritchie, J.R.B. and Zins, M. (1978) Culture as determinant of the attractiveness of a region. *Annals of Tourism Research* 5 (2), 252–67.

Ross, G.F. (1993) Service quality and management: The perceptions of hospitality employees. *Journal of Tourism Studies* 4 (2), 12–23.

Rovelstad, J.M. and Blazer, S.R. (1983) Research and strategic. Marketing in tourism: A status report. *Journal of Travel Research* 22 (2), 2–7.

Ryan, C. (1997) *The Tourist Experience: A New Introduction.* London: Cassell.

Sasser, W.E. and Morgan, I.P. (1977) The Bermuda Triangle of food service chains. *Cornell HRA Quarterly* (February), 56–61.

Sasser, W.E., Olsen, R.P. and Wyckoff, P.D. (1978) *Management of Service Operations: Text, Cases and Readings.* Boston: Allyn and Bacon.

Schmidhauser, H.P. (1962) *Markelforschung im Fremdenverkehrsverband.* Bern: Lang.

Schmoll, G.A. (1977) *Tourism Promotion.* London: Tourism International Press.

Seaburg, A.G. (1973) *Menu Design, Merchandising and Marketing* (2nd edn). Boston: CBI Publishing.

Selin, S. (2000) Developing a typology of sustainable tourism partnerships. *Journal of Sustainable Tourism* 7 (3, 4), 260–73.

Shames, G.W. and Glover, G. (1989) *World Class Service.* Yarmouth, Maine: Intercultural Press.

Shanklin, C.W. *et al.* (1987) Marketing in school food service – bibliography. *School Food Service Research Review* 11 (2), 120–6.

Sheldon, P.J. and Mak, J. (1987) The demand for package tours: A mode choice model. *Journal of Travel Research* 24 (4), 2–11.

Sheldon P.J. (1993) Destination information systems. *Annals of Tourism Research* 20 (4), 633–49.

Sheldon, P.J. (1997) *Tourism Information Technology.* Wallingford: CAB International.

Shoemaker, S. (1984) Marketing to older travelers. *Cornell HRA Quarterly* September, 84–91.

Shostack, L. (1977) Breaking free from product marketing. *Journal of Travel Marketing* 41 (4), 75–80.

Shostack, L. (1987) Service positioning through structural change. *Journal of Marketing* (January), 34–43.

Silberman, J. and Klock, M. (1986) An alternative to conversion studies for measuring the impact of travel ads. *Journal of Travel Research* 24 (2), 12–16.

Smith, S.L.G. (1983) *Recreation Geography.* London: Longman.

Smith, S.L.G. (1985) Location patterns of urban restaurants. *Annals of Tourism Research* 12 (4), 581–602.

Smith, S.L.G. (1986) Population threshold and capacity in the tourism and hospitality industry: Analysis of specialty urban restaurants. *Journal of Travel Research* 24, 29.

Smith, S.L.G. (1989) *Tourism Analysis – A Handbook.* Harlow: Longman.

Smith, V. (ed) (1977) *Hosts and Guests: The Anthropology of Tourism.* Philadelphia: University of Pennsylvania.

Snepenger, D.J. (1987) Segmenting the vacation market by novelty-seeking role. *Journal of Travel Research* 26 (2), 8–14.

Speelman, N. (1992) *Regional Tourism and Recreation Marketing: Theory and Practice.* Den Haag Stichting Recreatie Projecten.

Squire, S.J. (1988) Wordsworth and Lake District tourism: Romantic reshaping of landscape. *Canadian Geographer* 32 (3), 237–47.

Stabler, M.J. (ed.) (1997) *Tourism Sustainability Principles and Practice.* Wallingford: CAB International.

Stein, B. (1971) *Marketing in Action for Hotels, Motels and Restaurants.* New York: Ahrens Publishing.

Stringer, P.F. (1981) Hosts and guests: The bed-and-breakfast phenomenon. *Annals of Tourism Research* 8 (3), 357–76.

Summer, J.R. (1982) *Improve Your Marketing Techniques: A Guide For Hotel Managers and Caterers.* Sussex, UK: Northwood Publications.

Swan, J.E. *et al.* (1981) Effect of participation in marketing research on consumer attitudes toward research and satisfaction with a service. *Journal of Marketing Research* 28 (3), 356–63.

Swinyard, W. (1977) A research approach to restaurant marketing. *Cornell HRA Quarterly* (February), 62–5.

Swinyard, W.R. and Struman, K.D. (1986) Market segmentation: Finding the heart of your restaurants market. *Cornell HRA Quarterly* (May), 89–96.

Taylor, D. (1981) *How To Sell Banquets – The Key to Conference and Function Promotion* (2nd edn). Boston: CBI.

Taylor, P. and C. Gratton (1988) The Olympic Games: An economic analysis. *Leisure Management* 8 (3), 32–4.

Teare, R., Moutinho, L. and Morgan, N. (1990) *Managing and Marketing Services in the 1990s.* London: Cassell.

Teare, R., Bowen, J. and Hing, N. (1998) *New Directions in Hospitality and Tourism: A Worldwide Review.* London: Cassell.

Teare, R. and Calder, S. (1996) *Consumer Marketing: A Resource-Based Approach for the Hospitality and Tourism Industries.* London: Cassell.

Theobald, W. (1994) *Global Tourism: The Next Decade.* Oxford: Butterworth-Heinemann.

Theuns, H.L. (1989) Multidisciplinary focus on leisure and tourism. *Annals of Tourism Research* 16 (1), 189–204.

Thomas, D. (1978) Strategy is different in service businesses. *Harvard Business Review* (July–August), 58–65.

Thurot, J.M. and Thurot, G. (1983) The ideology of class and tourism: Confronting the discourse of advertising. *Annals of Tourism Research* 10 (1), 173–89.

Tighe, A.S. (1985) Cultural tourism in the USA. *Tourism Management* (Winter), 235–51.

Tinsley, H. and Kass, R.A. (1977) Leisure activities and need satisfaction. *Journal of Leisure Research* 9, 110–20.

Torkildsen, G. (1999) *Leisure and Recreation Management* (3rd edn). London: Spon.

Tremblay, P. (1998) The economic organization of tourism. *Annals of Tourism Research* 25 (4), 837–59.

Tribe, J. (2000) *Environmental Management for Rural Tourism and Recreation.* London: Cassell.

Uysal, M. and Crompton, J.L. (1985) An overview of approaches used to forecast tourist demand. *Journal of Travel Research* 23 (4), 7–15.

Uysal, N. (1986) Marketing for tourism – A growing field. *Parks and Recreation, USA* 21 (10), 57–61.

Uysal. M. and Fesenmaier, D.R. (1993) *Communication and Channel Systems in Tourism Marketing.* New York: Hayworth Press.

Uzzell, D. (1984) An alternative structuralist approach to the psychology of tourism marketing. *Annals of Tourism Research* 11 (1), 79–99.

Van Doren, C.S. and Lollar, S.A. (1985) The consequences of forty years of tourism growth. *Annals of Tourism Research* 12 , 467–89.

Var, T. *et al.* (1977) Determination of touristic attractiveness of the touristic areas in British Columbia. *Journal of Travel Research* 15 (3), 23–9.

Vellas, F. and Becherel, L. (1995) *International Tourism.* Houndsmills: Palgrave.

Vellas, F. and L. Becherel (1999) *The International Marketing of Travel and Tourism: A Strategic Approach.* Basingstoke: Macmillan.

Wahab, S. (1976) *Tourism Marketing – A Destination Oriented Programme for the Marketing of International Tourism.* London: Tourism International Press.

Wahab, S. and Cooper, C. ( 2001) *Tourism in the Age of Globalisation.* London: Routledge.

Wahab, S. and Pigram, J.J. (1997) *Tourism Development and Growth: The Challenge of Sustainability.* London: Routledge.

Wall, G. *et al.* (1985) Point pattern analyses of accommodation in Toronto. *Annals of Tourism Research* 12 (4), 603–18.

Weaver, P.A. and Mccleary, K.W. (1984) A market segmentation study to determine the appropriate and/model format for travel advertising. *Journal of Travel Research* 23 (1), 12–16.

Webster (1999) The media reader: Continuity and transformation. In H. Mackay and T. O'Sullivan (eds) *What Information Society.* London: Sage.

Wee, C.H. *et al.* (1986) Temporal and regional differences in image of a tourist destination: Implications for promoters of tourism. *Service Industries Journal* 6 (1), 104–44.

Welch, J.L. (1985) Focus groups for restaurant research. *Cornell HRA Quarterly* (August), 75–85.

Wilson, I. (1988) Competitive strategies for service business. *Long Range Planning* 21 (6), 10–12.

Wilensky, L. and Buttle, F. (1988) A multivariate analysis of hotel benefit bundles and choice trade-offs. *International Journal of Hospitality Management* 7 (1), 29–41.

Witham, G. (1985) Hotel companies aim for multiple markets: The current proliferation of brand names to an effort by hotels to become. *Cornell HRA Quarterly* (November), 39.

Witt, S.F. and Martin, C.A. (1987) Econometric models for forecasting international tourism demand. *Journal of Travel Research* 25 (3), 23–30.

Witt, S. F. and Moutinho, L. (1989) *Tourism Marketing and Management Handbook* New York: Prentice Hall.

Witt, S F. and Mouthinho, L. (1995) *Tourism Marketing and Management Handbook: Student Edition.* London: Prentice Hall.

Witt, S F., Brooke, M.Z. and Buckley P.J (1991) *The Management of International Tourism.* London: Unwin.

Witt, C.A. and Muhlemann, A.P. (1994) The implementation of total quality management in tourism: Some guidelines. *Tourism Management* 15 (6), 416–24.

Wolf, M.J. (1999) *The Entertainment Economy: How Mega-Forces are Transforming our Lives.* New York: Random House.

Wolf, S. and Latane, B. (1983) Majority and minority influence on restaurant preferences. *Journal of Personality and Social Psychology* 45 (2), 282–92.

Wood, R. (1999) Traditional and alternative research philosophies. In R. Brotherton (ed.) *The Handbook of Contemporary Hospitality Management Research* (pp. 3–18), Chicester: Wiley,

Woodside, A.G. (1984) How serious is non-response bias in advertising conversion research? *Journal of Travel Research* 22 (4), 34–7.

Woodside, A.G. and Jacobs, L.W. (1985) Step two in benefit segmentation: Learning the benefits realized by major travel markets. *Journal of Travel Research* 24 (1), 7–13.

Woodside, A.G. and Jeffrey, A. (1988) Consumer decision making and competitive marketing strategies: Applications for tourism planning. *Journal of Travel Research* 26 (3), 2–7.

Woodside, A.G. and Motes, W.H. (1981) Sensitivity of market segments to separate advertising strategies. *Journal of Marketing* 16 (1), 63–73.

Woodside, A.G. and Sherrell, D. (1977) Traveller evoked, inept and inert sets of vacation destinations. *Journal of Travel Research* 16 (1), 14–18.

Woodside, A.G. *et al.* (1987) Profiling the heavy traveller segment. *Journal of Travel Research* 25 (4), 9–14.

Woodside, A.G. and M.Y. Sakai (2001) Meta-evaluations of performance audits of government tourism-marketing programs. *Journal of Travel Research* 39 (4), 369–79.

Wyckoff, D.D. and Sasser, W.E. (1978) *The Chain-Restaurant Industry,* Vol. 2. Lexington, MA: Lexington Books.

Yaman, H.R. and R.N. Shaw (1998) Assessing marketing research use in tourism with the USER instrument. *Journal of Travel Research* 36 (3), 70–8.

Yesawich, P.C. (1977) Know your prime prospects: Marketing research for the lodging industry. *Cornell HRA Quarterly* (February), 11–16.

Yesawich, P.C. (1978) Post-opening marketing analysis for hotels. *Cornell HPA Quarterly* (November), 70–81.

Yesawich, P.C. (1979) The execution and measurement of a marketing program. *Cornell HRA Quarterly* (May), 41–52.

Yesawich, P.C. (1980) Marketing in the 1980s. *Cornell HRA Quarterly* (February), 35–8.

Yesawich, P.C. (1981) Marketing in an inflationary economy. *Cornell HRA Quarterly* (February), 35–8.

Yesawich, P.C. (1984) A market-based approach to forecasting. *Cornell HRA Quarterly* (November), 47–53.

Yesawich, P.C. (1987) Hospitality marketing for the 90s: Effective marketing research. *Cornell HRA Quarterly* (May), 48–57.

Yesawich, P.C. (1988) Planning: The second step in market development. *Cornell HRA Quarterly* (February), 71–81.

Yuan, Y. and Fesenmaier, D. (2000) Preparing for the new economy: The use of the internet and intranet in American convention and visitor bureaus. *Information Technology and Tourism* 3 (2), 71–86.

*Chapter 7*

# Comprehensive Human Resource Planning: An Essential Key to Sustainable Tourism in Small Island Settings

MICHAEL V. CONLIN and TOM BAUM

## Introduction

The concept of sustainability has its origins in the environmental movement which grew to prominence in the 1960s and which has now become a mainstream issue within most business communities. What began essentially as a fringe protest against the uncontrolled expansion of economic development and its negative impact upon the physical environment has now become a vital issue in national, regional and local planning in many areas, not the least of which is tourism.

Notwithstanding this growth, the debate about sustainable tourism policy generation and practice has matured significantly over the past decade and while it has generated a great deal of literature, the full relevance of its implication has probably only just begun to be understood by planners (McKercher, 1993). Sustainability, to be effective, needs to consider the overall 'environment' in which tourism development takes place, not just the physical environment. This chapter will suggest that human resource development and management are one area of the overall 'environment' which is critical for successful tourism development.

The case for the importance of human resource development for the success of tourism, particularly in those segments of the industry that are labour-intensive, has been made convincingly since the early 1990s (Baum, 1992; Enz & Fulford, 1993). These segments include the accommodation, food and beverage and transportation sectors, among others. Research in this area has included the development of planning models that seek to integrate all areas of human resource development (HRD) with the wider tourism environment. Baum's (1995) analysis includes a detailed comparison between features he describes as characteristic of 'traditional' approaches to HRD in tourism and the alternative sustainable models (Amoah, 1999; Amoah and Baum, 1997). The literature has also been developed through analysis in specific national or regional case studies (Jithendran & Baum, 2000). The debate has included a focus upon the impact of human resource management on levels of productivity and quality of service within various sectors of the industry. This emphasis is important particularly as the industry becomes more internationally competitive (Baum, 1992; Conlin, 1991; Goffe, 1993).

This chapter approaches the general theme of the importance of human resources for successful tourism from the narrower perspective of human resource development planning in island settings and from the emerging perspective of sustainability of the industry in this context (Guthunz & von Krosigk, 1996). The chapter will make the case that the special characteristics of island tourism call for a greater emphasis on the rational and culturally sensitive use of labour. Given the underlying concept of sustainable tourism, this approach to human resources must be considered as an essential key to sustainability. Ignoring comprehensive planning for human resources in island settings will have profound consequences not only for the local industry but also for the island community, as the experience of Pulau Langkawi in Malaysia demonstrates:

> What has emerged in Langkawi is a situation where most local people do not have the necessary experience or skills to take up many of the newly created jobs. Since training is not provided, the people can only fill unskilled positions as cleaners or general workers. Apart from a few . . . most islanders lack the contacts, credit, entrepreneurial flair, training and motivation to seize business opportunities. There are also cultural and religious reasons that discourage some locals from certain jobs. (Bird, 1989: 29)

Interestingly, Bird, albeit unwittingly, is alluding to ground covered by Guerrier and Lockwood (1989) in their discussion of the evolution of core and peripheral work roles within the hotel industry. It is clear that, in Bird's view, local islanders are obtaining jobs at the periphery, these being the poorest paid and the most vulnerable to cyclical fluctuations in demand. This 'marginalisation' of indigenous people is relatively common throughout the island tourism world. In the Caribbean, the industry has experienced difficulty attracting young people seeking to develop careers (Charles, 1992; Conlin & Baum, 1995; Conlin & Titcombe, 1995). The literature also confirms that in general, tourism is not seen as a high-status economic sector within which to develop a career (Airey & Frontistis, 1997;

Cooper & Shepherd, 1997). Although this view about career development is not unique to island destinations, it does serve to compound the challenges for developing indigenous island human resources.

The tourism industry is not generally considered to be a mainstream career opportunity, both in the developed and developing worlds. In the developed world, the industry has for many decades been seen as a part of the economy where work is short-term, transient and for the most part, not satisfying financially and psychologically. In the developing world, the situation is exacerbated by the practices of multi-national operators to view indigenous peoples as being incapable or undeserving of access to higher level occupation within the industry. Our concept of human resource development, therefore, seeks to counter traditional short-term, operationally orientated approaches to human resource planning and development within tourism that have failed to address the issues of sustainability in the broadest sense. Labour has been seen as a necessary support resource within efforts to develop a tourism industry that has been able to sustain itself in economic and environmental terms. The underpinning issue in this chapter is the need for tourism planning to give recognition to the impact of development on the character and balance within the labour market of local island economies. Lane (1992) touches on this issue by contrasting 'no career structure' and 'employees imported' features of non-sustainable tourism with those, of 'career structure' and 'employment according to local potential' in sustainable tourism development. Development from a human resource perspective should be 'of' island communities and not simply 'in' them as is frequently the case.

## The Concept of Sustainability

The origins of sustainable development, particularly in tourism, are to be found in concerns for the physical environment, as already mentioned. This concern began to broaden during the 1970s to include concerns about the negative impacts of tourism upon the culture of destinations and their indigenous populations. As far back as 1975, concerns about acceptable tourism development in the Caribbean began to include the impact of the industry upon cultural and sociological aspects of the region (Jefferson, 1975). As Butler (1993: 137) states in his analysis of the use of pre- and post-impact assessment of tourism development: 'It is more common now to see references to impact assessment, which implicitly includes both environmental impact assessment . . . and social impact assessment'.

The broadening emphasis of the sustainability concept to include cultural and social considerations is now widely accepted and has become a fundamental component of the concept. Several of the more widely accepted definitions of sustainable tourism clearly include this broad focus. The Action Strategy for Sustainable Tourism Development produced at the Globe '90 Conference in Vancouver in 1990 stated that:

> The concept of sustainable development explicitly recognises interdependencies that exist among environmental and economic issues and policies. Sustainable development is aimed at protecting and enhancing environment meeting basic human needs, promoting current and intergenerational equity, improving the quality of life of all peoples. (Action Strategy, 1990: 1)

The reference in this important definition to human needs, equity and quality of life is evidence of the broadening of the concept beyond the scope of the physical environment.

Bramwell and Lane (1993: 2), state that:

> Sustainable tourism is presented as a positive approach intended to reduce the tensions and friction created by the complex interactions between the tourism industry, visitors, the environment and the communities which are host to holiday makers It is an approach which involves working for the longer viability and quality of both natural and human resources.

Jithendran and Baum (2000: 404), however, note that the concepts and practices of sustainability are 'mired in contradictions and controversies'. Aronsson notes 'two seemingly paradoxical aspects, namely, preservation and development', while other writers (MacLellan, 1997; Wall, 1997) question whether sustainability as a concept has been hijacked by the tourism industry through eco-labelling and eco-selling. Butler makes the case bluntly:

> What is being criticized . . . is the hypocrisy and cant which is pontificated about tourism saving the environment through non-impacting forms of ecotourism, which is all too often an excuse for introducing tourism into areas where it may have been more appropriate for it not to have ventured, or where it should only have been allowed under conditions of control and management. Controls are exerted on most forms of activity yet tourism is one which frequently seems to avoid them, beyond those imposed on the actual construction of projects and appropriate labour and safety laws. Using the green banner and misusing the concept of sustainable development does not seem to make for what has also become termed 'appropriate' tourism (Butler 1996: 13)

Bramwell and Lane's definition is noteworthy because it stresses the need for long-term perspectives and a concern for the quality of human resources. It clearly underscores the need for the inclusion of human resource development within the ambit of the sustainable tourism philosophy. In the definitive text on sustainable tourism planning, Inskeep (1991: 461) cites the objectives of the concept as applied to the industry in the Action Strategy for Sustainable Tourism Development:

(1) to develop greater awareness and understanding of the significant contributions that tourism can make to the environment and the economy;
(2) to promote equity in development;
(3) to improve the quality of life of the host community;
(4) to provide a high quality of experience for the visitor; and
(5) to maintain the quality of the environment on which the foregoing objectives depend.

At least three of these objectives clearly involve the importance of comprehensive human resource development in tourism destinations. The notion of equity would seem to preclude tourism development that does not contribute as much to the indigenous population as is feasible. This was not the notion that the Strategy envisioned – it was concerned with equity relative to future generations of travellers – but it is no less relevant and probably more important. The quality of life in the host community is clearly interconnected with the patterns of employment of the host population. It can also be argued, as mentioned in the introduction to this chapter, that the human resource component is a vital element in the quality of the tourism product. In addition to these three objectives, it can also be argued that a comprehensive human resource development component in a tourism development plan may contribute to a higher degree of awareness and acceptance of the tourism industry on the part of the local population. This being the case, the first objective also can be seen to be linked with the comprehensive development of human resources in island settings.

The case for the inclusion of indigenous peoples in the tourism planning process has been made very convincingly over the past decade (Murphy, 1983). Much of the inclusion strategy, however, has been designed to generate a sympathetic understanding of the importance of tourism within the local community, primarily to ensure tourism's success (Inskeep, 1991; Lane, 1992; Murphy, 1983). As Murphy (1983: 118) states:

An industry claiming to be in the 'hospitality' business can find its product planning and marketing strategies laid to waste through bad service and a hostile reception from local residents.

Murphy appears to be simply confirming the traditional perspective of human involvement in tourism development, namely a 'bottom-line' orientation mainly concerned with marketing and financial considerations.

Indeed, the positive impact on the local community directly in the form of employment, and perhaps more importantly, career development, often seems to be peripheral. The Action Strategy for Sustainable Tourism Development, which provided the definition and objectives discussed above, never mentions employment in its 41 specific action recommendations to governments, National Tourist Organisations (NTOs), international organisations, the tourism industry and the individual tourist. Neither do the recommendations call for any educational or training activity other than those connected with tourism awareness programmes (Action Strategy Committee, 1990). Where planning does incorporate considerations of employment, such as in the development plan for Trinidad and Tobago, it is almost always confined to a call for the provision of education and training for the tourism industry (Williams, 1993).

Much of the discussion concerning community involvement in tourism planning stops short of providing an effective call for mechanisms to ensure that inclusion of local interests means full employment and career development opportunities for indigenous peoples. To date, the emphasis has been on stressing the need for greater education and training opportunities for indigenous populations, particularly in the development of lower-level skills and abilities (Mathiesen & Wall, 1990). This has been seen as the most effective means of incorporating locals into the industry and as a possible strategy for encouraging a sense of 'professionalism' in work which is traditionally seen as menial and demeaning (Burns, 1994). While no one would argue that the provision of the means for acquiring skills and abilities is not a positive step in involving local populations in the tourism industry, as a strategy it fails to take into consideration cultural and traditional barriers which mitigate against indigenous peoples entering the industry. The Langkawi example, already cited by Bird, addresses these very issues.

As a further concern, the use of expatriate labour has been identified as one of the factors which mitigates against significant economic impact by tourism on small islands (Fletcher & Snee, 1989). If the use of local labour is seen to be discriminatory in the sense that it confines locals to the 'peripheral' jobs, it is unlikely to become a positive force within the economic development of the island as a whole. It will generate employment but it will always be seen as a second-class industry for second-class persons.

Baum (1992) addresses this question, in part, when he identifies six characteristics of many island tourism destinations, especially in the developing world, which have particular significance in the human resource context. These can be summarised as follows:

- a high economic dependence on a small range of economic sectors, including tourism;
- a focused and limited range of tourism products, generally hedonistic rather than historic/cultural in nature;
- a focus on high-spend, international tourism, with the consequent requirement for five-star or equivalent product standards;
- a restricted pool of skilled labour; and
- limited education and training provision for tourism.

To these, we would also add, as pertinent in the present context,

- geographical remoteness;
- a small population base which demands the maximum development of skills, employment and career opportunities;
- political and economic insularity, mitigating against ready mobility of labour; and
- cultural intraversion, leading to suspicion and of even hostility to outsiders.

At a practical level, the impact of these characteristics may be manifested in a number of ways. First, economic dependence on tourism and a limited range of alternative economic activities may mean that the effects of the cyclical changes in demand on tourism employment cannot be readily absorbed elsewhere in the local economy. This can clearly be seen in St Lucia, for example, where agriculture is the only significant economic alternative to tourism. Second, political insularity and physical remoteness may restrict the options open to islanders, to seek alternative employment by moving elsewhere within the region in the manner that is open to people in larger land-mass locations. For example, if a hotel closes in St Kitts Nevis, the ability of the displaced local workers to seek employment elsewhere in the region is hampered by political obstacles relating to immigration policies, financial constraints upon travel and temporary residence, and pressure to maintain the family unit. Third, the factor of size may mean that educational and training opportunities in tourism are not available locally, while remoteness mitigates against accessing such provision elsewhere. The Maldives provides a good example in this context. Fourth, the impact of cultural intraversion, or a desire to protect aspects of an island's cultural or historic uniqueness, may act as a barrier to acceptance of the introduction of labour from elsewhere in a way that would not be so common within larger communities which have well developed land-based links at a regional or national level. The Aran Islands, for example, off the west coast of Ireland, have an Irish-speaking community and subscribe to traditional cultural values in many respects. Significant development of the tourism resources of the island would, inevitably, result in the importation of labour, especially on a seasonal basis, without the same cultural and linguistic background. Keane *et al.* (1992) argue the case for sustainability in tourism in the Aran Islands, and cultural aspects are very high on their agenda.

In addition, the emergence of tourism in small islands can have a disruptive effect on their traditional patterns of employment:

> large scale tourism development in the Caribbean is almost always accompanied by movement of workers out of agriculture into tourism-related activities to the detriment of the former . . . if the development of tourism is accompanied by the destruction of that sector, through the combined effects of changes in land use and movement of workers away from the farm, the incremental benefits will be minimal and possibly even negative. (Jefferson, 1975: 63)

Phuket, in Thailand, traditionally self-sufficient in meeting the food needs of the indigenous population, must now import foodstuffs, such as rice, for consumption by local people and visitors alike. Thus, the deployment of personnel, within a finite island labour market, can have an impact which reaches beyond its immediate ambit and impacts on the overall economic balance sheet of the location.

Island tourism is generally seasonal in nature. Thus, permanent full-time employment in the tourism industry is not always available. As a consequence, there is frequently seasonal migration of tourism labour from the island to other locations in search of work. Examples include the migration of workers from the Greek and Spanish islands to the mainland and to other parts of urban Europe, and from Ireland to the United Kingdom and Germany. This process, while ostensibly a balanced flow in both directions to reflect the demand for labour in the island's tourism industry, can, in situations where political considerations may allow, result in a net loss to the island, as staff settle permanently elsewhere. This haemorrhaging of skills effectively reduces the participation of the indigenous population in the industry with the same ultimate effect as not including them in the first place. A general discussion of this migratory process from peripheral to core tourism areas in the context of Europe is addressed by Baum (1993b). Island tourism is generally foreign-owned, at least in the accommodation area. This has always presented problems, two of which were identified in the Caribbean region in 1975:

> Foreign ownership represents a source of concentration, reduces the local contribution of any tourism expenditure and reduces the small potential for linkages in these small islands . . . Secondly, and this is most relevant, for Antigua and Barbados where tourism is the dominant economic activity, it encourages the renewal of concepts such as dependency, monoculture and centre/periphery relationship and, as such, inherits a legacy of intellectual criticism and popular hostility. (Carrington & Blake, 1975: 32)

An illustration of this relates to Bali, where it will be interesting to monitor the long-term impact on local businesses in locations such as Kuta and Sanur, or the continuing development of Nusa Dua as an international-standard resort. The contrast between traditional local ownership on the island and the more recent influx of international or at least non-Balinese investment, could not be starker and provides an important dimension in our consideration of sustainability in human resource terms. Guerrier (1993), however, discusses strategies which have been brought to bear in Bali designed in part to counter this process through local entrepreneurship training.

These island characteristics form what is essentially a touristic microcosm. This in turn results in a need to view the total touristic experience in holistic terms. Each experience of a 'moment of truth' has far more impact, positive or negative, than may be the case in a larger destination. Therefore, the role of human resources becomes vital to the delivery of a quality touristic experience and to the success of the community as a whole. This link is not always recognised, as Poon (1993: 258; see also Chapter 8 in this volume) argues:

> It seems paradoxical that employees hold the key to competitive success in an industry that has traditionally viewed labour as a cost of production, a replaceable item, an item to dispose of in the low season, an item that can be hired and fired at will. Yet for those companies that have stayed on top of the heap – from Disneyland to the Marriotts to Singapore Airlines – it is the unending drive toward quality and investment in human resources that has made the difference.

Generally, island tourism destinations compete at a disadvantage against comparable mainland locations as a consequence of structural and wider economic challenges. There are exceptions, however, and these include the Aland Islands (Baum, 1999) and Iceland (Baum, 1999). Features of the tourism sector in both these cold water island destinations is local ownership, control and management of the majority of tourism resources, including access transport and accommodation. The

structure of the industry illustrated in these cases has important implications for their HR environment which is likewise locally controlled
and orientated.

## The Sustainable Human Resource Agenda

The preceding sections have argued that sustainability is important in
island settings, that human resources need to be developed in a 'sustainable' manner, and that current tourism development practice does not
address fundamentally the issue of sustainable human resource development. What, then, needs to be done in order to ensure the sustainable
development of human resources in island settings?

## Recognition of the Value of Human Resources

Public sector policy-makers and private sector decision-makers need
to recognise that human resources are a necessary element of successful
tourism development, particularly that which is sustainable. This may
not be easy. Indeed, in a study of 66 national tourism administrations, a
surprising 14 indicated that they did not see human resource issues to be
of concern (Baum, 1994). Some NTOs indeed, do not see human resources
to be of concern and this suggests that there is a need to enhance awareness at this level as to the importance of human resources for success
(Baum, 1994).

This is essential if human resources are to be part of the overall planning
for tourism development and not simply an operational consideration after
the major policy and planning decisions have already been made. The
problem with the inclusion of human resources issues after the planning
has been completed is that fundamental changes in public policy and management thinking about human resources become difficult for host
countries to instigate.

International funding agencies may provide an incentive in this regard.
Generally, aid comes with the requirement for planning which must
include some consideration of the human resource factor in the project or
programme. To some extent, however, these requirements focus on the
need for the provision of education and training without putting into place
the necessary framework to motivate full integration. Simply calling for the
provision of education and training fails to account for the cultural barriers
that may exist in island locations.

## Public Policy Foundations for Human Resources

Recognition of the value of human resources in itself is not enough. A
regulatory framework which seeks to ensure the inclusion of host popula-

tions in the tourism industry to the fullest extent feasible is essential to operationalise this recognition at the highest level. The areas of immigration policy and education provide good examples.

Immigration policies generally provide for the training of counterparts. However, this provision can usually be sidelined by any number of clever tactics (Burns, 1994) and is generally not strictly enforced. What is needed is a balanced approach to immigration regulation which recognises the legitimate demands of the host population for an appropriate role in the tourism industry based upon ability, balanced against the industry's legitimate right to hire and fire in order to ensure the viability of its product and the sustainability of the economic contribution to the country. In order to obtain this balance, there must be trust and understanding on the part of both the public and private sector representatives.

In the past, governments and administrations in islands have tended to rely on the granting of work permits to promote the use and growth of local employees. At best, this is a confrontational situation which pits locals against expatriates with all its negative consequences. It gives rise to manipulatory practices by management and contributes to the probability of corruptive practices being employed. It is generally the case in island hotel industries that senior management comprises expatriates while the junior and supervisory posts are held by locals. The argument that multinational companies usually make to support this practice relates to their own policies for the training of senior managers. They value the far-ranging experience which short-term postings to different properties provide. Assuming that their position in this regard is valid, it would be appropriate for a host island to seek reciprocity whereby talented local employees would have the opportunity to participate in the process by being posted to foreign properties. Burns (1994) discusses the benefits of this process to Sri Lanka where the use of expatriate management is almost non-existent.

What is needed is a recognition that the employment and promotion of indigenous people has a wide range of benefits to both employers and the island communities at large. Greater appreciation of the industry, higher quality service, more authenticity in the product, and less likelihood of disruption combine with the financial benefits of lower human resource expense and the reduction of salary leakage, particularly at the higher levels of management, to justify changes in the industry's traditional approach to local employment and the use of expatriate labour. This approach would provide a rational basis for local human resource development as opposed to the legislated, coercive system that islands for the most part currently use.

## The Need for Integrated Human Resource Policy Structures

A further obstacle to the incorporation of human resource planning into the tourism development process is the fragmentation of responsibility that frequently exists in the public and private sectors for this area. For example, human resource concerns frequently fall within the ambit of several government units, be they ministries (education, labour, tourism, agriculture, home affairs), quangos such as NTOs, or diverse private sector interests (hotel associations, operators, consultants).

In order to counter the consequences of this fragmentation, there is a need for a comprehensive process through which to plan for the development of indigenous human resources in island tourism. Baum (1993a) provides an example of a comprehensive model that addresses many of the concerns mentioned above and that is readily applicable within island contexts. The model calls for the consideration of five areas:

- the tourism environment;
- tourism and the labour market;
- tourism and education;
- human resource practice in the industry; and
- tourism and the community – in a comprehensive, integrated and cohesive manner.

As Baum (1993a: 240) states:

> The value of the approach . . . is, primarily, as an aid to policy formulation and the establishment of national, regional and local priorities with respect to human resource concerns in tourism. Where this approach differs from that practised in most tourism environments is in its breadth. The approach is designed to incorporate as many as possible of the diverse influences and considerations which affect the development and management of an effective human resource policy in tourism.

An example of such an integrated approach to human resource development can be found in the Caribbean. There, the public and private sectors are collaborating to improve the nature of regional participation in the industry. This is being attempted through the use of regional public policy initiatives relating to such issues as immigration policy, the design and installation of coordinating structures and processes such as regional and national tourism education councils, and a prioritisation of education and training within national budgets (Conlin, 1993).

## Conclusion

This chapter has explored a number of seminal issues relating to the human resource environment within island tourism. It has recommended the use of a comprehensive approach incorporating public policy frameworks to ensure the integration of host populations within the industry. It has provided a model for achieving such integration. What is required is more detailed empirical and case-study research into the various dimensions of human resource policy and implementation which this chapter has addressed.

## Note

1.  This chapter first appeared as 'Comprehensive human resource planning: An essential key to sustainable tourism in island settings in Volume 6 of *Progress in Tourism, Recreation and Hospitality Management* (1994), pp. 259–70.

## Bibliography

Action Strategy Committee (1990) *An Action Strategy For Sustainable Tourism Development*. Tourism Stream, Action Strategy Committee, Globe '90 Conference, Vancouver, British Columbia, Canada, March.

Airey, D. and Frontistis, A. (1997) Attitudes to careers in tourism: An Anglo-Greek comparison. *Tourism Management* 18 (3), 149–58.

Amoah, V. (1999) Integrating tourism and education policy. Unpublished PhD thesis, University of Buckingham.

Amoah, V. and Baum, T. (1997) Tourism education: Policy versus practice. *International Journal of Contemporary Hospitality Management* 9 (1), 5–12.

Baum, T. (1992) Human resources: The unsung price-value issue. In *Proceedings of the First Island Tourism International Forum* (pp. 249–56). Paget, Bermuda: Centre for Tourism Research and Innovation, Bermuda College.

Baum, T. (1993a) *Human Resource Issues In International Tourism*. Oxford: Butterworth-Heinemann.

Baum, T. (1993b) Human resource concerns in European tourism: Strategic response and the EC. *International Journal of Hospitality Management* 12 (1), 77–88.

Baum, T. (1994) National tourism policies: Implementing the human resource dimension. *Tourism Management* 15 (4).

Baum, T. (1995) The role of the public section in the development and implementation of human resource policies in tourism. *Tourism Recreation Research* 20 (2), 45–63.

Baum, T. (1999) The decline of the traditional North Atlantic fisheries and tourism's response. *Current Issues in Tourism* 2 (1), 47–67.

Bird, B. (1989) *Langkawi from Mahsuri to Mahathir. Tourism For Whom?* Kuala Lumpur: INSAN.

Bramwell, W. and Lane, B. (1993) Sustainable tourism: An evolving global approach?' *Journal of Sustainable Tourism* 1 (1), 1–5.

Burns, P.M. (1994) Sustaining tourism's workforce: Cultural and social-values perspectives with special reference to the role of expatriates. *Journal of Sustainable Tourism* 1 (2), 14–19.

*Classic Reviews in Tourism*

Butler, R.W. (1993) Pre- and post-impact assessment of tourism development. In G. Pearce and R.W. Butler (eds) *Tourism Research: Critiques and Challenges* (pp. 112–34). London: Routledge.

Butler, R.W. (1996) Problems and possibilities of sustainable tourism: The case of the Shetland Islands. In L. Bruguglio, R. Butler, D. Harrison and W. Leal Filho (eds) *Sustainable Tourism in Islands and Small States: Case Studies* (pp. 11–31). London: Pinter.

Carrington, E.W. and Blake, B.W. (1975) Tourism as a vehicle for Caribbean economic development. In *Caribbean Tourism* (pp. 3–5). Caribbean Tourism Research Centre (now incorporated into the Caribbean Tourism Organisation).

Charles, K. (1992) Career influences, expectations and perceptions of Caribbean hospitality and tourism students: A Third World perspective. *Hospitality and Tourism Educator* 4 (3), 9–14.

Conlin, M.V. (1991) Credible higher education in tourism: A Caribbean example. In *Tourism: Building Credibility for a Credible Industry*. Proceedings of the 22nd Annual Conference of the Travel and Tourism Association, Long Beach, 1991.

Conlin, M.V. (1993) The Caribbean. In T. Baum (ed.) *Human Resource Issues in International Tourism* (pp. 147–60), Oxford: Butterworth-Heinemann.

Conlin, M.V. and Baum, T. (1995) Island tourism: An introduction. In M.V. Conlin and T. Baum (eds) *Island Tourism: Management Principles and Practice* (pp. 3–13). Chichester: Wiley.

Conlin, M.V. and Titcombe, J.A. (1995) Human resources: A strategic imperative for Caribbean tourism. In M.V. Conlin and T. Baum (eds) *Island Tourism: Management Principles and Practice*. Chichester: Wiley.

Cooper, C. and Shepherd, R. (1997) The relationship between tourism education and the tourism industry: Implications for tourism education. *Tourism Recreation Research* 22 (1), 34–47.

Enz, C.A. and Fulford, M.D. (1993) The impact of human resource management on organizational success: Suggestions for hospitality educators. *Hospitality and Tourism Educator* 5 (2), 29–37.

Fletcher, J. and Snee, H. (1989) Tourism in the South Pacific islands. In C.P. Cooper (ed.) *Progress in Tourism, Recreation and Hospitality Management* (pp. 67–79). Vol. 1, London: Belhaven.

Goffe, R. (1993) Managing for excellence in Caribbean hotels. In J.D. Gayle and J.N Goodrich (eds) *Tourism Marketing and Management in The Caribbean* (pp. 102–13). London: Routledge.

Guerrier, Y. (1993) Bali. In T. Baum (ed.) *Human Resource Issues in International Tourism* (pp. 108–15). Oxford: Butterworth-Heinemann.

Guerrier, Y. and Lockwood, A. (1989) Core and peripheral employees in hotel operations. *Personnel Review* 18 (1), 9–15.

Guthunz, U. and Von Krosigk, K. (1996) Tourism development in small island states: From Mirab to Tourab. In L. Bruguglio (ed.) *Sustainable Tourism in Islands and Small States: Issues and Policies* (pp. 34–48). London: Pinter.

Hawkins, D.E. (1983) Global assessment of tourism policy: Process model. In D.G. Pearce and R.W. Butler (eds) *Tourism Research: Critiques and Challenges* (pp. 167–78). London: Routledge.

Inskeep, F. (1991) *Tourism Planning*. Van Nostrand Reinhold, New York.

Jefferson, O. (1975) Some economic aspects of tourism. In *Caribbean Tourism*. Caribbean Tourism Research Centre (now incorporated into the Caribbean Tourism Organization).

Jithendran, K.J. and Baum, T. (2000) Human resource development and sustainability: The case of India. *International Journal of Tourism Research* 2 (6), 403–36.

Keane, M.J., Brophy, P. and Cuddy, M.P. (1992) Strategic management of island tourism *Tourism Management* 13 (4), 406–14.

Lane, B. (1992) *Sustainable Tourism: A Philosophy.* Rural Tourism Unit, Department of Continuing Education, University of Bristol.

Mathieson, A. and Wall, G. (1990) *Tourism: Economic, Physical and Social Impacts,* Harlow: Longman.

McKercher, R. (1993) The unrecognised threat to tourism: Can tourism survive 'sustainability'? *Tourism Management* 14 (2), 131–6.

Murphy, P. (1983) *Tourism: A Community Approach.* New York: Methuen.

Poon, A. (1993) *Tourism, Technology and Competitive Strategies.* Wallingford: CABI.

Williams, G. (1993) Formulating tourism development strategy in Trinidad and Tobago. In J.D. Gayle and J.N. Goodrich (eds) *Tourism Marketing and Management in the Caribbean* (pp. 76–81). London: Routledge.

## Chapter 8

# Competitive Strategies for a 'New Tourism'

AULIANA POON

## Introduction

International tourism is undergoing rapid and radical change – a transformation toward a new industry 'best practice'. This new 'best practice' holds a number of important implications for companies in the tourist industry. It also holds important consequences for developing countries, in Africa, Asia, the Caribbean and the Pacific regions that are growing increasingly dependent on the tourist dollar. This chapter examines the way in which the international tourist industry is being transformed from mass, standardised and rigidly packaged form into a new industry 'best practice' of flexibility, segmentation and diagonal integration. The implications of this new best practice for companies within the tourist industry as well as for destinations are considered.

## A Radically Changing Industry

The radical transformation of the international tourist industry can best be illustrated by what this author describes as 'old tourism' and 'new tourism'. Old tourism is the tourism of the 1950s, 1960s and 1970s. It is characterised by mass, standardised and rigidly packaged holidays, hotels and tourists. 'New tourism' is the tourism of the future. It is characterised by flexibility, segmentation and more authentic tourism experiences. It is also marked by a thrust toward the diagonally integrated organisation and management of the tourist industry, driven by the power of information technology.

### Old tourism

Old tourism was not only mass, it was standardised and rigidly packaged. Mass, standardised and rigidly packaged (MSRP) tourism was created and nurtured by a number of favourable post-war developments (Poon, 1987) These included:

- the arrival of the jet aircraft in 1958;
- promotional fares such as the Advance Purchase Excursion (APEX) fare;
- cheap oil;
- Keynesian-inspired economic growth;
- paid holidays; sun-lust tourists;
- the entry of multinational corporations;
- vertical and horizontal integration; and
- the ubiquitous franchise.

With respect to franchises, and the multinational hotel chains which perpetuated them, it is argued that their growth resulted in 'stultifying homogenization of products and communities. They destroy a sense of community by mass producing environments that minimize personal contacts' (Luxenberg, 1985: 10). By 1972, the 41 World Tourism Organisation (WTO) concluded that:

> the changes that have already taken place and the future investment plans and programmes of numerous travel enterprises leave no doubt that the travel sector will, in the main, be structural on the basis of *large owners* backed by strong financial interest, and in the selling of *standardized packaged deals at low rates to a large clientele*. (WTO, 1972: 39, emphasis added)

Not even sex tourism escaped this phenomenon.

## New tourism

In the 1990s these were already signs that the tourist industry was beginning to take on a different shape. International tourism was responding to, and internalising a number of signals – socially, culturally, technologically, ecologically, economically and institutionally – that emanated from the world environment. One was witnessing a transformation toward a new tourism, a tourism based upon a new 'common sense' or 'best practice' of 'flexibility, segmentation and diagonal integration' (FSDI). This new tourism was created by a number of factors, including:

- the diffusion of a system of new information technologies (SIT) in the tourist industry;
- deregulation of the airline industry and financial services;
- the negative impact of mass tourism on host countries;

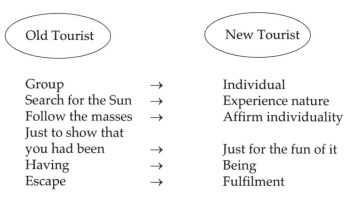

Figure 8.1 Old tourist versus new tourist
Source: *Tourism, Technology and Competitive Strategies,* Poon (1993)

- the movement away from sun-lust to sun-plus tourists;
- environmental pressures;
- technology competition; and
- changing consumer tastes, leisure time, work patterns and income distribution (Poon, 1987).

The factors that are engineering the transformation of the tourist industry can be seen in Figure 8.1. One can observe from this figure that it is the factors that facilitated the creation of mass tourism that have themselves been changing. With these changes come the transformation of the entire industry best practice. It can be seen in Figure 8.1 that the economics of new tourism is very different front the old: profitably no longer rests solely on economies of scale and the exploitation of mass undifferentiated markets. Economies of scope, systems gains, segmented markets, designed and customised holidays are becoming more and more important for profitability and competitiveness in tourism. Traditional managerial and organisational practices of vertical and horizontal integration are also giving way to diagonal integration. Tourists themselves are moving away from 'tinsel and junk' to more, real, natural and authentic experiences. There is also a movement away from mass, impersonalised services to 'high tech, high touch' (Naisbitt, 1984: 64) and there is greater care and concern for and conservation of the natural environment (Krippendorf, 1986). Flexibility, segmentation, diagonal integration and more authentic holiday experiences constitute the new tourism 'best practice' of the future.

## Evolution of a New Tourism Best Practice

The concept of 'best practice' refers to the set of principles and ingrained common sense that guide the everyday practices for profitability and competitiveness of the travel and tourism industry. A new best practice can be readily identified within the new tourism. Four elements of a new best practice are evident – flexibility, segmentation, diagonal integration and the evolution of tourism as a total 'system of wealth-creation'. These are explained below.

### Segmentation

The mass market in tourism is splitting apart. One of the profound changes in the travel marketplace comes from the consumers themselves. Tourists no longer have single, standardised and rigidly packaged wants. They never really had them. Tourists were simply forced by the economics of mass production to consume standardised and rigidly packaged holidays 'en masse'. However, the economics of new tourism allows suppliers to deal more effectively with the increasing complexity and diversity of consumer requirements. New technologies, coupled with diagonal integration, are making it possible to produce flexible and segmented vacations, which are price competitive with mass, standardised holidays (Poon, 1987).

It is interesting to observe, in addition, that segmentation in the travel environment is unique, unprecedented and infinitely more complex. In the past, it was common practice to segment the holiday market along traditional uni-dimensional lines of gender, age and income. Today, one has to be much more sophisticated when markets are segmented. Specifically, cluster segments of the vacation market must be catered to – that is, segments based on clusters of multi-optioned needs and consumer characteristics. This means that the choice is not between sun or sand holidays; young or old; male or female; but rather, exciting holiday combinations that incorporate a cluster of market requirements. For example, vacations must be provided which cater to Double Income No Kids (DINKS) couples, from the sunbelt region of the United States who seek sun plus windsurfing, plus bird watching, plus fresh air, plus Trinidad Carnival. Similarly, vacations tailored to the over–50s couples, who seek sun, plus sailing, plus educational tours, plus walking, plus healthy foods, etc. The key challenge for travel suppliers is to understand the components and composition of these cluster segments and to determine in which clusters an organisation can supply a competitive advantage. Today, in fact, one has to be surgically precise in defining markets. Some examples of these markets are gay and lesbians, vegetarian, sports, weddings and honeymoons, dive market and meetings and conventions.

### Flexibility

Flexibility, as a core element of the new tourism best practice, is reflected at four levels:

(1) Flexibility in the organization.
(2) Production and distribution of travel.
(3) Flexibility in the choice, booking, purchase and payment of holidays.
(4) Flexibility in the consumption and enjoyment of the holiday experience.

These aspects are all inter-linked. Information technology plays a major role in facilitating flexibility in the travel market-place. This is clearly evident in the case of time-share vacations.

Time-share, as its name implies, refers to the purchase of vacation time at a specified tourist resort. It amounts, for example, to owning time (usually one week) at the resort, for a number of years (spanning the life of the unit). The very concept of time-share is limited. It could mean, for example, that a retired couple would be limited to spending their vacation in the same room, in the same resort, in the same country for the rest of their lives. But information technologies have come to the rescue: it is now possible to facilitate the exchange of time and venue among time-sharing vacationers. For example, assuming that the correct matches can be made, it is possible for a couple who own a week in a villa in Spain to exchange this for a different week – at destinations from Tobago to Timbuktu. Information technologies have thus increased the flexibility, choice and variety with which time-share vacation can be produced, marketed and consumed.

Flexibility is also evident in the development of computerised reservation systems (CRS) which allow travel agents to look, book and sell in one call; in teleconferencing which allows meetings and conferences to take place from remote locations; in smart cards which can be used to purchase airline tickets outside normal working hours and outside travel agencies; and satellite printers which automatically deliver airline tickets to corporate offices. Flexibility too, is evident in the proliferation of all-inclusive, club vacations which emphasise a number of informal and flexible ways in which to 'spend' free time. Flexibility will increasingly be a key element of profitability and competitiveness in tourism.

## Diagonal Integration

Diagonal integration is created by new information technologies (computer and communications). It is the process whereby service firms move into new and different activities, with tremendous synergies, systems gains and scope economies to be derived from such integration (Poon, 1986). Synergies are benefits which accrue to the management, operation and organisation of interrelated activities, where each activity is capable of generating benefits that mutually reinforce each other. Each activity adds value to the other, thereby making the whole output greater than the sum of the discrete parts. Systems gains refer to the benefits or economies derived from creating and engineering linkages among design, production, marketing organisation and management. Examples of systems gains are networked activities, where each activity (or subdivision within an organisation) can share a common database or pool of knowledge. Economies of scope refer to the lower costs associated with the joint provision of more than one product or service, rather than producing each separately (Willig, 1979). With economies of scope, the joint production of two goods by one enterprise is less costly than the combined costs of two firms producing either goods 1 or goods 2. Assuming that scope economies existed in the provision of car rentals and hotel bed nights, for example, it would mean that the cost of adding the provision of car rentals to hotel bed nights would be cheaper than producing car rentals alone

The essence of diagonal integration is that 2 + 2 = 5. The economics of diagonal integration will lead to the increasing cross-fertilisation of many on unconventional services, with tremendous implications for travel suppliers. In tourism, therefore, it will no longer be best practice to produce single and unrelated items of tourism output. It is increasingly common sense to produce clusters of interrelated services (which may not all be tourism-specific) which are integrated into a total system of wealth creation. Perhaps the best way of defining diagonal integration is to explain what it is not. Table 8.1 explains the differences among vertical integration, horizontal integration, diversification and diagonal integration.

## Tourism as a Total System of Wealth Creation

One corollary of diagonal integration is that tourism is becoming a total system of wealth creation. In other words, wealth in tourism is created through the diagonal and synergistic integration of a number of activities into a total system. Within this total system of wealth creation, a computer and communications infrastructure provides the critical foundation from which a number of services can be spawned.

The fundamental backbone of this system of wealth creation is intelligence and information, i.e. the intelligent transaction in, and manipulation of, information. Information, as well as its intelligent manipulation, is of critical importance to the tourist industry – that is for understanding, ma-

**Table 8.1** Diagonal integration compared with other forms of integration

| Forms of Integration | | | | |
|---|---|---|---|---|
| Characteristics | Vertical integration | Horizontal integration | Diversification | Diagonal integration |
| Production focus | Many stages of production | Same stage of production | Many unrelated activities | Many tightly-related services |
| Objectives of integration | Control over stages of production | Monopoly power/ concentration | Spread risks | Get close to the consumer/ Lower costs of production |
| Integration mechanism | Acquisition/ start new businesses | Acquisition/ collusion | Acquisition/ start new activities | Information partnerships Strategic alliances Strategic acquisitions |
| Operational-ization | Integrated production and management | Operate as one entity | 'Arms Length' | Synergistic production/ shared networks |
| Orientation of production | Production-oriented | Supply-oriented | Investment-oriented | Consumer-oriented |
| Production concept | Economies of scale | Economies of scale | Production unrelated to markets | Economies of scale Economies of scope Synergies/ systems gains |

*Source: Tourism, Technology and Competitive Strategies, Poon (1993)*

nipulating and profitably satisfying the tourism market. The economics governing this system of wealth creation is very powerful. This can be seen both from the demand and supply imperatives of the system.

On the supply side, investment in a telecommunications infrastructure results in diminishing marginal costs with increasing utilisation. A computer-reservation system (CRS), for example, can market a number of travel services including airline and hotel reservations, flower and champagne services, cruises, car rental, restaurant bookings, etc. The beauty of these CRS however, is that once an initial investment is made in a computer and communications infrastructure, another group of services can be added at little or no marginal costs to the provider. Lastminute.com, for example certainly realises this. Since the users (travel agents) and other suppliers (co-hosts) pay market prices, rather than marginal cost prices, profitability to the suppliers (hosts) of the system is very great.

On the demand side, the wealth-creating potential of the tourism system lies in the character of demand for its output, i.e. the combinational and the lifetime character of demand for tourism and other related services. Travel is not consumed like washing machines, where relatively few purchases fix the need. Rather, it is purchased over one's lifetime. Travel, moreover, is not purchased by itself. It is usually purchased in combination with a number of other services such as travellers cheques, credit, insurance, investment services, ground tours etc. The profitability potential of producing and marketing a cluster of services which are effectively demanded by a targeted group of consumers is tremendous. Indeed, the economics of producing a whole range of services to a targeted market is different from providing the same item to a supermarket of clients. This American Express discovered a long time ago.

## Information Technology – a Vital Pillar of the New Tourism

In tourism, it is not a computer or a telephone or videotext that is being diffused, but a whole system of these technologies, based upon microelectronics (see Figure 8.2). The 'system of information technologies' (SIT) comprises computers, computerised reservation systems, digital telephone networks, videos, videotext (viewdata in the United States),

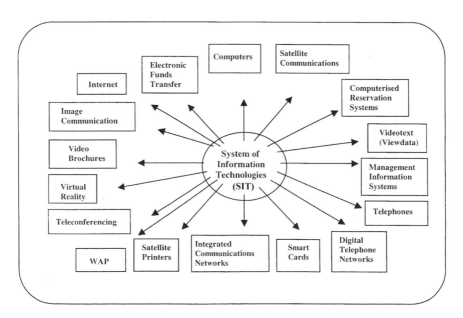

**Figure 8.2** The system of information technologies in tourism
*Source: Tourism, Technology and Competitive Strategies, Poon (1993)*

interactive videotext, teleconferencing, management information systems, energy management, and electronic locking systems. Moreover, this system of technologies is not being used by airline, or hotels or travel agents, but by all of them.

The diffusion of the system of information technologies in tourism will increase the efficiency, quality and flexibility with which travel services are supplied. It has already led to the generation of new services (teleconferencing, interactive videotext, video brochures and the Internet). Technology will have the greatest impact on the marketing and distribution of travel but will leave relatively untouched the human–intensive areas of guest–host relations and supplier consumer relationships (Poon, 1988b). Information technologies applied to the tourism system will increase the efficiency and quality of services provided and lead to new combinations of tourism services. This will be achieved without changing the manifestly human 'high touch' content of travel (Poon, 1988c).

It is the systematic use of the system of information technologies by all tourism suppliers, together with its profound impact on the travel industry that allows information technologies to create the foundation for a new tourism best practice and produce a total system of 'wealth creation'.

## Implications of the New Tourism Common Sense

### Competitors come from outside the industry

One of the implications of the diagonally integrating practices of companies and the evolution of tourism as a total system of wealth creation is that a firm's competitors will increasingly come from outside the tourism industry. This means that a firm's competitive advantages can be eroded not by obvious, readily identifiable competitors within its own market segment or industry, but from the entry of firms from completely unpredictable places (e.g. banks, telecommunication suppliers or real estate agents). This is clearly evident in the United Kingdom's travel market, for example, where banks, telecommunications providers and software companies have entered the travel market. The competitive threat of these suppliers that come from outside the traditional boundaries of the travel industry is potentially very great because firms from outside bring different experiences, resources, client bases and competitive strengths to the travel industry. In responding to increased competition from the outside, two complementary avenues are open to travel suppliers – industry monitoring and cross-fertilisation of travel services.

In the first option, systems of information provision, intelligence gathering, research and development, and market monitoring are necessary. Firms must be continuously on the lookout for changes and new developments, not just in their own market segment or industry, but from the entire tourism system. Information about markets and competitors must be intelligently utilised to render and reinforce competitive advantage.

Cross-fertilisation of services also provides an important opportunity for survival and competitiveness in the travel industry. In other words, just as other suppliers are entering the travel industry, travel suppliers must creatively enter other areas. This practice of cross-fertilisation is already being adopted by travel suppliers as they attempt to respond creatively and competitively to an increasingly dynamic, complex and changing travel environment.

### Innovation holds the key to survival and competitiveness

Survival within the transformed and continuously changing travel industry means that innovation is needed in order to survive. In today's tourism marketplace, a firm has virtually to run in order to stand still. Innovation is the essence of being creative and bringing new ideas and tourism services to the marketplace. Innovation must, however, be interpreted in the true Schumpeterian sense – encompassing innovations in goods, services, markets, methods of production, organizations, and sources of raw material (Schumpeter, 1965). It is necessary, therefore, to be totally innovative – not just in the marketing or vacation concepts, but also in the organisation, product blending, packaging, management of tourism (Poon, 1988a). A stand-alone or de-linked innovation is not likely to be as potent as a cluster of innovations related to different spheres of a firm's operation.

Innovation must not only be total; it must also be continuous. Indeed a company cannot hope to produce a single innovation and expect it to provide sustainable competitive advantages. The innovation itself has to be sustainable. With innovation, however, sustainability usually implies more innovation. Competitiveness then warrants the origination and sustenance of continuous clusters of innovation. A detailed comparative analysis of the Jamaican SuperClub hotel chain and the Benetton clothing concern in Italy revealed unambiguously that the ability of these organisations to evolve continuous clusters of innovation were vital ingredients in the success of both enterprises (Poon, 1988a).

### Get closer to the consumer

The complexity and unpredictability of tourists, coupled with the increasing diversity of their needs, mean that producers will have to get even closer to their customers. This closeness will be necessary in order to understand consumer demand, monitor its pattern and satisfy it competitively and at a profit.

A profound understanding of complex requirements, expectations and desires of consumers as well as their time and budget constraints is vital. Creating a travel option simply because it is sophisticated, or because the technology is available, or because the firm has some unused capacity simply will not work. Any innovation, new idea or concept must be grounded in the marketplace. It has to reflect the effective needs and requirements of consumers. It also has to be properly marketed in order to reach the target group. In this regard, choice of advertising mode and media is also important.

## Match the firm's skills and resources with the marketplace

While it is important to understand the travel market, to be creative and to utilize new information technologies, these activities constitute only half of the tourism profitability and competitiveness equation. The other half of the equation is related to the actual endowments of the firm, and how suited they are to the new requirements of the travel market-place. In other words, a firm may he very creative in thinking about a new service for the travel market; a proven demand for the service may exist; and the technology and software may be available to bring the new service to the market. However, the venture could fail if there is not a good match between the competitive strengths and resources of the enterprise and the requirements of the new travel services. New travel services as well as cross-fertilisations must be spawned from resources and competitive strengths already developed and acquired by a firm, (e.g. reputation, information, intelligence, vision, financial assets, software, skilled manpower. It is very easy to run into dis-economies of capital, skills and resources if an optimal match does not exist between the marketplace and the capabilities of a firm.

This is a very important point which should not be overlooked. Since the tourism system and its ancillary services are so complex and interrelated, just about any activity within the system can be perceived as related to any other (for example, hotels and theme parks; theme parks and cruise ships). Moreover, information technologies can easily make it possible to link just about any activity – from hotels to portfolio management – into a total system of wealth creation. However, this will not necessarily lead to market success.

The difficulty lies in the fact that for any given firm, this cross-fertilisation (diagonally integrating) process can be severely limited by the availability of human intelligence, skills, finance and other resources (political connections, contacts and information), some, all, or none of which a firm may possess. This seems to be the case with the Mariott hotel chain, for example, which succeeded in diversifying into restaurants and hotels but 'largely failed in gourmet restaurants, theme parks, cruise ships and wholesale travel agencies' (Porter, 1987: 56). Understanding the market, therefore, only constitutes half of the tourism profitability equation. The second half relates to harnessing the skills, resources and competitive strengths of the firm (augmenting them where necessary) to satisfy the market.

## Summary

International tourism is in metamorphosis and a new tourism is emerging – a tourism that promises flexibility, segmentation and diagonal integration; a tourism driven by information technologies and changing consumer requirements; a tourism that will produce an entire system of wealth creation. This new tourism has a number of profound implications for survival and competitiveness in the industry: competitors will increasingly come from outside the tourist industry; suppliers must get closer to the consumer; and firms have to match their skills and resources with the marketplace. Innovation holds the key to future survival and competitiveness in the dynamic and radically changing tourism environment.

## Note
1. This chapter first appeared as 'Competitive strategies for a new tourism' in Volume 1 of *Progress in Tourism, Recreation and Hospitality Management* (1989) pp. 91–102.

## Bibliography
Bush, M. (1984) *The Age of Market Segmentation – New Opportunities in Today's Market Place:* A special presentation at the American Society of Travel Agents' World Travel Congress, Las Vegas, Nevada, November.

Krippendorf, J. (1986) Tourism and the system of industrial society. *Annals of Tourism Research* 313 (4), 393–414.

Luxenberg, S. (1985) *Roadside Empires: How The Chains Franchised America.* New York: Viking.

Maccannell, D. (1973) Staged authenticity: Arrangements of social space for tourist settings. *American Journal of Sociology* 79, 589–603.

Mckean, P.F. (1978) Towards a theoretical analysts of tourism, economic dualism and cultural involution in Bali. In V.L. Smith (ed.) *Hosts and Guests: The Anthropology of Tourism,* London: Basil Blackwell.

Naisbitt, L. (1984) *Megatrends: Ten New Directions Transforming Our Lives.* London: Macdonald.

Noronha, R. (1977) *Social and Cultural Dimension, of Tourism: A Review of the IT Literature in English.* IBRD Draft Working Papers, May. Washington, DC: International Bank for Reconstruction and Development.

Poon, A. (1986) Diagonal integration – a new commonsense for tourism and services. Paper presented to the Fourth Annual Seminar on the Service Economy hosted by PROGRES Research on the Service Economy, Geneva, 30, 31 May, 1 June 1988.

Poon, A. (1987) Information technology and innovation in international tourism – implications for the Caribbean tourism industry. Unpublished PhD thesis, Science Policy Research Unit, University of Sussex, Brighton.

Poon, A. (1988a) *Flexible Specialization and Small Size – The Case of Caribbean Tourism.* Science Policy Research Unit, DRC Discussion Papers 57, February.

Poon, A. (1988b) The future of Caribbean tourism – A matter of innovation. *Tourism Management* 9 (3), 213–20.

Poon, A. (1988c) Information technology and tourism – Ideal bedfellow. *Annals of Tourism Research* 5 (4), 531–49.

Poon, A. (1993) *Tourism, Technology and Competitive Strategies.* Wallingford: CAB International.

Porter, M. (1987) From competitive advantage to corporate strategy. *Harvard Business Review* (May/June), 43–59.

Porter, M (1985) Technology and competitive advantage. *Journal of Business Strategy* (Winter), 60–78.

Schumpeter, J. (1965) *The Theory of Economic Development: An Enquiry Into Profit, Interest and the Business Cycle.* Oxford: Oxford University Press.

Turner, L. and Ash, J. (1975) *The Golden Hordes: International Tourism and the Pleasure Periphery.* London: Constable.

World Tourism Organization (1972) *Economic Review of World Tourism: A Study of the Economic Impact of Tourism on National Economies and International Trade.* Madrid: WTO.

Willig, R.I. (1979) Multiproduct technology and market structure. *American Economic Review, Papers and Proceedings* 346–51.

## Chapter 9

# Urban Tourism: Still an Imbalance in Attention?

GREGORY ASHWORTH

### Introduction: Was There an Imbalance?

The argument of the original 1988 paper in 'Progress' was simply that although academic interest in tourism had more or less paralleled its growth, this attention was, in at least one dimension, distinctly unbalanced (Ashworth, 1988). The paper argues that cities were the origin of most tourists and the destination of many. Much of the tourism industry was centred in cities even if rural attractions were part of the holiday package and the aggregate economic and social impacts of tourism were higher in urban than in rural areas. In a rapidly urbanising world this is not very surprising. However, surprise was expressed that despite this, the study of urban tourism did not exist in terms of specifically urban characteristics and attributes being recognised as creating a distinctive urban tourism product and experience in the same way as beach tourism and winter sports tourism. This mismatch between the study of tourism and the reality of the tourism industry was explained by the existence of a double neglect: those studying tourism neglected cities while those studying cities neglected tourism. The first proposition could be argued from the academic and policy literature itself; the second from the absence of such literature.

Stansfield (1964) was the first to draw attention to the almost exclusively rural focus of tourism studies and also the first to try to remedy this by identifying recreation business districts in cities. That tourism was seen as dominantly a temporary urban to rural migration can be illustrated by what must be the first spatial model specifically focused upon tourism, namely that proposed by the father of urban spatial modelling himself, Christaller (1966). Here tourism was added to the settlement networks, hierarchies and market areas as a function of the periphery. This idea has enjoyed a long, and probably continuing, application in the discovery and

143

mapping of various 'pleasure peripheries' around cities. 'Dart-board' models of recreational zones based usually on travel times were produced with the city as the origin of demand, usually reduced to a dot in the centre of a nodal region (Miossec, 1977; Yokeno, 1968).

Geographers in particular had come to an interest in tourism mostly through recreation studies – which itself originated largely from an interest in land economics, land-use and even nature conservation. Tourism was added to recreation just as a subcategory of leisure activity. Many courses in geography departments, and thus many of the textbooks, are still entitled 'A geography of recreation and tourism' (e.g. Hall & Page, 1999). This is thus not only a reflection of the historical origin of much of tourism study but also demonstrates the continuing inability of researchers to separate tourism from recreation. In retrospect, it could now be argued further that this was not just a neglect explainable, and excusable, though an historical accident of the development of academic disciplines. It was a symptom of a deep-seated anti-urban bias that was especially prevalent in the Western, English-speaking world. If cities are places for the serious tasks of work and government, then recreation – whether as rest or as the pursuit of more morally worthy rewards than wealth – must be sought elsewhere. For example, the social class bias that pervaded the establishment of the National Parks in England in the 1940s as places where the city's 'huddled masses' should engage in approved forms of outdoor recreation in selected landscapes is now more obvious than it was. Government provided moral and financial support for allotment gardens, green belts, country parks, nature trails and the like rather than for traditional urban leisure activities, whether sport or entertainment. The assumption was that not only cities were for work and the countryside for leisure, but also that a country rambler was to be encouraged and an urban flaneur was not. Geographers and planners not only accepted this official lead, and thus definition of the research agenda, they were themselves often a messianic part of it. The pioneering texts such as Dower's *Fourth Wave* (1965), Patmore's *Land and Leisure* (1970) and Coppock and Duffield's *Recreation in the Countryside* (1975) now read quite differently than they did on publication (see Glyptis' (1993) retrospective volume on this period).

The proposition that those studying cities neglected tourism was explained in my original 1988 paper by three related characteristics of urban tourism, all of which still seem as relevant. First, the tourist in the city was largely invisible. All cities are multifunctional, or they would not qualify as cities. Even resort towns are still towns and in most cities tourism was a marginal extra activity. If the tourist is invisible in all but a few selected districts of a very few remarkable cities at specific times then the study of tourist behaviour, tourism facilities, tourism impacts whether economic or social, and even the policy implications of tourism development will be itself of marginal interest in urban studies. A paradox is that tourism is proportionately least important in those cities attracting most tourists in absolute numbers. The large 'showcase' metropolitan centres, such as London and Paris, may accommodate more foreign tourists than their rural surroundings or even whole countries, yet their tourism industry is still a small proportion of their total economy. Conversely, tourism was likely to be proportionately dominant in small towns where the actual numbers and their economic importance were relatively small.

Secondly, and in part consequently, tourism is a poor indicator of intra-urban regionalisation. Attempts to delineate tourism districts resulted either in a fruitless search for the exclusively tourist, which was not to be found outside a holiday camp or theme park, or more usually the addition of the word tourism to other urban districts such as those for entertainment or culture.

Thirdly, and again in part derived from the above arguments, the invisibility of urban tourism and the near impossibility of demarcating it rendered it too difficult to study. Stansfield argued in 1964, reflecting the then current geographical fashion for quantification, that tourism was not quantifiable in cities as it was more readily in rural areas. Thus if you cannot count it then it does not exist, or at least should not be studied by 'real' scientists. This sounds an absurd exaggeration. However, if tourism could not be isolated as a function or set of facilities, the tourist not identified as a distinctly behaving and motivated individual and the 'tourism industry' was clearly not identifiable and located in space in the same way as other industries, then the neglect by urban studies becomes explainable if not excusable. Tourism in cities, whether analysed from the side of uses or users, was so embedded in the city as a whole that the 'tourist city' could only be conceived alongside and overlapping with, other 'cities' as shown in the much quoted Figure 9.1.

The brief of this chapter is not just to restate these arguments but to assess the extent to which they still apply. At the time, the charge of neglect was almost self-evidently true: no contradictory position was advanced in response to it. Some observers of tourism expressed surprise at the neglect; most accepted it as obvious but no one denied its existence, although it was suggested that this was more evidently a North American than continental European phenomenon (Jansen-Verbeke, 1990a). The answers sought here are to the questions: 'Does urban studies continue to neglect tourism and does tourism studies continue to neglect the city?'

The fundamental context for an investigation of the possible corrections to this spatial imbalance is that the urbanisation of the world has continued,

USERS
(demand)

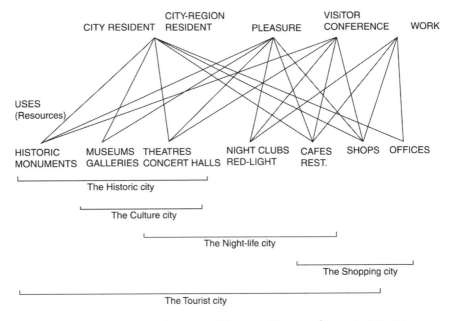

**Figure 9.1** Some users and users of the city (Burtenshaw *et al.*1991)

most strongly outside Europe and North America, and that cities have continued to increase their importance as places where tourism occurs.

## Is There Now an Urban Tourism?

The fragmentation of tourism studies is reflected in the use of the plural in the journal *Tourism Geographies* (1999), which does no more than echo the general rise in the importance of the study of 'adjectival tourisms'. In this context is there now a place for urban tourism? Adding the adjective urban to the activity noun tourism merely locates the activity in a geographical scene. 'If we already have 'mountain tourism' 'wilderness tourism' or 'seaside tourism' then surely urban tourism is equally a valid possibility' (Ashworth, 1992a:3). However, this leads either to further generally pointless refinements on the details of the spatial location such as 'metropolitan', 'suburban', 'peri-urban' or 'inner city'. More profoundly, such geographical descriptions do not in themselves help to focus the discussion on the urban nature of urban tourism. All activities occur somewhere: the important question is whether this somewhere is 'defining' or merely 'accommodating' the activity. The question should not be 'Does tourism occur in cities?' but 'What is particularly urban about urban tourism?' and; 'Which special characteristics of all or some cities are relevant to which kinds of tourism?'

Answers to the last question lead to the identification and analysis of 'cultural city tourism' (and its derivatives such as 'festival city tourism'), 'historic city tourism' (and all its many variants such as 'gem city tourism') and the like. Alternatively, does urban imply a range of activities different from rural so that urban tourism encompasses other activities such as shopping, gastronomy, cultural collections and performances, entertainment and many more that could be considered to belong specifically to cities.

In the past few years a number of textbooks specifically on urban tourism have appeared giving strong support to the notion that urban tourism now exists as a recognised and useful sub-discipline within tourism studies. In addition, there are some comparative studies of cities, such as Costa and Borg (1993), Borg (1994), Law (1993; 1995; 1996), Page (1993), Vanderborg (1996) and many individual case descriptions of urban tourism in Page (1992), Berg *et al.* (1995), Borg *et al.* (1996) and Borg (1998). The most notable books have been written by authors with an academic background in geography who thus are aware of the nature and role of the spatial setting. The most ambitious of these is Page (1995) which is uncompromisingly entitled *Urban Tourism* and which attempts to summarise for students all aspects of tourism in all types of cities. Law's (1995) book is more modest in that it confines itself to large cities and upon the economic roles of tourism in urban development. Both, however, find it logically impossible to explain urban tourism other than in the wider context of the functioning and management of cities as a whole. They both therefore become studies of urban planning and management in general and thus inevitably more concerned with the urban than the tourism.

The original 1988 paper was structured by four 'approaches' which provided a framework for analysis or at least a series of handy containers into which existing literature could be sorted. This sorting frame reflected the academic preoccupations of the time, especially in geography, and is not so apposite as it was. Human geography in particular was then dominantly concerned with either locational analysis ('where and why there?') or regionalisation ('can areal patterns be identified and mapped?). These concerns were reflected in the 'facility' and 'ecological' approaches. However, the contexts of both academic interest and policy are now significantly different from that of the 1970s and early 1980s. Current interests have focused much more on behaviour, phenomenology and management, which makes the last two approaches, namely that of 'users' and 'policy', more relevant than they were. This chapter will keep the original framework of approaches but inevitably will alter the balance and ultimately cannot refrain from adding some 'missing approaches'.

## Facility Approaches: In Search of the Tourism Facility

Perhaps an early phase of any new field of scientific endeavour involves taxonomic classification systems and inventorisations in an attempt to isolate the object of study. Certainly, most 'geographies of tourism' in the 1970s and 1980s were concerned with identifying, classifying, listing and counting tourism facilities. As many of these were inevitably located in cities, or were more easily exemplified by cities, it is not surprising that these sorts of studies, typified by Wall and Sinnot (1980), filled the reference list of the 1988 article. Not only were hotels, restaurants and historic buildings duly counted but so also were 'bed-spaces', 'restaurant seats' and even square metres of available space in historic cathedrals. Certainly, many subsequent studies have pursued this approach, concentrating upon inventorising and quantifying those urban facilities exclusively or dominantly used in tourism, or deliberately promoted as part of tourism products. Even then, however, it was difficult to take seriously many of the scrupulously researched attempts at inventorisation and quantification, because the facilities used by tourists were also to a greater or lesser degree also used by residents.

Attempts to move from locational description to explanation did result in the production of some location models, of which the most widely used subsequently has been the typology of urban hotel locations. This has been applied generally (Pearce, 1995; 1997), in medium-sized towns (Pearce, 1987) and in various national (Groote, 1987) or continental European contexts (Burtenshaw et al., 1991). North American studies have modelled urban-periphery hotel clusters in both the US (Wyckoff, 1992) and Canada (Bloomfield, 1996), and have related accommodation more generally to urban models (De Bres, 1994). Other urban tourism facilities modelled in this way have included shopping (Jansen-Verbeke, 1990b; 1991; 1994; English Historic Towns Forum, 1992), and cultural attractions (Townsend, 1992; Phelps, 1994).

Facility inventories and locational models were often related to comments upon urban tourism policy. The idea that resource surveys should precede industrial studies was prevalent and led to perhaps the single most used management tool in tourism, that of tourism carrying capacity, itself an idea, to revert to an earlier argument, imported from rural studies. If tourists were thought of as livestock and cities as pasture then it would be possible to calculate an optimum capacity which maximised tourism numbers in a sustainable way (although the word 'sustainable' was not yet in vogue). Numerous facility studies of cities were made through the 1980s in the hope that definitive figures of acceptable numbers of tourists could be calculated and which would then form the basis of local policy. Work on Venice was perhaps the most thorough, the most directly linked to various policy initiatives but also given the physical situation of this city, the least widely replicable (Borg, 1990, 1998). It was ultimately realised, however, that the capacity of tourism facility supply in cities was incalculable and not an aggregate of the calculable capacity of specific facilities at specific locations. In any event, demand and supply were not independent variables and that if capacity was largely a result of management and not an instrument independent of it, then it could not also be used as a guide to management strategy.

The conclusion even then was that this facility approach in general, despite its diligence and prodigious productivity, was getting nowhere because the separation necessary for this form of analysis made understanding urban processes almost impossible. Such a comment seems even more relevant now.

## Ecological Approaches: In Search of the Tourism City

One reaction to the futility of isolating supply features was the attempt to reintegrate tourism as a function into regions within the city. This led to what I then termed urban ecological approaches, in order to emphasis integration with the wider forms and functions of the city and contrast with the countervailing tendency to isolate the phenomenon of tourism. Even in 1988 it was noted that this came into vogue in tourism at the same time as it was becoming unfashionable in urban geography. It can be traced to two main origins, each of which goes back to the initial attempts of geographers to examine leisure. The logic of the Stansfield argument was that if a, so far undiscovered, urban tourism exists then it must be identifiable in intra-urban regions in the same way as only a few years earlier the 'Central Business District' had been discovered and mapped. This led to the delineation of 'Recreational Business District' (Stansfield & Rickert, 1970; Taylor, 1975) and later the 'Central Tourism District' alongside other functional areas such as shopping, office or nightlife entertainment districts. This search for the 'tourism city' as a definable functional region within the city, has been continued (Dewailly, 1990; Smith, 1991; Herbin, 1995), and the idea of the 'Tourism Business District' has been pursued (Meyer-Arendt, 1990; Getz, 1993). Variants that stretch the definition of the tourist more widely include the demarcation of restaurants and cafe districts (Chemla, 1990; Oosterman, 1993), entertainment districts (Burtenshaw et al., 1991; Ashworth, 1996) and recreational and souvenir shopping areas (Jansen, 1989; Jansen-Verbeke, 1990b, 1991, 1994; Pearce, 1995).

A second and quite independent line of enquiry, which also resulted in intra-urban regions, emerged from the study of seaside holiday resorts which had been a largely continental European preoccupation. For about 30 years from the early 1960s (from Defert 1966 to Faché, 1995) land-use models of seaside resorts had been created and these in many cases even outlasted the tourism significance of the actual resorts that inspired them. Although such ideas were first applied mostly to seaside resorts, similar models were proposed for winter sports resorts and spa towns: in all of which there was an economic and spatial dominance of tourism, and in all of which the type of city was seen as exceptional.

Stemming directly from this line of thought was the tourist-historic city model that was first produced in 1985 (Ashworth & de Haan, 1985) as a sort of inland variant on the then well-known, seaside resort models. It developed, however, quite differently and unexpectedly, largely because the tourist in the historic city was more diverse in motive and behaviour than the seaside holidaymaker. The resulting tourist city is thus not an exceptional kind of city, or even a homogeneous and exclusive mono-functional area within cities. It is a pattern of clustered sets of functional associations that describes the regionalisation of the activity of tourism in cities in general; thus allowing the tourist city to be compared to a wide variety of other possible 'cities'. The tourist-historic city model was not only applied world-wide, from Kansas cow towns to Japanese castle towns, but in the course of the 1990s, it spawned a whole family of derivative variants based upon the characteristics of the cities themselves, such as tourist historic waterfronts (Tunbridge & Ashworth, 1992), 'gem' cities, tourist-historic urban networks and regions. A comparison of Ashworth and Tunbridge (1990) with Ashworth and Tunbridge (2000) illustrates a shift way from regionalisation towards policy issues which relate more to the place of tourism within urban planning and management than to the role of cities within tourism policy.

## User Approaches: In Search of the Urban Tourist

The peopling of the locational and ecological models with tourists seemed in 1988 to be the most pressing necessity. The questions, 'who?', 'what?' and 'why?' had rarely been posed and never satisfactorily answered. Tourism statistics could demonstrate that cities were the most important destination for inter-continental visitors, among the two most important destinations for all foreign tourists and one of the important destinations for domestic tourists. But who exactly these visitors were could only be described in very general demographic, social class and locational terms and their motives could only be inferred from their location choices.

A strong plea was made in 1988 for studies of tourist behaviour within cities as this was the essential link between tourism facilities and tourism demands. There was then only the vaguest idea about this and only a handful of case studies in the literature. This existing work was richer in the local detail of a city than in informed comparative generalisation between cities. The starting point for this analysis of the tourist was generally that visitors, compared to locals, have more restricted knowledge and expectations and also thus practical constraints of time and mobility. Because tourists by definition have more limited time and generally less familiarity with local access and transport than residents, their action-space is more confined. This makes the understanding of time-space budgets of visitors in the city easier but also promises a potentially very powerful instrument for the management of visitors within the city. Understanding how tourists move around within cities provides not only information essential for reacting to their impacts, it also presents local managers with a potent method of influencing this behaviour. The very constraints on time and local knowledge, and the dependence on local marketing, provide the opportunity of using signage, trails and other information as an active management tool in the pursuit of improvements in the urban tourism experience as well as wider local planning objectives. Understandably therefore it has been the local urban managers, for example those operating within city centre management programmes, who have built up detailed local knowledge of tourist behaviour and its reaction to local management techniques rather than academics studying tourism as a spatio-social phenomenon. Among the latter, however, has been the notable work of Dietvorst on tourist behaviour in small Dutch tourist-historic cities (1994) and tourism regions (1995), and Flognfeldt (1996) and Jansen-Verbeke and Rekom (1996) on the wider urban behaviour of museum visitors.

In contrast to the paucity of informative studies on what visitors actually do in cities there was always a strong research line focusing on why they do it. The sociologists of tourism, led by MacCannell (1976), Cohen (1979), Dann (1981) and others who although they often disagreed among themselves nevertheless have laid a foundation for studies of visitor motives, attitudes and perceptions. This has been advanced by the renaissance of interest, among geographers in particular, in culture. As social and cultural geography has blossomed so has the interest in tourism as a reflection and expression of cultural values, identities and attitudes (e.g. Kinnaird & Hall, 1994; Shaw & Williams, 1994). Much of this has inevitably focused upon cities. However, it is evident that almost all of these studies use tourism to explain culture, not culture to explain tourism. There are often valuable insights usable in the analysis and management of urban tourism, but these are frequently not explicitly self-evident.

A fundamental assumption of both the industrial paradigm and the academic critics of that approach is that tourists are different from locals. For if they are not then there is little to be gained from studying them. Most studies not only depended upon the existence of this difference, they tended to focus upon it as the most significant aspect of tourist behaviour and consequent policy and management. However, trends in the nature of both tourism demand and tourism supply are rendering this distinction less tenable. Recent attention to 'special interest' tourism has overlooked the reality that cities have always offered a wide range of products and experiences to visitors and have always been capable of very rapid diversification in product supply. What seems to be now occurring is that visitors are pursuing while on holiday activities and interests that they also have at home. Expressed differently, our Western lifestyles have become more leisure oriented and defined and therefore the holiday becomes an extension of the home life, not a contrast to it. The tourist is then just a resident away from home: the resident is just a tourist between trips. If this is the case then the fundamental distinction between tourists and residents that has underpinned many behavioural studies fades away. Interestingly, many tourism studies dependent upon strong differences between the tourist and the local resident have been set in areas of the world where such differences are most pronounced. However, it can be argued that these studies, which tend to dominate anthropologies of tourism, are untypical. Most tourism flows are between origins and destinations that differ little in levels of economic, social or cultural development. The implications of this for future work on the users of the tourism city is not clear but it threatens to remove one of the easier frameworks of analysis.

## Policy Approaches: In Search of Urban Tourism Policies

A history of urban tourism policy would have to recognise that most cities, most of the time, have neither consciously developed such policies nor felt any particular need to do so. Tourism policy has generally been no more than *ad hoc* management strategies in the private as well as public sectors. There is a view that the accommodation of visitors is a traditional mundane urban function which, like the weather, cannot be influenced by local action. If there have always been and will always be tourists, why bother with tourism policy? Indeed the cynic could argue from historical cases that the success stories of urban tourism have occurred in the absence of policy, while policy has only been devised in the face of looming failure and thus the existence of a comprehensive local tourism policy is a good indicator of trouble. London, with no co-ordinated policy, little central public investment, and no unambiguous promotion far outstripped Paris, which had all of these in the 1970s to 1990s, in foreign visitor numbers (London Tourism Board, 1990; Pearce, 1997, 1999). Similarly Amsterdam without policy became a major international tourism centre in the 1960s and 1970s but devised a stream of local policies in the 1980s and 1990s as its tourism position was undermined and overtaken by Brussels. (These pairs of competitive cases are discussed in Ashworth & Tunbridge (2000)).

I have previously tried to argue that local public policies for tourism have followed the sequence, 'Everybody happy', Nobody happy', 'Everybody reconciled'. Unfortunately for the sake of temporal simplicity it has rarely proved to be so straightforward. The 'everybody happy' policies that were dominant until the 1970s keep re-emerging, although now not without challenge (Law, 1992; Jansen-Verbeke & Wiel, 1995). They depend upon a naive assumption of harmony between cities and tourism best expressed as the existence of a 'windfall gain model'. This assumes that tourism resources already exist for other purposes and are subsequently utilised for constructing products for sale on new tourism markets with beneficial local impacts which appear to deliver gain without cost. Tourists fill otherwise empty museums, galleries and monuments, as well as the tills of shops, restaurants and hotels. The tourism industry, constantly in search of new products to satisfy fickle demand, welcomes the offer of ubiquitous, often zero-priced, freely accessible, flexible and infinitely packagable urban resource. Tourism offers a profitable return on the use of a free existing resource with the additional benefits of enhanced local identity, social cohesion and favourable market images. It is assumed that extra consumption does not diminish or damage the resource, that an increase in one group of consumers does not lead to a diminution in access for others, and that the benefits and the costs accrued will be experienced equally by each of the parties involved. None of these assumptions is universally correct and the model is thus untenable in the longer term except in exceptional circumstances.

Local policies that could be labelled 'nobody happy' depended upon the reverse of the assumptions of automatic harmony, and were probably a reaction to them, namely automatic conflict between cities and tourism. Urban tourism development was cast as free-riding, irresponsible exploiter (Cheng, 1990), polluter (Jansen-Verbeke (1990c), irritator of residents (Dalibard, 1988), bowdleriser (Horne, 1984), commercialiser (Hewison, 1987), empoverisher (Mossetto, 1991), prostituter (Pfafflin, 1987) and many more villanous roles, of the city. These denigrating 'antigrockle' sentiments are not particularly recent (as Hunter & Green (1995) for example, have pointed out). The tourist in the city has always been both esteemed and despised, courted as opportunity and repelled as threat. The result has been an ambiguity in local policy which at the level of the individual city frequently resulted in policy that was little more than the management of actual or potential conflict.

A paradox, of course, is that the magnitude and type of tourism flows are more easily influenced at national level and largely uncontrollable at the local level. Cities have only very limited power to pick and choose their visitors (despite Borg's policy analysis and many suggestions for Venice (Borg, 1990, 1998)). However, tourism behaviour within the city is very amenable and responsive to local planning, marketing and management (see, among other examinations, Page, 1989; Jansen-Verbeke, 1992, 1997; Tyler et al., 1997). It is therefore not surprising that cities such as Venice (Westlake & White, 1992; Borg, 1998), Oxford (Glasson, 1994) or Canterbury (Page, 1992) have often viewed tourism as a planning problem to be contained, not a strategic opportunity to be welcomed. These are perhaps extreme, but inevitable, occurrences when the European heritage, concentrated in specific limited areas of historic towns, is visited by those on whose behalf, and with whose finance, it has been conserved.

However, the assumptions of automatic conflict are as naive as the assumptions of automatic harmony and were easier to justify in rural areas than in cities. They assume among others that:

- urban tourism resources are in fixed supply so that increases in demand lead automatically to a diminution of the resource;
- that the tourist use is essentially different, and by implication less worthy, from non-tourist uses; and
- that tourism as an economic activity should be evaluated on a different basis from other local economic activities.

Given both the continuing need for a mutually profitable symbiosis among the participants but also the increasingly evident context of conflict, it is not surprising that there has been a search for a new symbiosis in an 'everybody reconciled' policy. The idea of sustainable development was thus eagerly seized upon by the tourism industry, the resource providers and the destination place managers as a welcome solution and escape from the impasse. If sustainability is used as both a political commitment and a set of applicable management techniques, then we can all return to a previous state of profitable harmony without compromising the resource base.

Most European countries produced a spate of official documentation, usually using the word 'sustainable' in the title, that explored these issues in cities. In Britain the 'Tourism and Environment Task Force' of national agencies provided in 1991 accounts of working groups specifically upon tourism in historic towns and upon visitor management case studies, many of which were urban. Almost simultaneously the National Economic Development Council (Davies, 1991) reported upon 'the planning system and large-scale tourism and leisure developments'. Parallel reports appeared in many other countries at about the same time but most noticeable perhaps was the addition of the 'grey' environment to the 'green' in the fields of interest of a number of international agencies. The most potentially effective perhaps was the European Union (Commission of the European Communities, 1994). Green planning had become green/grey planning and tourism was recognised as an active ingredient in both. Sustainable tourism has more recently become responsible tourism as part of responsible planning. A pessimist might see this as just 'an industry running scared' (Ashworth, 1992b): an optimistic, some would say naive (Wheeller, 1991), view would be that tourists, and in response the commercial tourist industry, are becoming more aware of the threats that they pose to the environmental quality of the sites they visit (Hunter & Green, 1995, and see Chapter 12 in this volume). However, whether as part of a new 'urban renaissance' (City Fringe Partnership, 1997; Urban Task Force, 1999) or just urban cultural policy (Bianchini, 1993), at the very least, tourism is now, as it was not previously, firmly on the local policy agenda and not just in a handful of noted tourism towns.

## Some Missing Approaches

### Economics

Brief mention should be made of approaches missing in the 1988 paper which would now receive considerable attention. First, however, there should be a passing reference to the 'god that failed' namely economics. During much of the formative period of tourism as an academic study the subdiscipline of the economics of tourism offered much promise. There was an acceptance of the belief that tourism was in essence an economic phenomenon. It was an industry which had certain spatial dimensions, specifically those of the location of demand and supply, and undoubtedly some influences and impacts upon non-economic dimensions. However, as an economic activity it was reasonable to suppose that regional economics could provide not just answers to the questions on economic impact but also the management tools for regulating it. What happened in tourism studies as elsewhere was a failure of economic analysis to match the expectations that had been placed upon it. The economic region proved to be an abstraction that could not be operationalised and transformed into tools of analysis and management. The numerous studies throughout the 1970s and 1980s of local economic multipliers, input-output analysis, economic linkages and the like, never produced comparable results, usable quotients or any real basis for policy. Little of this approach survives in tourism (a rare exception is Sinclair and Stabler, 1997) and the economics of tourism has been mostly subsumed into business studies (e.g. Moutinho, 2000), which concentrates on practical considerations of the operation of tourism enterprises rather than sketching the workings of a local tourism economy (see Chapter 3 in this volume).

## City Marketing

There was some reference in the 1988 paper to the early work in city marketing but this was largely confined to a content analysis of promotional literature. This has now been swamped and largely superseded by a prodigious output of work on tourism marketing, tourism image creation and promotion and the semiotics of these. This productivity can be classified into two clear categories. The first is instrumental consisting effectively of handbooks of helpful hints. The goal of these 'how to do it' books (Witt & Moutinho, 1994; Middleton, 1999) is to increase the effectiveness of marketing, especially promotion, in influencing consumer behaviour to the benefit of the firm or indeed the public planning authority. That is not to denigrate their academic content as such but to place them within the study of marketing techniques rather than the specific marketed product – tourism.

The second category is quite different. Here studies are made of the images promoted to potential tourists as a means of entry into an examination of social or psychological attitudes, and thus discovery of trends and perceptions within society. Printed tourism promotional images lend themselves to work on historic attitudes and changes through time (Gold & Ward, 1994; Ward, 1998). Equally, tourism promotional material has been used as a means of investigating, through such images, how power is exercised in society (Morgan & Pritchard, 1998). Even more broadly many have used leisure studies as a peg upon which to hang feminist, 'post-colonial', or other 'discourses' (Aitchison *et al.*, 2000; Selwyn, 1996). The focus of interest in all of these is not in tourism as such, and certainly not in furthering the economic interests of the tourism industry that few such writers would wish to do: it is just that tourism represents a more extreme behaviour or attitude and is thus easier to study or recognise. The quantity and accessibility of material on the promotion, transmission and reception of tourism images renders it ideal for these purposes.

## Plus Ça Change . . .

One part of this chapter that is quite different from the earlier one is the list of references. In 1988 it was still possible to try to be comprehensive even if the attempt failed. Now the quantity of literature makes even the attempt quite futile. There is one significant difference between this and the earlier article which will pass unnoticed by many, especially younger researchers, for whom it is commonplace. The reference list in 1988, but not now, was partly in French and even German. This reflects either that the substantial contributions that had been made by continental European researchers in the 1960s and 1970s had largely ceased or at least were no longer produced in languages other than English. Either we have entered a world of an English-using monopoly or it may be one symptom of just a linguistic compartmentalisation.

The earlier paper concluded with the plea that what was required were new integrative approaches that could accommodate the distinctive characteristics of urban tourism and explain the multimotivated consumer in the multifunctional city. It would thus be correct to enquire whether these have emerged and whether indeed they were needed in the first place.

The answers can only be expressed through some paradoxes. On the one hand, there is an increasing realisation that the development of a diversified tourism product line, the economic well-being of places and the maintenance of local cultures, can all be related in joint policies profitable to all groups of actors in the city. On the other hand, it is all the more surprising that still very little is known about the detail of these relationships. The idea that there exists an automatic and universally harmonious symbiosis between all parties is still too often assumed rather than questioned or explained. The relationships between tourism and places pose more questions than can currently be answered with confidence. Why, and how, do tourists make use of cities? What are the implications for other urban functions of the addition of a tourism use? The effective management of tourism for local development goals depends upon answers to such questions.

The relationship of cities and tourism is asymmetrical. Cities are important to tourism but this does not automatically imply that tourism is important to cities. Tourism is highly selective and cities are only very rarely locked into an inevitable tourism development. Tourism may need the varied resources of the city but this does not imply that the city needs tourism. Although tourism is often a useful marginal economic activity (the 'windfall economic gain model') and sometimes the main support for local economies, there are actually only a few cases where a town has deliberately made tourism the leading economic sector as a compensation for economic failure elsewhere. The conditions for success are rigorous. These include an economic imperative with a severely limited range of alternative options; a surplus capacity especially of land, labour and supporting services; a set of resources capable of being commodified into products relevant to specific markets; a fortunate location relative to that market and also probably in the timing of a fortuitous initiative. Such a checklist of preconditions for an excess of economic benefits over costs explains why tourism development is not a priority in many cities and why failure in local tourism development is more likely than success.

There are now more courses in tourism at various educational and training institutions and at various levels of attainment, than ever before. There are more students, teachers, books and programmes. However, these are dominated by what can be termed 'the industrial paradigm'. Tourism is studied because commercial firms and governments need the information it generates or the skills it transfers to students for the furtherance of their economic goals. Unlike most academic studies, the dominant roles of most tourism studies is to act as provider of trained personnel and as a research section of a large industry. However, this may be regretted (see Hughes, 1991), it does define the horizons of most of those studying tourism. The agenda and to an extent the outcomes are predetermined. The implications of this are that the existence of tourism, the tourist and the industry are assumed into the paradigm. The first chapter of almost any textbook of tourism studies is concerned with the identification and recognition of these phenomena not a discussion of their possible existence.

The general conclusion is thus that the imbalance does still exist. However, previously I found this difficult to understand and felt it should be remedied by a more balanced approach within tourism through the development of the study of urban tourism. Now I accept that the imbalance is quite intrinsic to the nature of tourism studies and the nature of cities.

## Note
1. This chapter first appeared as 'Urban tourism: An imbalance in attention' in Volume 1 of *Progress in Tourism, Recreation and Hospitality Management* (1989), pp. 33–55.

## Bibliography

Aitchison, C., Maccleod N.E. and Shaw, S. (2000) *Leisure and Tourism Landscapes* London: Routledge.

Ashworth, G.J. (1989) Urban tourism: An imbalance in attention. In C.P. Cooper (ed.) *Progress in Tourism, Recreation and Hospitality Research* (pp. 35–54). London: Belhaven.

Ashworth, G.J. (1992a) Is there an urban tourism? *Tourism Recreation Research* 17 (2), 3–8.

Ashworth, G.J. (1992b) Planning for sustainable tourism. *Town Planning Review* 63 (3), 325–30.

Ashworth, G.J. (1999) Heritage, tourism and cities: A review. *Tourism Recreation Research* 24 (1), 19–29.

Ashworth, G.J. (1996) Managing night life in the city: The case of Groningen. In P. Pellenbarg, F. Schuurmans and J. De Vries (eds) *Reisgenoten: Liber Amicorum J.Van Der Bremen* (pp. 1–13). Groningen/Utrecht: Nederland Geografisch Studies.

Ashworth, G.J. and de Haan, T.Z. (1985) *The Tourist-Historic City: A Model and Initial Application*. Groningen: GIRUG.

Ashworth,G.J and Tunbridge, J.E. (1990) *The Tourist-Historic City*. London: Belhaven.

Ashworth, G.J. and Tunbridge, J.E. (2000) *The Tourist-Historic City: Retrospect and Prospect of the Management of Heritage Cities*. London: Elsevier.

Berg, L. Van Den, Borg, J. Van Der and Der Meer, J. Van (1995) *Urban Tourism: Performance and Strategies in Eight European Cities*. London: Avebury.

Bianchini, F. (1993) The role of cultural policies. In F. Bianchini and M. Parkinson (eds) *Remaking European Cities* (pp. 199–213). Manchester: Manchester University Press.

Bloomfield, G. (1996) Lodging at the interchange in London, Ontario. *Canadian Geographer* 40 (2), 173–80.

Boniface, P. and Fowler, P.J. (1993) *Heritage and Tourism in the Global Village*. London: Routledge.

Borg, J. Van Der (1990) *Tourism and Urban Development*. Faculty of Economics, Erasmus. Rotterdam: University of Rotterdam.

Borg, J. Van Den (1994) Demand for city tourism in Europe: Tour operators' catalogues. *Tourism Management* 15 (1), 66–9.

Borg, J. Van Der (1998) Tourism management in Venice, or how to deal with success. In D. Tyler, Y. Guerrier and M. Robertson (eds) *Managing Tourism in Cities* (pp. 125–35). Wiley, London.

Borg J. Van Den, P. Costa and G. Gotti (1996) Tourism in European Heritage Cities. *Annals of Tourism Research* 23 (2), 306–21.

Burtenshaw, D., Bateman, M. and Ashworth, G.J. (1991) *The European City: Western Perspectives*. London: Fulton.

Chemla, G. (1990) L'evolution récent des restaurants gastronomiques Parisiens. In P. Huetzdetemps and J.-R. Pitte (eds) *Les Restaurants dans le Monde et à Travers des Ages* (pp. 39–58). Paris : Edition Gelut.

Cheng, A. (1990) Tourism: How much is too much? *Canadian Geographer* 24 (1), 9–12.

Christaller, W. (1966) Some considerations of tourism locations in Europe. *Papers Regional Science Association* 12: 95–105.

City Fringe Partnership (1997) *Building on Success: City Fringe Partnership Review*. London: CFP.

Cohen, E. (1979) A phenomenology of tourist experiences. *Sociology* 13, 179–201.

Commission of the European Communities (1994) *Green Book on the Urban Environment*. Brussels.

Coppock, T. and Duffield B.S. (1975) *Recreation in the Countryside: A Spatial Analysis*. London: Macmillan.

Costa, P. and Van Der Borg, J. (1993) *The Management of Tourism in Cities of Art*. CIEST 2. Venice: University of Venice.

Crouch, D. (ed.) (1999) *Leisure/Tourism Geographies: Practices and Geographical Knowledge*. London: Routledge.

Dalibard, J. (1988) Can tourist towns be liveable? *Canadian Heritage* 14 (3), 3–4.

Dann, G. (1981) Tourism motivation: An appraisal. *Annals of Tourism Research* 8, 187–219.

Davies, H.W.E. (1991) *The Planning System and Large Scale Tourism and Leisure Developments*. London: National Economic Development Office.

De Bres, K. (1994) Cowtowns or cathedral precincts? Two models for contemporary urban tourism. *Area* 26 (1), 57–67.

Defert, P. (1966) *La Localisation Touristique: Problèmes Théorétique et Pratique*. Berne : Editions Gurten.

Department of the Environment (1990) *Tourism and the Inner City*. Inner Cities Directorate. London: HMSO.

Dewailly, J.M. (1990) *Tourisme et Amengement en Europe du Nord*. Paris : Masson.

Dietvorst, A. (1994) Cultural tourism and time-space behaviour. In G.J. Ashworth and P.J. Larkham (eds) *Building a New Heritage: Tourism, Culture and Identity in the New Europe* (pp. 69–89). London: Routledge.

Dietvorst, A. (1995) Tourist behaviour and the importance of time-space analysis In G.J. Ashworth and A.G.J. Dietvorst (eds) *Tourism and Spatial Transformation: Implications for Policy and Planning* (pp. 163–81). Wallingford: CAB International.

Dower, M. (1965) *The Fourth Wave: The Challenge of Leisure*. London: Civic Trust.

English Historic Towns Forum (1992) *Shopping and Tourism*. London.

Faché, W. (1995) Transformation in the concept of holiday villages in Northern Europe. In G.J Ashworth and A.G.J. Dietvorst (eds) *Tourism and Spatial Transformations: Implications for Policy and Planning* (pp. 109–28). Wallingford: CAB International.

Flognfeldt, T. (1996) Museum visitors and modes of travelling in Norway. In Robinson M. (ed.) *Tourism and Cultural Change* (pp. 113–26). Newcastle: University Of Northumbria.

Getz, D. (1993) Planning for tourism business districts. *Annals of Tourism Research* 20 (3), 583–600.

Glasson, J. (1994) Oxford: A heritage city under pressure. *Tourism Management* 15 (2), 137–44.

Gold, J.R. and Ward, S. (1994) *Place Promotion*. London: Belhaven.

Gyptis, S. (ed.) (1993) *Leisure and the Environment: Essays in Honour of J.A. Patmore*. London: Belhaven.

Groote, P. De (1987) *De Belgisch Hotelsector: Een Economische Geografisch Analyse*. Universitaire Pers K.U. Leuven.

Hall, C.M. and Page, S.J. (1999) *The Geography of Tourism and Recreation: Environment, Place and Space*. London: Routledge.

Herbin, J. (1995) Mass tourism and problems of tourism planning in French mountains. In G.J. Ashworth and A.G.J. Dietvorst (eds) *Tourism and Spatial Transformations: Implications for Policy and Planning* (pp. 93–105). Wallingford: CAB International.

Hewison, R. (1987) *The Heritage Industry: Britain in a Climate of Decline*. London: Methuen.

Horne, D. (1984) *The Great Museum: The Re-Presentation of History*. London: Pluto.

Hughes, G. (1991) Tourism: A comment. *Area* 23 (3), 263–7.

Hunter, C. and Green, H. (1995) *Tourism and the Environment: A Sustainable Relationship?* London: Routledge.

Jansen, A.C.M. (1989) Fun shopping as a geographical notion or the attitudes of the inner city of Amsterdam as a shopping area. *Tijdschrift Voor Economische En Sociale Geografie* 80 (3), 243–9.

Jansen-Verbeke, M. (1990a) The forum function of inner cities. *World Leisure and Recreation* 31 (4), 25–8.

Jansen-Verbeke, M. (1990b) Leisure + Shopping = Tourism product mix. In G. Ashworth and B. Goodall (eds) *Marketing Tourism Places* (pp. 128–37). London: Routledge.

Jansen-Verbeke, M. (1990c) Toerism in de Binnenstad van Brugge: Een Planologische Visie. *Nijmegse Planologische Cahiers* 35. Nijmegen: K.U.

Jansen-Verbeke M. (1991) Leisure shopping: A magic concept for the tourism industry. *Tourism Management* 12 (1), 9–14.

Jansen-Verbeke, M. (1992) Urban recreation and tourism: Physical planning issues. *Tourism Recreation Research* 17 (2), 33–45.

Jansen-Verbeke, M. (1994) The synergism between shopping and tourism: The Japanese experience. In T. Theobald (ed.) *Global Tourism: The Next Decade* (pp. 58–71). Oxford: Butterworth-Heinemann.

Jansen-Verbeke, M. (1997) Urban tourism: Managing resources and visitors. In S. Wahab and J. Pigram (eds) *Tourism, Sustainability and Growth* (pp. 237–56). London: Routledge.

Jansen-Verbeke, M. and Van Rekom, J. (1996) Scanning the museum visitor. *Annals of Tourism Research* 23 (2), 364–75.

Jansen-Verbeke, M. and Wiel, E. Van De (1995) Tourism planning in urban revitalisation projects: Lessons from the Amsterdam waterfront. In G.J. Ashworth and A.G.J. Dietvorst (eds) *Tourism and Spatial Transformation: Implications for Policy and Planning* (pp. 129–45). Wallingford: CAB International.

Kinnaird, V.H. and Hall, D. (1994) Tourism: A Gender Analysis London: Wiley.

Law, C.M. (1992) Urban tourism and its contribution to economic regeneration. *Urban Studies* 29 (3/4), 599–618.

Law, C.M. (ed.) (1993) *Urban Tourism: Attracting Visitors to Large Cities*. London: Mansell.

Law, C.M. (1995) *Urban Tourism*. London: Routledge.

Law C.M. (ed.) (1996) *Tourism in Major Cities*. London: Thomson.

London Tourism Board (1990) *Tourism Strategy for London 1990–3 Summary*. London: LTB.

MacCannell, D. (1976) *The Tourist: A New Theory of the Leisure Class*. New York: Schoken Books.

Meyer-Arendt, K. (1990) Recreational business districts in Gulf of Mexico seaside resorts. *Journal of Cultural Geography* 11, 39–55.

Middleton, V.T.C. (1999) *Marketing in Travel and Tourism*. Oxford: Butterworth-Heinemann.

Miossec, J.M. (1977) Un modèle de l'espace touristique. *L'Espace Géographique* 6, 41–8.

Morgan, N. and Pritchard, A. (1998) *Tourism Promotion and Power: Creating Images, Creating Identities*. Chichester: Wiley.

Mossetto, G. (1991) The economics of the cities of art: A tale of two cities. *Nota Di Lavoro* 91.10. Venice: Dept. of Economics, University of Venice.

Moutinho, L. (2000) *Strategic Management in Tourism*. Wallingford: CABI.

Oosterman, J. (1993) Welcome to the pleasure dome: Play and entertainment. In Urban public space: The example of the sidewalk café. *Built Environment* 18 (2), 155–63.

Page, S.J. (1989) Tourism planning in London. *Town and Country Planning* 12, 291–5.

Page, S.J. (1992) Managing tourism in a small historic town. *Town and Country Planning* 15, 82–102.

Page, S.J. (1993) Urban tourism in New Zealand. *Tourism Management* 14 (3), 211–18.

Page, S.J. (1995) *Urban Tourism*. London: Routledge.

Patmore, J.A. (1970) *Land and Leisure*. Newton Abbot: David and Charles.

Pearce, D.G. (1987) Motel location and choice in Christchurch. *New Zealand Geographer* 43 (1), 10–17.

Pearce, D.G. (1995) *Tourism Today: A Geographical Analysis* (2nd edn). London: Longmans.

Pearce, D.G. (1997) Analysing the demand for urban tourism: Issues and examples from Paris. *Tourism Analysis* 1 (1), 5–18.

Pearce, D.G. (1999) Tourism in Paris: Studies at the microscale. *Annals of Tourism Research* 26 (1), 77–97.

Pfafflin, G. (1987) Concern for tourism. *Annals of Tourism Research* 9 (3), 576–88.

Phelps, A. (1994) Museums as tourist attractions. In A.V. Seaton (ed.) *Tourism: The State of the Art* (pp. 169–77), London: Wiley.

Selwyn, T. (1996) *The Tourism Image: Myths and Myth Making in Tourism*. Chichester: Wiley.

Shaw, G. and Williams, A.M. (1994) *Critical Issues in Tourism: A Geographical Perspective*. Oxford: Blackwell.

Sinclair, M.T. and Stabler, M. (1997) *The Economics of Tourism*. London: Routledge.

Smith, R.A. (1991) Beach resorts: A model of development. *Landscape and Urban Planning* 21, 189–210.

Stansfield, C.A. (1964) A note on the urban–non-urban imbalance in American recreational research. *Tourist Review* 19 (4) / 20 (1), 196–200, 21–3.

Stansfield, C.A and Rickert, E.J. (1970) The recreational business district. *Journal of Leisure Research* 2 (4), 213–25.

Taylor, V. (1975) The recreational business district: A component of the East London urban morphology. *South African Geographer* 2, 139–44.

Townsend A. (1992) The attractions of urban areas. *Tourism Recreation Research* XVII 2, 24–32.

Tunbridge, J.E. and Ashworth, G.J. (1992) Leisure resource development in cityport revitalisation: The tourist–historic dimension. In D.S. Hoyle and D.A. Pinder (eds) *European Port Cities in Transition* (pp. 280–85). London: Belhaven.

Tyler, D., Guerrier Y. and Robertson, M. (1997) *Managing Tourism in Cities*. London: Wiley.

Urban Task Force (1999) *Towards An Urban Renaissance*. London: Department of Environment, Transport and the Regions.

Vanderborg, J. (1996) Tourism in European heritage cities. *Annals of Tourism Research* 23 (2), 306–21.

Wall, G. and Sinnot, J. (1980) Urban recreational and cultural facilities as tourist attractions. *Canadian Geographer* 24 (1), 50–9.

Ward, S.V. (1998) *Selling Places: The Marketing and Promotion of Towns and Cities 1850–2000*. London: Spon.

Westlake, T. and White, A. (1992) Venice: Suffering city of touristic dreams. *Town and Country Planning* 15, 210–11.

Wheeller, B. (1991) Tourism's troubled times. *Tourism Management* 12 (1), 91–6.

Williams, S. (1998) *Tourism Geography*. London: Routledge.

Witt, S. and Moutinho, L. (eds) (1994) *Tourism Marketing and Management Handbook*. Hemel Hempstead: Prentice-Hall.

Wyckoff, W. (1992) Denver's ageing commercial strip. *Geographical Review* 82, 282–94.

Yokeno, N. (1968) La Localisation de l'industrie touristique: Application de l'analyse de Thunen-Weber. *Cahiers de Tourism* série C 9, 1–18.

## Chapter 10

# Revisiting 'Heritage: A Key Sector of the (then) "New" Tourism' – Out With the 'New' and Out With 'Heritage'?

RICHARD PRENTICE

## The 1994 Paper in Historical Context

The first change to be noted in looking back to the 1994 paper that appeared in 'Progress' (Prentice, 1994) is the changed perspective now placed on non-standardised tourism products: these are now accepted as part of the tourism product-offering along with beach and pool-side holidays. Indeed, some forms of heritage tourism, such as visiting historic cities, are now forms of mass tourism, and no longer considered to be a curiosity of the elite. It is not simply that demand has changed: so have the conceptual perspectives through which demand is recognised and interpreted. Simply, to think of heritage tourism now as 'new' tourism is quaint, and frankly out-dated. Such has been the progress of disciplinary development in the intervening years. No longer are academics who are interested in battlefields, redundant factories, art galleries or nature trails as tourist attractions thought of as a little bizarre.

A second change concerns the term 'heritage'. This was a North American term, and incorporated into British and Antipodean use covered a wide range of attractions as set out in the 1994 paper. The term fitted well with the observed behaviour of North Americans trying to find their roots in Europe, and more recently in Africa. The term is still used, but the alternative, 'cultural', has increasingly supplanted it, other than in eco-tourism. In contemporary usage, 'heritage' implies an essentially past orientation: 'cultural' does not. The latter includes the contemporary and the futuristic, as well as the past within its scope. Indeed, this has been in the meantime reflected in the United Kingdom by the renaming of the (English) government Department of National Heritage, as the Department of Culture, Media and Sport, while retaining the same portfolio, including tourism de-

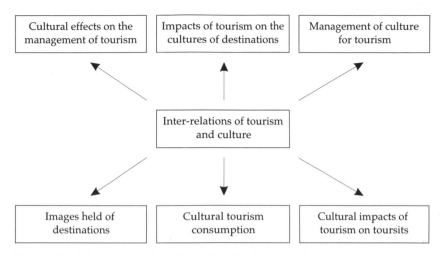

**Figure 10.1** Aspects of the dialectic of culture and tourism

velopment. In Britain the term 'heritage' had fitted well with Thatcherite 'Victorian' values, and the embracing of a constructed past: it fitted less well with the 'Cool Britannia' image proffered for Britain by the Blair government. The term 'cultural' implicitly recognises difference, evolution and change in what is imagined as authentic and in what is preferred.

The change in terminology is under-pinned by 'interactionist' concerns with the creation and change of symbolic orders via social interaction (Silverman, 1993). Interactionism has sought to show how meanings arise in the context of behaviour, focusing on the amenability of meaning to group members through socialisation. Meaning is recognised as inter-subjective and negotiable. The performing arts are readily recognisable as inter-subjective and interpretative: historical buildings perhaps less so. To ignore the latter as subject to this process is to fail to recognise the importance of communicative and contextual staging (Cohen, 1989; Cohen *et al.*, 1992): how cultural artefacts and behaviours are depicted to tourists. Such concerns include the '*whose* heritage?' questioning of the 1980s. With the incorporation of critiques of the construction of meaning into tourism during the 1990s, terminology has changed in favour of 'cultural tourism'.

The emergence of heritage/cultural tourism as a mainstream focus of tourism analysis during the 1990s has developed in several dimensions as a dialectic between culture and tourism (Figure 10.1). In terms of the focus of the 1994 paper, what it is to 'consume' as a heritage/cultural tourist is of most importance to the dimensions shown. Looking back over the past four

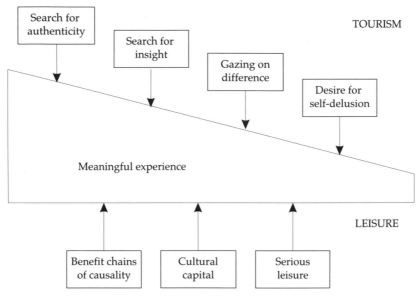

**Figure 10.2** Competing traditions in the conceptualisation of heritage cultural tourism consumption

decades of the development of tourism discourse at least seven 'traditions' can be identified in the conceptualisation of what drives heritage/ cultural tourism consumption (Figure 10.2). These 'traditions' are constructions to assist comparison, and are ultimately arbitrary. Indeed, some authors appear under more than one constructed 'tradition'.

Four of the traditions are from tourism discourses, and three from leisure: the 'traditions' overlap and compete, but are useful retrospective constructions in which to situate the 1994 paper. The four tourism traditions are: search for authenticity; search for insight; gazing on difference; desire for self-delusion. The three leisure traditions are: benefit chains of causality; cultural capital; serious leisure. The conceptualisations set out in Figure 10.2 are only now beginning to be brought together to demonstrate their variously supporting or conflicting theoretical assumptions and practical implications for tourism marketing. A challenge for the present decade is to resolve these differences both through theoretical comparison and empirical testing, not in a potentially fruitless quest to find 'the' universal model, but rather to create a bundle of perspectives as a tool-kit for analysis.

Because of their importance to the present agenda in cultural tourism the seven traditions of Figure 10.2 are usefully summarised in brief here.

### Search for authenticity

This tradition follows the seminal works of Berger (1973) and MacCannell (1973; 1976). Tourists are conceptualised as being driven by alienation from their everyday world into tourism as an attempt to find the profound in the lives of others, usually primitive others. In such a view what is real is looked for outside the person's immediate environment. Sites are sacralised as icons to visit as mass cultural tourism develops (Jacobsen, 1997); and as mass tourism develops, markers of sights to be enjoyed become standardised and tourists are offered only staged 'reality'. Their search for real experience was therefore considered to be futile in the earlier development of this tradition. However, more recently what is real to tourists, and consumers in general, has been considered a more relevant definition of authenticity (Wang, 1999). Namely, felt attributes of intensity and transformation, the 'presence' of history and morality, the perceived commitment of performers, immersion, and the context of production (Evans-Pritchard, 1993; Littrell _et al._, 1993; Daniel, 1996; Teo & Yeoh, 1997; Waller & Lee, 1999; Waitt, 2000). Authenticity has been a dominant anthropological / sociological tradition in tourism analysis.

### Search for insight

This tradition flows from Tilden (1957), and has been a dominant North American national parks discourse. It is a tradition concerned with facilitating insight through interpreting what is looked at (Pennyfather, 1975; Prentice, 1996; Prentice & Cunnell, 1997). As such, much emphasis has been placed on the effectiveness of interpretation. Initially, cognitive gains of tourists visiting sites were assessed; more recently, affective gains have also been considered (Prentice, 1993a; Beeho & Prentice, 1995 & 1997; Light, 1995a, b; Prentice, 1998; Prentice _et al._, 1998a, b; Schänzel & McIntosh, 2000). This tradition assumes that heritage tourists and other serious consumers demand informed experiences and wish to be mindful that they are itinerant encoders of information and are both associative and empathetic (Holt, 1995; Moscardo, 1996; McIntosh & Prentice, 1999; Prentice & Guerin, 1998). This is a perspective of mentally active consumption.

### Gazing on difference

This tradition follows Urry (1990; 1995), and is the consumption of difference and of the extraordinary. Even Central European heritage consumed by Western European tourists has been framed in such a way (Light, 2000). This tradition sees tourism as the collection of signs, and the opposite to work. Central to Urry's analysis is the social construction of gazes, dependent upon historical period: the romantic, collective and postmodern gazes. Whereas the 'insight' tradition has tended to focus on individuals as selectors, appraisers and constructors of meaning, the 'gaze' tradition has placed greater emphasis on how tourism styles are common to a society. The postmodern gaze comes closest to the 'insight' tradition as it recognises tourists' reflexivity: their ability to locate their own culture and to reflect upon it while consuming the aesthetics of another culture. However, Urry's postmodern gaze remains aesthetic in focus and emphasises semiotic skills (Urry, 1995).

## Desire for self-delusion

This tradition flows from Boorstin (1964) and Eco (1986). It emphasises tourists' desires to consume unreal experiences, and '. . . the dissociation between what is actual and what is believable' (McCrone *et al.*, 1995: 25). This tradition focuses on the contrived: 'pseudo-events' for tourists, the consumption of simulacra (iconic representations more 'real' than real) and SIMCITIES (urban environments of simulacra) (Meetham, 1996; O'Brien, 1997; Soja, 1997). Obvious cultural tourism examples are historical theme parks, such as *Rhegeg* in England and *Celtica* in Wales:

> The experience of several lifetimes . . . Named after the ancient Celtic kingdom, Rheged is Cumbria – The Lake District's newest, largest and most dramatic visitor attraction. And just what will you discover here? For starters you'll live a day in the life of Cumbria through the eyes of six local people as they share their moving and evocative tales in a stunning audiovisual spectacular. Then to the main attraction – a cinema screen as big as six double decker buses, where our 40 minute film will reveal a dramatic journey through time to discover myths, legends and history. You'll meet Rheged's ruler Urien . . . ride with fearsome Border Rievers and meet a larger than life Wordsworth. With a cinema screen this big you'll feel you're actually in the movie – flying high over the spectacular landscape – high over the fells and low over the lakes. (*Rhegeg* promotional brochure, 2000)

> The Celtica Experience brings the sights and sounds of Wales' Celtic past alive using the latest audio-visual technology. You are guided by commentary relayed to headsets by infra-red light as you go on an unforgettable journey portraying the Celtic spirit of the past, present and future. Starting in the Foundry you walk through to discover the Celtic Origins. Wander through the Corridor of Time to a re-creation of a Celtic Settlement and the Roundhouse where the characters tell you their own stories. You then venture into the Otherworld through a

mysterious and magical forest that leads you on to the Vortex where you join Gwydion and the Druid and look into the future! (*Celtica* promotional brochure, 2000)

Immersive attractions of this kind using fantasy to evoke emotions and convey information have now become a commonplace heritage offering, further emphasising the development of heritage tourism during the 1990s. But pseudo-events have a longer antecedence than modern electronic media: tourists photographing a piper in Edinburgh are participating in similar self-delusion. Many tourists to Scotland, especially first-timers, expect to see a piper in full Highland dress. They therefore compete to photograph a piper when they come across one in the Royal Mile tourist area, ignoring the hundreds of other Scots who are dressed in more everyday European fashions. These tourists have thereby in their imagination photographed a 'real' Scotsman by ignoring reality.

### Benefit chains of causality

This is the first of the three leisure traditions emphasised, and is a dominant North American leisure science tradition from the 1980s after Driver and Brown (Driver *et al.*, 1991). It has as its behavioural assumption the stance that all leisure behaviour is multiple goal orientated or needs satisfying (Manning, 1986). Four levels of analysis are postulated: activities, settings, experiences and benefits, with expected experiences and benefits the drivers to behaviour (Prentice, 1993b; Prentice & Guerin, 1998). The consumption experience is thereby extended beyond the engagement phase (actually doing the leisure activity): forwards by expectations, and subsequently by memories and lasting benefits. Combined with the 'search for insight' tradition it has been developed as a focused SWOT analysis (Beeho & Prentice, 1995, 1997; Schänzel & McIntosh, 2000). An alternative benefit chain analysis is found in consumer behaviour, as the Means-End Chain (Gutman, 1982), where consumers are asked to explain why what they are doing is important (Davies and Prentice, 1995).

### Cultural capital

Cultural capital is the notion that consumers not only have money capital as resources, they also have other sorts of capital, including that derived from their cultural background. This tradition flows from the work of Bourdieu (Holt, 1998; Robbins, 2000) and identifies three kinds of cultural capital used in competition for social status: embodied, objectified and institutionalised cultural capitals. Embodied cultural capital is that of practical knowledge, skills and dispositions. Objectified cultural capital is that of cultural objects; and institutionalised cultural capital that of official qualifications. Of central importance to heritage tourism is the stance that in postmodern societies as income levels generally rise, objectified cultural capital is increasingly being supplanted by embodied capital. For example, from such a perspective, museum access and appreciation is a learned and socialised behaviour which for any point in time implies that different tourists will have different accumulations of embodied capital. Art has become 'sacralised' (Fowler, 1997) and thereby accessible only through religious-like devotion. Those with inadequate embodied capital pertinent to museum visiting may feel nervous or bored during a visit, or too daunted and may not visit in the first place. By extension, the same applies to more popular pursuits, such as travelling to attend a football match.

## Serious leisure

This is the final of the seven traditions identified. It flows from the work of Stebbins, who has defined serious leisure as the

> systematic pursuit of an amateur, or hobbyist, or a volunteer activity sufficiently substantial and interesting for the participant to find a career there in the acquisition and expression of a combination of its special skills, knowledge, and experience. (Stebbins, 1997a: 17)

Dimensions of serious leisure include perseverance, a non-work career in endeavour, personal effort, lasting benefits, a social world and an identity (Stebbins, 1997b; Baldwin, 1999). Stebbins has distinguished cultural dabblers from cultural tourists (Stebbins, 1996, 1997a). The former are casual leisure pursuers; the latter, serious leisure pursuers. In Stebbins' terminology, therefore, by definition all cultural tourists are serious in their activities. This is an opposite stance to Urry's tourists visiting under the collective gaze, and ignores a middle range of motivation between the determined and the accidental or entertainment-seeking tourist. Stebbins' definition would seem to exclude many tourists seeking transient self-delusion, and thereby define many tourists attending contrived attractions as cultural dabblers. This is in contrast to my 1994 'Progress' paper which adopted a more encompassing definition of heritage tourists from the empathetic to the serious.

The seven traditions provide a range of sometimes conflicting perspectives whereby contemporary heritage/cultural tourism can be analysed. Largely based on fieldwork of the 1980s, the 1994 paper sought to resolve the conflicting perspectives of a search for insight and the collective gaze. It conceptualised heritage tourists as usually mindful in motivation, generally not serious in the Stebbins sense, but subject to gazing rather than participating or amassing cultural capital. In part this was due to the quality of interpretation and staging frequently proffered to tourists at the time. Developments in the intervening years have necessitated revisions to this overall conceptualisation. During the 1990s, the market progressively fragmented into segments, with some emergent as amassers of cultural capital, and others otherwise serious in their consumption. In essence, the market has matured, and rapidly so. Similarly, the lure of conceptualising 'the' tourist and generic 'touristic' practices has been surpassed in the sweep of academic discussion.

## The Significance of Heritage Tourism

In 1994, heritage tourism was usefully seen as one element of supply and demand within the wider 'new' tourism industry. Poon (1989) described this 'new' industry as characterised by flexibility, segmentation and diagonal integration, in contrast to the mass, standardised and rigidly packaged 'old' tourism of the three decades preceding the 1980s (see chapter 8). As noted above, what was new a decade ago has now been in-corporated into standard product offerings and into mainstream academic debate. Important to the understanding of contemporary tourism is that the mass market has been splitting apart and that products are being devel-oped to meet this diverse market. 'Heritage' and other cultural attractions proffered as tourism products are one such development. Even potentially negative images can be positively sold under the heritage theme; and, for example, redundant coal-mining infrastructure and waterfronts have been offered in large number as part of a heritage product since the 1980s. The selling of Cape Breton Island in Nova Scotia as a tourist destination is a seminal example of the power of heritage imagery. Cape Breton Island has its own tartan, evoking both Scottish and landscape heritage. The colours of this tartan, which is essentially green in colour, have been poetically de-scribed to tourists as:

> Black for the wealth of our coal mines,
> Grey for our Cape Breton steel,
> Green for our lofty mountains;
> Our valleys and our fields;
>
> Gold for the golden sunsets
> Shining bright on the lakes of Bras d'Or,
> To show us God's hand has lingered
> To bless Cape Breton's shores

In this way even the island's heavy industrial past is evoked as a 'posi-tive' part of the tourism place-image of Cape Breton Island. The presumed power of heritage imagery can be seen likewise in the case of England and

**Figure 10.3** A 1990's geography of England and Wales of tourism countries

Wales, which in the 1990s became a land of 'tourism countries' (Figure 10.3) and other proffered associations (Figure 10.4). This new proffered geography has been dominated by reference to historic and literary figures or landscape features. Associations of this kind are not peculiar to Britain; for example, Oklahoma has been promoted as 'Native America', exploiting its Indian heritage for tourism. England and Wales have both 'heritage coasts' and 'heritage landscapes', the former an official and the latter an unofficial labelling (Countryside Commission, 1988, 1989). References and labels of

**Figure 10.4** Some other heritage associations used in the 1990s for tourism promotion in England and Wales

this kind unambiguously confirm that for promotional as well as protective purposes, heritage associations have become a central element of contemporary tourism. However, the promotional value of heritage associations does not end with tourism, and thus tourism needs to be seen as part of a wider usage. For example, one British clearing bank has offered a National Trust credit card, making payments to the Trust as the card is used; 'So, the more you use your card, the more you help to keep our country beautiful'.

Among other uses, Stonehenge has been used to promote the image of reliability and chunkiness for biscuits, the permanency of double-glazing and perfection in surveying competence (Crouch & Colin, 1992).

'Heritage' is in the literal sense something that is inherited: 'The word 'heritage' means an inheritance or a legacy; things of value which have been passed from one generation to the next' (Parks Canada, undated, p. 7). In this sense cultural heritage is cultural 'property', and in extreme cases may be fought over or otherwise physically appropriated (Eirinberg, 1992). As a relationship of the present with the past it can be contested and revised (Light, 2000). However, this is only loosely how the term 'heritage' has in the past 25 years come to be used in tourism. Essentially in tourism the term has come to mean not only landscapes, natural history, buildings, artefacts, cultural traditions and the like, which are either literally or metaphorically passed on from one generation to the other, but those among these things which can be portrayed for promotion as tourism products.

As a term, 'heritage' came to the fore in the 1970s in Europe, and throughout the 1980s expanded increasingly to encompass other aspects and to be used increasingly for commercial purposes. In the developing world 'ecotourism' is now an established mass tourism sector with markets in the developed world. Ecotourism may be considered a form of heritage tourism based on the natural ecological attractions of developing countries, with tourist activities ranging from snorkelling off coral reefs to game viewing in savanna grasslands, to Antarctic viewing (Cater, 1992; Davis, 1999). As such, limits to acceptable changes are equally pertinent in both treasured built and treasured 'natural' environments.

If a benchmark for the start of heritage consumption as a mass demand in Europe is desired, however imperfect this benchmark might be, European Architectural Heritage Year of 1975 is probably the best claimant for this. Not only was building conservation promoted, but 'heritage centres' were frequently founded on the North American model to 'tell the story' of an historic town (Dower, 1978). However, cathedrals and castles have for several generations been popular places for tourist visits and popular demands for access to upland landscape in Britain predate 1975 by four decades or more. Indeed, by the 1880s the working class of Lancashire and Durham were making day-trips by train to the English Lake District to enjoy the beauty of the landscape, as the middle classes had begun in volume to do as tourists 50 years previously (Marshall & Walton, 1981). Victorian souvenirs included needle-work embroidery packs of place-images and site-images, vases and other items made out of local stone, 'geological' jewellery of semi-precious stones and brooches and rings characterising particular places, such as 'luckenbooth' brooches from Scotland and 'claddagh' rings from Ireland (Gurvod, 1976). These souvenirs were intended to fix the associations of places in the minds of visitors long after their return home. As such, we should be careful in interpreting contemporary demands for the consumption of heritage as distinctly novel, at least in quality if not in quantity. Heritage may be said, therefore, to have had some place in the 'old' tourism and its evolution. It was part of the collective gaze as well as the earlier romantic gaze into which Urry (1990) located it.

Heritage tourism and leisure is undoubtedly now big business. The number of visits recorded at historic buildings, gardens and museums and galleries in the United Kingdom in 1998 gives some indication of the scale of demand for heritage. Visitor figures do not distinguish between tourist and leisure visitors, and as such it would be wrong to equate visitor figures with tourist demand alone. However, in 1998 some 63 historic properties in the United Kingdom were each visited by in excess of 200,000 visitors, and likewise 16 gardens and 72 museums and galleries (English Tourism Council *et al.*, 1999). These figures reveal little medium term changes in preferences, as in 1990 some 57 historic buildings attracted over 200,000 visitors (English Tourist Board *et al.*, 1991a). Likewise, the figures for gardens and museums and galleries have remained much the same with 13 and 63 respectively attracting this level of visitation in 1990. In overall terms, visits to historic houses within the United Kingdom would appear to have suffered from the increase in competing tourist attractions in the 1990s. Whereas visits to all historic houses in 1998 were only 1% greater in volume than in 1990, visits to gardens were 18% greater and visits to museums and galleries were 8% greater (English Tourism Council *et al.*, 1999).

However, although such figures give some indication of the scale of demand for heritage by tourists visiting the United Kingdom and residents, they give no indication of the proportion of tourists expressing their desire to visit sites of the kind described. Some indication of background demand for heritage in Europe can be gained from surveys of people's participation in types of activities. For the Isle of Man, effective demand for museum visiting has been estimated at around two-thirds of the population, and convertible latent demand at about a further sixth of residents (Prentice, 1998). For 1986 it was estimated that on average each adult in Great Britain was involved in walking (including rambling and hiking) over two miles as an outdoor activity on 20 days of the year, visiting historic buildings or like sites on 3.7 days and visiting museums and art galleries on 0.8 days (Office of Population Censuses and Surveys, 1989). These background attributes of demand can in some cases be made more specific to tourists. Similarly, for 1990 alone it is estimated that 7% of holiday trips in the United Kingdom involved as their 'main' purpose hiking, hill walking, rambling or orienteering, that 4% of trips involved as their main purpose a visit to a castle, monument or church and similar heritage site, and that 2% of trips included as their main purpose visits to museums, galleries and heritage centres (English Tourist Board *et al*, 1991b). Of Canadian tourists, one in 12 has been classified through their activities as a heritage tourist and a further one in twelve as a city culture tourist (Taylor, 1986). Moreover, it would be wrong to think that heritage demands are solely a European and North American phenomenon. Of tourists from Hong Kong it is estimated that upwards of three-quarters visit places of historical significance when on holiday, and almost all of those tourists who can be classified as sightseers (Hsieh *et al.*, 1992). When asked 'why' heritage places were being visited, Japanese independent travellers to Scotland have been found to be almost all seeking to learn about local culture (Andersen *et al.*, 2000). This was particularly so for those classified as careerists seeking to improve their employment prospects through overseas travel and those classified by the researchers as collectors of experiences.

## A Heterogeneity of Supply

Walsh-Heron and Stevens commented that 'Attractions come in all shapes and sizes, catering to a wide variety of tastes and leisure requirements' (Walsh-Heron % Stevens, 1990: 2). Much the same comment has been made about heritage attractions, which have been described as 'a bewildering variety' (Light, 1989: 130). In response to this heterogeneity, a typology of attractions was presented by Prentice (1993a). Such a typology has of necessity to reflect the range of attractions visited by tourists and other visitors; as such, it has to include some attractions for which this very term may seem inappropriate, and the inclusion of some types of site may be distasteful to some. Foremost among such sites are those commemorating genocide, so-called 'dark tourism' sites. Updated to include developments since, the typology is shown in Table 10.1.

The 23 types of heritage attraction shown in Table 10.1, and their potential subdivisions, clearly illustrate the diversity of the heritage 'product', giving further confirmation of Poon's stance (Chapter 8). However, this diversity has been masked by the prevalence of the term 'heritage industry', to describe heritage attractions. The categorisation of this diverse group of attractions as one 'industry' (Hewison, 1987) groups together attractions of varying compatibility in terms of size, theme, management objectives and funding. Categorisation of all attractions as one industry can easily lead to the limitations of some attractions being universally attributed to all, and implicitly denies the diversity inherent in contemporary tourism. The heterogeneity of heritage attractions also has implications for our ability to make generalisations about their markets. Despite research attention

**Table 10.1** A typology of heritage attractions

*Natural history attractions,* including nature reserves, nature trails, aquatic life displays, rare breeds centres, wildlife parks, zoos, butterfly parks, waterfowl parks; geomorphological and geological sites, including caves, gorges, cliffs, waterfalls.

*Science-based attractions,* including science museums, technology centres, 'hands-on' science centres, 'alternative' technology centres.

*Attractions concerned with primary production,* including agricultural attractions, farms, dairies, farming museums, vineyards, fishing, mining, quarrying, water impounding reservoirs.

*Craft centres and craft workshops,* attractions concerned with hand-made products and processes, including watermills and windmills, sculptors, potters, woodcarvers, hand-worked metals, glass makers, silk working, lace making, handloom weaving, craft 'villages'.

*Attractions concerned with manufacturing industry,* including the mass production of goods, e.g. pottery and porcelain factories, breweries, cider factories, distilleries, economic history museums.

*Transport attractions,* including transport museums, tourist and preserved railways, canals, civil shipping, civil aviation, motor vehicles.

*Socio-cultural attractions,* prehistoric and historic sites and displays, including multi-media presentations, dark rides, domestic houses, social history museums, costume museums, regalia exhibitions, furnishings museums, museums of childhood, toy museums.

*Attractions associated with historic persons,* including sites and areas associated with writers and painters.

*Performing arts attractions,* including theatres, street-based performing arts, performing arts workshops, circuses.

*Pleasure gardens,* including ornamental gardens, period gardens, arboreta, model villages.

*Theme parks,* including period and nostalgia parks, 'historic' adventure parks, fairy tale parks for children (but excluding amusement parks, where the principal attractions are exciting rides and the like).

*Galleries,* principally art galleries.

**Table 10.1** (*cont.*)

---

*Festivals and pageants,* including historic fairs, festivals, 'recreating' past ages, countryside festivals of 'rural' activities.

*Fieldsports,* traditional fieldsports, including fishing, hunting, shooting, stalking.

*Stately and ancestral homes,* including palaces, country houses, manor houses.

*Religious attractions,* including cathedrals, churches, abbeys, priories, mosques, shrines, wells, springs.

*Military attractions,* including castles, battlefields, military airfields, naval dockyards, prisoner of war camps, military museums.

*Genocide monuments,* sites associated with the extermination of other races or other mass killings of populations.

*Towns and townscape,* principally historic townscape, groups of buildings in an urban setting.

*Villages and hamlets,* principally 'rural' settlements, usually of pre-1940s architecture.

*Countryside and treasured landscapes,* including national parks, other countryside amenity designations, 'rural' landscapes which may not be officially designated but are enjoyed by visitors.

*Seaside resorts and 'seascapes',* principally seaside towns of past eras and marine 'landscapes'.

*Regions,* including *pays, landes,* counties, or other historic or geographical areas identified as distinctive by their residents or visitors.

---

during the 1990s, as yet insufficient survey evidence exists from which generalisations can safely be made. Our knowledge-base favours certain types of attraction and, in consequence, present generalisations may be attributing market characteristics falsely to those un-researched attraction types.

In 1999, England had 1989 historic buildings advertised as regularly open to the public (English Tourism Council, 1999). This total excludes museums and galleries. With the exception of historic properties, most British heritage attractions open in 1998 had been opened to the public since 1970 (English Tourism Council *et al.*, 1999). Whereas museums might popularly be thought to be 'old', 64% of those open in 1998 had in fact been opened since 1970. The mixed bag of 2101 attractions surveyed other than historic properties, gardens, museums and galleries, or wildlife sites demonstrates this expansionist trend even more, although not all are heritage sites. Of these 'other' attractions, 82% had been open since 1970, and 30% in the 1990s alone. Among the latter are many attractions proffering self-delusion as 'info-tainment': information given in an entertaining way.

Of concern is whether or not the numbers of heritage attractions can be sustained. As part of its embodied capital an increasingly discerning market has now accrued experiences of some of the best attractions in the world: however, such visitors cannot indefinitely demand widespread up-grading of attractions without large investment. However, concern is wider than commercial viability alone. Tourists can degrade the attractions they visit. A scarcity of material to interpret and a shortage of both trained staff and conservation facilities can counter integrity and authenticity in presentation, particularly where several minor attractions compete in a locality to present the same theme. For example, the slate-quarrying industry of North Wales and the coal-mining industry of South Wales are arguably already over-supplied with heritage attraction developments, each competing to present the same regional industrial and social past. Nor may attractions be welcome if they contravene the heritage values of minority populations, as for example in conflicts over developments between Australians of Aboriginal and European descent (Davis and Weiler, 1992).

## Consuming Heritage Products

A recurrent and long-standing feature of surveys and visitors to heritage attractions is their disproportionately middle-class profile, although as noted above the deficiencies in our present knowledge-base need to be acknowledged. In terms of expressed demand, heritage is frequently a middle-class product. Heritage tourism is no exception; equally, it would be incorrect to equate heritage consumption solely with middle-class tourists, for the market bias found does not mean that other sections of the population are totally excluded. Concerns of the 1990s in Europe for social inclusion have not altered this general pattern, implying the importance of cultural capital in facilitating heritage consumption through visiting historic sites.

A survey of visitor surveys at heritage attractions over a decade ago (Prentice, 1989a) confirms the view that holiday tourists visiting heritage sites are likely to be of a socially unrepresentative social class profile, with a substantial bias to non-manual worker social groups. Further support for such an inference is provided by other studies not summarised in this composite source or published since. For example, only a quarter of tourists visiting Dylan Thomas's boathouse at Laugharne in Dyfed were found by a 1983 survey to be from manual-worker households (Wales Tourist Board, 1984a); in contrast, a third of all tourists surveyed at the attraction were from professional or senior managerial households. More recently, surveys of art exhibitions in Edinburgh in the mid-1990s found that between 73% and 83% of visitors were from non-manual households (Andersen *et al.*, 1997). Similarly, fewer than one in five visitors surveyed at the research ship *Discovery* in 1996 were found to be from manual worker households (Prentice *et al.*, 1998a). The socially unrepresentative profile of heritage consumption is also confirmed for holiday-maker tourists visiting heritage attractions on the Isle of Man. Upwards of 6 out of 10 holiday tourists visiting Manx attractions were found to be from non-manual households (Prentice, 1993a).

Social or economic history museums of working-class life might be thought an exception to the general profile. This is often not the case. For example, only one in 10 visitors to Edinburgh's *The People's Story* have been found to be of manual worker status (Prentice & Cunnell, 1997). Even at the primary production industrial heritage attractions of Big Pit and the Rhondda Heritage Park in South Wales, manual workers have not been disproportionately more prevalent than non-manuals among visitors. A survey at Big Pit in the first year of its operation confirms this. This survey found that three out of 10 of its tourist visitors were from professional or senior managerial households, and a further third were from other non-manual households (Wales Tourist Board, 1984b). This pattern has continued. At the Rhondda Heritage Park in 1993, only 30% of visitors were found to come from manual worker households (Prentice *et al.*, 1993).

Despite the impression given by many conservators of historic sites, a recurrent characteristic of visitors to historic sites is their general interest in what they are visiting, rather than a historical interest. Motivations to broaden general knowledge and to satisfy curiosity have been found to be generic for heritage site visits (Prentice *et al.*, 1997; Prentice, 1998). The prevalence of 'generalist' interest has been known for at least two decades. English Heritage addressed this imprecise motivation in an archaeological management review:

> The past means different things to different people, and many consider the presence of the past as somehow improving the quality of life. Beneath this general concept, however, there is a rather more fundamental trait of human nature which attracts people to ancient monuments.
>
> Understanding, exploring, and conquering the mystery of the past,

and seeking answers to the questions posed by ancient monuments . . . is something inbuilt in human nature. For many people, the remains of the past provide a sense of security and continuity in an uncertain world, a thread of timelessness running through a rapidly changing environment' (Darvill, 1987: 167)

Millar made a similar point: 'Broadly defined, heritage is about a special sense of belonging and of continuity' (Millar, 1989: 13). But visits are recalled for many reasons other than a sense of history alone (Masberg & Silverman, 1996; Prentice, 1998). Indeed, such motivations are integral to serious leisure as identity forming. For visitors to attractions less 'authentic' than archaeological or historical sites, motivations other than historical interest are even more likely. For example, concerning heritage events which celebrate or display some theme, Getz (1989) identified five benefits, only one of which is authenticity, the others being belonging, spectacle, ritual and games. Joy, celebration and excess may dominate at such events, rather than learning. Such motivations dominate festival consumption (Getz, 1991; Williams-Braun, 1994; Formica & Uysal, 1996, 1998; Atkinson, 1997; Grant & Paliwoda, 1998; Krausse, 1998). For natural heritage visits, studying wildlife is only one benefit. Others include hunting, viewing wildlife or natural features of the landscape, perceived as varyingly beneficial or non-beneficial in meeting expectations as diverse as to be in a natural setting, to have fun, or to take chances (Kuentzel & Heberlein, 1992; Kuentzel & McDonald, 1992). For the wider tourist market a wide range of benefits may be postulated for casual heritage consumption; for example, tourists visiting North Carolina have been segmented on the basis of 26 benefits perceived from holidaying (Gitelson & Kerstetter, 1990). As well as intellectual needs to be met when on holiday, those of competence mastery, social interaction or stimulus avoidance compete for prominence among this wider market of potentially casual visitors to heritage attractions among holiday makers (Lounsbury & Polik, 1992).

As an example of visitor motivation at formally 'authentic' heritage attractions (castles and the like), surveys in Wales have shown that tourists visit heritage attractions out of general, rather than specific, interests or to enjoy sightseeing. Interest in archaeology, architecture, culture or other specific interest in a site are only secondary reasons (Thomas, 1989). The same was shown for visitors to the research ship *Discovery* (Prentice *et al.*, 1998a). Similarly, at Big Pit only around a quarter of visitors surveyed in 1983 gave educational reasons for their visit and even fewer, about one in seven, gave an interest in industrial archaeology as a reason. In contrast, three-quarters of all visitors gave 'to see how coal is mined' as a reason (Wales Tourist Board, 1984b). The dominance of sightseeing and a 'general' interest has also been found among tourists' reasons for visiting attractions on the Isle of Man (Prentice, 1993a). A 'particular' interest in castles or historic places and the visit as one part of a day out were secondary reasons given for visiting. In contrast, a particular interest in Manx culture and history formed only a third-order reason for visiting the Manx attractions. Taken together, these studies raise the question of the appropriateness of categorising, implicitly or otherwise, all tourists visiting heritage attractions as heritage specialists or enthusiasts. Contemporary heritage consumption includes casual as well as serious leisure consumers. Equally of importance, among so-called specialists most would seem to be members of heritage rather than historical or archaeological societies, even when interviewed at castles or museums (Prentice, 1993a). Such findings suggest that we should be careful in assuming preferences for education rather than insight on the bases of arguments made from standpoints of cultural capital, serious leisure or aesthetic cosmopolitanism.

## Future Use and Role of Heritage in Tourism

For many tourists a general wish to see sights or to become aware of a destination area's heritage is a sufficient motivation for their visit to a heritage attraction, and sets the context for attraction managers in supplying 'products' to benefit their customers. Equally, such visitors are not the sole segment of any size. The diversity of attractions which has emerged during the 1990s has informed some consumers, and encouraged fragmentation of motivations. However, other than in terms of the authenticity debate, the dimensions of how tourists seek to benefit from visiting attractions are as yet insufficiently researched for different types of attraction. Much progress has been made in the past decade, as reflected in the volume of material this chapter has reviewed when compared to its 1994 predecessor. However, it is the fuller understanding of the types of benefits sought by tourists through visiting heritage attractions that still forms a major research challenge. In particular, such research needs to be contextualised within the seven traditions outlined at the beginning of this chapter.

The primacy of a general interest in heritage attractions by many of their visitors has important implications for how such attractions should be presented to these visitors, not least in that prior information about an attraction cannot be assumed, nor a demand for detailed information at the attraction. The importance of the leisure context of tourist visits to attractions may be seen from a study in Wales, which included a case assessment of the effectiveness of site interpretative media for higher educational visitors – in this case, undergraduates on a field visit (Prentice, 1991). A general conclusion from this case study of particular pertinence to the present discussion was that even when given a learning task, many students through lack of thorough attention to the media around the castle failed to recall correctly, or at all, much of the information presented. The predominantly leisure context of tourist visits to heritage attractions sets an even greater challenge for the designers of presentational media, for a learning objective cannot be assumed to be to the fore, as it would be in the case of a university field excursion.

The social bias in the profile of tourists visiting heritage attractions also has important implications for the development of heritage and other cultural 'products'. First among these is the question of how members of the working class appropriate their heritage and relate to that of others. Are the heritage products on offer uninviting, presenting middle-class views of social and economic affairs, or do members of working-class households choose other leisure pursuits or appropriate their heritage in other ways, such as attending a football match, for example? What is known is that the prices generally charged for heritage attraction admission do not seem to discriminate socially in terms of their deterrence, at least to potential visitors at their gates (Prentice, 1989b).

The second implication for heritage 'product' development of the social bias among the visitors to heritage attractions is the disproportionate bias towards a market with formal educational qualifications, or institutional-ised cultural capital to use Bourdieu's terminology. This relationship should not be exaggerated, however, for it can depend upon the tourist profile of a destination area and on the range of competing attractions. For those tourists with formal educational qualifications, a different site presentation may be desirable than for those visitors without such back-grounds. Doubly so, as embodied and institutionalised capital may compound through serious tourism.

These conditions have important implications for providing the benefi-cial experiences sought by those visiting heritage attractions. Principal among the benefits offered to visitors by the managers of heritage attrac-tions is that of information to encourage empathy, an 'informed visitor experience', as it is often termed. The prevalence of tourists' generally un-specific and often uninformed interest in particular sets a pertinent context in which information is to be presented. Information needs to be provided in a manner compatible with the leisure context in which it is generally to be consumed if it is to be of benefit in helping visitors to understand, however superficially and transiently, what they are visiting. The means of providing this benefit, 'interpretation', has become increasingly diverse and multimedia (Alderson & Low, 1986; Uzzell, 1989; Jenkins, 1992; Prentice *et al.*, 1998a, b; McIntosh & Prentice, 1999). However, it is still dependent for its messaging on agendas set largely by academics rather than by popular interest (Prentice, 1997). The study of the information benefits provided at many attractions is not without ethical consideration as to which benefits 'ought' to be presented, and how far art may be 'de-sacralised'. In particular, the benefit of authenticity has been a recurrent concern of historians and museum curators alike, who have found the subject matter of their discipline and conservation increasingly becoming a recreational resource. Jenkins is far from alone in the standpoint evident in the following:

> One reason why Big Pit, Blaenafon, one of South Wales's principal tourist attractions, falls short of expectations is that it consists merely of a pit-head gear with associated colliery buildings around it, stuck in the middle of a reclaimed, featureless industrial desert. Equipped with safety helmets and cap lamps, visitors get a taste of life underground; yet because they can walk comfortably upright along well-lit corridors the reality of coal mining can hardly be presented to them. Most of the pits of South Wales were damp and low-ceilinged with noise, coal-dust laden air and little light. If the visitor relies on impressions of the coal industry gathered from a visit to Big Pit, then he or she will hardly understand why coal miners throughout history fought employer and government over the wretched conditions of work in the mines. (Jenkins, 1992: 83)

Concerns such as these reflect the traditional view of heritage as providing educational benefits to its consumers. That such benefits may not be uppermost in the minds of many visitors to attractions, with many as, outlined above, preferring instead to consume constructed images or to have fun, sets a challenge for the providers of attractions who seek to present authentic experiences.

For the future development of heritage attractions, a fuller understanding of the comparative effectiveness of different interpretative media is also important. Techniques for investigating the effectiveness of presentational media are severalfold:

- studies of non-verbal communication as a means of feedback from visitor to guides providing verbal information (Risk, 1989);
- the unobtrusive recording and subsequent analysis of visitors' conversations at attractions (McManus, 1989);
- time-lapse photography (Vander Stoep, 1989);
- the reports made by visitors on the media seen (Herbert, 1989; Prentice, 1993a; Prentice & Cunnell, 1997; Prentice *et al.*, 1998a);
- visitors' descriptions of their experiences (Beeho & Prentice, 1995, 1997; McIntosh & Prentice, 1999); and

- unobtrusively tracking visitors and recording their behaviour (Russell, 1989).

However, the basic point to be made is that studies of the effectiveness of different types of media at attractions are even now insubstantial in number compared to the usage of interpretative media. Recent studies at best provide limited guidance as to how beneficial visitors to attractions find the variety of media used in the presentation of attractions, and give some guidance as to future development. These findings would concur with the stance that media are quite different in their effectiveness.

## Conclusions

Heritage attractions are part of Poon's 'new' tourism, and are now an established part of tourism provision (see Chapter 8). So much so, that the term 'new' is no longer apposite. Areas of countries have now been relabelled for tourism purposes, to invoke an integrative heritage theme for their localities. The emphasis on heritage and other cultural products has become a phenomenon across the world, and a heterogeneity of attraction types has developed. So, out with the 'new' of the 1994 paper!

However, it would be wrong to assert that heritage, or cultural, tourism was a universal phenomenon across all social classes, for it is unquestionably disproportionately a middle-class interest for those types of heritage attraction for which we have data. This social bias in consumption has important implications both for how the heritage 'product' is presented, and for the content of the heritage presented. The pervasive leisure context of heritage attraction visits also has important implications for attraction development. So have the differing theoretical perspectives on consumption represented by the seven traditions identified earlier. Taking the social class and leisure contexts for product development together, it seems that the commercial fortunes of the heritage part of the tourism sector will be dependent upon the leisure budgets and preferences of the middle classes of the developed world. Equally, the current social bias in consumption sets a challenge for finding product-types which may appeal to other social classes. How these products are designed, presented and promoted will depend on which conceptualisation of consumption is considered pertinent.

Product development strategies will increasingly need to be based upon an understanding of the motivations of tourists when visiting attractions. Otherwise, in what is now a crowded market, as competition increases through the development of new attractions, business failures will increase among those enterprises providing less-wanted 'products'. Our understanding of these benefits is as yet under-developed, and frequently still constrained for many traditional sites by the doubly presumptive view that tourists are seeking the twin benefits of an objectively authentic and learning experience, and that if they are not, they ought to be. Conversely, many 'high-tech', publicly funded projects in the United Kingdom have been recent failures in terms of visitor numbers. Failings of these attractions in terms of visitor experiences and non-visitor perceptions have not been extensively researched: blame has been placed on projection error and feather-bedding from public funding, not on whether the products are actually wanted, and by whom and for what purposes.

Rather than curator-led as in the past, new attractions today are often technology-led. As in many booms, much less attention has been given to market research. Sub-optimal performance in product design and delivery has until recently often been masked by apparently boundless unmet demand. The sheer volume of attractions now means that visitors can choose: the days of the collective view are over for many destinations. The research agenda for heritage tourism still needs more fully to address how heritage is consumed, and the benefits perceived by heritage tourists, within the wider context of benefits perceived generally from cultural tourism. Indeed, by focusing attention on 'heritage' we may be misdirecting ourselves for cultural imagining is unlikely for most tourists to end with things past. Similarly, as the practical usage of 'heritage' has associated it strongly with physical assets (museums, audio-visual technologies, historic houses and the like), its usage impels a supply-driven perspective. Market-based product development is needed instead. So, out with 'heritage' too?

## Note
1.  This chapter first appeared as 'Heritage: A key sector of the "New" Tourism' in Volume 5 of *Progress in Tourism, Recreation and Hospitality Management* (1994), pp. 309–24.

## Bibliography
Alderson, W.T. and Low, S.P. (1986) *Interpretation of Historic Sites* (2nd edn). Nashville: American Association for State and Local History.

Andersen, V.A., Prentice, R.C. and Guerin, S. (1997) Imagery of Denmark among visitors to Danish fine arts exhibitions in Scotland. *Tourism Management* 18, 453–64.

Andersen, V.A., Prentice, R.C. and Watanabe, K. (2000) Journeys for experiences: Japanese independent travellers in Scotland. *Journal of Travel and Tourism Marketing* 9 (1 & 2), 129–51.

Atkinson, C.Z. (1997) Whose New Orleans? Music's place in the packaging of New Orleans for tourism. In S. Abram, J. Waldren and D.V.L. Macleod (eds) *Tourists and Tourism. Identifying with People and Places* (pp. 91–106). Oxford: Berg.

Baldwin, C K. (1999) Exploring the dimensions of serious leisure. *Journal of Leisure Research* 31, 1–17.

Beeho, A.J. and Prentice, R.C. (1995) Evaluating the experiences and benefits gained by tourists visiting a socio-industrial heritage museum. *Museum Management and Curatorship* 14, 229–51.

Beeho, A.J. and Prentice, R.C. (1997) Conceptualising the experiences of heritage tourists. *Tourism Management* 18 (1), 75–87.

Berger, P.L. (1973) 'Sincerity' and 'Authenticity' in modern society. *Public Interest* Spring, 81–90.

Boorstin, D.J. (1964) *The Image: A Guide to Pseudo-Events in America.* New York: Harper.

Cater, E. (1992) Profits from Paradise. *Geographical Magazine* 64 (3), 16–21.

Cohen, E. (1989) 'Primitive and remote': Hill tribe trekking in Thailand. *Annals of Tourism Research* 16, 30–61.

Cohen, E., Nir, Y. and Almagor, U. (1992) Stranger-local interaction in photography. *Annals of Tourism Research* 19 (1), 213–33.

Countryside Commission (1988) *Heritage Landscapes Management Plans.* CCP 205. Cheltenham: Countryside Commission.

Countryside Commission (1989) *Heritage Coasts in England and Wales.* CCP 252, Cheltenham: Countryside Commission.

Crouch, D. and Colin, A. (1992) Rocks, rights and rituals. *Geographical Magazine* 64 (6), 14–19.

Daniel, Y.P. (1996) Tourism dance performances. *Annals of Tourism Research* 23 (4), 780–97.

Darvill, T. (1987) *Ancient Monuments in the Countryside.* London: English Heritage.

Davies, A.J. and Prentice, R.C. (1995) Conceptualizing the latent visitor to heritage attractions. *Tourism Management* 16 (4), 491–500.

Davis, D. and Weiler, B. (1992) Kakadu National Park – conflicts in a world heritage area. *Tourism Management* 13 (4), 313–20.

Davis, P.B. (1999) Beyond guidelines: A model for Antarctic tourism. *Annals of Tourism Research* 26 (4), 516–33.

Dower, M. (1978) *The Tourist and the Historic Heritage.* Dublin: European Travel Commission.

Driver, B.L., Brown, P.J and Peterson, G.L. (eds) (1991) *Benefits of Leisure.* State College: Venture.

Eco, U. (1986) *Travels in Hyper Reality.* Orlando: Harcourt Brace Jovanovich.

Eirinberg, K. (1992) Culture under fire. *Geographical Magazine* 64 (12), 24–8.

English Tourism Council (1999) *The Heritage Monitor 1999.* London: English Tourism Council.

English Tourism Council, Scottish Tourist Board, Northern Ireland Tourist Board and Wales Tourist Board (1999) *Sightseeing in the UK 1998.* London: English Tourism Council.

English Tourist Board, Northern Ireland Tourist Board, Scottish Tourist Board and Wales Tourist Board (1991a) *Sightseeing in the UK 1990.* London: English Tourist Board.

English Tourist Board, Northern Ireland Tourist Board, Scottish Tourist Board and Wales Tourist Board (1991b) *The UK Tourist Statistics 1990.* London: English Tourist Board.

Evans-Pritchard, D. (1993) Ancient art in modern context. *Annals of Tourism Research* 20 (1), 9–31.

Formica, S. and Uysal, M. (1996) A market segmentation of festival visitors. *Festival Management and Event Tourism* 3, 175–82.

Formica, S. and Uysal, M. (1998) Market segmentation of an international cultural-historical event in Italy. *Journal of Travel Research* 36 (4), 16–24.

Fowler, B. (1997) *Pierre Bourdieu: A Cultural Theory.* London, Sage.

Garrad, L.S. (1976) *A Present From.* Newton Abbot: David & Charles.

Getz, D. (1989) Special events. Defining the product. *Tourism Management* 10 (2), 125–37.

Getz, D. (1991) *Festivals, Special Events and Tourism.* New York: Van Nostrand Reinhold.

Gitelson, R.J. and Kerstetter, D.L. (1990) The relationship between socio-demographic variables, benefits sought and subsequent vacation behaviour. *Journal of Travel Research* 28 (3), 24–9.

Grant, D. and Paliwoda, S. (1998) Segmenting Alberta arts and festival consumers. *Festival Management and Event Tourism* 5, 207–20.

Gutman, J. (1982) The means–end chain model based on consumer categorisation processes. *Journal of Marketing* 46, 60–72.

Herbert, D.T. (1989) Does interpretation help? In D.T. Herbert, R.C. Prentice and C.J. Thomas (eds) *Heritage Sites: Strategies for Marketing and Development* (pp. 191–230). Aldershot: Avebury.

Hewison, R. (1987) *The Heritage Industry. Britain in a Climate if Decline.* London: Methuen.

Holt, D.B. (1995) How consumers consume: A typology of consumption practices. *Journal of Consumer Research* 22, 1–16.

Holt, D.B. (1998) Does cultural capital structure American consumption? *Journal of Consumer Research* 25, 1–25.

Hsieh, S., O'Leary, J.T. and Morrison, A.M. (1992) Segmenting the international travel market by activity. *Tourism Management* 13 (3), 209–23.

Jacobsen, J.K.S. (1997) The making of an attraction. The case of North Cape. *Annals of Tourism Research* 24 (3), 341–56.

Jenkins, J.G. (1992) *Getting Yesterday Right. Interpreting the Heritage of Wales.* University of Wales Press, Cardiff.

Krausse, G.M. (1998) Waterfront festivals. *Festival Management and Event Tourism* 5, 171–84.

Kuentzel, W.F. and Heberlein, T.A. (1992) Does specialisation affect behavioural choices and quality judgments among hunters?. *Leisure Sciences* 14, 211–26.

Kuentzel, W.F. and McDonald, C.D. (1992) Differential effects of past experience, commitment, and lifestyle dimensions on river use specialization. *Journal of Leisure Research,* 24, 269–87.

Light, D. (1989) The contribution of the geographer to the study of heritage. *Cambria,* 15, 127–36.

Light, D. (1995a) Visitors' use of interpretative media at heritage sites. *Leisure Studies* 14, 132–49.

Light, D. (1995b) Heritage as informal education. In D.T. Herbert (ed.) *Heritage, Tourism and Society* (pp. 117–45). London: Mansell.

Light, D. (2000) Gazing on communism. *Tourism Geographies* 2, 157–76.

Littrell, M.A., Anderson, L.F. and Brown, P.J. (1993) What makes a craft souvenir authentic? *Annals of Tourism Research* 20 (1), 197–215.

Lounsbury, J.W. and Polik, J.R. (1992) Leisure needs and vacation satisfaction. *Leisure Sciences* 14, 105–19.

MacCannell, D. (1973) Staged authenticity: Arrangements of social space in tourist settings. *American Journal of Sociology* 79,589–603.

MacCannell, D. (1976) *The Tourist. A New Theory of the Leisure Class.* London Macmillan.

Manning, R.E. (1986) *Studies in Outdoor Recreation.* Corvalis: Oregon State University Press.

Marshall, J.D. and Walton, J.K. (1981) *The Lake Counties From 1830 to the Mid-Twentieth Century.* Manchester: Manchester University Press.

Masberg, B.A. and Silverman, L.H. (1996) Visitor experiences at heritage sites. *Journal of Travel Research* 34 (4), 20–5.

McCrone, D., Morris, A. and Kiely, R. (1995) *Scotland – The Brand.* Edinburgh: Edinburgh University Press.

McManus, P. (1989) What people say and how they think in a science museum. In D. Uzzell (ed.) *Heritage Interpretation* (vol. 2) (pp. 156–65). London: Belhaven.

McIntosh, A.J. and Prentice, R.C. (1999) Affirming authenticity: Consuming cultural heritage. *Annals of Tourism Research* 26 (4), 589–612.

Meethan, K. (1996) Consuming (in) the civilized city. *Annals of Tourism Research* 23 (3), 322–40.

Millar, S. (1989) Heritage management for heritage tourism. *Tourism Management* 10 (1), 9–14.

Moscardo, G. (1996) Mindful visitors. *Annals of Tourism Research* 23 (3), 376–97.

O'Brien, C. (1997) Form, function and sign. *Journal of Urban Design* 2, 163–78.

Office of Population Censuses and Surveys (1989) *General Household Survey 1986.* SS4570, London. London: HMSO.

Parks Canada (undated) *Parks Canada Policy.* Ottawa: Parks Canada.

Pennyfather, K. (1975) *Interpretative Media and Facilities.* Edinburgh: HMSO.

Poon, A. (1989) Competitive strategies for a 'New Tourism'. In C. Cooper (ed.) *Progress in Tourism, Recreation and Hospitality Management 1* (pp. 91–102). London: Belhaven.

Prentice, R.C. (1989a) Visitors to heritage sites. In D.T. Herbert, R.C. Prentice and C.J. Thomas (eds) *Heritage Sites: Strategies for Marketing and Development.* Aldershot: Avebury.

Prentice, R.C. (1989b) Pricing policy at heritage sites. In D.T. Herbert, R.C. Prentice and C.J. Thomas (eds) *Heritage Sites: Strategies for Marketing and Development* (pp. 231–71). Aldershot: Avebury.

Prentice, R.C. (1991) Measuring the educational effectiveness of on-site interpretation designed for tourists. *Area* 23, 297–308.

Prentice, R.C. (1993a) *Tourism and Heritage Attractions.* London: Routledge.

Prentice, R.C. (1993b) Motivations of the heritage consumer in the leisure market: An application of the Manning-Haas demand hierarchy. *Leisure Sciences* 15, 273–90.

Prentice, R.C. (1994) Heritage: A key sector of the 'New' Tourism. In C.P. Cooper and A. Lockwood (eds) *Progress in Tourism, Recreation and Hospitality Management 5* (pp. 309–24). Chichester: John Wiley.

Prentice, R.C. (1996) Managing implosion: The facilitation of insight through the provision of context. *Museum Management and Curatorship* 15, 169–85.

Prentice, R.C. (1997) Cultural and landscape tourism. In S. Wahab and J.J. Pigram (eds) *Tourism, Development and Growth* (pp. 209–236). London: Routledge.

Prentice, R.C. (1998) Recollections of museum visits. *Museum Management and Curatorship* 17, 41–64.

Prentice, R.C. and Cunnell, D. (1997) Response to interpretative media as a basis of multi-variate market segmentation for museums and heritage centres. *Museum Management and Curatorship* 16, 233–56.

Prentice, R.C. and Guerin, S. (1998) The romantic walker? A case study of users of iconic Scottish landscape. *Scottish Geographical Magazine* 114, 180–91.

Prentice, R.C., Davies, A. and Beeho, A. (1997) Seeking generic motivations for visiting and not visiting museums and like cultural attractions. *Museum Management and Curatorship* 16, 45–70.

Prentice, R.C., Guerin, S. and McGugan, S. (1998a) Visitor learning at a heritage attraction: A case study of *Discovery* as a media product. *Tourism Management* 19 (1), 5–23.

Prentice, R.C., Witt, S.F. and Hamer, C. (1998b) Tourism as Experience: The case of heritage parks. *Annals of Tourism Research* 25 (1), 1–24.

Prentice, R.C., Witt, S.F. and Hamer, C. (1993) The experience of industrial heritage: The case of black gold. *Built Environment* 19, 137–46.

Risk, P. (1989) On-site real-time observational techniques and responses to visitor needs. In D. Uzzell (ed.) *Heritage Interpretation* (Vol. 2) (pp. 120–8). London: Belhaven.

Robbins, D. (2000) *Bourdieu and Culture*. London: Sage.

Russell, T. (1989) The formative evaluation of interactive science and technology centres. In D. Uzzell (ed.) *Heritage Interpretation*, Volume 2 (pp. 191–202). London: Belhaven.

Schänzel, H.A. and McIntosh, A.J. (2000) An insight into the personal and emotive context of wildlife viewing at the Penguin Place, Otago Peninsula, New Zealand. *Journal of Sustainable Tourism*, 36–52.

Silverman, D. (1993) *Interpreting Qualitative Data. Methods for Analysing Talk, Text and Interaction*. London: Sage.

Soja, E.W. (1997) Six discourses on the postmetropolis. In S. Westwood and J. Williams (eds) *Imagining Cities: Scripts, Signs, Memory*. London: Routledge.

Stebbins, R.A. (1996) Cultural tourism as serious leisure. *Annals of Tourism Research* 23 (4), 948–50.

Stebbins, R.A. (1997a) Casual leisure: A conceptual statement. *Leisure Studies* 16, 17–25.

Stebbins, R.A. (1997b) Identity and cultural tourism. *Annals of Tourism Research* 24 (3), 450–2.

Taylor, G.D. (1986) Multi-dimensional segmentation of the Canadian pleasure travel market. *Tourism Management* 7 (2), 146–53.

Teo, P. and Yeoh, B.S.A. (1997) Remaking local heritage for tourism. *Annals of Tourism Research* 24 (1), 192–213.

Thomas, C.J. (1989) The roles of historic sites and reasons for visiting. In D.T. Herbert, R.C. Prentice and C.J. Thomas (eds) *Heritage Sites: Strategies for Marketing and Development*. Aldershot: Avebury.

Tilden, F. (1957) *Interpreting Our Heritage* (3rd edn, 1977). Chapel Hill: University of North Carolina Press.

Urry, J. (1990) *The Tourist Gaze*. London: Sage.

Urry, J. (1995) *Consuming Places*. London: Routledge.

Uzzell, D. (ed.) (1989) *Heritage Interpretation* (2 vols). London: Belhaven.

Vander Stoep, T. (1989) Time-lapse photography. In D. Uzzell (ed.) *Heritage Interpretation* (Vol. 2). London: Belhaven.

Waitt, G. (2000) Consuming heritage: Perceived historical authenticity. *Annals of Tourism Research* 27 (4), 835–62.

Wales Tourist Board (1984a) *Survey of Visitors to Dylan Thomas' Boathouse, Laugharne.* Cardiff: Wales Tourist Board.

Wales Tourist Board (1984b) *Survey of Visitors to Big Pit Mining Museum, Blaenafon.* Cardiff: Wales Tourist Board.

Waller, J. and Lea, S.E.G. (1999) Seeking the real Spain? *Annals of Tourism Research* 26 (1), 110–29.

Walsh-Heron, J. and Stevens, T. (1990) *The Management of Visitor Attractions and Events.* Englewood Cliffs, NJ: Prentice Hall.

Wang, N. (1999) Rethinking authenticity in tourism experience. *Annals of Tourism Research* 26 (2), 349–70.

Williams-Braun, B. (1994) Situating cultural politics. *Environment and Planning D: Society and Space* 12, 75–104.

## Chapter 11

# Environmental Auditing: A Means to Improving Tourism's Environmental Performance

BRIAN GOODALL

## Tourism and Environment

Environmental issues in the modern global economy are just as likely to arise from consumption, as from production. The last quarter of the twentieth century witnessed society, governments, businesses and individuals becoming increasingly aware of the environmental issues emanating from current lifestyles. Accounting for the environment has therefore become a major growth area of business, especially during the last decade, against a background of worldwide interest as epitomised by United Nations conferences on Environment and Development at Rio (1992), Kyoto (1996), The Hague (2000) and Johannesburg (2002).

Environment is a core feature of the tourism product. Tourists are therefore 'consumers of environment', travelling to the producer's location, the tourist destination, in order to consume the product. Thus tourism is dependent upon the attractive power of a destination's environment, that is, its primary resources of climate, scenery, wildlife, cultural and historic heritage. Often much of that environment takes the form of open-access resources, which are not owned by anyone and for which no market exists, so making avoidance of overuse more difficult. That tourism, as not only the world's largest industry but also one whose rationale embraces commodification of the environment, should come under close scrutiny was inevitable. Attitudes towards the environment within the tourism industry are changing – initially the mode was reactive, as to be expected in a fiercely competitive industry which is private sector driven, incredibly diverse, being fragmented into micro-businesses and reflective of the high degree of product substitutability.

The rapid global growth of tourism has led to a devastating impact on the environment. Growth creates problems, especially where fragile and remote environments are visited. To enable tourists to experience a destination's primary resources, secondary resources, such as accommodation, transport facilities and service infrastructure have to be provided, resulting in the major physical restructuring of the destination by the extension of its built environment (Cater & Goodall, 1992). Such mass market and other environmentally destructive forms of tourism continue to dominate the industry worldwide. There exists a circular and cumulative relationship between tourism development, the environment and socio-economic development in the destination area: most tourism development places additional pressures on the environmental resources upon which it is based, compromising the future prospects of the host population.

Tourism's environmental impacts continue to be well documented although the underlying reasons for their apparent inevitability are not well understood beyond pointing to the variable structure and scale of tourism as a resource-based industry (natural, built and cultural) requiring additional infra/superstructure provision and producing wastes typical of urban lifestyles (McKercher, 1993; Butler, 2000). Emphasis is still placed on the local/destination impact which may be accepted in certain cases as a necessary part of the activity, e.g. creation of skiing pistes and trails, or may pass unacknowledged by tourists making only a single visit to a destination. Wider ramifications are, however, inescapable following from tourism's significant linkages with other economic sectors, especially transport. Environmental footprints, extending spatially well beyond destinations, are now acknowledged: the global impact of inputs to and outputs from tourism in origin and transit regions as well as destinations is now recognised. For example, less than a quarter of the total fossil fuel used by a tourist taking a two-week package holiday to a developing country is consumed within the destination – over three-quarters is accounted for by the long-haul air travel, with significant consequences for global warming (Gössling, 2000a). Environmental impacts ascribable to tourism are not unique, being the same as or similar to outcomes of other human activity, but their spatial and temporal incidence may well be so.

Increased awareness of environmental issues has been accompanied by a realisation of the complexity of tourism–environment relationships, prompting further debate about tourism's dependence upon environment (Butler, 2000). Not only is an understanding required of what attracts tourists to destinations if the latter are to retain their market share but also of the process of environmental change initiated by tourism. Due recognition is accorded to the fact that tourism normally shares the use of an area with other economic activities as well as being dependent upon other economic sectors, such as energy, transport, agriculture and manufacturing, which invariably extends its environmental footprint well beyond destinations. Where, previously, tourism has been viewed as a low-impact, non-consumptive activity, environmental resources have been undervalued, treated as an externality leading to inevitable consequences of over-exploitation of natural resources and a steady increase in pollution levels. The criticality of natural resource capital, especially at the global scale, has not yet been fully appreciated by major parts of the tourism industry. Indeed implications of global climate change for tourism may well be considered without acknowledging the extent of tourism's contribution to the problem (Wall & Badke, 1994).

The debate about tourism and environment is ongoing, set in the context of sustainability and embraces various interpretations of sustainable tourism development (Goodall & Stabler, 1994; Hunter & Green, 1995; Mowforth & Munt, 1998; Sharpley, 2000). The implication is that tourism development can be reconciled with environmental protection and social justice, at least at destination level, even though the increasing popularity of ecotourism pressurises fragile destinations. Application of the environmental efficiency concept to tourism's economic use of resources is still largely theoretical (Steele, 1995) and the danger is that pro-environmental awareness becomes lip service without corresponding action (Wheeller, 1997 and see Chapter 12 in this volume). The challenge is to put theory into practice in ways which are sympathetic to the structure of the tourism industry, that is, a large industry globally dominated by micro-businesses in most destinations. All tourism businesses are capable of improving upon their current level of environmental performance.

Even though not all forms of tourism, for example visiting friends and relatives, have a dependent relationship with environment, all forms of tourism interact with natural environmental systems and have a capacity to initiate environmental change. The tourism industry is therefore expected to be concerned about natural resource and cultural heritage conservation, and about maintenance and enhancement of global ecosystems and environmental quality. As quality of life and quality of service become increasingly important to consumers, so tourism firms and organisations in both public and private sectors will seek to act in more environmentally responsible ways. Indeed market research suggested evidence of consumers' concern for the environment and human relations was strong and thought to be sufficiently deeprooted to influence purchasing behaviour and product development throughout the 1990s (Gordon, 1991). Thus there is both a push factor away from environmentally destructive tourism and a pull factor towards green or sustainable tourism which makes sensitive use of natural environments and cultural heritage attractions.

Sustainable tourism requires that the demands of increasing numbers of tourists are satisfied in a manner that continues to attract them while meeting the needs of the host population by delivering improved standards of living, yet safeguarding the destination environment and cultural heritage. Although this view of sustainable tourism is generally accepted, how it can be implemented, given the loose and fragmented structure of the tourism industry, including the public sector, is another matter. Ideally, the principle of sustainability should be central to the tourism policies of both tourism-generating and tourism-receiving countries, embracing concepts of environmental efficiency and improvement of tourism's environmental performance. However, what does it entail in practice for tourism firms and organisations? What constitutes good environmental practice by the tourism industry and how can tourism firms and organisations monitor their activities in this context?

## Tourism's Environmental Objectives (and Responsibilities)

Society demands products which are supplied (for tourists this means holidays and other travel products), and accepts, albeit sometimes involuntarily, that there are environmental risks in so doing. However, tourist destinations, the tourism industry and the tourists themselves appear to share a common interest in ensuring that the environment, their primary resource, is sustained. In essence the constant natural assets rule applies, whereby the overall stock of environmental assets available to future generations (of tourists and non-tourists) must not be reduced (Pearce, 1991). This implies minimisation of loss of stock of non-renewable resources and an emphasis on efficiency in use, re-use and recycling of such resources, while ensuring the rate of use of renewable resources does not exceed their regenerative capacity, and thereby maintaining the integrity of the global resource system. Thus the overall objective of the tourism industry, including private firms and public sector organisations, must be to conduct business in an environmentally acceptable manner which is not only compatible with the character of destinations, on a scale which their host environments and cultures can absorb and welcome, but also compatible with the global environment and the needs of future generations. Too often to date the approach has been tourism-centric, that is destination focused (Hunter, 1995).

Is the tourism industry ready to accept its responsibility for the environment? This question needs to be answered from a global, not just a destination perspective, because tourism in its use of transport services and associated energy demands contributes to global environmental change (pollution). The diversity and fragmentation of the industry is important in considering its response: in particular, recognition of the very different roles performed by commercial firms (whether tour operators, travel agents, transport carriers, attraction or accommodation operators, etc.) and the public sector (whether national, regional or local governments or agencies such as national tourist offices or local tourist information centres). The former will be supplying a total tourism product or some component of the product to make profits. Increased environmental awareness provides a rationale to stay in business and gain competitive advantages through innovative behaviour (Hjalager, 1996). The latter do not, usually, have a tourism product *per se* to sell, although they may participate in promotional activities and supply infrastructure and public services. Their role, however, may be crucial on the destination scale where tourism development and expansion proposals emanating from many, small, independent firms can have a substantial environmental impact in the aggregate. Regulatory and planning roles of public sector organisations therefore have a particular role to play in safeguarding primary resources on the destination scale.

A distinction needs to be made between existing tourism activity and proposed tourism development. The latter, as a condition of proceeding, can be made to conform more readily to current 'best' standards of environmentally acceptable practice. Full advantage can be taken of the latest technical advances for example, in energy-efficient buildings, vehicles and other equipment. Large-scale development proposals can be made the subject of, as in the European Community, an environmental impact assessment (EIA) – a balanced appraisal of the 'potential' total effects of the proposed development on the natural and human environments. Only where the result of the EIA clearly demonstrates that the development will be environmentally responsible and sustain the destination's primary tourism resources should planning permission to proceed normally be granted. Planning authorities in destination areas are therefore in an influential position to ensure new tourism development maintains and enhances environmental quality (although it has to be admitted that destination planners and politicians have to balance environmental and other priorities).

Existing tourism activities and facilities, however, would at best have been developed to past standards (if any such existed) at a time when environmental considerations may not have been a factor in the development decision. Indeed, given that normal business practice is designed to maximise profits, commercial tourism firms are unlikely to take environmental externalities resulting from their activities into account when calculating their costs. Many established tourism businesses may be operating in an environmentally inefficient, even polluting, manner. Continuing profitability, unexpired economic lives of indivisible factors of production (buildings, equipment, etc.), habit and inertia make it difficult to change the nature of existing tourism activities. Indeed, the capital cost of any change for environmental reasons and/or loss of revenue can be a deterrent. Nevertheless opportunities for (environmental) improvement do occur when equipment needs replacing, buildings refurbishing and supply contracts renewing. For example, a cruise business replacing one of its cruise-ships could specify diesel engines with smokeless performance, i.e. clean exhaust under all load conditions. Ongoing tourism activities therefore need to be subjected to 'environmental audit' which is a management tool providing a systematic, regular and objective evaluation of the environmental performance of the organisation, its plant, buildings, processes and products. In essence, environmental audit and EIA have the same goals and are complementary tools in the struggle to achieve sustainable tourism.

Increasingly there is evidence that the tourism industry is seeking to act in environmentally responsible ways. The pressures for change are compelling and from many sources. As Figure 11.1 shows, there are many stakeholders with interests overlapping tourism's environmental performance. The consequences of poor environmental performance for destination place and corporate business images, and hence their commercial success, is a spur to action. The early lead often came from national government. In the United Kingdom, for example, the Tourism and Environment Task Force (1991) was established to draw up guidance on how the tourism industry might ensure that their present activities and policies as well as future tourism developments harmonise with the need to conserve and preserve the environment and to serve the well-being of the host populations. Elsewhere in Europe, national tourism plans and policies sought to conserve natural and cultural resources and regulate tourism development, e.g. in Portugal (Lewis & Williams, 1991), Switzerland (Gilg, 1991) and France (Tuppen, 1991). Further afield similar action sought to conserve, protect and improve the environment in Cyprus (Witt, 1991), Kenya (Dieke, 1991) and the Philippines (Choy, 1991).

While there is concern within the tourism industry about environmental trends and issues and agreement that co-ordinated action is necessary to sustain the environment, there is a certain reluctance to admit tourism's contribution to environmental degradation (Goodall, 1995; Stabler & Goodall, 1997) and therefore debate about who takes responsibility for initiating action (Kavallinis & Pizam, 1994), particularly in developing countries (King & Weaver, 1993). Often the tourism industry's position views the solution of environmental problems as the responsibility of government and society (Hashimoto, 2000).

However, the tourism industry has been more than just responsive to

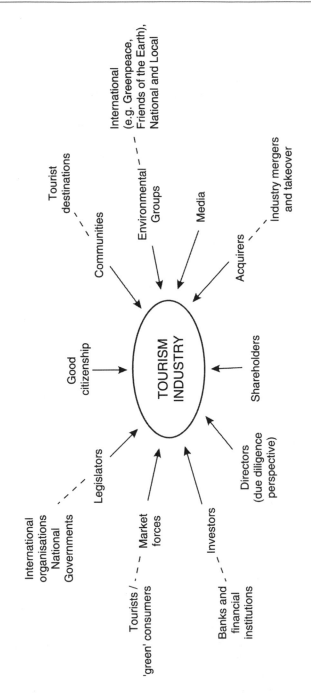

**Figure 11.1** Spurces of pressures on the tourism industry to act in an environmentally responsible way

government policies over the past decade. Efforts to translate the industry's recognition of its environmental responsibility into action have produced a multiplicity of advisory codes of conduct (Mason & Mowforth, 1995; UNEP/IE, 1995). While such codes may emanate from government sources at national, regional and local levels, as many come from international and non-governmental organisations, including the World Tourism Organization and the World Travel and Tourism Council, as come from the tourism industry, especially its sectoral trade associations (Hawkins & Holtz, 2001). Codes may be targeted not only at tourism businesses but also directed at tourists and host communities: all seek to influence attitudes and behaviour and implementation is usually voluntary. Those directed at tourism firms emphasise environmental commitment and responsibility, and highlight the consideration of environmental factors in the planning and development of tourism facilities, and in the development of environmentally sound products, operations and processes (Goodall, 1997). Most frequently these codes are 'statements of ideal' (Mason & Mowforth, 1995) or principles: they do not give practical advice, so badly needed by many tourism firms and destinations, on how to measure environmental performance and implement best environmental practice at business unit or site scales.

Principles enunciated within codes of conduct need to be translated into implementable 'green' practices by the tourism industry at business unit and site scales. Practical advice for existing tourism businesses and destinations is forthcoming in an increasing number of technical advisory manuals made available through trade associations, e.g. the Hotel Catering and Institutional Management Association (1991), International Association of Antarctic Tour Operators (1993), Canadian Restaurant and Foodservices Association (Wight, 1994a), British Holiday and Home Parks Association (Mason & Mowforth, 1995), and the International Hotels Environment Initiative (1993). Such advice may also come from public sector tourism organisations, including destination authorities, e.g. Scottish Tourist Board (1993), RDC/ETB/CC (1995), and even in the form of user-friendly do-it-yourself green audit kits (Dingle, 1995; Beioley, 1995). This demonstrates that knowledge exists to improve tourism's environmental performance but take-up or implementation is normally voluntary and, as discussed below, there may be barriers to (early) implementation. Still lacking, however, is guidance on how to assess current environmental performance, on what constitutes appropriate environmental performance standards for businesses or destinations, and how to calculate the feasibility of making improvements. Measurement of environmental performance and especially the interpretation of the results can be beset with problems (Goodall & Stabler, 2000).

Improvement of environmental performance is but a step on the path to sustainable tourism, and the implementation of policies and practices to achieve such ends requires tourism development to be subject to EIA and existing tourism activity to environmental auditing. Since the general principles of EIA application to tourism have been outlined elsewhere (see Green & Hunter, 1990; Hunter & Green, 1995), the emphasis here is on environmental auditing as a management tool for monitoring the environmental performance of existing tourism activity. Tourism activity and development in both the public and private sectors are equally amenable to environmental audit and environmental impact assessment.

There are certain implications which follow from the adoption of an environmentally responsible code of behaviour by tourism firms and organisations. At the development proposal stage particular attention has to be paid to choice of location and site selection in relation to environmental capacity concepts and to the design and integration of any buildings and infrastructure. During the construction phase efforts have to be made to minimise environmental disturbance and to ensure restoration where any environmental damage has occurred. Once operational, it requires adherence to appropriate on-site landscape and ecological management practices and the choice of working processes and routines with respect to principles of natural resource conservation, e.g. entailing energy efficiency, waste management (recovery and recycling), and source reduction of inputs. This is where environmental auditing comes into its own for the individual tourism business or organisation: although such businesses and organisations have to comply with various health, safety and environmental legislation, environmental auditing goes much further.

The introduction of environmental auditing into tourism business and destination practices demands far-reaching changes in the way most currently operate. The vision of environmental auditing is a full understanding of all environmental costs and benefits within a tourism business or destination by its management from both an operational and a product perspective, i.e. the 'greening' of the business (tourism firm or destination) and of the product (holiday or activity) are complementary. Environmental auditing therefore provides an understanding of environmental management controls, processes and systems, allowing a true verification of a tourism business's or destination's environmental performance.

## Principles of Environmental Auditing

The Commission of the European Communities (1993, based largely on the International Chamber of Commerce, 1989) defines environmental auditing as a management tool comprising a systematic, documented, periodic and objective evaluation of the performance of the organization, management system and processes designed to protect the environment with the aim of (i) facilitating management control of practices which may impact on the environment; and (ii) assessing compliance with company environmental policies.

Environmental auditing, it must be emphasised, is a means to an end – a combination of standardised testing and verification procedures. Such regular and comprehensive audits are applicable not only at business and establishment levels (i.e. the hotel chain and the individual hotel) but also to public sector tourism organisations (e.g. national tourist offices, tourist information centres) as well as destinations as a whole. The ensuing discussion concentrates upon the adoption and use of environmental auditing by tourism businesses.

Audits are likely to be undertaken voluntarily as part of normal business practice only by a corporate tourism businesses committed to acknowledging its environmental responsibility. These businesses will, therefore, have already formulated an environmental policy as an integral part of their overall business strategy, designed to deliver total quality management. The place of environmental auditing within the operating structure of a business is highlighted in Figure 11.2.

What objectives are likely to be contained in the environmental policy of businesses committed to 'green' or 'environmental' corporatism? Their policy statements should indicate, for both current and future activities:

(1) compliance with the spirit as well as the letter of environmental legislation and participation in the development of reasonable and workable environmental regulations;
(2) avoidance of negative environmental impacts of their proposed developments and reduction of any negative impacts of current activities (e.g. emission of pollutants);
(3) promotion of increased efficiency in the use of resources, including waste minimisation, the substitution of environmentally benign inputs and equipment wherever feasible, and the safe disposal of waste where the latter is unavoidable;
(4) development of products which are environmentally friendly; and
(5) fostering among staff, and maybe also customers and the communities in which they function, an understanding of environmental issues.

Having formulated an environmental policy, containing specific goals and targets, the key purposes of environmental auditing as an integral part of a tourism business's environmental management system, are to:

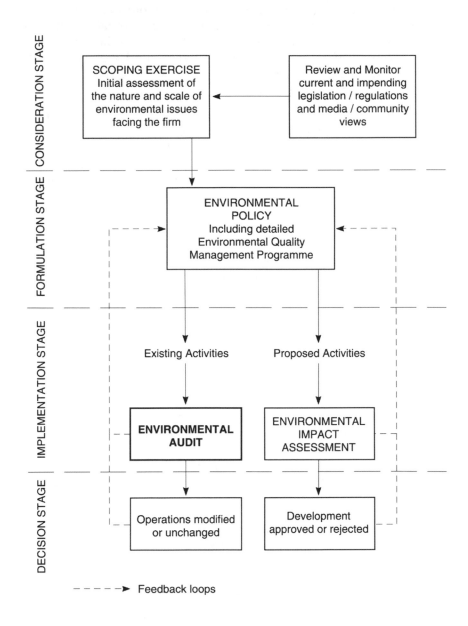

**Figure 11.2** Corporate environmentalism – the place for environmental auditing

(1) determine whether the environmental management system of the tourism business is performing satisfactorily;
(2) verify compliance with relevant environmental legislation;
(3) verify compliance with the tourism business's corporate policy;
(4) assess impact on the environment, both local and global, of the tourism business's operations;
(5) minimise human exposure to risk from the environment and to ensure appropriate health and safety provision, i.e. prevention of accidents;
(6) identify and assess the tourism business's risk resulting from environmental failure of its activities;
(7) advise the tourism business on environmental improvements it could make; and
(8) review the tourism business's internal procedures needed to achieve its environmental objectives (after Welford & Gouldson, 1993).

Why should tourism businesses voluntarily adopt environmental auditing? In addition to the benefits which accrue to the global, as well as the local, environment, there are realisable commercial benefits for individual tourism businesses. Such benefits include:

(1) cost savings from more efficient use of resources and effective minimisation of waste;
(2) marketing advantages relating to acceptance and projection of brand image;
(3) identification of environmental problems before they become liabilities, facilitating insurance cover and saving on litigation and clean-up costs;
(4) acquiring confidence of investors and lenders, facilitating raising of loan capital;
(5) better employee motivation and recruitment of higher quality staff;
(6) acquiring confidence of regulators as well as the community within which to operate; and
(7) improved corporate image.

In addition, environmental auditing provides each tourism business with an up-to-date environmental database for future planning (and for use in emergencies), as well as a framework for measuring environmental performance and developing benchmarks of good environmental practice.

For auditing to be effective, a tourism business must have established its baseline performance by means of an environmental review and have introduced a clear managerial responsibility for environmental issues. The general structure of an audit trail is outlined in Figure 11.3. Although it was suggested above that environmental auditing should be comprehensive, it

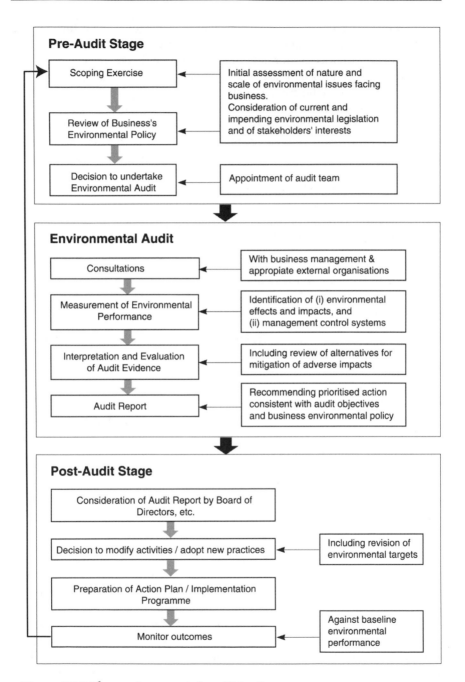

**Figure 11.3** The environmental audit trail

is possible for businesses to carry out a narrower assessment of only part of their activities (see below for types of audit), hence the requirement at the pre-audit stage to determine the nature and scope of the audit. This stage provides a framework within which objectives are set and accountability specified for accomplishing the task, including appointment of an audit team and scheduling of the audit process.

There is no uniform methodology for conducting an environmental audit and no set checklist of environmental performance indicators to be evaluated. This is not surprising because the potential environmental impacts/footprints of a charter airline and a hotel chain are obviously very different. However, in general, the last decade has witnessed a change in environmental auditing: originally it focused on technical issues and legal compliance and was frequently undertaken by professionals external to the business. Now, however, it is accepted that auditing extends to the environmental management systems and controls within a business. Also, coupled with the need to review these on a regular basis, more environmental auditing is undertaken internally, subject to external verification by attestation (Medley, 1997).

The audit exercise generates a report in which findings and recommendations (after consideration of alternatives) are prioritised in relation to audit objectives and the tourism business's environmental policy. The report provides significant feedback to management about overall environmental performance, flagging specific problem areas, especially concerning compliance status, and including recommendations for corrective action. At the post-audit stage, consideration of the report by the board of the business leads, after balancing environmental against other business goals, to an action plan or implementation programme to rectify any deficiencies and improve internal environmental management.

Regular auditing encourages a consistent approach towards managing tourism's environmental impacts and further develops integrated environmental management systems at the levels of the individual tourism business and establishment. Within any tourism business the effectiveness of environmental management itself should be ascertainable over time, not only in terms of increased trade and reduced costs but also via improvements in its compliance record, reductions in environmental accident/incident statistics, and lowering of risk of exposure to environmental hazards. Maintaining an environmental auditing system may have other spin-offs, improving management generally and so assist the achievement of other objectives, e.g. a British Standard BS 5750 quality management certification or an ISO 14001 as external attestation of its environmental claims.

Activities of all tourism businesses, organisations, and even destina-

**Table 11.1** Types of environmental audit and possible applications within the tourism industry

| Audit type | Scope | Use in tourism |
|---|---|---|
| A: Full Audits | | |
| Corporate | Entire business – all aspects of its environmental impacts and environmental management systems | A multi-establishment business, e.g. national restaurant chain, to ensure consistency of environmental performance across all their establishments. |
| Life cycle | 'Cradle to grave' assessment of environmental impact of a product/service over its life-span | Car hire firm evaluating purchase, use and disposal of vehicles in its fleet. |
| Site | Environmental impact of operations at a specific site | Car wash evaluating water use and recycling, energy consumption and effluent disposal. |
| State of the environment | Assessment of the environmental quality of an area | Destination public authority reviewing its environmental performance. |
| B: Partial Audits | | |
| Activity | Overview of activity or process across a business | Hotel chain reviewing staff travel on company business(may be extended to include journey to work). |
| Associate(or Supplier) | Supply chain linkages | Airline checking how green its in-flight caterers are. |
| Compliance | Checks to ensure business complies with relevant current environmental regulations affecting its operations | Fast-food takeaway ensuring its street frontage is not persistently littered. |
| Divestiture liability | Assessment of environmental costs of disposing of subsidiary businesses | Hotel chain selling its in-flight catering subsidiary. |
| Health and safety | Identification of hazards and quantification of risks associated with production processes and occupational health of workers | Review of hotel fire escape routes and staff awareness of fire precautions and drill routines. |

Table 11.1 (*cont.*)

| Audit type | Scope | Use in tourism |
|---|---|---|
| Issues | Assessment of consequences of business for a specific environmental issue | Airline considering its output of $CO_2$ and $NO_x$ in relation to global warming. |
| Pre-acquisitional (or Transactional) | Assessment of environmental liability of businesses involved in merger, take-over or other joint ventures | Airline taking over a regional carrier. |
| Product | Ensuring existing and proposed products meet environmental policy criteria | Tour operator reviewing package holiday impact on destination resources. |

tions can be reviewed under environmental auditing. Indeed, annual environmental audits of all ongoing tourism activities are viewed by the World Travel and Tourism Council (1991) as an integral management tool in a tourism industry with a proactive commitment to environmentally responsible tourism. In practice, not all environmental audits undertaken are fully comprehensive. Table 11.1 lists and describes the scope of the different types of audit and illustrates possible applications within tourism.

Clearly all aspects of a business's operations may be reviewed under environmental audit. Inputs, in varying forms and amounts are required by all businesses and organisations, and where a business 'thinks green' the use of environmentally benign materials, substances and equipment will be encouraged. This means that inputs are selected which are environmentally beneficial because they reduce demand on natural resources, e.g. recycled paper, or which do not contain environmentally damaging ingredients, e.g. phosphate-free detergents and cleaners, CFC-free aerosols, while environmentally unfriendly inputs, such as asbestos, pesticides, toxic and corrosive materials are phased out. In the production of a good or the rendering of a service, the resource efficiency of the processes, particularly their energy efficiency (including that of buildings and vehicles), will be evaluated. In addition, the generation and disposal of wastes from production will be examined with a view to source reduction, recovery and reuse within the business and recycling off-site where disposal is necessary. Where any wastes are potential pollutants, particular attention will be given to controlling, progressively reducing and ultimately eliminating such emissions. Similarly the business's product can be designed to meet higher environmental standards, e.g. motor vehicles which run on unleaded petrol, or to be *green*, e.g. walking or cycling holidays.

What is feasible? Acting in an environmentally responsible way has consequences for a business's costs and revenues, the incidence of which may vary over time. For example, improving the energy efficiency of an existing hotel by installing wall and roof insulation and double-glazed replacement windows will incur an immediate capital outlay in anticipation of lower, future annual fuel costs. There may also be changes to revenues: positive if the higher comfort standard attracts more visitors; negative if average occupancy declines because of any associated price increase. Elimination of all pollution or environmentally damaging action is therefore neither technologically nor economically feasible. Even where technologically feasible, the adoption of environmentally friendly practices and materials will reflect the trade-off between costs and benefits of such action, particularly for private sector businesses. Thus, in the situation of an optimum use of the environment, the marginal pollution abatement costs are equal to the marginal environmental damage costs.

The principles evolved under industrial pollution control can be used to demonstrate the minimum that can be expected of tourism businesses and organisations volunteering to act in an environmentally responsible way and the considerations that should exercise public authorities when formulating environmental regulations that impinge upon tourism activity. The fundamental basis of the British approach to anti-pollution legislation for a century and a half has been the 'best practicable means' (BPM) which took account of the cost of pollution abatement and its effect on the viability of the industry. This led to presumptive emission limits, set and updated by HM Inspectorate of Pollution (HMIP) after consultation with industry. Compliance with the set limit value was normally taken as evidence that the BPM were being used. This approach was refined in the proposals for 'integrated pollution control' (Royal Commission on Environmental Pollution, 1976) incorporated into the 1990 UK Environmental Protection Act. Integrated pollution control was to have been based on the concept of the 'best practicable environmental option' (BPEO), i.e. that option which provided the most benefit or the least damage to the environment as a whole, at acceptable cost, in the long term as well as the short term. A BPEO pollution control strategy for a particular industry could be so expensive as to be uneconomic, e.g. a technique which reduced emissions by 95% although it was four times as expensive as an alternative which reduced emissions by only 90%, could be judged as acceptable if the emissions were particularly hazardous. In fact, the 1990 UK Environmental Protection Act incorporated the EC Directive on combating industrial pollution which is based on the 'best available technique not entailing excessive cost' (BATNEEC). This is a concept not far removed from the BPM. Under the BATNEEC, the HMIP again impose conditions specifying emission levels from plants which can be up-graded in line with technological developments from time to time. The BAT will normally apply, although the presumption can be modified where it can be shown that the costs of applying the BAT would be excessive compared with the environmental protection achieved. Even so there may be a further 'let-out' albeit temporary, via derogation, entailing the modification of legislation (specifically for application of EC directives), e.g. relaxing of emission standards, compliance dates, etc.

Even allowing for acceptance of the 'polluter-pays principle' (whether interpreted as the polluter paying for the cost of prevention or the cost of the environmental damage), tourism businesses and organisations may be expected, as part of their environmental policy, to behave according to the BPM/BATNEEC principles.

It therefore has to be admitted that while such behaviour will mitigate the environmentally damaging consequences of tourism, it will not necessarily eliminate them. For example, if tourism is expanding at a particular destination, even though existing businesses comply with emission standards and similar (or more stringent) standards are imposed on new businesses, incremental growth of the tourism industry could still lead to the capacity of the destination environment to absorb potential pollutants, such as sewage effluent, being exceeded. Environmental deterioration may ensue unless emission standards for existing businesses and new entrants are tightened further. But, implicit in the BPM/BATNEEC reasoning, some human-induced change to the natural environment is allowable. While all tourism impacts upon the environment the change initiated is not necessarily permanently damaging so the question becomes what are the 'limits of acceptable change' (Wight, 1994b). Various interpretations exist, not surprising given that value judgements are involved, ranging from the 'no observed effect level' (NOEL), to the 'no observable adverse effect level' (NOEAL), and the 'lowest observable adverse effect level' (LOEAL), to 'as low as reasonably achievable' (ALARA) (UNEP/GESAMP, 1986). ALARA is certainly consistent with BPM/ BATNEEC.

Environmental auditing will therefore allow a tourism business to evaluate the environmental consequences of its current range and level of activities, to determine the extent to which its current operations measure up to the BPM/BATNEEC principles, and therefore to project an environmentally responsible image.

## Applying Environmental Auditing Within Tourism

Theoretically environmental auditing can be applied to the activities of any tourism business, organisation and destination at any spatial scale from site, through neighbourhood to regional, national and global levels. Although there is limited evidence of tourism businesses undertaking comprehensive corporate and life cycle audits, many have drafted or are formulating environmental policies and partial audits (especially product, operational activity and site ones) are becoming increasingly common-place. Thus individual tourism businesses undertake, at least on specific occasions if not regularly, environmental audits of their products, for example:

- package holiday;
- for essential activities; e.g. energy use and transport;
- for buildings, especially hotels;
- for waste management, e.g. disposal and/or recycling of paper, glass, etc.;
- for linked firms, e.g. suppliers of foodstuffs and furniture to hotels;
- for broader issues, e.g. their contribution to global warming;
- for compliance purposes.

It should be noted that the nature of the environmental impact differs between scales of production of the same product because of different technologies used (compare a seaside holiday taken in a guesthouse or self-catering cottage with one taken in a resort hotel complex) and that this can have repercussions for the nature and extent of any environmental auditing undertaken. The environmental auditing appropriate to a transnational company, such as an international hotel chain, will differ from that relevant to a small family business, such as a guesthouse. Some (e.g. McKercher, 1993) argue that the very nature of the tourism industry makes even voluntary compliance with environmental legislation extremely difficult.

Consider tourism products. A product audit will reveal how environmentally responsible the business's present product range is and suggest how products can be adapted to make them environmentally more friendly. For example, tour operators offering hire cars as part of a package holiday can ensure that they operate on lead-free petrol; those operating coach tours can arrange that routes in historic towns are selected so as not to damage the foundations of medieval buildings. Tour operators can also select accommodation that is owned and managed locally: this helps sustain the local economy, the more so where hotels in particular use mainly local produce (the latter having a further environmental benefit as fewer transport inputs are used). Opportunities to substitute local produce arise in certain destinations, e.g. the Caribbean region where, in resorts and on cruise ships, tourists are more likely to eat tropical fruits imported from other parts of the world than produced locally (Pattullo, 1996). Tour operators may encourage the restoration of derelict, vernacular properties for use as tourist accommodation. A product audit may therefore lead to a change in both the width and depth of the business's product range, with new or revamped products formulated to be environmentally friendly such as the introduction of wildlife conservation working holidays, or restricting the numbers participating in particular wildlife and natural history tours. Anecdotal examples of tourism businesses formulating clear environmental mission statements as part of their business plans and developing simple but effective environmental monitoring and control systems using both internal and external audits can be found even among small businesses, e.g. Treadsoftly, a family-owned and operated, back country mountain biking company in Alberta, Canada adopted such an approach from start-up (Herremans & Welsh, 1999, 2001).

Formulating an environmentally friendly tourism product may be only half the battle, since there is the matter of how that product is 'consumed' by the holiday makers, some of whom are less environmentally aware than others. It may therefore be argued that tour operators have a duty of care towards destination environments and their host populations, which requires tour operators to help educate holidaymakers about the customs, culture and environmental issues of those destinations. Thus, tour operators like Saga Holidays, Eurocamp and Thomson include briefing packs and/or advice on a destination's cultural and ecological background among the information they distribute to their tourists. Such 'consumer education' in the form of tour operator-issued codes of conduct for behaviour at a destination is becoming increasingly common.

Tourism businesses can also 'go green' operationally by seeking to minimise their use of resource inputs (i.e. source reduction), by substituting environmentally benign inputs, by controlling waste discharges and encouraging recovery and reuse, and by giving staff 'environmental' training. This operational context applies to all activities of tourism businesses, including those that take place in tourist origin areas or entail transport between tourist origins and destinations. The hotel sector, particularly transnational corporations (WTTERC, 1993), has made most progress in using regular audits to implement and review environmental strategy, e.g. Canadian Pacific Hotels (Troyer, 1992) and Inter-Continental Hotels, whose environment manual was made available worldwide acting as the catalyst for the International Hotels Environment Initiative (Black, 1995). Hotels concentrate their environmental auditing upon energy and water conservation and waste reduction, while restaurants emphasise energy and solid waste reduction and airlines fuel efficiency, noise and emissions reduction (Todd & Williams, 1996). Occupancy-linked controls in hotel heating/lighting/ventilation/air conditioning systems can generate significant energy savings. Source reduction of inputs presents the tourism industry with considerable difficulty where the transport component of the product is concerned (see also Gössling, 2000a, 2000b). While some saving may be possible by substituting public for private transport and increasing load factors, all fossil fuels contribute to global warming. Hence any increase in the long-haul tour market adds to that problem, however well-maintained the aircraft engines. Certain tourism businesses have reduced or are seeking to reduce energy consumption in their buildings. For example, Disney World have reviewed all building specifications at both their California and Florida sites from the viewpoint of electrical energy (and water) conservation (Woolf, 1991). On a much smaller scale the Hotel Ucliva, Waltensberg, Switzerland installed a heating system which uses locally grown wood, managed on sustainable forestry principles and burnt in a pollution-free, high temperature furnace (Lane, 1990).

The importance of employee support for environmentally responsible working practices is increasingly recognised, as in Canadian Pacific Hotels' Green Partnership Phase II (WTTHRC, 1998b) and in British Airways' environmental policy and training programmes (British Airways, 1999).

Substitution of environmentally benign for environmentally harmful inputs is also taking place, although the availability of such inputs depends on the environmental policies adopted by firms in other industries. However, large tourism businesses, e.g. Disney World, use the power of their massive purchasing budget to make suppliers provide environmentally friendly products. Toiletries and cleaning materials that are CFC and phosphate-free are insisted upon by some businesses, e.g. Consort Hotels. Organic produce is appearing on certain hotel and restaurant menus. Many businesses run their motor vehicles on unleaded petrol, e.g. British Airways and Consort Hotels. Indeed, the latter provide staff living within five miles of their York hotel with bicycles, as well as having two courtesy bicycles for guests' use (Evans, 1990). Stationery and other paper products used by hotels (e.g. Consort), tour operators (e.g. Saga Holidays) and airlines (e.g. British Airways), is made increasingly from recycled paper. These examples illustrate the possibilities; activity and site audits would confirm whether, and the extent to which, tourism businesses operate in a fully environmentally responsible manner.

An integral part of a tourism business's corporate environmental policy will be a positive attitude towards minimising waste and encouraging recycling. Much waste from tourism businesses, especially from hotels and other tourist accommodation, is similar in composition to domestic household rubbish and is normally disposed of by burial at landfill sites. Even where the waste is biodegradable this is not a totally satisfactory solution to waste disposal, since landfill sites are in increasingly short supply, there is some danger of pollution from leachate, and even vegetable waste is hard to break down in a landfill site when surrounded by plastic and lacking oxygen. If biodegradable rubbish does eventually decompose it still releases methane (which contributes to global warming). However, waste minimisation and pollution reduction is a step in the right direction. British Airways, for example, continuously reviews its operations, seeking to reduce aircraft noise, CFC emissions from its engineering processes, and toxic paint wastes, as well as its catering operations, where increasing use is made of reusable crockery. The Las Vegas Flamingo Hilton Resort and Casino has demonstrated the potential of solid waste minimisation practices, backed by continuous monitoring, to reduce costs and defuse regulatory pressures (Cummings, 1997).

Recyclability is preferable to biodegradability. Efforts should therefore be made to recycle as many materials as possible, e.g. aluminium and 'tin' (steel) cans, paper and cardboard, glass, plastic, other scrap metals, cooking oils and lubricants, etc. Even energy can be 'recycled' in a sense, e.g. heat energy from refrigeration units can be used to heat water and buildings. Recycling has the advantage that it may also reduce primary resource consumption, e.g. if a car hire firm installs a car wash that cleans and recycles its water (rather than discharging dirty water into mains drainage) it will use only 9 litres of fresh water per wash (instead of the usual 210 litres where there is no recycling). In particular recycling can save on energy use (although these benefits are only indirect to the tourism industry) e.g. the energy consumed in making one new aluminium can would make 20 recycled ones. Hotels and other tourist buildings can fit low-energy compact fluorescent bulbs which not only use far less energy but last up to eight times longer than standard light bulbs (although they do cost more initially). Such reductions in energy consumption will assist in stemming global warming.

However, recycling opportunities may be differentially available to tourism businesses, a reflection of their size. Small firms, such as independent hotels and guest-houses would need to sort, store and either arrange collection or delivery of recyclable materials, whereas large businesses, such as transnationals, may have 'in-house' opportunities, based on scale economies, to benefit from recycling. For example, Disney World in Florida has its own sewage works linked to an organic composting factory which converts sewage sludge into organic fertiliser for use on the flower-beds and trees of the Magic Kingdom and also recycles irrigation water to reduce demand on water supply while a large reverse osmosis plant enables recycled water to be used in swimming pools (Woolf, 1991). A study of business attitudes towards sustainable tourism in the UK outbound tourism industry revealed very limited adoption of environmental management and auditing, with recycling being the most commonly practised action (Forsyth, 1995). Again, activity and site audits would indicate how 'green' a business was operationally and target processes and activities for improvement.

Tourism businesses, especially those in the accommodation and attractions sectors, are also concerned about the wider aspects of the environmental quality of their sites, not just aesthetic, landscaping issues. Center Parcs, for example, have enhanced the biodiversity of their holiday village sites as a result of annual ecological monitoring carried out by local Wildlife Trust naturalists and English Nature. This demonstrates a particular, albeit narrow, value of site audits.

While all tourism businesses can undertake the range of internal environmental audits, the tour operators are in a position to influence the environmental friendliness of the total tourism product by carrying out associate audits of businesses acting as their agents or subcontractors in supplying the components of their package holidays. Leading tour operators are increasingly using environmental advisers to monitor the environmental practices of hotels and resorts (Inskeep & Kallenberger, 1992). There is also evidence to suggest that some tour operators, especially smaller specialist ones, select tourist accommodation on the basis that it is locally owned and managed, is of vernacular design and construction, etc. (e.g. Saga Holidays, Pure Crete, Arctic Experience, Sunvil Travel and VFB Holidays), even if they do not go so far as to undertake associate audits. In Europe at least, EC Directive 990/314/EEC on Package Travel, Package Holidays and Package Tours (implemented from 31 December 1992), that clearly imposes certain responsibilities on tour operators (and/or travel agents) regarding their products, encourages European tour operators to consider such audits. Thus British Airways Holidays has instituted supply chain audits of the hotels it uses in Bali, Mauritius, the Seychelles and Thailand (British Airways, 1999).

Corporate audits *per se* are probably redundant where a tourism business has a fully comprehensive environmental management system which implements corporate environmental policy, consults with stakeholders, has developed environmental performance indicators, audits progress and reviews targets and whose efficacy is attested annually by external verification. This is likely to be the case only with the largest tourism businesses, such as British Airways, where its original Environment Branch has evolved into its Sustainable Business Unit (British Airways, 2000). Corporate audits are hardly appropriate for the many small businesses which form a large part of the fragmented tourism industry. It would therefore be sufficient if such small independent businesses carried out activity, product and site audits as part of their regular management function. However, for large businesses, especially transnationals, with numerous 'local bases', e.g. multiple travel agencies, hotel chains and mass tour operators, the role of the corporate audit assumes importance in ensuring knowledge of the business's environmental policy and comparability of implementation in each of the business's operative bases or establishments. In practice this may focus on internal communications and on the training and motivation of all company staff. The latter is perhaps the one area where many businesses are showing an awareness of their wider environmental responsibilities, although the fact that tour operators, such as Eurocamp, provide a range of environmental training for their staff (including destination representatives and agents) cannot be represented as even an embryo corporate audit.

Issues audits are likely to adopt a rather different format, not least because they do not need to be undertaken as part of a regular environmental monitoring schedule, being required only when a particular (new) environmental issue is recognised. In all other respects, if a business has adopted regular environmental monitoring, employing the other forms of audit, then issues audits could well be redundant. Within the tourism industry many businesses, especially tour operators, are demonstrating an awareness of wider environmental issues such as wildlife conservation and global warming: for example, Moswin Tours provide their tourists who visit the Black Forest in Germany with an opportunity to learn about acid rain. Tour operators also participate in a practical way at the destination scale, e.g. CV Travel has been advising communities in certain destinations about rubbish disposal; Sunvil Travel assisted, with staff time and other aid in kind, in the creation of Cyprus's first national park on the Akemas peninsula; and Turkish Delight have provided financial support to the conservation foundation attempting to save the Dalyan Delta (important for loggerhead turtles) from development. Similarly, other tour operators offer general (financial) help to wildlife conservation, e.g. Arctic Experience support both the Wildlife Trust and the Whale and Dolphin Conservation Society, although they may link such support to the numbers of tourists purchasing their package holidays. Cox & Kings will buy one acre of Belize rainforest for conservation for every traveller on their wildlife programme, or offer a week's sponsorship for a researcher from the Whale and Dolphin Conservation Society for each tourist on one of their whale-watching holidays.

Given the emphasis there has been on strategic planning for sustainable tourism (e.g. Inskeep & Kallenberger, 1992; IFTO, 1994; Inskeep, 1998; Simpson, 2001) and the fact that environmental audit preparation has been included in training programmes, such as the Green Management Strategic Planning Workshops run by ecoplan:net ltd. for the Bahamian government with participants from 11 Commonwealth Caribbean countries (WTTHRC, 1998a), it is surprising that auditing has not been practised to the same extent at tourist destinations as in tourism businesses. The advantages of undertaking state of the environment auditing should be clear but it has only been carried out in the case of restricted destination sites usually under single ownership, e.g. Cape Byron Headland Reserve, New South Wales, Australia (Brown & Essex, 1997) and Aanuka Beach Resort, Coffs Harbour City, New South Wales, Australia (Pigram, 1996). It may be suggested that environmental monitoring is akin to partial auditing, i.e. focusing on a particular environmental medium/issue in a destination, is practised under environmental quality grading schemes, such as the European Blue Flag beaches which has evolved more stringent and inclusive indicators over time (UNEP/WTO/FEEE, 1996) or where the benefits of traffic calming have been assessed for resort quality (and business levels) (Langer, 1996). Academic studies have demonstrated the potential of destination level environmental management systems in the case of ski areas (Todd & Williams, 1996) and small islands (Stabler & Goodall, 1996) and also of 'state of the environment' auditing, e.g. for Molyvos, a resort on the Greek island of Mytilini (Diamantis & Westlake, 1997), although the latter was restricted to water quality/supply and waste generation/disposal issues. Indeed, particular issues have been singled out, such as the role of integrated water management at Banff, Canada (Draper, 1997) in promoting destination water sustainability via water conservation, protection of natural water quality and wastewater treatment.

## Conclusion – Steps in the Right Direction

Environmental auditing offers management a procedural framework within which judgements can be made on how environmentally responsible a tourism business's or organisation's current operations and products are. It is a means to an end, providing post-development assessment identifying environmental damage emanating from present activities. Implementation of environmental auditing is dependent upon a clear commitment by tourism businesses and organisations to total quality management, of which environmental policy is an integral part. The response of the tourism industry has been mixed. Despite encouragement and guidance at international, national and sectoral levels as outlined above, the evidence of positive response is largely anecdotal. Many commentators suggest both awareness of environmental issues and especially innovation in environmental management has been limited, confined predominantly to large tourism businesses (Leslie, 1995; Pigram, 1996), although mass tour operators are not viewed as responsive as specialist/niche ones (Carey *et al.*, 1997). More generally, small and medium-sized enterprises are seen as complying with environmental law more by good luck than conscious action (Petts *et al.*, 1998) so small tourism businesses are no exception. Product innovation has also been restricted since ecotourism or sustainable tourism products command only a small share of the market (while their use of energy and its global consequences is ignored). Very few tourism businesses can therefore be categorised as green innovators, many are 'conventionals' supplying a traditional product not perceived for its environmental-friendly qualities, and most remain 'underperformers' (Goodall, 1995). Eco-labelling has a role to play in this context but there is a clear differentiation between eco-labels, which reflect environmental impact of a tourism product, and eco-quality indicators, which identify the environmental quality of the tourism business/organisation or destination (Mihaliè, 1996). Most labels used to date in tourism are of the latter type, e.g. ISO 14001, Green Globe, PATA Green Leaf, (Hawkins, 1997; Hawkins & Holtz, 2001).

At first sight it appears obvious that the long-term common interest of the tourism industry is the adoption of policies which conserve tourism's primary resource base, the environment, since this must underpin the sustainability of tourism at any destination. However, environmental auditing itself requires a commitment of resources and the question must be asked whether the benefits and costs of taking action consequent upon the results of an environmental audit are clear-cut. Aside from any lack of awareness of environmental issues and of commitment to environmental policy, tourism businesses frequently perceive the costs of implementing environmentally friendly changes to their products, operations, buildings and equipment as prohibitive, as well as arguing a lack of demand for environmentally friendly tourism products (Forsyth, 1995; Goodall, 1995, 1997). Indeed, McKercher (1993) reported that tourism businesses could not afford the high cost of installing pollution control systems. It is further suggested that, given the highly competitive nature of the industry, tourism businesses fear taking action not matched by competitors and believe themselves powerless to influence improvements (Forsyth, 1995). Environmental 'commitment' has been viewed as a public relations exercise to 'green' a tourism business's image: according to Dann (1996: 257) some tour operators use 'greenspeak' – 'promotional hype (which) simply reinforces the old myths of paradise and unspoiled nature' – while concealing their own material goals from tourists. This leads, at best, to cosmetic rather than genuine changes in environmental practices of tourism businesses (Mowforth & Munt, 1998).

Although environmental auditing may identify why and where tourism products, activities and processes are damaging the environment, remedial action may be another matter. If a compliance audit shows a business is failing to meet legal requirements, immediate action can be expected (otherwise the business risks prosecution and fines). However, where activity, associate, product and site audits indicate environmentally damaging consequences, a positive response can clearly be expected where a business's profitability will benefit, which may be true where a hotel reduces its energy consumption. Cost-cutting is the favoured form of changes to practice among tourism businesses, as Forsyth (1995) confirms. This is consistent with a tourism industry driven more by short-term reaction to competition and crisis than by longer-term strategic considerations. Indeed, for tourism's many small businesses it is a rational way forward, i.e. a reactive mode where adoption of environmental practices lags behind other business objectives.

Action may be less likely, though, where the benefits are largely enjoyed by third parties or the general public, such as the reduction of pollution from motor vehicle emissions. In these cases, if remedial action entails greater costs, the individual business could be at a disadvantage *vis-à-vis* competitors (who take no action) unless it is able to offset these higher costs by even greater revenue. Can more tourists be attracted if the business markets its products as 'greener' than those of its competitors? Herein lies the uncertainty! If consumers' current search for quality embraces an increasing environmental awareness, the tourism industry would face demand-led pressure to adopt environmental auditing more widely. But holidays are still sold largely on the basis of destination, value for money, excitement and quality rather than on environmental sustainability. There is evidence in the United States that consumers are willing to pay a premium for environmentally responsible hospitality products (Cummings, 1997).

Where environmental auditing has been adopted as part of business practice it normally follows that there is an improvement in the environmental performance of that tourism business. But there is no guarantee: environmental auditing may give tourism businesses greater access to information on the environmental impacts of their activities but that information may still not be comprehensive, nor wholly accurate, nor fully reflect social concerns. Moreover it cannot be guaranteed that tourism decision-makers will understand or act upon the information available.

Environmental auditing undoubtedly has the potential to improve tourism's environmental performance, as the anecdotal evidence above highlights, but the hopes have yet to be fully realised. Corporate environmental management (and green consumerism) in tourism is not sufficiently widespread to have brought about fundamental change throughout the industry. The reasons are several: some generic, others specific to tourism. It has to be acknowledged that no significant advances in the valuation of environmental externalities and their internalisation (other than through legislation and auditing) have been made recently and, therefore, environmental costs are not automatically factored into accountability systems at all levels by all businesses and organisations in all sectors and in all countries. Standard decision-making relies on quantifiable and objective facts but falters where there is uncertainty. Unquestionably environmental problems and their solutions are beset by long-term uncertainty being highly complex, value-laden and subjective and not conforming to set assessment criteria. Given the lack of understanding within tourism of the actual and potential criticality of natural capital, the precautionary or proactive approach to environmental management now commonly required of decision-makers is a daunting prospect for much of the tourism industry. The user-friendly system of environmental auditing demonstrating benefits at defined scales of operations needed by tourism, especially its smaller businesses, is at least a decade away.

It has already been emphasised above that the nature of the tourism industry constrains what can be achieved in the environmental context. In supplying a positional good, subject to the dictates of fashion, tourism operates in a fiercely competitive market system which is largely insensitive to environmental priorities (Gössling, 2000a), especially the use of common environmental resources on the part of any one tourism business. For countries in the developing world with a significant tourist trade, environment-based growth constraints represent a highly contentious issue. For destinations experiencing loss of market share the reaction may be further investment in environmentally damaging development, as in the case of ski resorts responding to snow-deficient winters by investing in artificial snow-making equipment (Koenig & Abegg, 1997).

Attitudes to environmental auditing and management in tourism remain equivocal, with the industry on the one hand viewing action as the responsibility of others, particularly government, yet recognising this as a driver of improved environmental performance, while, on the other hand regarding government regulation as a nuisance, imposing costs and stifling innovation, and preferring environmental regulation to be 'controlled' by the industry itself in order to reflect business reality (Forsyth, 1995). Leaving the means of compliance to self-regulation by the tourism industry is likely to entail an enforcement deficit (Goodall, 1997) and suggests some command-and-control powers need to be exercised by government (Goodall & Stabler, 1997, 2000; Stabler & Goodall, 1997).

Progress in improving tourism's environmental performance via environmental auditing has been piecemeal – in essence the tourism industry has moved from one sub-optimal position to another. Whether the latter is superior from a purely environmental viewpoint is inconclusive given the long-term uncertainties surrounding environmental change and also the fact that while the environmental performance of many tourism businesses has improved considerably, the overall environmental impact of tourism may have increased as the industry expanded, i.e. an increase in the number of tourists/bednights/distances travelled more than offsets any per capita reduction in the use of energy or water or emission levels. Indeed, it begs the question as to what constitutes an improvement in environmental performance (Goodall & Stabler, 2000) and points to the frailty of the concept of sustainable tourism. How far can the environmental impact of tourism be reduced without damaging business performance? Will the impact level consistent with concepts such as sustainable tourism and limits to acceptable change support a tourism industry as large and diverse as the present one? The answers are not obvious, nor straightforward.

In the meantime the way forward is for tourism businesses to strive to improve further their environmental performance, in conjunction with action by and encouragement from the tourism industry and its various trade associations. Environmental auditing provides the databases for identifying best environmental management practice (Goodall, 1994; Pigram, 1996) and therefore the introduction of performance and process benchmarking. Simply extending current best practice throughout the industry would bring marked improvement in tourism's environmental performance and reduction in its environmental impact. Benchmarking provides a continuous management procedure whereby a tourism business can compare its level of environmental performance and rate of improvement in that performance with that of the best or leading tourism businesses. This is 'competitive benchmarking' but there is no reason why the comparison should not be with the best performers among service industry businesses in general, i.e. 'functional benchmarking' (see also Coker, 1996). 'Best practice benchmarking' is increasingly common in many sectors of advanced economies, including the voluntary and public sectors, although seldom adopted by very small firms. Tourism is beginning to embrace benchmarking in the assessment of total management quality, with a focus on customer satisfaction: for example, in the hospitality sector, including smaller hotels (Department of National Heritage, 1996; Phillips & Appiah-Adu, 1998), at visitor attractions (Young & Ambrose, 1999), and quality of services in destinations (Thomason *et al.*, 1999a, 1999b; Thomason *et al.*, 2000). In the United Kingdom, from 1 April 2000, all authorities providing local public services have a new statutory duty of 'best value': measured by a combination of 170 Best Value Performance Indicators and a further 54 Audit Commission Performance Indicators. This is an approach designed to promote continuous improvement in service delivery (Grant *et al.*, 2000). The indicators cited are not specific to tourism and certainly not to purely environmental objectives but the approach does provide a structured framework within which destinations could evolve environmental best practice benchmarking.

The future prospect is of continuous improvement in tourism's environmental performance and further reduction in its negative environmental impacts as management tools such as environmental auditing and environmental best practice benchmarking are integrated into environmental management systems applied regularly by tourism businesses, organisations and destinations – the more so if life cycle principles are incorporated into the equation. The rate of overall improvement will depend, of course, upon further exhortation, incentives and enforcement by the tourism industry, its trade associations and, in the last resort, by governments. Even though sustainable tourism development may be unachievable (Sharpley, 2000), highly significant and continuing environmental benefits can be delivered by a tourism industry committed to the use of environmental auditing, life cycle analysis and best practice benchmarking.

## Note
1. This chapter first appeared as 'Environmental auditing for tourism' in Volume 4 of *Progress in Tourism, Recreation and Hospitality Management* (1992), pp. 60–71.

## Bibliography
Beioley, S. (1995) Greening tourism – soft or sustainable. *Insights* 7 (May), B75–89. English Tourist Board.

Black, C.W. (1995) The Inter-Continental Hotels Group and its environmental awareness programme in the hotel industry. In D. Leslie (ed) *Promoting Environmental Awareness and Action in Hospitality, Tourism and Leisure* (pp. 31–46). Environment Papers Series No. 1, Department of Hospitality, Tourism and Leisure Management. Glasgow: Glasgow Caledonian University.

British Airways (1999) *Annual Environmental Report 1999*. Harmondsworth: British Airways.

British Airways (2000) *Social and Environmental Report 2000*. Harmondsworth: British Airways.

Brown, G. and Essex, S. (1997) Sustainable tourism management: Lessons from *The Edge* of Australia. *Journal of Sustainable Tourism* 5 (4), 294–305.

Butler, R.W. (2000) Tourism and the environment: A geographical perspective. *Tourism Geographies* 2 (3), 337–58.

Carey, S., Gountas, Y. and Gilbert, D. (1997) Tour operators and destination sustainability. *Tourism Management* 18 (7), 425–32.

Cater, E. and Goodall, B. (1992) Must tourism destroy its resource base? In A.M. Mannion and S.R. Bowlby (eds) *Environmental Issues in the 1990s* (pp. 97–114). Wiley: London.

Choy, D.J.L. (1991) National tourism planning in the Philippines. *Tourism Management* 12 (3), 245–52.

Coker, C. (1996) Benchmarking and beyond. *Insights* 7 (March), A139–44. English Tourist Board.

Commission of the European Communities (1993) Council Regulation (EEC) No. 1836/93 of 29 June 1993 allowing voluntary participation by companies in the industrial sector in a Community Eco-Management and Audit Scheme. *Official Journal* L168, Vol. 35, 10 July.

Cummings, L.E. (1997) Waste minimisation supporting urban tourism sustainability: A mega-resort case study. *Journal of Sustainable Tourism* 5 (2), 93–108.

Dann, G.M.S. (1996) Greenspeak: An analysis of the language of ecotourism. *Progress in Tourism and Hospitality Research* 2 (3/4), 247–60.

Department of National Heritage (1996) *Benchmarking for Smaller Hotels*. London: Department of National Heritage.

Diamantis, D. and Westlake, J. (1997) Environmental auditing: An approach towards monitoring the environmental impact in tourism destinations, with reference to the case of Molyvos. *Progress in Tourism and Hospitality Research* 3 (1), 3–14.

Dieke, P.U.C. (1991) Policies for tourism development in Kenya. *Annals of Tourism Research* 18 (2), 269–94.

Dingle, P.A.J.M. (1995) Practical green business. *Insights* 7 (March), C35–45. English Tourist Board.

Draper, D. (1997) Touristic development and water sustainability in Banff and Canmore, Alberta, Canada. *Journal of Sustainable Tourism* 5 (3), 183–212.

Evans, M. (1990) Green tourism – a hotelier's view. *Insights* 2 (September), D9–11. English Tourist Board.

Forsyth, T. (1995) Business attitudes to sustainable tourism: Self-regulation in the UK outgoing tourism industry. *Journal of Sustainable Tourism* 3 (4), 210–31.

Gilg, A.W. (1991) Switzerland: Structural change with stability. In A.M. Williams and G. Shaw (eds) *Tourism and Economic Development: Western European Experiences* (pp. 130–52). London: Belhaven.

Goodall, B. (1994) Environmental auditing: Current best practice (with special reference to British tourism firms). In A.V. Seaton (ed.) *Tourism: The State of the Art* (pp. 655–64). Chichester: Wiley.

Goodall, B. (1995) Environmental awareness and management response in the hospitality industry. *Revista Portuguesa de Gestão* 2/3, 35–45.

Goodall, B. (1997) The role of environmental self-regulation within the tourism industry in promoting sustainable development. In W. Hein (ed.) *Tourism and Sustainable Development* (pp. 271–93). Hamburg: Deutschen Übersee-Instituts.

Goodall, B. and Stabler, M. (1994) Tourism-environment issues and approaches to their solution. In H. Voogd (ed.) *Issues in Environmental Planning* (pp. 78–99). Pion European Research in Regional Science Series, Vol. 4. London.

Goodall, B. and Stabler, M.J. (1997) Principles influencing the determination of environmental standards for sustainable tourism. In M.J. Stabler (ed.) *Tourism and Sustainability: Principles to Practice* (pp. 279–304). Wallingford: CAB International.

Goodall, B. and Stabler, M.J. (2000) Environmental standards and performance measurement in tourism destination development. In G. Richards and D. Hall (eds) *Tourism and Sustainable Community Development* (pp. 63–82). London: Routledge Advances in Tourism.

Gordon, C. (1991) Sustainable leisure. *Ecos* 12 (1), 7–11.

Grant, M., Human, B. and Le Pelley, B. (2000) Sustainable tourism indicators – their importance at local level. *Insights* 12 (September), A47–54. English Tourism Council.

Green, D.H. and Hunter, C. (1990) Assessing the environmental impact of tourism. *Proceedings of the Tourism Research into the 1990s Conference* (pp. 338–53). University College, Durham Castle, 10–12 December.

Gössling, S. (2000a) Sustainable tourism development in developing countries: Some aspects of energy use. *Journal of Sustainable Tourism* 8 (5), 410–25.

Gössling, S. (2000b) Tourism – sustainable development option. *Environmental Conservation* 27 (3), 223–24.

Hashimoto, A. (2000) Environmental perception and sense of responsibility of the tourism industry in mainland China, Taiwan and Japan. *Journal of Sustainable Tourism* 8 (2), 131–46.

Hawkins, R. (1997) Green labels for the travel and tourism industry. *Insights* 9 (July), A11–19. English Tourist Board.

Hawkins, D.E. and Holtz, C. (2001) Environmental policies and management systems related to the global tourism industry. In S. Wahab and C. Cooper (eds) *Tourism in the Age of Globalisation* (pp. 261–89). London: Routledge Advances in Tourism.

Herremans, I.M. and Welsh, C. (1999) Developing and implementing a company's ecotourism mission statement. *Journal of Sustainable Tourism* 7 (1), 48–76.

Herremans, I.M. and Welsh, C. (2001) Developing and implementing a company's ecotourism mission statement. Treadsoftly revisited. *Journal of Sustainable Tourism* 9 (1), 76–84.

Hjalager, A-M. (1996) Tourism and the environment: The innovation connection. *Journal of Sustainable Tourism* 4 (4), 201–18.

Hunter, C. (1995) On the need to re-conceptualise sustainable tourism development. *Journal of Sustainable Tourism* 3 (3), 155–66.

Hunter, C. and Green, H. (1995) *Tourism and the Environment: A Sustainable Relationship*. London: Routledge

IFTO (International Federation of Tour Operators) (1994) *Planning for Sustainable Tourism: The Ecomost Project*. Lewes: IFTO.

Inskeep, E. (1998) *Guide for Local Authorities on Developing Sustainable Tourism*. Madrid, World Tourism Organization.

Inskeep, E. and Kallenberger, M. (1992) *An Integrated Approach to Resort Development*. Madrid: World Tourism Organization.

International Association of Antarctic Tour Operators (1993) *Guidelines of Conduct for Antarctic Tour Operators as of November 1993*. Kent, WA: IAATO.

International Chamber of Commerce (1989) *Environmental Auditing*. Publication 468. Paris: International Chamber of Commerce.

International Hotels Environment Initiative (1993) *Environmental Management for Hotels: The Industry Guide to Best Practice*. Oxford: Butterworth-Heinemann.

Kavallinis, I. and Pizam, A. (1994) The environmental impacts of tourism – whose responsibility is it anyway? The case study of Mykonos. *Journal of Travel Research* 33 (2), 2–20.

King, B. and Weaver, S. (1993) The impact of the environment on the Fiji tourism industry: A study of industry attitudes. *Journal of Sustainable Tourism* 1 (2), 97–111.

Koenig, U. and Abegg, B. (1997) Impacts of climate change on winter tourism in the Swiss Alps. *Journal of Sustainable Tourism* 5 (1), 46–58.

Lane, B. (1990) Green accommodation. In B. Bramwell (ed.) *Shades of Green: Working Towards Green Tourism in the Countryside* (pp. 81–3). Conference Proceedings. Cheltenham: Countryside Commission, English Tourist Board, Rural Development Commission.

Langer, G. (1996) Traffic noise and hotel profits – is there a relationship? *Tourism Management* 17 (4), 295–306.

Leslie, D. (1995) Promoting environmentally friendly management and practices. In D. Leslie (ed.) *Promoting Environmental Awareness and Action in Hospitality, Tourism and Leisure* (pp.11–30). Environment Papers Series No. 1, Department of Hospitality, Tourism and Leisure Management. Glasgow: Glasgow Caledonian University.

Lewis, J. and Williams, A.M. (1991) Portugal: Market segmentation and regional specialization. In A.M. Williams and G. Shaw (eds) *Tourism and Economic Development: Western European Experiences* (pp. 107–29). London: Belhaven.

McKercher, B. (1993) Some fundamental truths about tourism: Understanding tourism's social and environmental impacts. *Journal of Sustainable Tourism* 1 (1), 6–16.

Mason, P. and Mowforth, M. (1995) *Codes of Conduct in Tourism*. Occasional Papers in Geography No. 1. Plymouth: Department of Geographical Sciences, University of Plymouth.

Mason, P. and Mowforth, M. (1996) Codes of conduct in tourism. *Progress in Tourism and Hospitality Research* 2 (2), 151–68.

Medley, P. (1997) Environmental accounting – what does it mean to professional accountants? *Accounting, Auditing and Accountability Journal* 10 (4), 595–600.

Mihalič, T. (1996) Ecological labelling in tourism. In L. Briguglio, B. Archer, J. Jafari and G. Wall (eds) *Sustainable Tourism in Islands and Small States: Issues and Policies* (pp. 197–265). London, Pinter.

Mowforth, M. and Munt, I. (1998) *Tourism and Sustainability: New Tourism in the Third World*. London: Routledge.

Pattullo, P. (1996) *Last Resorts: The Cost of Tourism in The Caribbean*. New York: Monthly Review Press.

Pearce, D. (1991) Towards the sustainable economy: Environment and economics. *Royal Bank of Scotland Review* 172, December, 3–15.

Petts, J., Herd, A., Gerrard, S. and Horne, C. (1998) The climate and culture of environmental compliance in SMEs. *Business Strategy and the Environment* 8 (1), 14–30.

Phillips, P. and Appiah-Adu, K. (1998) Benchmarking to improve the strategic planning process in the hotel sector. *Service Industries Journal* 18 (1), 1–17.

Pigram, J.J. (1996) Best practice environmental management and the tourism industry. *Progress in Tourism and Hospitality Research* 2 (3/4), 261–71.

RDC/ETB/CC (Rural Development Commission/English Tourist Board/Countryside Commission) (1995) *The Green Light: A Guide to Sustainable Tourism*. London: ETB.

Royal Commission on Environmental Pollution (1976) *Air Pollution Control: An Integrated Approach*. Fifth Report. London: HMSO.

Scottish Tourist Board (1993) *Going Green: Guidelines for the Scottish Tourism Industry*. Edinburgh: Scottish Tourist Board.

Sharpley, R. (2000) Tourism and sustainable development: Exploring the theoretical divide. *Journal of Sustainable Tourism* 8 (1), 1–19.

Simpson, K. (2001) Strategic planning and community involvement as contributors to sustainable tourism development. *Current Issues in Tourism* 4 (1), 3–41.

Stabler, M.J. and Goodall, B. (1996) Environmental auditing in planning for sustainable island tourism. In L. Briguglio, B. Archer, J. Jafari and G. Wall (eds) *Sustainable Tourism in Islands and Small States: Issues and Policies* (pp. 170–96). London: Pinter Island Studies Series.

Stabler, M.J. and Goodall, B. (1997) Environmental awareness, action and performance in the Guernsey hospitality sector. *Tourism Management* 18 (1), 19–33.

Steele, P. (1995) Ecotourism: an economic analysis. *Journal of Sustainable Tourism* 3 (1), 29–44.

Thomason, L., Colling, P. and Wyatt, C. (1999a) Benchmarking – an essential tool in destination management and achievement of best value. *Insights* 10 (January), A111–17. English Tourist Board.

Thomason, L., Colling, P. and Wyatt, C. (1999b) Destination benchmarking II – evaluating the 1998 pilot. *Insights* 10 (May), A173–80. English Tourist Board.

Thomason, L., Colling, P. and Baker, P. (2000) To market we go – benchmarking Lincolnshire market towns. *Insights* 12 (November), A65–72. English Tourism Council.

Todd, S.E. and Williams, P.W. (1996) From white to green: A proposed environmental management system for ski areas. *Journal of Sustainable Tourism* 4 (3), 147–73.

Tourism and Environment Task Force (1991) *Tourism and the Environment: Maintaining the Balance.* London: English Tourist Board and Employment Department.

Troyer, W. (1992) *The Green Partnership Guide.* Toronto: Canadian Pacific Hotels and Resorts.

Tuppen, J. (1991) France: The changing character of a key industry. In A.M. Williams and G. Shaw (eds) *Tourism and Economic Development: Western European Experiences* (pp. 191–206). London: Belhaven.

UNEP/GESAMP (United Nations Environment Programme/Joint Group of Experts on the Scientific Aspects of Marine Pollution) (1986) *Environmental Capacity: An Approach to Marine Pollution Prevention.* UNEP Regional Seas Reports and Studies No. 86. Geneva: UNEP.

UNEP/IE (United Nations Environment Programme: Industry and Environment) (1995) *Environmental Codes of Conduct for Tourism.* UNEP Industry and Environment Technical Report No. 29. Paris: UNEP.

UNEP/WTO/FEEE (United Nations Environment Programme/World Tourism Organization/Foundation for Environmental Education in Europe) (1996) *Awards for Improving the Coastal Environment: The Example of The Blue Flag.* Paris: UN Publications.

Wall, G. and Badke, C. (1994) Tourism and climate change: An international perspective. *Journal of Sustainable Tourism* 2 (4), 193–203.

Welford, R. and Gouldson, A. (1993) *Environmental Management and Business Strategy.* London: Pitman Publishing.

Wheeller, B. (1997) Here we go, here we go, here we go eco. In M.J. Stabler (ed.) *Tourism and Sustainability: Principles to Practice* (pp. 39–49). Wallingford: CAB International.

Wight, P. (1994a) The greening of the hospitality industry: Economic and environmental good sense. In A.V. Seaton (ed.) *Tourism: The State of the Art* (pp. 665–74). Chichester: Wiley.

Wight, P. (1994b) Limits of acceptable change: A recreational-tourism tool in cumulative effects assessment. Paper presented at Cumulative Effects in Canada: from Concept to Practice, National Conference of the Alberta Society of Professional Biologists and the Canadian Society of Environmental Biologists, Calgary, Canada, 13–14 April.

Witt, S.F. (1991) Tourism in Cyprus – balancing the benefits and costs. *Tourism Management* 12 (1), 37–46.

Woolf, J. (1991) The greening of Mickey Mouse. *Observer* (10 February), 57.

WTTC (World Travel and Tourism Council) (1991) *WTTC Policy-Environmental Principles.* Brussels: World Travel and Tourist Council (mimeo).

WTTERC (World Travel and Tourism Environment Research Centre) (1993) *Travel and Tourism: Environment and Development.* Oxford: WTTERC.

WTTHRC (World Travel and Tourism Human Resource Centre) (1998a) Environmental tourism training for the Bahamas and Caribbean Nations. *Steps to Success* 2 (2), 13–5.

WTTHRC (World Travel and Tourism Human Resource Centre) (1998b) Canadian Pacific Hotels Green Partnership Phase II. *Steps to Success* 2 (2), 20–2.

Young, S. and Ambrose, T. (1999) Benchmarking visitor attractions – Hampshire Pilot Project. *Insights* 11 (November), A71–80, English Tourism Council.

## Chapter 12

# Alternative Tourism – A Deceptive Ploy

BRIAN WHEELER

Nearly 10 years on, the validity of the arguments outlined in the original 1992 paper in 'Progress' remain fundamentally robust. Indeed, as the problems become more acute, the intervening decade has added substance, further weight and a prescient resonance to the message. None of the issues raised then seem, in the interim, to have been satisfactory addressed. Rhetoric is still rife; action lamentable. Riddled with hypocrisy selfish, vested interest holds sway. Tourism numbers have escalated. Tourism remains unmanageable and the spatial spread of tourism continues unabated. As Mike Robinson recently remarked 'The sustainable tourism debate has developed little over the last ten years' (Robinson, 2001). In effect, it is yesterday once more. So let's go back in time – to the present and, even more depressingly, to the future.

Over the last few years there has been a growing general awareness, and a belated acknowledgement by the tourist industry itself, of the impact problems that have invariably accompanied tourism growth. Tourism clearly brings benefits to the recipient region and of course to the tourists themselves. However, though sometimes the scapegoat for other negative forces, there is a catalogue of impact catastrophes that provide graphic evidence of tourism's destructive power.

Much of the blame for the current situation has (simplistically) been attributed to the demands of mass tourism. A school of thought has developed that appears to be based on the fundamental premise that changing those demands would somehow provide the solution to tourism impacts. Apparent hope lies (an appropriate word here) in the new forms of tourism being lauded by tourist practitioners, the media and many academics. Lane (1989), writing on the effects of mass tourism, believed that 'Perhaps the saddest feature of contemporary tourism is that there is an alternative, but we are ignoring it'.

227

If the 'alternative' was being ignored then, it certainly is not now. Currently, there is no shortage of verbose rhetoric in support of this new 'alternative' as a requisite for tourism planning and development.

To suggest that there is only one alternative might seem to be misleading. Indeed, the bewildering variety of names allocated to the numerous strands of the new tourism movement is somewhat confusing – soft, green, eco, gentle, appropriate, responsible, sustainable, quality, harmonious, community, progressive – the list of names given to this new 'aware' tourism seems endless. Nevertheless, although the nomenclature continually changes to reflect what appears to be little more than fine-tuning, the overall message coming through is roughly the same. What is needed, it is argued by many, is:

- a more caring, aware form of tourism-industry-small-scale developments;
- ecologically sound, local integration with indigenous ownership and control;
- seasonal and spatial spread of demand, etc. and
- a more caring, aware tourist well versed in the ethics of 'travel'.

The pace of any tourism development should be slow, controlled, sympathetically planned and managed and, of course, sustainable.

Although numerous writers have obviously contributed significantly in raising tourism awareness and consciousness, arguably the two seminal pieces of work, both emanating from the mid-1980s, were Krippendorf's *Holidaymakers* (1987) and Murphy's *Community Approach* (1985). Even so, most of the ideological roots underlying this new aware tourism are, in fact, nothing new. It is however only relatively recently that they have, for a combination of reasons, been applied to tourism and gained acceptability and popularity in that context. Seaton (1992), in a brief, erudite exposition of what he calls 'Quality Tourism', highlights the fact that the concept of sustainability has long been associated with development economics although it has only over the last few years become in vogue in tourism.

The emphasis has been on the environment with eco-tourism receiving a high profile. However, discussions on sustainability should not be restricted to ecological issues but should also, as Sofield (1991) believes, incorporate the environment as a whole, including culture. He develops this argument in his search for principles of sustainable ethnic tourism.

The surge of support for the movement is now in full flow. Warnings such as 'making simplistic and idealised comparisons of hard and soft on mass and green tourism, such that one is obviously undesirable and the other close to perfection is not only inadequate, it is grossly misleading'

(Butler, 1990) are being ignored. New tourism is being ecstatically embraced with unbridled enthusiasm by virtually all sections of tourism – the thinking tourist/traveller; the tourism industry (both private and public); the media; and many academics. Apparently there is enough vociferous, vanguard support to endorse it fully as the green way forward. However, such wholehearted and unquestioning acceptance is desperately disturbing, although not at all surprising if one considers the power of vested interest. For the educated tourist/traveller, for instance, it is immediately appealing, for it conveniently appeases any guilt while simultaneously providing the increased holiday options and experience desired.

A deluge of material endorsing green sustainable tourism is currently flooding the tourism consciousness. The industry, increasingly 'sensitive to criticism that it is in the business of destroying the very world it encourages us to see, is desperately trying to appear ecologically responsible' (Wickers, 1992). It is becoming difficult to find a brochure that does not allude to green tourism. However, Wickers explains:

> Much of the noise is marketing babble – another front on which to fight the competition – and many companies are simply slapping the green label on any destination where nature is more rampant than concrete. What will happen to that nature as a result of their promotion of it is not a question they care to address.

The cynicism is well founded. To put into some perspective industry's support for the new tourism it is worth considering how selective they have been in deciding which components of new tourism to overtly adopt. International tour operators, for example, while ostentatiously (and ostensibly) going green do not seem too keen on relinquishing control to the local community.

In the United Kingdom, material produced by official tourist and related bodies in the late 1990s vigorously wave the green flag – witness *Tourism in the National Parks. A Guide to Good Practice* (ETB, 1990), and the much vaunted *The Green Light. A Guide to Sustainable Tourism* (ETB, 1991a). Superficially both look good. However, do they actually deal with the issue of coping with increasing numbers of mass tourists, the real crux of the problem, or are they just glossy, sleek brochures – the public sector equivalent of private sector marketing hype? A similar question mark must also surely hang over the British government's 'Task Force' Publication, *Tourism and the Environment* (ETB, 1991b). Other examples include the Tourism Society (1991), the main tourism professional body in the United Kingdom that has produced a short document on sustainable tourism setting out in a straightforward manner some of the considerations and examples of good practice, and suggesting principles to adopt. Tourism

Concern (1991), a growing voice in the tourism debate, has also produced material suggesting the way forward. However, there remains the void between words – however genuine and well intentioned – and harsh reality.

There is also a spate of articles and books advocating the ethics of the new tourism and urging tourists to behave correctly (see, for example, Stevens, 1990; Bramwell, 1991, Anscombe, 1991; Platt, 1991; Wood and House, 1991). Wood and House' book, *The Good Tourist* described as 'a world-wide guide for the green traveller' is dedicated to all travellers of the next generation. Unfortunately for those believing that 'green behaviour' will solve the problem, it seems highly probable that the next generation will, globally, consist of a large number – the critical mass – of tourists not behaving correctly. Would-be travellers will be vastly outnumbered by mass tourists. It must be doubtful that Western tourists, experienced in the culture of going abroad, will radically change their holiday behaviour patterns unless it meets their immediate personal interest to do so.

It seems unrealistic to believe that all tourists from countries new to the international tourism scene will behave sensitively and sympathetically. For them it is a new experience and in the circumstances they will want as much from it as possible at as little cost (to themselves) as possible. Recent behaviour patterns of tourists from eastern Europe suggest this to be, understandably, the case (Wheeller, 1992).

We have moved from travel, to tourism, to mass tourism. Pundits of the green movement advocate a kind of 'back to travel' except the reality is that globally we are moving toward mega- tourism. The gap between the solution and the problem is again alarmingly though conveniently forgotten. Of particular concern to some critics of the new movement is this very gap, some would say chasm, between the appealing though theoretical notions of good tourism and the practical realities of its implementation. Cazes (1989) warns of the danger of 'insidious distortions between the ideological discourse on the one hand, and the effective practices in places of tourism on the other'. In the Third World, he laments, 'there are no examples of significant size that fully meet the requirements of the alternative model'.

Pigram (1990) also argues cogently that though worthwhile policy statements may be espoused, they encounter formidable barriers when attempts are made to translate them into action. The problem is not deciding what should be done, but actually making it happen. His perceptive paper on sustainable tourism concludes with the stark prospect that without the development of effective means of translating the ideal into action, sustainable tourism 'runs the risk of remaining irrelevant and inert as a feasible policy option for the real world of tourism development'. The irony here should not be lost. Usually academics are criticised, often with justification, for theoretical ivory tower mentality. In this particular case, however, several academics are arguing that it is the limited practical application of alternative tourism, and the constraints that prevent wider actual adoption, make the new tourist movement so questionable as a way forward for tourism planning and management.

I have argued previously (Wheeller, 1991) that the practical issues of implementation are being ignored by many advocates of the new movement. Glib, general assertions are frequently incorporated into policy statements without any attention being given to defining in a practical sense such phrases as, for example, the local community, tourism education or good visitor management. Who actually decides what is required? If, for example, authenticity is the objective, then the popular assumption that indigenous ownership and control will automatically ensure its maintenance is, as Sofield (1991) illustrates, sadly misplaced. How are new forms of tourism to be co-ordinated and who is to be responsible and accountable for its success? Difficult questions remain unanswered.

That such criticism is being swamped is not surprising given the concerted support for new tourism – the easy comfortable answer that does not address the central issue. It must be stressed that the main problem with tourism is 'numbers', the sheer volume and their continued spatial spread – yet the solution identified by many seems to be small-scale, slow, restricted development. Hardly an answer, given the problem. True, examples of supposed good tourism practice being cited have included Disney and Centre Parcs (ETB, 1991, Tourism Society, 1991). By citing these honey-pots (itself to an extent at odds with the spread the load, spread the jam philosophy), advocates go some way to dealing with numbers. It is, however, going to take a considerable number of 'Centre Pares' to siphon-off mass demand on a global basis. And where, of course, does the ghettoisation of tourism fit in with the notion of being at one with the indigenous population, so important to our new code of behaviour for the traveller. Surprise, surprise, it seems the ghettos are for the masses and the undiscovered (and as yet unspoilt) for the sensitive traveller.

However, are these really examples of what is meant by green, sustainable tourism? Are they examples of the mysterious, ubiquitous, good visitor management? Or are these synonymous? Improvements at Benidorm, Ibiza and Magaluf are also being cited as good examples of the new tourism. In reality, are they not all just good examples of attempts at providing a quality product, or upgrading an existing one, for the quality market? (Now, is this what is meant by alternative tourism?) The policy of upgrading fits perfectly with the tourism industry's continued obsession with growth. To counterbalance the hackneyed argument of the danger of killing the goose, the equally hackneyed Pavlovian response is that the product must be continually enhanced. Always an emphasis on quality for the discerning quality market. Unfortunately, while there might well be a quality market, all the market is not quality. As, worldwide, the tourist numbers grow, are all these new tourists going to be up-market, quality tourists? The uncomfortable answer must certainly be no. If say, Magaluf is successful in changing its 18–30 image and goes up-market, ridding itself of the undesirable, holiday hooligan as it does so, will this solve the problem of tourism? Current thinking would have us believe so. However, although it might solve the problem for Magaluf, it just shifts the problem elsewhere. The lower end of the market will, presumably, go elsewhere for their pleasure – possibly somewhere even less able to cope than Magaluf. A case of passing the buck. A solution, or survival of the fittest?

Although numbers are of critical importance, it is not simply mass tourism that is the problem. So too is the pseudo-sophisticated, sensitive traveller: 'the vanguard of the package tour, where he or she goes others will, in every increasing numbers, eventually follow. They are forever seeking the new, the exotic, the unspoilt – the vulnerable' (Wheeller, 1991). Alternative tourism is somewhat vague in dealing with this matter of the desire for the new. Apparently it endorses it and the concomitant opening up and development of new destinations, provided this is undertaken sensitively, sensibly and is appreciated by those travelling. (Read the books before you go, behave with respect, etc. – for eco-tourism, read ego-tourism.) If this sensitive development can be achieved, which I doubt, surely this will only encourage more to travel anyway. It seems most likely that destinations will continue to be developed and planning and regulatory standards relaxed under pragmatic pressures, as demand increases. Either way, prospects are bleak. What seems certain, though, is that the traveller/tourist, seeking the new, will continue to fan outwards, one step beyond tourism's new frontier.

According to Butler (1990), 'Claiming one form of tourism is all things for all areas is not only pious and naive, it is unfair, unrealistic and unwise.' Alternative tourism is not the answer to the negative impacts of tourism. It must be treated with caution, indeed scepticism, scrutinised and critically analysed from a realistic, practical perspective. Its ineffectiveness is its popularity, enabling the tourist/traveller to enjoy the holiday experience they want with a clear conscience, impunity and no sacrifice. It provides the tourist lobby with the perfect foil to allay fears (superficially) while enabling the industry to continue its growth, spread and development, swathed in a green mantle. Cohen (1989), in an excellent review of alternative tourism argues that as 'contemporary tourism is an extremely varied and many-sided phenomenon its indiscriminate criticism and total repudiation stand in danger of being rejected as tendentious and inadequate . . . as stale and unconvincing'.

Although there is much truth in this, it must surely also be true that this very complexity and heterogeneity render tourism unmanageable. The main protagonists in tourism are now behaving much as before, although, thanks to alternative tourism, with a renewed vigour borne out of self-righteous virtue.

On reflection, there is little in the original 1992 paper that I would wish to change. Possibly more on domestic tourism, in that there has tended to be overemphasis on the international dimensions of sustainability when a considerable proportion of tourism is domestic in nature. And maybe the title, given that alternative could be construed as 'alter-native' which was not, superficially at least, what new forms of tourism were necessarily supposed to be about (in itself is a moot point).

To the majority of mass tourists (and the majority of tourists are surely mass) sustainability is of little import – far more pressing are matters of price, value for money and fun! fun! fun!. For the 'believers', I contend, the ineffectiveness of sustainable tourism is its strength and remains, perversely, core to their acceptance of it. No change here then. Or elsewhere.

Just as in the early 1990s, the futility of sustainable tourism is around us for all to see. Most are, understandably, not remotely interested. For those that are, the sham could not be more apparent. But shame. Even now we just cannot face up to seeing it for what it is. Or, actually, what it isn't. The Emperor's Clothes – though now no longer new – show no signs of wearing thin. Unlike my patience.

## Note
1. This chapter first appeared as 'Alternative tourism – a deceptive ploy' in Volume 4 of *Progress in Tourism, Recreation and Hospitality Management* (1992), pp. 140–45.

## Bibliography
Anscombe, J. (1991) The gentle Traveller. *New Woman* (June), 51–3.

Bramwell, B. (1991) Shades of green tourism. *Leisure Management* (February), 40–1.

Butler, R. (1990) Alternative tourism: Pious hope or Trojan horse? *Journal of Travel Research* (Winter), 40–5.

Cazes, G. (1989) Alternative tourism: Reflections of an ambiguous concept. In T. Singh and L. Theuns *et al.* (eds) *Towards Appropriate Tourism* (pp. 117–126). Frankfurt: Lang.

Cohen, E. (1989) Alternative tourism – a critique. In Singh, Theuns *et al.* (eds) *Towards Appropriate Tourism* (pp. 127–42). Frankfurt: Lang.

English Tourist Board (1990) *Tourism: The National Parks. A Guide to Good Practice.* London: ETB.

English Tourist Board (1991a) *The Green Light. A Guide to Sustainable Tourism.* London: ETB.

English Tourist Board (1991) *Tourism and the Environment – Maintaining the Balance.* London: ETB.

Lane, B. (1989) Modern mass tourism: A critique. *Independent* (13 May).

Krippendorf, J. (1987) *The Holidaymakers.* London: Heinemann.

Murphy, P. (1985) *Tourism. A Community Approach.* London: Routledge.

Pigram, J. (1990) Sustainable tourism, policy considerations. *Journal of Tourism Studies* 2 (November), 2–9.

Platt, S. (1991) The tender tax. *New Statesman and Society* (9 August), 19–20.

Seaton, A. (1992) Quality tourism sustained. *Tourisme Qualitatife Aiest Annual* 33, 209–37.

Robinson, M. (2001) The future of tourism. Lecture delivered at College of St John and St Mark, Plymouth, UK.

Sofield, T. (1991) Sustainable ethnic tourism in the South Pacific: Some principles. *Journal of Tourism Studies* 2 (1) (May), 56–72.

Stevens, T. (1990) Greener than green. *Leisure Management* (September), 64–6.

Tourism Society (1991) *Sustainable Tourism. Development in Balance with the Environment.* London: Tourism Society.

Tourism Concern (1991) *Himalayan Code.* Tourism Concern. London: Roehampton Institute.

Wheeller, B. (1991) Tourism: Troubled times. *Tourism Management* 12 (1), 91–6.

Wheeller, B. (1992) Is progressive tourism appropriate? *Tourism Management* 13 (L), 104–5.

Wickers, D. (1992) Whither green. *Sunday Times* (5 January).

Wood, K. and House, S. (1991) *The Good Tourist.* London: Mandarin.

*Chapter 13*

# Gender and Tourism

GEOFF WALL and JOANNE NORRIS

## Introduction

The purpose of this chapter is to present a synthesis of research on tourism and gender from a feminist perspective. It is argued that feminist scholarship and research on tourism have both been growth areas in the past decades but, until relatively recently, few attempts have been made to establish relationships between them. While the potential links are wide-ranging and far-reaching, emphasis is placed in this chapter on development studies which have been a focus of attention in both fields. Unfortunately, it is not possible to provide conclusive answers concerning the nature of connections between gender and tourism. Rather the intent is to create a consciousness that such relationships exist and should be addressed. The challenge is to improve clarity in thinking about the experience of tourism for women – women as tourists, women as workers in the tourism industry and women as a constituent of tourism products. However, while the emphasis of this contribution is on women, it is important to acknowledge that gender studies are also about men and, furthermore, there has been growing interest in a diversity of sexual orientations and these perspectives are slowly finding their way into the tourism literature.

As in other explorations into the meaning and reasons behind goings-on in society, the perspective that is offered stems from particular assumptions. The first and most explicit is the need to study women and women's points of view. The second is the value of studying women and men, and their relations as they are expressed in tourism. The third is to situate tourism, tourists and tourism development within a feminist framework.

The structure of this chapter is as follows. In the next section it is claimed that, until quite recently, few links had been made between tourism research and gender studies. However, in the time since the original paper appeared in *Progress*, the situation has changed somewhat. Not only has there been a proliferation of publications on gender studies, there has also been a fragmentation of feminist scholarship into different camps. Furthermore, useful compendiums of research on women, gender and tourism have also begun to appear (see, for example, Kinnaird & Hall, 1994: Sinclair, 1997; Swain, 2001; Swain & Momsen, in press), including a special issue of *Annals of Tourism Research* devoted to the subject (Swain, 1995). The third section outlines the growth of feminist studies in Western societies: various perspectives that come under the umbrella of feminist studies, the evolution and growth of gender studies in development and the emerging literature concerning gender and leisure studies. A case will then be made for making a connection between gender and leisure studies when conducting research on tourism, regardless of whether a 'developed' or 'developing' society is under consideration. Examples of research that might be conducted under the umbrella of gender and tourism are then presented. It should be kept in mind that the purpose of this chapter is to suggest possibilities for future research, rather than to draw conclusions from research already completed.

## Tourism Studies

The purpose of this section is to present evidence of the slow growth of studies which incorporate gender perspectives on tourism. However, it is much easier to demonstrate the presence of something than its absence, and space does not permit a detailed examination of the burgeoning tourism literature or even that specifically devoted to development. Fortunately, there are now numerous texts available which address these topics and a growing number of review papers assess the status of tourism research from different disciplinary perspectives. For example, an issue of *Annals of Tourism Research* was devoted specifically to assessments of the contributions to and status of tourism research of a number of social science disciplines (Graburn & Jafari, 1991). A reading of such documents confirms the limited number of references to feminist scholarship.

The broader field of leisure studies, of which tourism can be considered a part, has begun to incorporate a feminist perspective; this will be discussed in greater detail later in the chapter. However, it continues to he a distinct strand of research which has not yet been well integrated into mainstream leisure research. Thus, the comprehensive review of leisure and recreation research edited by Jackson & Burton (1989), which includes chapters on tourism, contains one chapter on women and leisure (Bella, 1989). However, this chapter presents a separate perspective which is not incorporated into other contributions.

Of course. tourism researchers have not totally ignored women in their studies: it is an unusual questionnaire which does not ascertain the sex of respondents! However, the resulting data are seldom analysed and presented in a meaningful way. For example, where differences in participation between women and men are sometimes identified, they tend to be noted rather than explained. Such research is seldom undertaken from a feminist perspective and indirectly may promote the *status quo* in that it usually ignores the different constraints and opportunities to which women and men are exposed.

Tourism, tourists and tourism development have each been explored in various ways, depending upon the disciplinary orientations of the researchers. In much research, elements and approaches from several disciplines have been linked and combined so that it can be argued that tourism is an interdisciplinary subject. Feminist scholarship, too, is interdisciplinary but the link with tourism is only now becoming firmly established.

# Gender Studies

One wonders if women still exist, if they will always exist, whether or not it is desirable that they should, what place they occupy in this world, what their place should be, (de Beauvoir, 1971)

### Growth of feminist studies

Feminist studies emerged as a result of the lack of representation of women in many aspects of political, economic and social life. Although there is a direct connection between feminist writings and the women's liberation movement, the intent here is only to discuss feminism in its literary expression.

Hess and Ferree (1987) see the study of men and women as passing through three distinct phases since the early 1970s. The first phase emphasised the sex differences between men and women. Maleness and femaleness were viewed as biological properties of individuals with clear implications for social behaviour. Those within this perspective who proposed equality between men and women downplayed biological differences, claiming that they 'are rarely relevant for important behaviours. and that the differences are as likely to be instances of female superiority as male' (Hess & Ferree, 1987: 14). Actual historical experience, though, has clearly indicated a non-egalitarian view of sex differences to be much more prevalent, keeping those who do promote the possibility of egalitarian biological determinism continually on the defensive.

The second phase was marked by a preoccupation with sex roles whereby the biological determinants of maleness and femaleness were combined with social determinism via upbringing in any proportion of nature and nurture that seemed appropriate. Sex differences were no longer intrinsically important issues, since both large and small differences could be explained by socialisation (Hess and Ferree, 1987: 14–15). In this phase, then, socialisation practices became the culprit. Childrearing was studied to explore the occurrence of sex-specific socialisation practices. A strong critique of this line of reasoning is that when one stresses the importance of sex role socialisation, especially in the socialisation of young children, one assumes continuity throughout the life course (Hess & Ferree, 1987: 15). In other words, this approach does not take into account the innumerable life experiences that affect the way we think and act. Also, sex role explanations do not give much credence to adult learning or our ability to have control in our lives.

The third phase is one which has ignited an explosion of feminist studies in diverse research areas. A new perspective with a new conceptual locus has been created: the centrality of gender. Gender is seen as 'a principle organizing social arrangements, behaviour, and even cognition' (Hess & Ferree, 1987: 16). Gender itself is a socially constructed system which suppresses any natural similarities that may occur between men and women. It is a property of systems, rather than people.

Because gender is relational rather than essential, structural rather than individual, analysing gender requires consideration of changes in systems over time. The alteration in social structures themselves, as well as variation in individual relations within these gender systems, demand attention to both macro and micro levels of structure and change (Hess & Ferree, 1987: 17). This perspective has been employed to examine many aspects of society: gender stratification in economic relations; gender relations in the family; gender and the state; gender and ideology, to name but a few. These explorations have led to further, more refined, approaches which focus on particular aspects of the gender system. The conceptualisation of patriarchy, the function of domestic labour in capitalist society, and distinctions between 'private' and 'public' spheres were three early areas of investigation which provided a more systematic approach to gender studies. As conceptual and analytical depth grew, particular frameworks, or paradigms, became distinguishable.

## Streams of thought in feminism

> . . . feminism is a philosophical framework that has application to numerous facets of society, yet is reflective of each individual's unique life experiences and values. (Henderson *et al.*, 1989: 47)

This quotation attempts to capture the essence of feminism by stressing the all-encompassing nature of a feminist framework that coexists with personal experience and expression. Although women such as Tong (1989) have provided outlines of various frameworks that discuss this multifaceted subject, it is difficult to make general statements about feminist theory or review it comprehensively as a single body of work.

Approaches to the study of gender span liberal, socialist and Marxist perspectives. Each is attached to particular conceptual and analytical abstractions which are offered to explain the structure of society and relationships between the men and women in it. Bearing this in mind, Stanley and Wise (1982) have identified three widely accepted assumptions about women that are common to all feminist theories:

- women are oppressed and share a common set of oppressions;
- the personal is political in that personal experience is affected by the 'system' in everyday life; and
- a feminist consciousness and an understanding of what it means to be a woman can be developed.

These assumptions suggest that, in any discussion of theory, it is essential that women not be simply *added in* to what already exists in a patriarchal world.

The above assumptions can be related to common goals. Henderson *et al.* (1989) recognise the different foci of feminist researchers, but suggest that, despite this, feminism and feminist writings are united in the quest for specific goals:

- to make visible women's power and status;
- to redefine existing societal structures and modes of existence; and
- to enable every woman to have equity, dignity and freedom of choice through power to control her life and body, both within and outside the home.

As the feminist literature has increased, so it has also fragmented into different schools of thought. For example, eco-feminists suggest that the male desire for domination and oppression of women also applies to the environment and is an important cause of its degradation (Mellor, 1992; Zimmerman, 1994). Others point out that ideas emanate from minds that are situated in bodies and, therefore, knowledge is embodied. It follows that greater attention should be given to the bodies in which experiences and knowledge are situated (Veijola & Jokinen, 1994; Lewis & Pile, 1996). Johnston (2001) has studied gay parades from both participants' and observers' perspectives and, through this, has criticised the numerous dualisms that pervade much rational thought, including those between mind and body, and between women and men. The next two sections will outline more specifically gender orientations in two particular areas of study: development studies and leisure studies.

### Gender studies in development

Boserup (1970) provided the first overview of women's role in the development process in a comparative analysis of women in Asia, Africa and Latin America. Her thesis was that women were being ignored in the development of the Third World. Therefore, 'development' was gender-specific – specifically beneficial to men. Her analysis was not critical of the development process itself, for she remained quite firmly within the neo-classical modernisation paradigm and she did not present a clear-cut feminist analysis of women's subordination. Her work did provide, though, a starting point for the next decades of feminist research in development studies.

A school of thought that was established after this pioneering research was the liberal, feminist, Women in Development School (WID), which parallels the liberal modernisation perspective. Their philosophy of development for women lies in the diffusion of values, capital, technology and political institutions from the West (Bandarage, 1984: 497). They argue that integration of women into the development process will facilitate their participation in the formal (public) economy. The limitations of this perspective stem from a lack of class analysis, combined with the fact that women are already integrated into the development process but their work is invisible.

The Marxist perspective differs from the liberal in that it sees the poverty of women and men as a structural feature of capitalism as a social and economic system (Bandarage, 1984: 500). Marxists agree with liberal WID thinkers that economic modernisation (capitalist development) marginalises Third World women, but they believe that, to understand this inequality, one must look at social class inequality and the unequal and uneven development of capitalism world-wide. Marxists also acknowledge, unlike liberal WID advocates, that not all men benefit from technological innovations, nor are all women similarly affected by technological and other aspects of change (Bandarage, 1984: 501). Comparing the two approaches to gender in development, the Marxist is superior in that it comes from a materialist perspective and is less prone to generalise about men and women as homogeneous groups. Marxism is deficient, however, because its position on women's oppression, like men's, is based on the abstract forces of capitalism, commercialisation and proletarianism, thereby ignoring women's oppression by men (Bandarage, 1984: 505).

The birth of radical feminism challenged this omission by introducing personal relations as political issues. The focus on the domestic sphere of life and personal relationships between men and women opened up for debate areas that had been previously ignored by both liberalism and Marxism (Bandarage, 1984: 505). Radical feminism, focusing on the 'universality of patriarchy', tends to overlook the interrelations between sexual and other forms of social oppression such as class, race and nationality (Bandarage, 1984: 506). In attempting to bridge this gap, a theoretical perspective has been created to synthesise Marxist theory on capitalism and radical feminist theory on patriarchy. This is socialist feminism or the analysis of gender and class in the political economy.

Theories of gender in development have provided a body of literature which illuminates the invisibility of women. Although there are conflicting ideologies within the general paradigm, the growth of this literature confirms the appropriateness of making gender central to development studies. The revolutionary nature of the growth of this field of study is apparent, but its limitations to date are also evident. There is a lack of systematic research on the consequences of rapid growth and technological change on women and on gender relationships. Heyzer (1987), focusing specifically on women in South East Asia, identified two main areas of study which need to be enhanced: the reactions of women to technological and other kinds of production changes, and the resulting conflict and contradictions that occur at both macro and micro levels as a result of these changes. The view of women as agents of change rather than as merely passive victims of circumstances animates research into how women themselves interpret and respond to structures of opportunity and constraint. It also forces recognition of the limited alternatives for action facing women who wish to resist oppression (Hess & Ferree, 1987: 14).

## Gender and leisure

In the mainstream leisure studies texts of the 1970s, women's experience was not considered at all; if mention of women was made, it was only in reference to the family. Talbot (1979) produced the first study that focused on women's leisure. This served as an impetus for additional research in the 1980s. In 1980, Stanley (cited in Stanley & Wise, 1982: 6–7) made a major contribution concerning the 'meaning of leisure'. She proposed that women are not to be viewed as 'deviant' from men, but that women are a heterogeneous group with many, different interests (Wimbush & Talbot, 1988: 7–8).

As a result of the relationship between women and leisure being brought to the forefront, writers in leisure studies attempted to use less sexist language. Although this may he viewed as a progressive step, the drawback was that their inclusion of gender produced a series of even more pluralistic analyses which treated class, age, race and gender as though they were similar and cumulative factors (Winbush & Talbot, 1988: 9). Gender became an additional component which was noted in participation in sex-typed activities, but little was known about why or how this related to gender differences and inequalities in society in general. Results were not interpreted in light of the different personal and social contexts of women and men (Henderson *et al.*, 1989: 100). Therefore, what feminist contributions to the sociology of leisure have done is to stress the importance of analysing leisure in the context of individuals' lives as a whole. This holistic approach makes one more aware of why, for instance, women spend more of their leisure time at home than men do (Wimbush & Talbot, 1988: 121).

Conceptual frameworks that are relevant to the study of women and leisure and the comparative study of men's and women's leisure are being developed to provide more fruitful analyses of the context and meaning of leisure. An area within the study of women's leisure that is drawing attention is constraints on leisure. Women's experience of *time* is a particular focus. Women are, in general, the facilitators of others' leisure – husbands, children and parents – rather than the recipients of leisure (Wimbush & Talbot, 1988: 14). When do women have the time to partake in their own leisure? Do they feel there is time to spare to explore activities solely for their own individual enjoyment? Research studies have shown that women's experiences of time are much more fragmented than those of many men, particularly for women not in any form of paid employment (Wimbush & Talbot, 1988: I1). An historical analysis of leisure illustrates that women have not had the same opportunity for leisure as men. Some of the constraints include: economic oppression in the workforce; family obligations; and maintaining responsibility for the family as well as being an economic provider. A feminist perspective on leisure provides a means to address and attempt to understand women's experience of leisure, as well as a push for social change that will recognise women's leisure needs. Feminism and leisure are inextricably linked by components of choice and freedom (Henderson *et al.*, 1989: 45).

If work is viewed as being the antithesis of leisure, then changes in the labour market, including the allocation of time between productive and reproductive labour, have implications for leisure and, by extension, for tourism. McDowell (2001) provides a useful review and discussion of relevant literature.

If one takes leisure and feminism and puts them on a series of continua, there are many similarities. Both are more visible today than at any other time in history, both as movements and as streams of thought. At the core of leisure are the elements of freedom and choice, while at the core of feminism are the elements of freedom and integrity; thus, freedom is central to both concepts (Henderson *et al.*, 1989: 51). It has been hypothesised that if women are given opportunities to take control of their leisure, they may be able to create social changes in other aspects of their lives (Henderson *et al.*, 1989).

No attempt has been made here to define leisure or to categorise and compare the experience of leisure for women and men. Rather, the objectives have been to make explicit the relationship between gender and leisure and to illustrate how a feminist perspective can shed some light on the subject (Fox, 1992).

The purpose of exploring research in the areas of development and leisure studies in greater depth stems from their relevance to gender and tourism studies. The gender and development literature has contributed greatly to a better understanding of women's work in so-called 'developed' and 'developing' societies (Leacock & Safa, 1986). However, technological change and the forces of modernity have been viewed through a limited lens with emphasis mainly on work in agricultural and factory production. The rapid growth of international tourism to developing countries since the 1950s is only starting to be broached by gender and development researchers. In the growing gender and leisure material, the beginnings of rigorous conceptual and analytical frameworks are emerging, but most definitions and discussions of what leisure means to women do not include women as tourists. Much of the literature focuses on gendered leisure in everyday life, and how women and men differ in what they like to do in leisure time as it relates to their daily routine. This is a legitimate area for research but it has limitations as a basis for discussion of women as tourists and women workers in the tourism industry.

## Tourism, Gender and Development: Why Make the Connection?

Thus far, it has been argued that neither the general area of tourism studies nor the general area of gender studies provides a coherent, systematic overview of relationships between gender and tourism. Kinnaird and Hall (1996) have proposed a 'gender-aware framework' for understanding tourism processes but, while their paper is an excellent and concise introduction to relevant tourism literature, their framework is not fully developed and really consists of three broad topics. However, these topics are important as points of departure and they are briefly stated here:

(1) The activities and processes involved in tourism are constructed out of gendered societies and, consequently, the masculine and feminine

identities articulated by both host and guest societies are important components of the types of tourism taking place.

(2) Gender relations both inform and are informed by the practices of all societies. Therefore, economic, social, cultural, political and environmental aspects of tourism-related activity interact with the changing gendered nature of individual societies.

(3) Discussions of gender and gender relations are concerned with issues of power and control. Tourism involves power relations between groups of people from nations to households and, as such, revolves around social interactions and articulations of motivations, desires, traditions and perceptions, all of which are gendered.

In this chapter, because the volume of relevant material is now substantial, for purposes of explication, six topics which exhibit gender-tourism relationships will be outlined briefly. Within each topic, references are illustrative rather than comprehensive.

### The participants

There is little doubt that women and men have different leisure budgets (Thrane, 2000), holiday involvements (Deem, 1996) and activity preferences. Similarly, it will be no surprise to readers to be told that there are different participation patterns and degrees of involvement in and commitment to sports (Wiley *et al.*, 2000) and that provision of recreation opportunities is often determined by policy makers that are predominantly male (Yule, 1997). Scraton and Watson (1998), through work on women's leisure and public space in urban areas, have suggested that women share gendered experiences related to safety, financial constraints and sexual divisions of labour and they also share adaptive strategies. However, there are many complexities and it is easy to over-generalise about such matters. There may be differences in preferred landscapes and scenery (Kay, 1991). For example, Virden and Walker (1999) showed that there are different preferences for natural environments, women more than men in their study sharing a preference for the presence of managers, development for visitor convenience (as compared to more remote natural settings), and environments offering intimacy with close friends and family.

Typologies have been devised to describe variations among tourists. For example, Cohen (1972) devised a typology of four tourist roles which makes a distinction between more *organised* types of tourist and the more *exploratory*. These types relate to demands for particular kinds of tourist experience and facilities, such as accommodation and modes of travel. Although such typologies provide useful insights into some aspects of tourism, they have not attempted to distinguish between motivations of male and female tourists. In fact, no research has been located which focuses specifically on this particular area. Yet this is a worthy area of study because as women gain more diverse opportunities in the fields of education, sexual relations and employment, new (leisure) lifestyles emerge.

> . . . a number of social forces have been instrumental in changing the lives of women . . . technology that can potentially free women from housework and unwanted pregnancies; liberalization of divorce and abortion laws; new views on sexual morality and an increasing emphasis on permissiveness and individualism; and the women's movement with egalitarian educational and economic goals. (Henderson *et al.*, 1989: 4)

An historical perspective on tourism reveals that women, just as men, have been concerned travellers. Russell (1988) examined women travellers from as far back as the seventeenth century and found numerous reasons why particular women decided to travel to a distant land:

> to escape from domesticity or the drudgery of a routine job; to recover from a broken love affair; to experience the thrill of danger; to demonstrate that women's name is definitely not frailty; to bring the Bible to China; to study plant life or unknown peoples; to delve into the past; to expiate a private guilt; to honour a dead partner; to glorify their country; to find something interesting to write about – or simply to have fun. (Russell, 1988: 15)

Russell's book is anecdotal, not theoretical. She does not interpret the meaning or significance of the various reasons women had for travelling, nor does she attempt to draw any conclusions concerning women travellers through history. However, she does contribute a detailed, thorough account of the experiences of several women travellers. In fact, examination of the observations and experiences of women travellers, particularly as they related to colonialism and scientific exploration, have attracted a growing number of researchers (for example, Middleton, 1965; Birkett, 1990; Mills, 1991; Robinson, 1990; Blunt & Rose, 1994; Morgan, 1996; and Guelke & Morin, 2001). Somewhat similarly, their involvement in such activities as mountaineering has also received scholarly attention (Squire, 1995; Morin, 1999). Kroller (1987) has documented the journeys and experiences of Canadian women travellers in Europe between 1851 and 1900. While virtually all such women were members of the elite, often travelling for substantial periods of time and perhaps uncharacteristic in that they kept records and wrote about their experiences, these studies are welcome additions to literature on the history of tourism as, until recently, mention was rarely made of women travellers in the past.

In a study of long-term budget travellers, Riley (1988) attempted to distinguish the motives of young, educated, mainly middle-class travellers. She found that most of them were escaping from the dullness and monotony of their everyday routine, their jobs, from making decisions about careers, and desired to postpone work, marriage and other responsibilities (Riley, 1988: 317). Riley mentions escaping constraints of marriage and romantic relationships, but not in a gender-specific sense. There is potential to extend her analysis to distinguish whether more women than men, or vice versa, turn to travel as a form of escapism and to determine what it is that they are escaping to and from. She 'suprisingly' reports that a large number of budget travellers. perhaps a quarter, are women, but that is the extent of her analysis by gender. However, she does note in passing that women more than men said that they wanted to travel to establish independence from their families and feel comfortable with doing things alone (Riley, 1988: 324). Both Beezer (1993) and Elsrud (1998) have also studied female adventure travellers and backpackers.

A number of studies address the gendered use of leisure space (Henderson, 1994a; 1994b; Aitchison, 1999). However, Carr (1999) has suggested that it remains to be determined whether there are significant differences between women and men in terms of holiday patterns that cannot be accounted for by other factors, such as socio-economic status or age. Not only is it necessary to explore the nature of female tourists to recognise and appreciate women's experiences, but the patterns of travel and tourist wants of women are also of direct interest to the tourist industry. Types of accommodation and kinds of attractions can be oriented to gender-specific wants. For example, a number of hotel chains now set aside particular floors solely for female customers. The industry has adapted to the growth of sex tourism in particular regions, usually but not always catering to the sexual needs of male tourists (see below). However, not all gender-oriented tourist activities and services need have negative connotations.

## Tourism employment

This section examines the employment of women in the tourist industry. Although there has yet to be a systematic, wide-ranging study of relationships between gender and tourism, a number of unconnected empirical case studies has been undertaken which incorporate women tourism workers or focus upon women workers in the tourist industry (Armstrong, 1978; Samarasuriya, 1982; Rupena-Osolnik, 1983–1984; Lever, 1987; Miller & Branson, 1989; Swain, 1989, Levy & Lerch, 1991). The number of references indicates that this is an emerging area of study, and a concise introduction to this work, with examples from both the developed and developing world, can be found in Meethan (2001: 147–53). Also, a number of case studies of tourism employment from both developed and developing countries can be found in the books edited by Kinnaird and Hall (1994) and Sinclair (1997). Nevertheless, it is still appropriate to suggest that most gender-related studies concentrate upon the developing world and the provision of accommodation for visitors and the creation of souvenirs. The work of the present authors in Bali, Indonesia, generally fits this statement (Cukier & Wall, 1995; Cukier *et al.*, 1996), as does the study by Wilkinson and Pratiwi (1995) which was also undertaken in Indonesia. However, the work of Phillimore (1998), which examines women as managers of attractions in the United Kingdom, is an interesting exception.

Most of these studies concentrate upon the introduction of tourism into rural rather than urban areas. All of them note that, in spite of potential increases in economic standing that women may attain due to employment in tourism, strong cultural barriers, the lack of government initiatives and the lack of organisation among the women workers themselves inhibit women from aspiring to leadership roles both in the political and community senses. Armstrong's study in highland Scotland found that women were the main workers in the industry (especially in the bed and breakfast sector) and, because of this, they had become involved in local politics to protect their interests (Armstrong, 1978: 63). Their only avenue to pursue this was through organising voluntary associations. These voluntary organisations were not recognised as legitimate political parties. Therefore, women could only enter politics informally, 'through the back door'. The primary organisation, the Women's Rural Institute (WRI), despite repeated efforts, remained powerless due to many social and economic factors, the main one being that traditional male leadership and male networking systems did not acknowledge the head of the WRI as a legitimate political figure. The result was that women remained in informal politics and, although important locally, had little influence beyond their village.

Swain's (1989) study of the Cuna ethnic group in Panama also focuses on indigenous tourism development and the role opportunities that tourism generates for women and men. Swain details the division of labour in the production of mola artwork of fabric applique and the gendered access to political roles. Cuna women produce mola artwork of fabric applique and maintain a marketable image of ethnicity; Cuna men produce and maintain the political forum that shapes the group's interactions with outside interests, including tourism (Swain, 1989: 83).

Despite this strict demarcation of gendered roles, Swain describes the division of labour as reflecting an interdependence of the sexes. She discusses bilateral inheritance among Cuna people which is reinforced by an individual's right to personal earnings (Swain, 1989: 92). Cuna women have organised cooperatives and working groups to support themselves economically and socially. Swain's optimistic account emphasises the importance of local control in tourism, and she suggests that local employment in indigenous tourism could affect the evolution of Cuna gender roles. Maybe one day mola-making may be considered Cuna work, not women's work (Swain, 1989: 103).

Lcvy and Lerch (1991) and Samarasuriya (1982) provide the most detailed studies on women and employment in the tourism industry: the former investigate women workers in Barbados; and the latter examines women workers in a small, coastal village in Sri Lanka. Both studies focus upon the relationships among gender, employment in tourism and status in society. They discuss the limitations and barriers women face in light of the positions they are able to enter in the labour market, potential income attainment, job security, work satisfaction, access to resources, social mobility and socio-economic class. The studies adopt a 'development' perspective (development for whom?). However, they differ with respect to the type of tourist development under scrutiny. In Barbados, employment in large-scale hotels was the focus; whereas in Sri Lanka, more small-scale, locally controlled (guest house) tourism was under study.

Levy and Lerch offer more information concerning gender relations than Samarasuriya, looking at employment of both men and women, whereas Samarasuriya only considers women's employment. The advantage of Samarasuriya's study is that it provides greater depth by categorising and detailing several occupational relations women have to the tourism industry.

Despite the different types of development in the two case studies, many similar consequences affected women workers in both regions. In both cases, access to tourist employment was more limited for women than men. In the Barbados study, none of the women sampled entered tourism employment in a managerial position. Those who were able to attain supervisory positions were in traditional women's areas, such as housekeeping and reception (Levy & Lerch, 1991: 78). In the Sri Lankan study, socio-economic class was the factor most constraining where women could enter the labour market. Only middle-class women ran officially registered guest houses, while the poorest women hawked their wares on the beach or by the roadside. Despite class differences, most of the women, regardless of the nature of their employment, did not profit front their endeavours.

Reproductive roles of women, including childcare and household domestic duties, were emphasised as necessarily being combined with women's work in tourism. In Barbados, women relied on social networks to help with the burden of domestic duties: 35% of all women sampled and 50% of female household heads reported that problems with childcare were their biggest concern (Levy & Lerch, 1991: 81). Women's employment, income, and job security were all noted as being significantly inferior to those of men, and many women took on additional earning strategies, such as baking and sewing, because their remuneration from tourism was not sufficient to make ends meet. Women in the Sri Lankan study also had the primary responsibility of domestic duties and childcare, with implications for their tourism employment. Samarasuriya describes the situation as it relates to women shopkeepers engaged in petty trading:

> Most of the women in the business continue to do so even with little profit because it does not hinder their tasks as mother and housewife. As the shop is part of the house, or garden, they can still look after children. cook the meals and attend to other household chores. (Samarasuriya, 1982: 45)

In both studies it is evident that there are areas of employment deemed 'women's work'. In hotels in Barbados, most of the women employed worked in housekeeping, reception and other service occupations with the lowest job security (due to a lack of unionised women workers) and income levels. In the Sri Lankan study, it is noted that even the women who did own and manage their own guest house or restaurant (there were only a few) did not gain increased status, due to the low value ascribed to women's work. In short, women's mode of reproduction defines the nature of women's mode of production

The unstable nature of women's employment in the tourist industry is similarly expressed in Lever's (1987) study of Spanish migrant workers. Much of the seasonal, unskilled employment, with long hours and low pay, is undertaken by rural women who migrate due to lack of stable employment at home. The exploitation of what is deemed women's work is again expressed in a different regional context. In Lloret de Mar, a Costa Brava resort, women are seen as 'cheaper' than men, not in terms of pay, but because they sweep and tidy up at the end of the day and do other little jobs men refuse to do (Lever 1987: 453). Women predominate in the more precarious occupations that have no job security and low hourly wages, and their work again is a continuation of household and domestic duties, such as chambermaiding and dishwashing. Women view the work as backbreaking and poorly paid, but they see it as a way to enter a career in tourism. Management is happy because there is no need to offer training for these jobs and thus workers (women) can be easily replaced (Lever, 1987: 454). The lack of unionised women workers was also noted in this study. Lever commented that women are likely to see unions as potentially useful but were less likely to join because men dominated the more stable jobs and were more likely to stay away from their *pueblo* for the whole year

(Lever, 1987: 563). Lever concludes by viewing tourism migration as bringing temporary improvement for individual migrants but representing no more than a 'half-way house'. She sees migration as 'a way of shelving the problem of long-term development of rural areas' (Lever, 1957: 470).

The last study that will be mentioned is that of Miller and Branson (1989) on women and tourism in Bali, Indonesia. The historical and cultural perspective that is adopted provides an appropriate context in which to approach and attempt to understand women, men, and economic and social change. They discuss the forces of culture on women in Bali: religious, ideological and political. They postulate that the current processes of economic and political change transform women's roles but warn against the assumption that economic autonomy for women automatically leads to political or religious freedom.

> The changes increasingly domesticate women, threatening their economic autonomy in and beyond markets and redefining familial responsibilities to fit a view of the family in which the man is the 'breadwinner'. Men are increasingly evident in trading activities at both the administrative and commercial levels. The Balinese view of commercial activity of trading as 'female' is being redefined in line with the government's stress on the need for economic initiative and for men to lead in development. Both the nation state and the national economy are viewed, by the government and Western advisors alike, as 'male'. (Miller and Branson, 1989: 111)

This paper illustrates that there is little to be gained from examining women's roles in economic production, without also considering their definition according to the dominant religious and political traditions, and their place in the household. Recognition must he accorded to the mutual influence of these ideological and institutional factors to avoid an ahistorical and incomplete analysis of women's experiences.

The nature of the tourist industry is such that various types of development can occur (this is discussed in the next section) which determine options for direct employment and also affect potentials for indirect employment. Regional differences, diverse tourist wants and types of tourism all affect women's employment opportunities. Despite these variations in the manifestations of tourism, similar cultural and societal constraints were apparent in all of the studies reviewed. Traditional views concerning what is defined as 'women's work' limited the avenues women could pursue for employment: domestic and childcare duties were the responsibility of women and either had to be combined with tourist employment or extended to other family members (usually daughters or grandmothers);

and lack of organisation among women workers, either through unionisation, access to political power or government initiatives, prevented women from 'getting ahead' in the tourism industry.

## Type of Tourist Development

This topic is closely related to tourist employment in that the type of tourist development largely determines employment opportunities that exist for women and men. The scale of development has implications for gender relations.

A general distinction can be made between large-scale and small-scale tourism. The former refers to large complexes associated with mass tourism. Such places have the capacity to accommodate a large number of visitors, supply a variety of recreational opportunities and are often largely self-contained. Critics of large-scale development come from both developing and developed countries (Turner & Ash, 1975; de Kadt, 1979; Holden, 1984; English, 1986; Singh *et al.*, 1989; Weaver, 1991). They postulate that the benefits of large-scale development do not trickle down to the local population receiving tourism. In fact, this kind of tourism development may even make many people worse off than before its introduction. Therefore, small-scale or alternative tourism development which is locally and/or nationally controlled, that involves direct employment of the local population. and distributes the benefits of tourism among the local population is viewed by many as the *appropriate* type of tourist development. The distinction between small-scale or alternative tourism development and large-scale or mass tourist development has provoked many commentators and critics to debate the usefulness of such a distinction (Cazes, 1989; Cohen, 1989; Wheeller, 1991). However, a question which has yet to be addressed is where gender fits in this debate.

In the previous section, gendered employment patterns were examined in various tourist settings. It was distinguishable that women in both large-scale (Barbados) and small-scale (Sri Lanka) tourist developments experience constraints which affect the avenues they can pursue in tourism employment. Such research should be extended to compare the experiences of women in both situations. A superficial analysis suggests that women have more opportunity in small-scale tourist developments because of the emphasis on local control; however, as was illustrated in the case of women in rural Scotland, while women were the majority of workers in the tourist industry, that did not give them access to political power.

Tourism development under local control does not necessarily lead to benefits for local women. The majority of political and community leadership in most societies is male so that, whether power is in the hands of locals or foreigners, many of the effects on women may be similar.

## Images in Tourism

This section will critique marketing and advertising in tourism promotion (Bolla, 1990). It is argued that depictions of 'woman' as 'native' in traditional anthropology are maintained in modern tourism advertising. In fact, Pritchard and Morgan (2000: 115) have argued that 'tourism promotion reflects a privileged white, male, heterosexual gaze'. Such imagery and ideology have relationships to sex tourism. Tiffany and Adams (1985) critique the depiction of women in accounts of traditional anthropologists and attempt to demystify romanticised images of so-called 'primitive' women.

In their search for the primitive, anthropologists have succeeded in reinforcing this contrast to Western men's lives. Like non-Western peoples, women are the losers in these invidious comparisons. Women, the archetype of what men are not, provide the focus of a political inequality that is general among men. Appearing in various roles as Amazons, virgins and matriarchs, women represent a projection of civilised men's imagination (Tiffany & Adams, 1955: xi).

The objectification and dichotomisation of women has been prevalent in images of society throughout history. Women are constantly depicted in relation to something else: in relation to men, sexuality, motherhood and domesticity. In other words, women present a problem which is addressed through patriarchal structures or explained by biological determinism. Tiffany and Adams discuss the evolution of the discipline of anthropology and the nature of the 'civilised' male anthropologist versus the 'primitive' local female, and demonstrate that the historical roots of female images as mothers, virgins and whores predominated in early Western thought and continue to be the dominant cultural representations of women today.

It is especially relevant to be aware of this context when discussing images of women in tourism because images of First World women tourists and Third World women hosts to tourism are frequently compared and contrasted. Common themes in tourism brochures are the passive, yet alluring, native woman versus the active, sexually provocative, white woman tourist. In both instances women are being defined sexually, but on different levels. In the first case, there is an objectification of women and the native host woman is portrayed as being submissive and as promising something male tourists can control and dominate. In the second case, the sexy, yet independent, white female tourist is active rather than passive and promises a potential sexual liaison with other male tourists on more equal grounds. This separation between women in the West and women in the East also makes an ideological distinction between those women who are 'emancipated' and those women who are not. This theme is further explored in the next section on the growth of prostitution in developing countries.

The ideological constructs of the advertising industry infuse the tourism industry. Advertising is a form of discourse which provides the recipient with a range of cultural elements with which fantasy, meaning and identity can be constructed and created. Without advertising, the tourism product often means little other than household-related services, such as food, accommodation and shelter, which are provided to the traveller away from home (Truong, 1990: 124). The possibility of sexual liaisons with non-white native women as well as with more promiscuous women tourists is portrayed in the mysterious, alluring, black woman, on the one hand, and the buxom, bikini-clad, white woman, on the other. The presentations imply that there is freedom for the white woman tourist to express her sexual desires (away from potential constraints at home) while the black woman provides sexual pleasure for white male tourists.

Britton (1979: 326) calls for a dramatic 'reorientation of image'. He does not specifically discuss the depiction of women in advertising but provides a more general commentary upon the advertising of destinations in the Third World. He critiques the imagery of the paradisiacal, utopian societies that have never existed anywhere and demands a more diverse, realistic depiction of destinations and their peoples. However, he does not discuss gendered representations as a central feature of his analysis, thereby limiting his case for a more humane form of advertising.

## Prostitution and Tourism

> They were poor girls whom fortune failed in need:
> They sold their charms and threw their youth away.
>   Old age caught them alone and desolate –
> Unmarried, childless, where could they seek help?
>   Alive, they drained the cup of bitter dregs;
> And dead, they eat rice mush in banyan leaves.
>   How sorrowful is women's destiny.
> Who can explain why they are born to grief?
>
> (Nguyen Du, quoted in Truong. 1990: 131)

Prostitution is one topic which has attracted attention in the tourism literature to the role of women and the literature continues to proliferate (Oppermann, 1998; Schwartz, 1997; Jeffreys, 1999; Clift & Carter, 2000;

Ryan & Hall, 2001). However, because it usually operates on the margin of legality, neither service providers nor customers are likely to be open informants and many studies are based on thin data sets and resort to stereotypes. A result of this situation is that the women involved in the industry are given inadequate opportunity to express their views. It is insufficient to generalise about the oppression of women without being aware of the various reasons why particular women enter prostitution. There are many instances of forced, violent, exploitative subjugation of Third World women, but if stereotypical assumptions and depictions about Third World women are to be avoided, what they have to say must be heard in their own voices.

Although it is important to understand the meaning of prostitution to the individual women and men who work in the industry, one should be aware of the organisational links between prostitution and the sex-related entertainment industry to distinguish the various forms of prostitution involved. Oppermann (1999) has examined the overlap between prostitution and sex tourism and has proposed a sex tourism framework consisting of a number of continua that describe variations in the relationships between provider and customer. There are organised sex package tours which are an extreme form of the merging of prostitution and tourism. These tours involve tour operators, airlines, hotels and entertainment establishments and require a high degree of coordination among the components of the tourism industry (Truong, 1990: 127). Sex tours to Thailand, the Philippines and South Korea are frequently advertised, especially through large Japanese and German travel agencies (English, 1986: 51). One German travel agent advertised that:

> Thailand is a world full of extremes and the possibilities are limitless. Anything goes in this exotic country. Especially when it comes to girls . . . Rosie travel has come up with the answer. For the first time in history, you can book a trip to Thailand with erotic pleasure included in the price. (English, 1986: 51)

There are other forms of prostitution that have less overt linkages to the tourism industry. 'Services' are purchased locally in various locations, such as bars, nightclubs and massage parlours, and then carried out by individual purchase of the means of transport and accommodation, or individual purchase of a package tour (Truong, 1990: 127). In this situation, there is no formal link between prostitution and tourism, except through the supplying of information on prices, locations, and the forms of sexual services available at the destination.

There is a tension between the morality of selling sex and the potential revenues that such a practice generates. The concurrent existence of established and casual workers in the industry is one outcome of this (Truong, 1990: 127). The economic potential of prostitution forces governments either to turn a blind eye or to try to regulate the activity. At the same time, the moral issues surrounding prostitution impose limits on the degree of public tolerance. In developing countries especially, there are many vested interests in this practice: many people and organisations, both foreign and domestic, want a piece of the pie. Complete regulation of prostitution is seldom possible because the labour force, female labour in particular, is not well organised.

Female prostitution in developing countries signifies the continuous interplay between the new international division of labour and the manipulation of the sexual division of labour (Mies, 1986). The mobilisation of female labour in the entertainment industry has become integral to government policies and business practices. In short, female sexuality has become an economic asset. The Philippines offers one example of government involvement in regulating female sexuality in efforts to bring in foreign exchange. During the 1970s, the Filipino government established what was called the 'hospitality' industry and proceeded to license, train and give regular medical check-ups to 'hospitality girls' working in bars and massage parlours. A specific division of government, the Bureau of Women and Minors, was responsible for this (Holden *et al.*, 1986: 61–2). The Bureau developed a training course as a prerequisite to licensing. Most of the girls come from poor, farming families or destitute families living in urban slum areas. 'Employment agencies' recruit women in the provinces promising jobs in the city, paying their parents an amount in advance and then forcing the young women into prostitution (Holden *et al.*, 1986: 63–4). The number of 'girls' increased from 10,000 in 1976 to approximately 300,000 in 1986, with an estimated 20,000 child prostitutes (girls and boys) between the ages of 9 and 12 (Holden *et al.*, 1986: 62). The Bureau director refuses to acknowledge these women as prostitutes but prefers to refer to them as 'workers'.

Government involvement, combined with less explicit organisation in the exploitation of female sexuality, creates an ideological depiction of the traditional female role in conjunction with the ideologies of nationalism and development. This presents a contradiction for the female (or male) prostitute because, even though the 'glorification of self-sacrifice for the household and nation justifies the act of prostitution . . . the criminalization of prostitutes makes labour organization impossible' (Truong, 1990: 128).

Thus far prostitution has been discussed in the form of Third World women servicing First World men. This form has been the most evident in tourist destinations and continues to be, but a form of prostitution which should also be explored is Third World men servicing First World women.

Dahles and Bras (1999) have adopted this perspective in their work in Indonesia and have interviewed 'wild guides' who provide a wide variety of services to mostly Western women. Their work is important not only because of the perspective that is adopted but also because they link their works to broader concepts, particularly entrepreneurship. Pruitt and LaFont (1995) in Jamaica and Herold *et al.* (2001) have undertaken a somewhat similar study in the Dominican Republic. To date, although the latter researchers interviewed both tourists and beach boys, no material on this subject has been found which explores the phenomenon from the First World women's point of view. This is a relevant area of research because women tourists are a growing phenomenon, travelling alone, in pairs or in groups. Is there a demand for male sexual services in tourist destinations in the Third World? If so, where and to what extent? How does this relationship fit into the more 'traditional' organisational structure for satisfying male tourists? Much of the literature which addresses the motivations of male tourists seeking the services, company and even long-time companionship of Third World women, explains that women in the West are too 'feminist' or 'emancipated' and that they want a woman who will cater to them and not make any particular demands The ideological distinction between women who are emancipated and those who are not, and how imagery in tourism advertising feeds off this distinction, was mentioned in the previous section. What, we ask, does the emancipated female tourist want? Does she also seek out sexual services to fulfil desires which she cannot satisfy at home? Is she looking to dominate and control the male gender, but only able to do so in a context in which she is viewed as having high status?

Bowman (1989) explored sexual relationships between Palestinian merchants and female tourists in Jerusalem, but he discussed it only from the perspective of the male merchants. He reported that sexual relations with female tourists were a way of gaining status among fellow merchants. Their failure to gain economically was compensated by their (imagined or real) masculine mastery over foreign women. Bowman (1989: 84–5) acknowledged his difficulty with exploring the motivations of women tourists in relationships with the merchants, thus limiting his account to 'the domain of male tales'.

This paper demonstrates the need to understand situations from the perspectives of both genders. While Bowman's account was legitimate and well expressed, the women tourists. who were so central to the situation, had no voice. A similar situation was mentioned previously in reference to female prostitutes in developing countries. It is also the case with respect to the sexual exploitation of children in tourism which is a cause of growing concern, especially among church organisations, and has been the subject of an international campaign that is co-funded by the European Commission. The dissemination of AIDS through tourism has also been the subject of some research (Cohen, 1988; Arvidson *et al.*, 1996). It is also worthwhile to explore less extreme situations. For example, Ryan and Martin (2001), in an exploration of striptease, have shown that simple dominant male–subordinate female or dominant female–submissive male explanations are inadequate interpretations of complex situations.

Research on prostitution is appropriate and should be continued, but it is also necessary to research relationships which are less exploitative and in which women, especially Third World women, are not commonly viewed as being continually oppressed.

## Tourism and the Family

In previous sections, some aspects of tourism and the family have been mentioned and attention has been drawn to the danger of viewing topics and situations in isolation. In the case of tourism employment, family situations and household status largely determine employment opportunities for women who often combine reproductive and productive duties in order to access the market. In Sri Lanka. this entailed working out of the home or taking children to work and, in Barbados, family networks were set up to help with childcare responsibilities.

Tourism has a demonstration effect with implications for the cultural institution of the family in host societies. One among many issues which deserve attention is contact between local and travelling youth. What kinds of relationships develop? Are authentic exchanges of cultural beliefs and values possible? Is there a move away from traditional ways of life on the part of local youth, towards emphasis on consumerism and Western attitudes? Does tourism have dramatic effects on the moral and sexual conduct of a community? What about changes in work ethics? These are very broad questions which demand systematic investigation to see if they apply in particular situations. A drawback of much of the literature is that many generalisations have been made concerning tourism and its effects, without a clear specification of the type and stage of tourism, and overlooking the importance of regional specificity and the dynamics of culture.

Kousis (1989), in her study of tourism and the family in a rural Cretan community, concludes that tourism can cause family change but that it is economic not ideological factors which induce this change. Her data reveal that the influence of family control, the importance of marital arrangements, and the dowry system have not lost the significance they enjoyed before tourism (Kousis, 1959: 318). What has changed are employment patterns, family size and land-holding and wealth-owning patterns. Again it is noted that females constitute the majority of both women who are self-employed and those who work for an employer. This article also touches on the presence of single female tourists in the Cretan community and how they affect the sexual, moral codes. The relationships between local males and female tourists involve a delicate and controversial issue. Some of the local men, often called *kamakia* or harpoons (metaphorically implying that the male was the harpoon and the female was the fish), systematically dated foreign women. In the full-scale tourism phase, there were about 10 groups (or cliques) of single males between the ages 16 and 30 who regularly dated female tourists (Kousis, 1989: 329). Although the sexual, moral codes changed with the introduction of tourism. the effect was restricted to male Cretans. Strict sexual conduct of local females was unchanging, despite the relaxed relationships between local males and foreign women. Thus, the gap in sexual codes for men and women was widened.

Kousis's paper raises issues which are rarely considered before tourist development takes place or when tourism policies are being implemented. Systematic exploration of the interaction between factors of change, the local socio-cultural context and family relations is often lacking. Gender is central to all of these concerns.

Another neglected area of research concerns gender and family relations while families are on vacation. Women are often caretakers of others' leisure, especially that of husbands and children. Does being in the tourist role modify women's 'fragmented' leisure time? Are women still in charge of the family's leisure satisfaction first and their own second? Do women organise the family holiday – destination, accommodation, leisure activities – from start to finish? Numerous questions could be explored in this area, many of which would be of interest to those in the industry. Work done in feminist leisure studies, which has explored the nature of female leisure experiences. may provide a useful starting point for such investigations.

It is common knowledge that the constitution of families is becoming increasingly diverse as is the attempt by tourism providers to cater to niche markets. Thus, there is growing interest in the provision of tourism and recreation opportunities for specialised markets: young singles, honeymooners (Dubinsky, 1999), businesswomen and the gay and lesbian markets (Pritchard *et al.*, 2000) are examples (Holcomb & Luongo, 1996; Hughes, 1997; Johnston, 2001).

## Discussion

Six topics have been discussed which exhibit relationships between gender and tourism. A distinct theoretical framework has not been provided, nor have all aspects of such relationships been covered. The topics were selected because of their importance for understanding the gendered processes which are apparent in tourist development but, in many cases, they have yet to be addressed as a primary focus in tourism studies. By including women's perspectives, understanding of human behaviour can be broadened and improved. Women need to become a subject of discourse as they experience tourism and should be involved in the formation of ideas about themselves: as tourists, tourism employees and hosts to tourism. Women need to be placed at the centre of thinking, having the right to define and decide what is valid, true and meaningful about their lives (Henderson *et al.*, 1989). The practice and investigation of tourism, at both theoretical and empirical levels, should move beyond its androcentric orientation and incorporate female perspectives.

## Which Way To Go?

The need to incorporate a gender perspective in tourism studies and to make a commitment to the systematic study of women and tourism has been pointed out. This having been said, where should one begin and how is it to he done? Much can be drawn from previous work in the areas of gender in leisure and development studies, as well as in the general feminist studies literature. Feminist leisure studies have viewed leisure from the angle of the social division of labour and stratification which provide guidelines for an analysis of leisure in terms of the historical specificities of production and reproduction (Truong, 1990: 97). This perspective on leisure can be extended to applications in the study of tourist behaviours and practices to explore implications for gender. 'Social time' is another conceptual addition that stems from feminist leisure studies. New patterns of leisure (or tourism) may promote more leisure for one part of society at the expense of the remainder. Truong (1990) puts forth particular questions which address this issue. Who has access to leisure and 'free time'? To what extent can 'free time' be considered unproductive? Does 'free time' have a liberating effect? In the context of this chapter, tourism can be substituted for 'free time'. A gender perspective on these questions could be very illuminating concerning the nature of tourism.

The gender in development literature provides analytical constructs with which to examine the international gendered division of labour, and women's experiences in changing economic, political, social and technological times. Tourism constitutes the entry of leisure into the international division of labour and creates an interplay between discourse, culture, economy and technology and between the developed and developing countries. It has been shown that women from developing countries are being integrated into the structure of production of the tourist industry, but in particular ways. It follows that the study of tourism must be placed within the relationship between reproduction and production, and be analysed in historically specific terms, taking into account social differentials on the basis of class, gender, race and age (Truong, 1990: 97).

The theoretical and empirical contributions to tourism research studies that have come from many disciplines also have much to contribute to gender and tourism studies. Even though gender has not been a central construct in many analyses, models and theoretical frameworks can be modified and extended to include women's perspectives. They also provide a base against which the lack of gender attention can be assessed. Understanding tourism within a feminist framework goes beyond stereotypical images and accounts, and moves towards understanding the symbolic meanings of tourism for women and the social issues surrounding tourism. If tourism has the ability to promote dramatic social, cultural, economic, geographical and political changes, then gender relations among those in host communities, gender relations among tourists, and relations between the two should be investigated. If gender relations are not an integral part of such investigations, then they will be incomplete.

**Note**
1.  This chapter first appeared as 'Gender and tourism' in Volume 6 of *Progress in Tourism, Recreation and Hospitality Management* (1994), pp. 57–78.

**Bibliography**
Aitchison, C. (1999) New cultural geographies: The spatiality of leisure, gender and sexuality. *Leisure Studies* 18 (1), 19–40.
Armstrong, K. (1978) Rural Scottish women politics without power. *Ethnos* 43 (1–2), 51–72.
Arvidson, M., Hellberg, D. and Mardh (1996) Sexual risk behavior and history of sexually transmitted diseases in relation to casual travel sex during different types of journeys. *Acta Obstetricia et Gynecologica Scandinavia* 75, 490–94.
Bandarage, A. (1984) Women in development: Liberalism, Marxism and Marxist-feminism. *Development and Change* 15 (3), 495–515.
Beezer, A. (1993) Women and 'Adventure Travel' tourism. *New Formations* 21, 119–130.
Bella, L. (1989 Women and leisure: Beyond androcentrism. In E.L. Jackson and T.L Burton (eds) *Understanding Leisure and Recreation: Mapping the Past and Charting the Future*. State College, Pennsylvania: Venture Publishing.
Birkett, D. (1990) *Spinsters Abroad: Victorian Women Explorers*. Oxford: Basil Blackwell.
Blunt, A. and Rose, G. (eds) (1994) *Writing Women and Space: Colonial and Postcolonial Geographies*. London: Guildford Press.
Bolla, P.A. (1990) Media images of women and leisure: An analysis of magazine advertisements. *Leisure Studies* 9 (3),241–52.

Boserup, E. (1970) *Women's Role in Economic Development.* St Martin's Press: New York.

Bowman, G. (1989) Fucking tourists: Sexual relations and tourism in Jerusalem's Old City. *Critique of Anthropology* 9 (2), 77–93.

Britton, R.A. (1979) The image of the Third World in tourism marketing. *Annals of Tourism Research* 6 (3), 318–29.

Carr, N. (1999) A study of gender differences: Young tourist behaviour in a UK coastal resort. *Tourism Management* 20 (2), 223–28.

Cazes, G.H. (1989) Alternative tourism: Reflections on an ambiguous concept. In T.V. Singh, H.L. Thuens and F. Go (eds) *Towards Appropriate Tourism: The Case of Developing Countries* (pp. 117–26). Frankfurt-am-Main: P. Lang.

Clift, S. and Carter, S. (2000) *Tourism and Sex: Culture, Commerce and Coercion.* London: Pinter.

Cohen. E. (1972) Towards a sociology of international tourism. *Social Research* 39, 64–182.

Cohen, E. (1988) Tourism and AIDS in Thailand. *Annals of Tourism Research* 15 (4), 467–86.

Cohen, E. (1989) Alternative tourism – a critique. In T.V. Singh, H.L. Thuens and F. Go (eds) *Towards Appropriate Tourism: The Case of Developing Countries* (pp. 127–42). P. Lang. Frankfurt-am-Main.

Cukier, J. and Wall, G. (1995) Tourism employment in Bali: A gender analysis. *Tourism Economics* 1 (4), 389–401.

Cukier, J., Norris, J. and Wall, G. (1996) The involvement of women in the tourism industry of Bali, Indonesia. *Journal of Development Studies* 33 (2), 248–70.

Dahles, H. and Bras, K. (1999) Entrepreneurs in romance: Tourism in Indonesia. *Annals of Tourism Research* 26 (2), 267–93.

De Beauvoir, S. (1971) *The Second Sex.* Edited and translated by H.M. Parshley. New York: Alfred A. Knopf.

De Kadt, E. (1979) *Tourism: Passport to Development?* New York: Oxford University Press.

Deem, R. (1996) Women, the city and holidays. *Leisure Studies* 15 (2), 105–19.

Dubinsky, K. (1999) *The Second Greatest Disappointment: Honeymooners, Heterosexuality and the Tourist Industry in Niagara Falls.* New Brunswick, NJ: Rutgers University Press.

Elsrud, T. (1998) Time creation in traveling: The taking and making of time among women backpackers. *Time and Society* 7 (2), 309–34.

English, P.E. (1986) *The Great Escape? An Examination of North-South Tourism.* Ottawa: North-South Institute.

Fox, K. (1992) Choreographing differences in the dance of leisure: The potential of feminist thought. *Journal of Leisure Research* 24 (4), 333–47.

Graburn, N.H.H. and Jafari, J. (eds) (1991) Tourism social science. *Annals of Tourism Research* 18 (1) 1–169.

Guelke, J.K. and Morin, K.M. (2001) Gender, nature, empire: Women naturalists in nineteenth century British travel literatures. *Transactions of the Institute of British Geographers* 26 (3), 306–26.

Henderson, K. (1994a) Broadening an understanding of women, gender and leisure. *Journal of Leisure Research* 26 (1), 1–7.

Henderson, K. (1994b) Perspectives on analysing women, gender and leisure. *Journal of Leisure Research* 26 (2), 119–37.

Henderson, K.A., Bialeschki, M.D., Shaw, S.M. and Freysinger, V.J. (1989) *A Leisure of one's Own: A Feminist Perspective on Women's Leisure.* Pennsylvania: State College, Venture Publishing.

Herold, E., Garcia, R. and Demoya, T. (2001) Female tourists and beach boys: Romance or sex tourism. *Annals of Tourism Research* 28 (4), 978–97.

Hess, B. and Ferree, M.M. (1987) *Analyzing Gender: A Handbook of Social Science Research.* London: Sage.

Heyzer, N. (1986) *Working Women in South-East Asia: Development, Subordination and Emancipation.* Milton Keynes: Open University Press.

Holcomb, B. and Luongo, M. (1996) Gay tourism in the United States. *Annals of Tourism Research* 23 (3), 711–12.

Holden, P. (ed.) (1981) *Alternative Tourism. Report of the Workshop on Alternative Tourism with a Focus on Asia.* Chiang Mai, Thailand: Ecumenical Coalition on Third World Tourism.

Holden, P., Pfafflin, G.F. and Horlemam, J. (1986) *Third World People and Tourism.* Bangkok: Ecumenical Coalition on Third World Tourism and the Third World Tourism Ecumenical European Network.

Hughes, H. (1997) Holidays and homosexual identity. *Tourism Management* 18 (1), 3–7.

Jackson, E.L. and Burton, T.L. (eds) (1989) *Understanding Leisure and Recreation. Mapping the Past and Charting the Future.* Pennsylvania: State College, Venture Publishing.

Johnston, L. (2001) (Other) bodies and tourism studies. *Annals of Tourism Research* 28 (1), 180–201.

Jeffrey, J.R. (1988) There is some splendid scenery: Women's responses to the Great Plains landscape. *Great Plains Quarterly* 8, 69–78.

Jeffreys, S. (1999) Gobalizing sexual exploitation: Sex tourism and the traffic in women. *Leisure Studies* 18 (3), 179–96.

Kay, J. (1991) Landscapes of women and men; rethinking the regional geography of the United States and Canada. *Journal of Historical Geography* 17 (4), 435–52.

Kinnaird, V. and Hall, D. (1994) *Tourism: A Gender Analysis.* Chichester: Wiley.

Kinnaird, V. and Hall, D. (1996) Understanding tourism process: A gender aware framework. *Tourism Management* 17 (2), 95–102.

Kousis, M. (1989) Tourism and the family in a rural Cretan community. *Annals of Tourism Research* 16 (3), 318–32.

Kroller, E.-M. (1987) *Canadian Travellers to Europe 1851–1900.* Vancouver: University Of British Columbia Press.

Leacock, E. and Safa, H.I. (1986) *Women's Work: Development and the Division of Labour by Gender.* South Hadley, MA: Bergin and Garvey.

Lever, A. (1987) Spanish tourism migrants: The case of Lloret de Mar. *Annals of Tourism Research* 14 (4), 449–70.

Levy, D.E. and Lerch, P.B. (1991) Tourism as a factor in development: Implications for gender and work in Barbados. *Gender and Society* 5 (1), 67–85.

Lewis, C. and Pile, S. (1996) Woman, body, space: Rio Carnival and the politics of performance. *Gender, Place and Culture* 3 (1), 23–41.

McDowell, L. (2001) Father and Ford revisited: Gender, class and employment change in the new millennium. *Transactions of the Institute of British Geographers* 26 (4), 448–65.

Meethan, K. (2001) *Tourism in Global Society: Place, Culture, Consumption.* Basingstoke: Palgrave.

Mellor, M. (1992) *Breaking the Boundaries: Towards a Feminist Green Socialism.* London: Virago Press.

Middleton, D. (1965) *Victorian Lady Travellers.* London: Routledge and Kegan Paul.

Mies, M. (1986) *Patriarchy and Accumulation on a World Scale.* London: Zed Book.

Miller, D.B. and Branson, J. (1989) Pollution in Paradise. Hinduism and the subordination of women in Bali. In P. Alexander (ed.) *Creating Indonesian Cultures* (pp. 91–112). Sydney: Oceania Publications.

Mills, S. (1991) *Discourses of Difference: An Analysis of Women's Travel Writing and Colonialism,* London: Routledge.

Mohanty, C.T., Russo, A. and Torres. L. (1991) *Third World Women and the Politics of Feminism.* Indianapolis: Indiana University Press.

Morgan, S. (1996) *Place Matters: Gendered Geography in Women's Travel Books About Southeast Asia.* New Brunswick, NJ: Rutgers University Press.

Morin, K.M. (1999) Peak practices: Englishwomen's 'heroic' adventures in the nineteenth-century American West. *Annals of the Association of American Geographers* 89 (3), 489–514.

Oppermann, M. (1998) *Sex Tourism and Prostitution: Aspects of Leisure, Recreation and Work.* Elmsford, NY: Cognizant Communication.

Oppermann, M. (1999) Sex tourism. *Annals of Tourism Research* 26 (2), 251–66.

Phillimore, J. (1998) Gender, employment and training in rural tourist attractions: The case of Herefordshire, England. *Tourism Recreation Research* 23 (2), 53–60.

Pritchard, A. and Morgan, N.J. (2000) Constructing tourism landscapes – gender, sexuality and space. *Tourism Geographies* 2 (2), 115–39.

Pritchard, A., Morgan, N.J., Sedgeley, D., Khan, E. and Jenkins, A. (2000) Sexuality and holiday choices: Conversations with gay and lesbian tourists. *Leisure Studies* 19 (4), 267–82.

Pruitt, D. and S. Lafont (1995) Love and money: Romance tourism in Jamaica. *Annals of Tourism Research* 22 (2), 422–40.

Riley, P.J. (1988) Road culture of international long-term budget travelers. *Annals of Tourism Research* 15 (3), 313–28.

Robinson, J. (1990) *Wayward Women: A Guide To Women Travellers.* Oxford: Oxford University Press.

Rupena-Osolnik, M. (1983–1984) The role of farm women in rural pluriactivity: Experience in Yugoslavia. *Sociologia Ruralalis* 23–24, 89–94.

Russell, M. (1988) *The Blessings of a Good Thick Skirt: Women Travellers and Their World.* London: Collins.

Ryan, C. and Hall, C.M. (2001) *Sex Tourism: Marginal People and Liminalities.* London: Routledge.

Ryan, C. and Martin, A. (2001) Tourists and strippers: Liminal theater. *Annals of Tourism Research* 28 (1), 140–63.

Samarasuriya, S. (1982) *Who Needs Tourism? Employment for Women in the Holiday Industry of Sudugama, Sri Lanka.* Colombo and Leiden: Research Project Women and Development.

Schwartz, R. (1997) *Pleasure Island, Tourism and Temptation in Cuba.* Lincoln: University of Nebraska Press.

Scraton, S.A. and Watson, B. (1998) Gendered cities: Women and public leisure space in the 'Postmodern City'. *Leisure Studies* 17 (2), 123–37.

Sinclair, M.T. (ed.) (1997) *Gender, Work and Tourism.* London: Routledge.

Singh, T.V., Thuens, H.L.and Go, F.H. (eds) (1989) *Towards Appropriate Tourism: The Case of Developing Countries.* Frankfurt-am-Main: P Lang.

Squire, S. (1995) In the steps of 'Genteel Ladies': Women tourists in the Canadian Rockies 1885–1939. *Canadian Geographer* 39 (1), 2–15.

Stamp, P. (1990) *Technology, Gender and Power in Africa*. Ottawa: International Development Research Centre.

Stanley, L. and Wise, S. (1982) *Breaking Out: Feminist Consciousness and Feminist Research*. London: Routledge and Kegan Paul.

Swain, M.B. (1989) Cuna women and ethnic tourism: A way to persist and an avenue to change. In V.L. Smith (ed.) *Hosts and Guests: The Anthropology of Tourism* (pp. 71–81). Philadelphia: University of Pennsylvania Press.

Swain, M.B. (1995) Gender in tourism. *Annals of Tourism Research* 22 (2), 247–66.

Swain, M.B. (2001) Gender, tourism and tourism research: Of waitrons and patrons, paradigms and praxis. In G. Wall (ed.) *Contemporary Perspectives on Tourism* (pp. 233–53). Occasional Paper No. 17. Waterloo: University of Waterloo.

Swain, M.B. and Momsen, J. (eds) (in press). *Gender Tourism, Fun?* Elmsford, New York: Cognizant Communication Corporation.

Talbot, M. (1979) *Women and Leisure*. London: Sports Council/Social Sciences Research Council.

Thrane, C. (2000) Men, women, and leisure time: Scandivian evidence of gender inequality. *Leisure Sciences* 22 (2), 109–22.

Tiffany, S.W. and Adams, K.J. (1985) *The Wild Woman: An Inquiry into the Anthropology of an Idea*. Cambridge, MA: Schenkman Publishing Company.

Tong, R. (1989) *Feminist Thought*. Boulder, CO: Westview Press.

Truong, T.-D. (1990) *Sex, Money and Morality: Prostitution and Tourism in Southeast Asia*. London: Zed Press.

Turner, L. and Ash, J. (1975) *The Golden Hordes*. London: Constable.

Veijola, S. and Jokinen, E. (1994) The body in tourism. *Theory, Culture and Society* 11 (3), 125–51.

Virden, R.J. and Walker, G.J. (1999) Ethnic/racial and gender variations among meanings given to, and preferences for, the natural environment. *Leisure Sciences* 21 (3), 219–39.

Weaver, D.B. (1991) Alternative to mass tourism in Dominica. *Annals of Tourism Research* 18 (3), 414–32.

Wheeller, B. (1991) Tourism's troubled times: Responsible tourism is not the answer. *Tourism Management* 12 (2), 91–6.

Wiley, C.G.E., Shaw, S.M. and Havitz, M.E. (2000) Men's and women's involvement in sports: An examination of the gendered aspects of leisure involvement. *Leisure Sciences* 22 (1), 19–31.

Wilkinson, P.F. and Pratiwi, W. (1995) Gender and tourism in an Indonesian village. *Annals of Tourism Research* 22 (2), 283–99.

Wimbush, E. and Talbot, M. (1988) *Relative Freedoms: Women and Leisure*. Milton Keynes: Open University Press.

Yule, J. (1997) Engendered ideologies and leisure policy in the UK. Part 1: Gender Ideologies. *Leisure Studies* 16 (2), 61–84.

Zimmerman, M.E. (1994) *Contesting Earth's Future: Radical Ecology and Postmodernity*. Berkeley: University of California Press.